Les Guédry et Petitpas d'Asteur
Generations

This book is one in a series of five books that includes newsletters published by Les Guédry et Petitpas d'Asteur between the years 1998 and 2018. These newsletters were published for the descendants of Claude Guédry & Marguerite Petitpas, and Claude Petitpas & Catherine Bugaret, who lived in a land called Acadia in the 1600's. The first three newsletters published in 1998 and 1999 were called *La Gazette des Guidry-Petitpas*, and put together by Daniel 'Chuck' Guidry. Then, starting in the winter of 2003, a series of newsletters called *Generations* were published by the team of Marty Guidry, Allie Guidry, Lindsey Hardee and Rachel Hardee.

These newsletters are now being published in these series of five books so that the numerous stories and family information included in them will be available for the ages.

Copyright 2018

Self-Published by Les Guédry et Petitpas d'Asteur

Books compiled by Mark Labine and Marty Guidry

ISBN : 9781791704582

BISAC: History/United States

The cover includes a background picture by James Peachy, d.1797, painted in 1785 titled "Vue sur le pont de la riviere Berthier". The painting is in the public domain.

Forward
by Marty Guidry

In late 1996 articles appeared in newspapers throughout southern Louisiana announcing the coming of the Congrès Mondial Acadien to Louisiana in August 1999. At least one of the articles emphasized that family reunions would play a major role in the 1999 Congrès and listed Acadian surnames found throughout southern Louisiana that were having reunions. Daniel "Chuck" Guidry of Houma, LA read the article and, being a genealogist, called the contact telephone number to determine where the Guidry reunion would be held and on what date. The pleasant voice on the telephone asked him where he lived and then announced that it would be in Houma, LA on the date of his choosing since he was the first to call about the Guidry reunion and thus would be the organizer. Chuck took the challenge and began in earnest to plan the Guidry reunion.

He immediately held a well-advertised organizational meeting in Bourg, LA. Five folks attended. Thus the "bones" of an organizing committee formed. After several additional organizational meetings in the next few months with the same level of attendance, an organizing committee developed that eventually would host the Guidry reunion in Houma, LA on Saturday, August 7, 1999. The organizing committee members were: Daniel Charles "Chuck" Guidry (President), Warren Lorenzo Guidry (Vice-President), Richard Martin Guidry (Secretary), Wayne Gregory Simoneaux (Treasurer), Ewell Thomas "E.T." Guidry (Board Member), Gayle Paul Guidry (Board Member), Richard James Guidry (Board Member) and Roland Joseph Guidry (Board Member). Since the Board needed an official charter to hold the reunion, they decided the name of the Guidry family association would be Les Guidry d'Asteur (The Guidry of Today). In addition, the Board decided to invite our sister family, the Petitpas, to join us at the reunion. Thus the reunion officially became the Guidry-Petitpas Reunion.

After applying for a charter in mid-1997, the Board began holding informational meetings monthly throughout southern Louisiana from Lafourche Parish to Calcasieu Parish and all points between. Never did more than ten people attend these meetings and that included four to five Board members making the presentation. On October 22, 1998 Les Guidry d'Asteur, Inc. received its official charter from the State of Louisiana. This did not increase attendance at the informational meetings. Always optimistic, Chuck Guidry insisted that 500 folks would attend the Guidry-Petitpas Reunion. Unfortunately he was wrong – the official attendance role showed that 499 folks attended the Reunion on August 7, 1999. Interest at the Reunion was so great that an additional Guidry-Petitpas Reunion was organized overnight and held at the Acadian Village in Lafayette, LA on August 10, 1999. It too was a huge success.

During 1998 and 1999 Chuck Guidry published three newsletters to inform potential and registered attendees about the Guidry-Petitpas Reunion and information about the Guidry family. He called these gems La Gazette des Guidry-Petitpas.

After the 1999 Guidry-Petitpas Reunion Chuck Guidry stepped down as President, but has remained Treasurer until the present day. Les Guidry d'Asteur remained dormant for a few years until activities for the Congrès Mondial Acadien 2004 in Nova Scotia came to the forefront. Martin Guidry then decided to fill the void as President. With an outstanding organizing committee the Guidry and Petitpas families have had reunions for the Congrès Mondial Acadien 2004 in both Meteghan, Nova Scotia and Lunenburg, Nova Scotia; Congrès Mondial Acadien 2009 in Bathurst, New Brunswick; La Grand Réveil Acadien 2011 in Cutoff, Louisiana; Congrès Mondial Acadien 2014 in Van Buren, Maine and La Grand Réveil Acadien 2015 in Henderson, Louisiana. Plans are being made to host another reunion at the Congrès Mondial Acadien 2019 in Summerside, Prince Edward Island.

Over time the name of our family association has changed slightly to accommodate the various enclaves of our family. Besides our officially-registered name Les Guidry d'Asteur, Inc., it has been Les Guédry d'Asteur; Les Guédry-Labine d'Asteur; Les Guédry-Labine et Petitpas d'Asteur and Les Guédry et Petitpas d'Asteur – our current name. Our current name reflects the surnames of our founding families – Claude Guédry dit Grivois & Marguerite Petitpas and Claude Petitpas & Catherine Bugaret.

To provide information about our ancestors and current family members and to announce our upcoming family reunions, the Board has published an online journal Generations three to four times a year since 2003. To preserve the family information in both the La Gazette des Guidry-Petitpas and Generations for our future family members, the Board is publishing all of the past newsletters in these bound volumes. They are as published, blemishes and all. No corrections or updates to the articles have occurred except for the few updates made in the actual journals during the period of publication.

Since 2003 Allie Guidry has edited Generations with the assistance of Rachel Hardee and Lindsey Hardee. We thank Allie, Rachel and Lindsey for their outstanding support and for editing a superb informational and entertaining journal for our family. Also since 2003 Becky Boggess has managed our Guédry-Labine Family website – a major part of which is making Generations available online and extracting key articles to highlight from each issue. Thanks, Becky, for your outstanding work on the website and with the journal. We also thank several members of our family for sharing their knowledge through articles they have written for Generations. They include Mark Labine, Sandra Pettipas Perro, Bernard L. Geddry, Jo Ann Guidrey Aulick, Art Guidry, Velma Guidry Beauxis, Rev. Mitchell Guidry, Allison Guidry, André Labine, Albert & Simone Geddry, Martin Guidry, Robert Choate, Barry Guidry, Christine Guidry Law, Claudette Mancini, Marvin Guidry and Jude Avery. We also thank the many fabulous chefs in our family who shared their recipes with us all.

Finally, in 2011 we instituted the Les Guédry et Petitpas Circle of Distinction to recognize those members of our family who have brought distinction to the Guédry and Petitpas families. Read their accomplishments as they represent the best of our families. We have so many outstanding individuals in our families that we will continue to induct members into the Circle of Distinction for years to come.

We hope you enjoy perusing the articles, recipes, historical tidbits, book reviews and other areas of these journals. Good reading.

The Guédry and Petitpas Crest
The Story of Our Family

The Guédry and Petitpas Crest tells the story of the Guédry and Petitpas family from its French origins through the struggle of its exile and eventually its resettlement throughout North America and Europe. It is the crest of the Guédry and Petitpas family in all of its name variations. Each item and color on the crest has special significance. Below is an explanation of the colors and components of the Guédry and Petitpas crest as they tell the story of the Guédry and Petitpas family.

ESCUTCHEON – The field of the escutcheon (shield) is divided into two parts: the chief (broad band across the top) and the field per quarterly with simple cross charge.

CHIEF – The chief is divided into three sections per pale (vertical lines) of blue, white and red tinctures (colors). Blue, white and red are the colors of the Acadian flag. These colors, the same as the Tricolor of the French flag, signify the French origins of the Acadians and the Guédry and Petitpas family.

BLUE represents the personal color of the Holy Virgin Mary – the patron saint of the Acadians. It also signifies loyalty and truthfulness – traits the Guédry and Petitpas family exhibited throughout their lives in Acadie and during the bleakness of deportation.

WHITE represents peace. In Acadie our Guédry and Petitpas forefathers remained neutral between the English and French, striving for peaceful lives. Even while being deported, they maintained their peaceful demeanor.

RED represents fortitude – the strength of mind that enabled our Guédry and Petitpas ancestors to endure the almost unbearable treatment by the English and emerge a stronger people.

The YELLOW STAR symbolizes Our Lady of the Assumption (the Virgin Mary), the patron saint of the Acadians.

The CREEL (fish basket) symbolizes the unique relationship between the Guédry and Petitpas family of Merliguèche and the Mi'kmaq nation. The Mi'kmaq taught their Guédry and Petitpas neighbors how to survive the harsh Merliguèche environment using the bounty of the land and sea.

The FIDDLE symbolizes the unique culture of the Guédry and Petitpas family - their music, their food, their faith, their joie de vivre. Although their culture has evolved and changed through the generations and where they may live, it has remained uniquely theirs. An old musical instrument, the fiddle has remained a constant of this culture wherever the music is played: in old Acadie, in Louisiana, in Nova Scotia, on Prince Edward Island, in New Brunswick or in France.

CHARGES – The four symbols in the quarterly fields represent the evolution of the Guédry and Petitpas family from the days of Old Acadie to today. The silver tincture of two fields represents the neutrality and peace that our ancestors strove to maintain during their two hundred years in Acadie. The blue tincture of two fields represents loyalty and truthfulness – qualities exhibited by our Guédry and Petitpas forefathers through much adversity.

The FLEUR-DE-LIS symbolizes the French origins of the Guédry and Petitpas ancestors, the North American forefathers of our family.

The GOLD color symbolizes the generosity of our ancestors toward others – striving for better lives for all.

The COAST-PILOT (boat) represents the early life of the Guédry and Petitpas family in North America. Settled near the Mi'kmaq at Merliguèche, the Guédry's and Petitpas's were excellent coasting pilots – plying the waters between Merliguèche and Île Royale. They lived a difficult life – learning critical skills from the Mi'kmaq, harvesting their needs from the land and sea, growing strong as a family.

The weather-beaten OAK TREE symbolizes the difficult days of deportation for our Guédry and Petitpas ancestors and their survival through it. It represents the strength of our family as they were uprooted and exiled, separated from mother and father, brother and sister, cousin and friend; spread throughout the world. They endured the hardships, the persecution and the oppression; they survived and they spread their roots firm and deep.

The BLACK color denotes the grief experienced during the dark days of exile.

The GLOBE symbolizes the worldwide breadth of our family today – throughout the United States, Canada, the Caribbean, Europe and even the Southern Hemisphere. Because of the firm, deep roots laid by our Guédry and Petitpas ancestors, we are truly a global family today tied closely together by the strong beliefs, characteristics and traits of our forefathers and passed along to us – generation by generation.

GOLD CROSS – The cross quartering the field symbolizes the strong Christian faith of our Guédry and Petitpas forefathers – the faith that helped them survive the early days of Acadie, endure the difficult years of deportation and overcome the struggle for survival afterwards to build the strong family that we are today. The gold tincture represents the generosity of our forefathers throughout their lives – a cornerstone of their faith.

MOTTO – The motto "Dieu, Famille, Acadien" translates to "God, Family, Acadian" – the guiding lights that have held our Guédry and Petitpas family together for over three hundred years and will continue to serve us well in the future.

The Guédry and Petitpas Crest represents all direct descendants of Claude Guédry and & Marguerite Petitpas and Claude Petitpas & Catherine Bugaret. The Guédry and Petitpas names have many variations in spelling today. All variations are represented by the Guédry and Petitpas Crest. These variations include:

Guédry	Guildry	Geddry	Jeddry	LaBean	Petitpas
Guedry	Guildrie	Geddrie	Jeddrie	LaBeau	Petit Pas
Guedrie		Gedry	Jedry	Labeau	Petit-Pas
		Gaidry	Gedrie	Jedrie	Pettipas
Guidry	Gaidrie	Lledre	Petipas		
Guidery		Gettry	Labine		Petitpa
Guidrey	Gidry		LaBine	Yedri	Pitts
Guidrie	Gidrie		Labene		
Guiddry			Labeen		
Guiddery	Guitry				
Gudiry					

R. Martin Guidry designed the elements and composition of the Guédry and Petitpas Crest in 2003 as he was preparing for the 2004 Congrès Mondial Acadien and the Guédry & Petitpas Reunion. Lindsey Hardee using the rough sketch and her graphic arts expertise created the beautiful Guédry and Pettipas Crest that our family shares today.

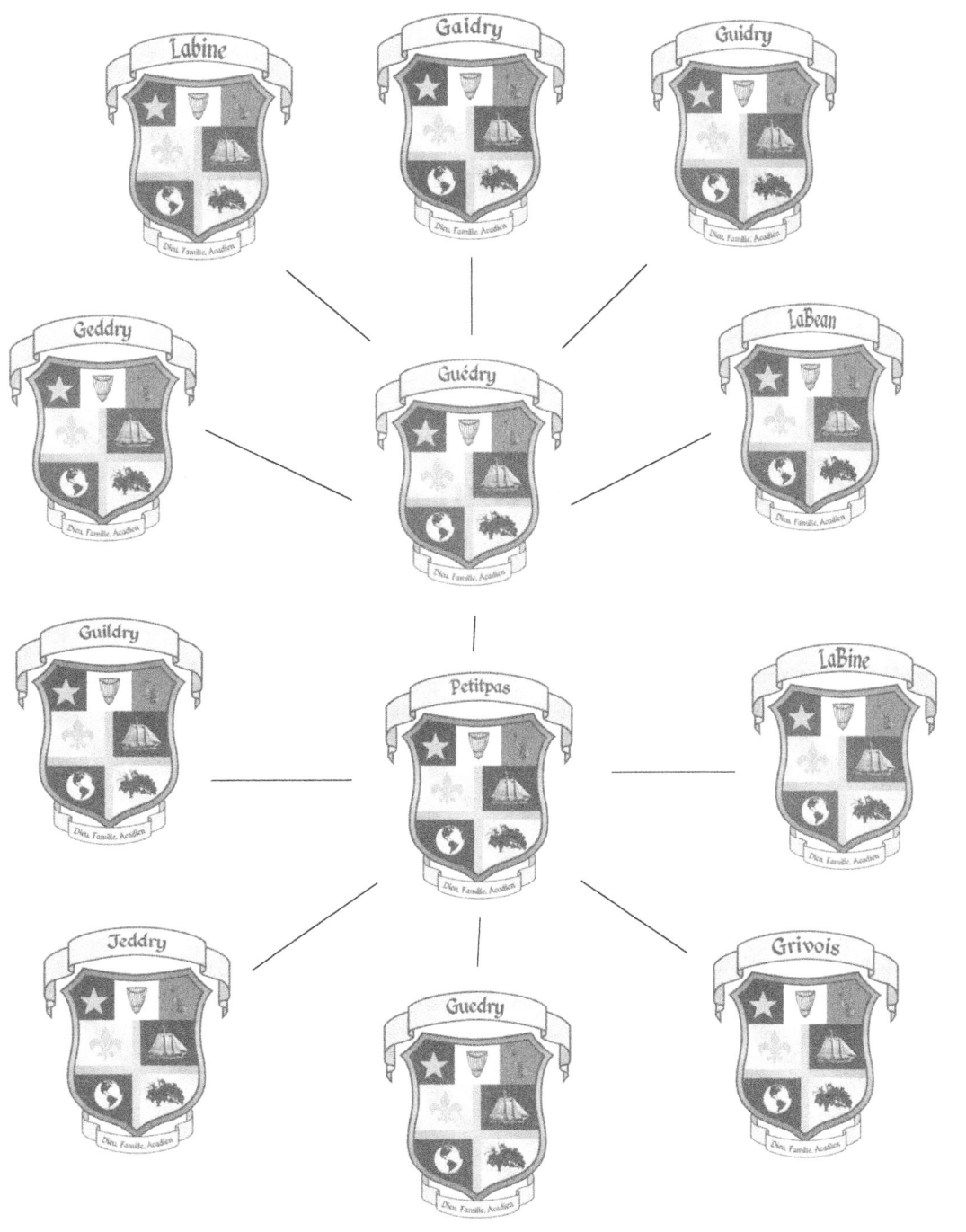

Family Crests of families who descend from Claude Guédry & Marguerite Petitpas and Claude Petitpas & Catherine Bugaret.

Table of Contents- Book One

Description	Pages	Page #
Forward by Marty Guidry	3	3
Guédry et Petitpas Crest- The Story of our Family	4	6
Table of Contents	3	10
Gazette Table of Contents by Newsletter and Topic	3	13
Generations Table of Contents by Newsletter	15	16
Generations Table of Contents by Topics	14	31
La Gazette- Vol 1, No. 1, January 1998 issue	8	45
La Gazette- Vol 1, No. 2, Avril 1998 issue	10	53
La Gazette – January 1999 issue	19	63
Generations- Vol 1, Issue 1 Winter 2003	9	82
Generations- Vol 1, Issue 2 Spring 2003	10	91
Generations- Vol 1, Issue 3 Summer 2003	11	101
Generations- Vol 1, Issue 4 Fall 2003	11	112
Generations- Vol 2, Issue 1 Winter 2004	9	123
Generations- Vol 2 Issue 2, Spring 2004	11	132
Generations- Vol 2, Issue 3, Summer 2004	20	143
Generations- Vol, 2 Issue 4, Fall 2004	16	163
Generations- Vol 3, Issue 1, Winter 2005	7	179
Generations- Vol 3, Issue 2, Summer 2005	12	186
Generations- Vol 3, Issue 3, Winter (Fall) 2005	14	198
Generations- Vol 4, Issue 2, Summer 2006	26	212
Generations- Vol 4, Issue 3, Fall 2006	15	238
Generations- Vol 5, Issue 1, Winter 2007	42	253
Generations- Vol 5, Issue 2, Summer 2007	48	295

Table of Contents- Book Two

Description	Pages	Page #
Forward by Marty Guidry	3	3
Guédry et Petitpas Crest- The Story of our Family	4	6
Table of Contents	3	10
Gazette Table of Contents by Newsletter and Topic	3	13
Generations Table of Contents by Newsletter	15	16
Generations Table of Contents by Topics	14	31
Generations- Vol 5, Issue 3, Fall 2007	21	45
Generations, Vol 6, Issue 1, Winter 2008	35	66
Generations, Vol 6, Issue 2, Summer 2008	18	101
Generations, Vol 6, Issue 3, Fall 2008	23	119
Generations, Vol 7, Issue 1, Winter 2009	54	142
Generations, Vol 7, Issue 2, Spring 2009	29	196
Generations, Vol 7, Issue 3, Summer 2009	21	225
Generations, Vol 7, Issue 4, Fall 2009	15	246
Generations, Vol 8, Issue 1, Winter 2010	36	261
Generations, Vol 8, Issue 2, Summer 2010	25	297
Generations, Vol 8, Issue 3, Fall 2010	32	322

Table of Contents- Book Three

Description	Pages	Page #
Forward by Marty Guidry	3	3
Guédry et Petitpas Crest- The Story of our Family	4	6
Table of Contents	3	10
Gazette Table of Contents by Newsletter and Topic	3	13
Generations Table of Contents by Newsletter	15	16
Generations Table of Contents by Topics	14	31
Generations, Vol 9, Issue 1, Winter 2011	39	45
Generations, Vol 9, Issue 2, Summer 2011	60	94
Generations Vol. 9, Issue 4, Fall 2011	25	154
Generations, Vol 10, Issue 1, Spring 2012	40	179
Generations, Vol 10, Issue 2, Summer 2012	57	219
Generations, Vol 10, Issue 3, Fall 2012	25	276
Generations, Vol 11, Issue 1, Spring 2013	45	301

Table of Contents - Book Four

Description	Pages	Page #
Forward by Marty Guidry	3	3
Guédry et Petitpas Crest- The Story of our Family	4	6
Table of Contents	3	10
Gazette Table of Contents by Newsletter and Topic	3	13
Generations Table of Contents by Newsletter	15	16
Generations Table of Contents by Topics	14	31
Generations, Vol 11, Issue 2, Summer 2013	38	45
Generations, Vol 11, Issue 3, Fall 2013	26	85
Generations, Vol 12, Issue 1, Spring 2014	24	112
Generations, Vol 12, Issue 2, Summer 2014	18	136
Generations, Vol 12, Issue 3, Fall 2014	27	155
Generations, Vol 13, Issue 1, Winter 2015	26	182
Generations, Vol 13, Issue 2, Summer 2015	31	208
Generations, Vol 13, Issue 3, Fall 2015	30	239
Generations, Vol 14, Issue 1, Winter 2016	18	269
Generations, Vol 14, Issue 2, Summer 2016	33	285
Generations, Vol 14, Issue 3, Fall 2016	26	320

Table of Contents - Book Five

Description	Pages	Page #
Forward by Marty Guidry	3	3
Guédry et Petitpas Crest- The Story of our Family	4	6
Table of Contents	3	10
Gazette Table of Contents by Newsletter and Topic	3	13
Generations Table of Contents by Newsletter	15	16
Generations Table of Contents by Topics	14	31
Generations, Vol 15, Issue 1, Spring 2017	18	45
Generations, Vol 15, Issue 2, Summer 2017	26	63
Generations, Vol 15, Issue 3, Fall 2017	69	89
Generations, Vol 16, Issue 1 Spring 2018	37	158
Generations, Vol 16 Issue 2, Summer 2018	28	195
Generations, Vol 16 Issue 3, Fall 2018	23	222

La Gazette des Guidry-Petitpas- 1998-99

Table of Contents by Newsletter

&

Index by Topic

TABLE OF CONTENTS INDEX TO
"LA GAZETTE DES GUIDRY-PETITPAS" - THE NEWSLETTER OF LES GUIDRY D'ASTEUR
(Prepared by Martin Guidry)

TITLE	Page
Volume 1 No. 1 (Jan-Mar 1998)	
The President's Message	1
Congrès Mondial Acadien - Louisiane 1999	2
How Do We Fit In?	3
So What's in a Name?	3
Board of Directors - Ewell T. Guidry; Gayle P. Guidry; Daniel 'Chuck' Guidry; Richard J. Guidry; Warren L. Guidry; R. Martin Guidry	4
The Case of Jean-Baptiste Guédry and His Son: Pirates or Heroes? (R. Martin Guidry)	6
We Are On The Web	7
Coming Next Issue	8
Volume 1 No. 2 (Apr-Jun 1998)	
The President's Message	1
Acadian Families Remembered - Guédry	2
Louisiana in Summer	3
Family Cookbook	4
Corn and Crab Bisque (Daniel "Chuck" Guidry)	5
Pierre Guédry: The Sojourns of an Early Louisiana Acadian (R. Martin Guidry)	6
Earl V. Guedry. - Corporate Sponsor	9
Earl V. Guedry - Business Card	10
Volume 2 No. 1 (Jan-Mar 1999)	
The President's Message	1
Congrès Mondial Acadien - Facts	4
"Genealogy of the Acadian People" Conference	6
"Genetics of the Acadian People" Symposium	7
Earl V. Guedry - Business Card	10

TOPICAL INDEX TO
"LA GAZETTE DES GUIDRY-PETITPAS" - THE NEWSLETTER OF LES GUIDRY D'ASTEUR
(Prepared by Martin Guidry)

TITLE	Volume	Issue	Page	Year	Season
Board of Directors - Ewell T. Guidry; Gayle P. Guidry; Daniel 'Chuck' Guidry; Richard J. Guidry; Warren L. Guidry; R. Martin Guidry	1	1	4	1998	Jan-Mar
Guédry - Acadian Families Remembered	1	2	2	1998	Apr-Jun
Guedry, Earl V. - Corporate Sponsor	1	2	9	1998	Apr-Jun
Guedry, Earl V. - Business Card	1	2	10	1998	Apr-Jun
Guedry, Earl V. - Business Card	2	1	10	1999	Jan-Mar
Guédry, Jean-Baptsite - Case of Jean-Baptiste Guédry and His Son, The: Pirates or Heroes? (R. Martin Guidry)	1	1	6	1998	Jan-Mar
Guédry, Pierre - The Sojourns of an Early Louisiana Acadian (R. Martin Guidry)	1	2	6	1998	Apr-Jun
Coming Next Issue	1	1	8	1998	Jan-Mar
Congrès Mondial Acadien - Louisiane 1999	1	1	2	1998	Jan-Mar
Congrès Mondial Acadien - Facts	2	1	4	1999	Jan-Mar
Corn and Crab Bisque (Daniel "Chuck" Guidry)	1	2	5	1998	Apr-Jun
Family Cookbook	1	2	4	1998	Apr-Jun
"Genealogy of the Acadian People" Conference	2	1	6	1999	Jan-Mar
"Genetics of the Acadian People" Symposium	2	1	7	1999	Jan-Mar
How Do We Fit In?	1	1	3	1998	Jan-Mar
Louisiana in Summer	1	2	3	1998	Apr-Jun
President's Message, The	1	1	1	1998	Jan-Mar
President's Message, The	1	2	1	1998	Apr-Jun
President's Message, The	2	1	1	1999	Jan-Mar
So What's in a Name?	1	1	3	1998	Jan-Mar
We Are On The Web	1	1	7	1998	Jan-Mar

Table of Contents by Newsletter

TABLE OF CONTENTS INDEX TO "GENERATIONS" -
THE NEWSLETTER OF LES GUÉDRY ET PETITPAS D'ASTEUR
(Prepared by Cheryl Tholen; Updated by Martin Guidry)

TITLE	Page
Volume 1 No. 1 (Winter 2003)	
Richard Martin "Marty" Guidry (Meet Our Members)	1
The Guédry-Labine Family and the World's First Atomic Bomb (Marty Guidry)	2
Ronald (Ron) Ames Guidry (Baseball)	5
Kevin Dale Guidry (Football)	6
Paul Michael Guidry (Football)	6
The Cajuns - Essays on Their History and Culture (Glenn R. Conrad)	7
The Cajuns: From Acadia to Louisiana (William Faulkner Rushton)	7
Cajuns on the Bayous (Caroline Ramsey)	7
Cajun Sketches from the Prairies of Southwest Louisiana (Lauren C. Post)	7
People of the Bayou: Cajun Life in Lost American (Christopher Hallowell)	7
The Truth about the Cajuns (Trent Angers)	7
Family Associations - An Oft-Overlooked Resource (Betty Jo Stockton)	8
Guédry-Labine & Petitpas Reunion - Clare & Lunenburg, Nova Scotia, August 5 & 7, 2004 (Marty Guidry)	8
Volume 1 No. 2 (Spring 2003)	
Michael G. C. Guidry (Meet Our Members)	1
Early Guedry Family of Southeast Texas (Marty Guidry)	2
Michael Guidry & Barbara Hall (The Enablers)	6
Clement (Clem) Walter Labine (Baseball)	7
Mike Guidry (Raquetball)	8
Leo Gerald Labine (Ice Hockey)	8
Guédry-Labine Genealogy	
The Guédry, Guidry, Geddry, Jeddry, Guildry dit LaBine, LaBine and LaBean Family - Descendants of Claude Guédry and Marguerite Petitpas (Daryl LaBine)	9
The Ancestors and Family History of Brady W. Guidry and Siblings (Holly Newhouse-Guidry)	9
The Guidry's (Guédry's) (Eunice Helen Barber)	9
The Guidry Family (Geneva Seymour)	9
Ancestors of the Guidry Family of Orange, Texas (Marshall Villeré Woolner)	9
Guidry - Ancestors of John Guidry and Descendants of John Guidry & Rosa LeJeune (Roland Guidry)	9
La Verdure de Mirligueche - The Story of the Guidry dit Labine Family in North America (Mark Labine)	9
Guédry-Labine & Petitpas Reunion - Clare & Lunenburg, Nova Scotia, August 5 & 7, 2004 (Marty Guidry)	10
Volume 1 No. 3 (Summer 2003)	
Cynthia Kay Guidry Herdt (Meet Our Members)	1
Ancestry of the Guedry Family of Clare, Nova Scotia (Jeddry, Geddry) (Marty Guidry)	3
Carlette Guidry (Track & Field)	7
Phyllis Marie Guedry (Softball)	8
Battle of Baton Rouge - 1862 (W. A. Spedale)	9
Compendium of the Confederate Armies Louisiana (Stewart Sifakis)	9
Portraits of Conflict - A Photographic History of Louisiana in the Civil War (Carl Moneyhon & Bobby Roberts)	9
Reminiscences of Uncle Silas: A History of the 18th Louisiana Infantry Regiment (Silas T. Grisamore)	9
Shiloh to Stones River: The True Story of Private John H. Sullivan of the 16th Louisiana Regiment CSA (Travis L. Ayers)	9
The Story of the 26th Louisiana Infantry - In the Service of The Confederate States (Winchester Hall)	9
Civil War Soldiers (Reid Mitchell)	10
The Confederate Nation: 1861-1865 - The New American Nation Series (Emory M. Thomas)	10
Crucible of Reconstruction - War - Radicalism and Race in Louisiana 1862-1877 (Ted Tunnell)	10
Guide to Louisiana Confederate Military Units, 1861-1865 (Arthur W. Bergeron)	10
Acadians in Gray (On The Web)	10
The Civil War in Louisiana (On the Web)	10
Eighteeth Louisiana Infantry Regiment (On the Web)	10
Louisiana Military Units (On the Web)	10
The Seventh Louisiana Cavalry (On the Web)	10
Guédry-Labine & Petitpas Reunion - Clare & Lunenburg, Nova Scotia, August 5 & 7, 2004 (Marty Guidry)	11
Volume 1 No. 4 (Fall 2003)	
Daniel Charles "Chuck" Guidry (Meet Our Members)	1
The Last Guedry's in Merligueche or The Labrador and Guedry Family (Marty Guidry)	3
Mark Guidry (Horseracing)	7
Fodor's Nova Scotia, New Brunswick, Prince Edward Island (Fodor's Gold Guides)	8
Moon Handbooks Atlantic Canada: New Brunswick, PEI, Nova Scotia, Newfoundland and Labrador (3rd Edition) (Mark Morris, et. al.)	8
Nova Scotia: A Colour Guidebook (Stephen Poole)	8
Acadians of Nova Scotia: Past and Present (Sally Ross & Alphonse Deveau)	9
Notes from Exile: On Being Acadian (Clive Doucet)	9
An Unsettled Conquest: The British Campaign Against the Peoples of Acadia (Geoffrey Gilbert Plank)	9
Guédry-Labine & Petitpas Reunion - Clare & Lunenburg, Nova Scotia, August 5 & 7, 2004 (Marty Guidry)	10

TABLE OF CONTENTS INDEX TO "GENERATIONS" -
THE NEWSLETTER OF LES GUÉDRY ET PETITPAS D'ASTEUR
(Prepared by Cheryl Tholen; Updated by Martin Guidry)

TITLE	Page
Volume 2 No. 1 (Winter 2004)	
Jack Anthony Guidry (Meet Our Members)	1
Who Was The First Guedry in Louisiana? (Marty Guidry)	2
Bread and Respect: The Italians of Louisiana (A. V. Margavio & Jerome J. Salomone)	6
Century of Acadian Culture. The Development of a Cajun Community: Erath 1899-1999 (General Curney J. Dronet)	6
Spanish in New Orleans and Louisiana (Jose de Montero Pedro, Marques de Casa Mena, Richard E. Chandler)	6
Louisiana History: An Annotated Bibliography (Florence M Jumonville)	7
The Louisiana Purchase: An Historical and Geographical Encyclopedia (Rodriguez, Junius P.)	7
Louisiana, Yesterday and Today: An Historical Guide to the State (John Wilds, Charles L. Dufour & Walter G. Cowan)	7
George T. Guidry (Golf)	8
Michael Guidry (Golf)	8
Vernon A. Guidry (Rodeo Stockman)	8
Dennis LaBean (Fishing Guide)	8
Guédry-Labine & Petitpas Reunion - Clare & Lunenburg, Nova Scotia, August 5 & 7, 2004 (Marty Guidry)	9
Volume 2 No. 2 (Spring 2004)	
The LaBeans of Michigan - Another Branch of the Guédry Family (Marty Guidry)	4
Jules "Nonc Jules" Guidry (Cajun Band Leader and Musician)	6
Sidney Guidry (Guitarist, Vocalist, Songwriter)	7
Wes Guidry (Rock Disk Jockey)	7
Randy Jeddry (Disk Jockey)	7
The Seven Acadian Expeditions of 1785 (Marty Guidry)	8
Guédry-Labine & Petitpas Reunion - Clare & Lunenburg, Nova Scotia, August 5 & 7, 2004 (Marty Guidry)	1,11
Volume 2 No. 3 (Summer 2004)	
Claude Guedry dit Laverdure & The Origins of the Guedry Family in North America (Marty Guidry)	2
Mickey Guidry (Football)	8
Orun "Doc" Guidry (Cajun Fiddler)	9
Gregory M. "Greg" Guidry (Singer and Songwriter)	10
Genealogical Research in Nova Scotia (Terrence M. Punch)	11
Gentlemen and Jesuits - Glory and Adventure in the Early Days of Acadia (Elizabeth Jones)	11
History of the County of Lunenburg (1895) (M. B. DesBrisay)	12
Tracking Doctor Lonecloud Showman to Legend Keeper (Ruth Holmes Whitehead)	12
Acadian Awakenings - France & Acadie: Routes & Roots; International Links; An Acadian Family in Exile (William D. Gerrior)	13
Politics of Nova Scotia 1710-1896 (J. Murray Beck)	13
Acadian Legends, Folktales, and Songs from Prince Edward Island (Georges Arsenault)	14
Historic Yarmouth - Town & Country (Eric Ruff & Laura Bardley)	14
Guédry-Labine & Petitpas Reunion - Clare & Lunenburg, Nova Scotia, August 5 & 7, 2004 (Marty Guidry)	15
Volume 2 No. 4 (Fall 2004)	
Guédry-Labine & Petitpas Tour of St. Mary's Bay - Clare Region, Nova Scotia, August 4, 2004 (Marty Guidry)	2
Guédry-Labine & Petitpas Reunion - Meteghan, Nova Scotia, August 5, 2004 (Marty Guidry)	5
Guédry-Labine & Petitpas Tour - Clare Region Photo Gallery - August 4, 2004 (Marty Guidry)	7
Augustin Guedry - Hero of the Expulsion (Bernard L. Geddry)	11
Old Fashioned Crackling Cornbread (Charlene Guidry Lacombe, Iota, LA)	12
Pan Fried Haddock (Nathalie Geddry, Halifax, Nova Scotia)	12
Hear What You See Along Baie Sainte-Marie (Alexander C. Axent-Hilton)	13
The Guedry-Labine Cookbook (Jack Guidry, Editor)	13
Fortune & LaTour - The Civil War in Acadia (M. A. MacDonald)	14
Lunenburg - Then and Now (Brian Cuthbertson)	14
Acadia - A Novel (Alfred Silver)	15
Six Micmac Stories (Ruth Holmes Whitehead)	15
"A Hard Day's Work" (A Poem by Marvin 'Mark' Guidry) (Submitted by Allison Guidry)	16
Volume 3 No. 1 (Winter 2005)	
Guédry-Labine & Petitpas Reunion - Lunenburg Nova Scotia, August 7, 2004 (Marty Guidry)	1
Guédry-Labine & Petitpas Tour - Lunenburg Area, August 8, 2004 (Marty Guidry)	1
Survival of a Family: The Migration of the Guedry Family during the 18th Century (Marty Guidry)	2
Nathalie Geddry (Acadian Singer)	2
Michael Guidry & Barbara Hall (The Enablers)	2
Brisket (Maundry Guidry Viator, Abbeville, LA)	3
Myra's Scalloped Potatoes (Marie-Claude Geddry, Gagetown, New Brunswick)	3
"Reunion" (A Poem by Marvin 'Mark' Guidry) (Submitted by Allie Guidry)	3
Belle's Bayou Bounty (Belle Guidry)	4
Belle's Country Cooking (Belle Guidry)	4
Best of Everything: Mama's Creolebook (Marilyn Goudeau Guidry)	4
Yoga Kitchen: Recipes from the Shoshoni Yoga Retreat (Faith Stone and Rachel Guidry)	4
Clans Guidry	5

TABLE OF CONTENTS INDEX TO "GENERATIONS" - THE NEWSLETTER OF LES GUÉDRY ET PETITPAS D'ASTEUR
(Prepared by Cheryl Tholen; Updated by Martin Guidry)

TITLE	Page
Volume 3 No. 2 (Summer 2005)	
Survival of a Family: The Family of Augustin Guedry & Jeanne Hebert (Marty Guidry)	1
Ron "Black" Guidry (The Cajun Man)	2
Creamy Pralines (Charlene Guidry Lacombe, Jennings, LA)	3
HodgePodge (Susan Corkum-Greek, Lunenburg, Nova Scotia)	3
Stuffed Catfish Fillets (Wayne Simoneaux, Montegut, LA)	3
The Acadians - The Historical Basis for Longfellow's Poem of Evangeline (George P. Bible)	4
Historic LaHave River Valley (Sheila Chambers, Joan Dawson & Edith Wolter)	4
A Land of Disocrd Always - Acadia from Its Beginnings to the Expulsion of Its People, 1604-1755 (Charles D. Mahaffie, Jr.)	4
Volume 3 No. 3 (Fall 2005)	
Survival of a Family: The Family of Paul Guedry dit Jovial & Anne Mius d'Entemont d'Azit de Pobomcoup (Marty Guidry)	1
Survival of a Family: Update - The Family of Augustin Guedry & Jeanne Hebert (Marty Guidry)	1
Mama's Fricassee du Poulet (Loyd J. Guidry, Waco, TX)	3
Maque Choux (Alice Matte Guidry, Lake Charles, LA)	3
L'Ouragan de la Cheniere Caminada de 1893 (The Hurricane of Cheniere Caminada of 1893) (Marty Guidry)	4
Marie Lucien Guidry	6
Clare- 2005 Festival Acadian de Clare (Al & Simone Geddry)	7
Acadian Homecoming - 2004 Congrès Mondial Acadien (Clive Doucet)	9
A Great and Noble Scheme - The Tragic Story of the Expulsion of the French Acadians from their American Homeland (John Mack Faragher)	9
Port-Royal Habitation - The Story of the French and Mi'kmaq at Port-Royal (1604-1613) (W. P. Kerr)	9
Volume 4 No. 1 (Winter 2006)	
Survival of a Family: The Family of Pierre Guedry dit Labine & Marguerite Brasseau (Marty Guidry)	1
Iced Tea (Charlene Guidry Lacombe, Jennngs, LA)	3
Stuffed Mirlitons (Jack Guidry, Lafayette, LA)	3
O. G. Guidry	6
Acadian Root Baskets of Atlantic Canada (Joleen Gordon)	10
From Migrant To Acadian (A North American Border People, 1604-1755) (N.E.S. Griffiths)	10
The Forge in the Forest (Charles G.D. Roberts)	11
The History of Louisiana: From the Earliest Period (Francois-Xavier Martin)	11
Father Mitchell Guidry Tours Italy and France (Father Mitchell Guidry)	12
Laura Jane LaBine (Singer & Songwriter)	15
Volume 4 No. 2 (Summer 2006)	
Survival of a Family: The Family of Jean-Baptiste Guedry & Madeleine Mius d'Azy (Marty Guidry)	1
Broccoli Salad (Ron and Joanne Pitts, Toronto, Ontario)	3
Fish Cakes (Simone Comeau Geddry, St. Benoni, Nova Scotia)	3
Lemonade (Marie-Claude Geddry, Gagetown, New Brunswick)	3
Alcee Guidry	6
Survival of a Family: Update on Pierre Guedry dit Labine and Marguerite Brasseau (Marty Guidry)	8
Commemoration of the Guedry-Labine-Petitpas Reunions of August 2004 (Marty Guidry)	10
Bell Terre Acadie (A.K. Keller)	12
Louisbourg - The Phoenix Fortress (Photograhs-Chris Reardon; Text - A.J.B. Johnston)	12
Acadian Redemption - From Beausoleil Broussard to the Queen's Royal Proclamation (Warren A. Perrin)	13
Two Beginnings - A Brief Acadian History (Deveau Alphonse Deveau)	13
A Search for the Father of Claude Guedry, Grandson of Claude Guedry and Marguerite Petitpas (Marty Guidry)	14
Kyle Labine	21
Tyler Labine	22
DNA & Genealogy (Colleen Fitzpatrick)	25
Forensic Genealogy (Colleen Fitzpatrick)	25
Volume 4 No. 3 (Fall 2006)	
Survival of a Family: The Remaining Sons of Claude Guedry and Marguerite Petitpas (Claude, Charles, Alexis, Claude and Joseph) (Martin Guidry)	1
Banana Nut Bread (Maudry Guidry Viator, Abbeville, LA)	3
Navy Bean Soup (Allie Guidry, Springfield, VA)	3
The Virgin of Mount Gédry [La Vierge du Mont Gédry] (Bernard L. Geddry)	4
Archange Guidry	6
Acadian-Cajun Genealogy & History (Tim Hebert) (On the Web)	8
Acadians in Gray (Steven A. Cormier) (On the Web)	8
The Cajuns - Genealogy, History and Culture (Stanley LeBlanc) (On the Web)	8
Claude Petitpas, Sr. and Catherine Bugart (Parents of Maguerite and Claude Petitpas, Jr.) (Sandra Pettipas Perro)	9
Acadian Lives in Cape Breton Island (Ronald Caplan with Rose Aucion Grace)	11
Olde St. John's - Stories from a Seaport City (Frank Galgay & Michael McCarthy)	11
Stir the Pot: The History of Cajun Cuisine (Marcelle Bienvenu, Carl Brasseaux, Ryan A. Brasseaux)	12
Talking Acadian: Communication, Work, and Culture (John Chetro-Szivos)	12
Joseph Guedry and Acadian Card Money (Marty Guidry)	13
Frank Guidry (Guitar, Singer)	15

TABLE OF CONTENTS INDEX TO "GENERATIONS" -
THE NEWSLETTER OF LES GUÉDRY ET PETITPAS D'ASTEUR
(Prepared by Cheryl Tholen; Updated by Martin Guidry)

TITLE	Page
Volume 5 No. 1 (Winter 2007)	
Survival of a Family: The Family of Francoise Guedry & Jean LeJeune (Marty Guidry)	1
Ray's Cajun Hot Brisket (Ray Guidry, Lafayette, LA)	3
Malvina Menard Labine (1893-1967) - Reeve of Azilda, Ontario (Claudette Mancini - her granddaughter)	5
Ozair Guidry	6
Tragedy for the Guedry Family - An Act of Piracy On The High Seas - Part 1 of 2 (Marty Guidry)	7
Trials of Five Persons for Piracy, Felony and Robbery - Part 1 of 2 (Marty Guidry)	9
Acadians in Gray (Steven A. Cormier) (On the Web)	27
Archives Nationales (French National Archives) (On the Web)	27
La Ferme Acadienne (On the Web)	27
The National Archives (On the Web)	27
Accordions, Fiddles, Two Step & Swing - A Cajun Music Reader (Ryan A. Brasseaux & Kevin S. Fontenot)	30
Louisiana Families in Southeast Texas (1840s - 1940s) (Rev. Donald J. Hebert)	30
A History of Port-Royal, Annapolis Royal, 1605-1800 (Brenda Dunn)	31
La Fleur du Rosier - Acadian Folksongs (Helen Creighton)	31
Origins of the Guedry Family in Louisiana, 1765-1785 (Marty Guidry)	32
Guedry-Labine & Petitpas Mini-Reunion - Acadian Village at Lafayette, LA, October 13, 2007 (Marty Guidry)	40
Volume 5 No. 2 (Summer 2007)	
Survival of a Family: The Family of Marie-Josephe Guedry and Philippe Doiron (Marty Guidry)	1
Blueberry Cake (Bernie & Barbara Geddry, Peoria, AZ)	4
Easy and Delicious Seafood Casserole (Aurore Comeau, Comeauville, Nova Scotia)	4
Tragedy for the Guedry Family - An Act of Piracy On The High Seas - Part 2 of 2 (Marty Guidry)	8
The Louisiana State Archives (On the Web)	9
The National Archives (On the Web)	9
The National Archives of Quebec (On the Web)	9
John Jeddry Murdered in St. Alphonse	11
Trials of Five Persons for Piracy, Felony and Robbery - Part 2 of 2 (Marty Guidry)	12
The Encyclopedia of Cajun & Creole Cuisine (John D. Folse)	28
Histoire de l'Acadie (Nicolas Landry & Nicole Lang)	28
A Man For Two Peoples - Pierre-Amand Landry (Della M. M. Stanley)	29
A Song For Acadia (Mary Alice Downie & George Rawlyk)	29
An Exciting Find About Helene and Marie-Josephe Guedry - Twin Daughters of Augustin Guedry & Jeanne Hebert (Marty Guidry)	30
Guédry-Labine & Petitpas Mini-Reunion - Acadian Village at Lafayette, LA, October 13, 2007 (Marty Guidry)	35,45
The Guidry (Guedry) Family of Vermilion (Velma Guidry Beauxis)	36
Origins of the Guédry Family in Louisiana, 1765-1800 - Amended (Marty Guidry)	37
Volume 5 No. 3 (Fall 2007)	
Dedication of Plaque to Augustin Guédry and Marie Jonson - (Marty Guidry)	2
Persimmon Cake (Charlene Guidry Lacombe, Jennings, LA)	4
Rappie Pie (Vawn Jeddry, Edmonton, Alberta)	4
Malvina Menard Labine - The Woman Who Can Do Anything (Marty Guidry and André Labine)	5
Guédry-Labine & Petitpas Mini-Reunion - Acadian Village at Lafayette, LA, October 13, 2007 (Marty Guidry)	11
Edwin Joseph (E.J.) Guidry Sr. and Leon Graugnard - Terre Haute (High Grounds) Plantation (Marty Guidry)	14
The Louisiana State Archives (On the Web)	17
The National Archives (On the Web)	17
The National Archives of Quebec (On the Web)	17
Louisiana's German Coast - A History of St. Charles Parish (Harry E. Yoes III)	18
The Mississippi and the Making of A Nation (Stephen E. Ambrose)	18
My Acadian Heritage (Leonie Comeaux)	19
The Island Acadians, 1720-1980 (Georges Arsenault)	19
Volume 6 No. 1 (Winter 2008)	
The Acadians of Québec (Adrien Bergeron) & Short Genealogy Commentaries: France, Acadia, Quebec (Sandra Pettipas Perro)	2
Oyster Soup (Jack Guidry, Lafayette, LA)	4
Pumpkin Mousse (Jim Graham, Kemah, TX)	4
Antoine Guedry - An Intriguing Acadian (Marty Guidry)	5
Library & Archives - Canada (On the Web)	9
The Louisiana State Archives (On the Web)	9
The National Archives (On the Web)	9
Guédry-Labine & Petitpas Reunion - Bathurst, New Brunswick, August 16, 2009 (Marty Guidry)	10
Ron Guidry - Books featuring baseball	13
Guidry (Ron Guidry & Peter Golenbock)	13
Sports Hero Ron Guidry (Marshall Burchard)	13
Ron Guidry Louisiana Lightning (Maury Allen)	13
Louisiana's Athletes - The Top Twenty (Marty Mule with Bob Remy)	13
Louisiana Sports Legends - The Men and Women of The Louisiana Sports Hall of Fame (Jerry Byrd)	13
Louisianians All (Jeanne Frois)	13
New York Yankees - Players in Pinstripes (Mark Vancil & Mark Mandrake)	13

TABLE OF CONTENTS INDEX TO "GENERATIONS" -
THE NEWSLETTER OF LES GUÉDRY ET PETITPAS D'ASTEUR
(Prepared by Cheryl Tholen; Updated by Martin Guidry)

TITLE	Page
Volume 6 No. 1 (Winter 2008) (Continued)	
The New York Yankees - The Greatest Yankees Teams (Mark Vancil & Mark Mandrake)	13
Clem Labine - Books featuring baseball	14
Brooklyn Dodgers in Their Original Voices (Vince Scully)	14
The Boys of Summer (Roger Kahn)	14
When the Cheering Stops…Former Major Leaguers Talk About Their Game & Their Lives (Lee Heiman, Dave Weiner & Bill Gutman)	14
"That Was Part of Baseball Then" - Interviews with 24 Former Major League Baseball Players, Coaches and Managers (Victor Debs, Jr.)	14
Mark Guidry - Books featuring horseracing	14
Ride of Their Lives -The Triumphs and Turmoil of Today's Top Jockeys (Lenny Shulman)	14
The Original 2004 Thoroughbred Times Racing Almanac (The Staff of Thoroughbred Times)	14
Hon. Albert Guidry - Citizens Meeting	34
Volume 6 No. 2 (Summer 2008)	
Captain Joseph J. Guidrey USNR - Saga of the USS YMS-378, June-July 1944 (as told to his daughter, Jo Ann Guidrey Aulick)	2
Crawfish Etouffee - Creole Style (Jack Guidry, Lafayette, LA)	6
Scott Guidry - Local Man Researches History of Lockport Church (Thad Angelloz & Marty Guidry)	7
H. D. Guidry, M.D. - Advertisement	8
Felix Guidry - Claim Allowed	9
Felix Guidry - Shot Accidentally	9
Oleus Guidry - Refugees from Coast Jam Inland Shelters	9
Woody Guidry, Jr. - Skating Rink Dance Ad	9
Diane Adair Gaidry (Actress and Producer)	10
Jeff Guidry - Freedom and Jeff (Marty Guidry)	12
Library & Archives - Canada (On the Web)	14
The Louisiana State Archives (On the Web)	14
The National Archives (On the Web)	14
Guedry-Labine & Petitpas Reunion - Bathurst, New Brunswick, August 16, 2009 (Marty Guidry)	15
Yankee Autumn in Acadiana: A Narrative of the Great Texas Overland Expedition through Southwestern Louisiana October-December 1863 (David C. Edmonds)	17
Cajuns and Their Acadian Ancestors - A Young Reader's History (Shane K. Bernad)	17
Volume 6 No. 3 (Fall 2008)	
The D-Day Landing and POW Experience of Emery J. Guidry from Cow Island, LA (as told to his nephew Jeffrey Guidry)	2
Pork Chop - Squash Casserole (Carol Leger (Don)-Jeanette Leger, Rayne, LA)	6
Pumpkin Pie (Jim Graham, Kemah, TX)	6
The Guedry Crest (Marty Guidry)	7
A. A. Guidry - Guidry's Seafood Invites Public to Open House; Kerrville, Texas	9
"Petitpas Restaurant" - About Town	9
And How Did I Get That Name? Summerall Martin Guidry (Marty Guidry)	10
The Old Man Told Us - Excerpts from Micmac History - 1500-1950 (Ruth Holmes Whitehead)	12
Louisiana Indian Tales (Elizabeth Mooe & Alice Couvillon)	12
The Vaudville Team of Jim Jedrey and Little Eddie Kelly (Bernard Geddry)	15
H. D. Guidry, M.D. - Advertisement	17
Jewel and Johnnie Guidry - Jewel's Lounge, Kerrville, Texas - Advertisement	18
The Guedry-Labine Family Genealogical Database (On the Web)	19
Les Guidry d'Asteur (On the Web)	19
The Louisiana State Archives (On the Web)	19
Guédry-Labine & Petitpas Reunion - Bathurst, New Brunswick, August 16, 2009 (Marty Guidry)	20
Volume 7 No. 1 (Winter 2009)	
Charlene Guidry Lacombe - Les Guédry d'Asteur Membership Chair Recognized Nationally (Marty Guidry)	2
Charles Guildry dit Labine - Voyageur (Mark Labine)	3
New Research Reveals Guédry's Exiled to North Carolina (Marty Guidry)	12
Frannie's Beer Bread (Charlene Guidry Lacombe, Jennings, LA)	15
Taco Beef Soup (Carolyn Guidry Hilderbran, Uvalde, TX)	15
Mr. Guidry - Scott Scrapings	18
Aynar Guidry - Ad for Order of Wood and Coal	18
Ethel Guidryl - Hadacol Helps Thousands of All Age Groups	18
Hilda and Isaure Guidry - Sisters are Injured When Train Hits Buggy	18
Miss Mary Mae Guidry - 14th Surprise Birthday Party	18
Discovering New Brunswick (Marianne and H.A. Eiselt)	21
New Brunswick Book of Everything (Edited by Martha Walls)	21
Judge Greg G. Guidry - Associate Justice - Louisiana Supreme Court	40
Guédry-Labine & Petitpas Reunion - Bathurst, New Brunswick, August 16, 2009 (Marty Guidry)	41
The Guédry-Labine Family Genealogical Database (On the Web)	43
Les Guidry d'Asteur (On the Web)	43
The Louisiana State Archives (On the Web)	43

TABLE OF CONTENTS INDEX TO "GENERATIONS" -
THE NEWSLETTER OF LES GUÉDRY ET PETITPAS D'ASTEUR
(Prepared by Cheryl Tholen; Updated by Martin Guidry)

TITLE	Page
Volume 7 No. 2 (Spring 2009)	
An Interesting Genealogical Puzzle: Using Land Records to Determine Parentage - Jean-Baptiste Guédry, husband of Anne Magdeleine Dupuis (Marty Guidry)	2
Ray Labine - Dual Roles, His Job & His Lifelong Love (Marty Guidry)	5
Aubrey Guidry - Back Home After Detention	9
Jules Guidry - Short Note To Him	9
William Guidry - Baby Falls Three Stories, Uninjured	9
Hormidas G. Labine - Husband Is Absolute Boss	9
Chicken Fricot (Margaret Jeddry, Nahant, MA & Meteghan, Nova Scotia)	10
Smothered Okra (Alice Matte Guidry, Lake Charles, LA)	10
Labine Hotel - Fort Coulonge, Québec, Canada (Marty Guidry)	11
The Siege of Fort Beauséjour 1755 The (Chris M. Hand)	13
An Unsettled Conquest: The British Campaign Against the Peoples of Acadia (Geoffrey Gilbert Plank)	13
Les Filibustiers de l"Acadie - Coureurs des Mers (Armand G. Robichaud)	14
History of the Cajuns - From Ancient France to Nova Scotia to Louisiana to Colonial Texas (Alex Loya)	14
Census of Acadians at Port Tobacco, Maryland Desiring to Go to France, 7 July 1763 (Marty Guidry)	15
Arrival in New Orleans, 1768 (Marty Guidry)	17
Permit to Sail to New Orleans for the "Jane" - 2 March 1767 (Marty Guidry)	19
Distribution of Land to the Acadians Settling at Fort San Luis de Natchez, February 1768 (Marty Guidry)	20
Inventory of Joseph Guédry's Estate (Marty Guidry)	21
Guédry-Labine & Petitpas Reunion - Bathurst, New Brunswick, August 16, 2009 (Marty Guidry)	26
The Archives of Canada (On the Web)	28
The Guédry-Labine Family Genealogical Database (On the Web)	28
Les Guidry d'Asteur (On the Web)	28
The Louisiana State Archives (On the Web)	28
Volume 7 No. 3 (Summer 2009)	
Michel Cantrelle - Commandant of the First Acadian Coast (Marty Guidry)	2
Acadians To Have Music At Reunion	9
Frank Guidry - Birds Make A Refuge From Farm Swampland	9
Mystery Shrouds Fate of Pennsylvania's "Cajuns"	9
Longfellow Memorial for Evangeline Park at Grand Pré	10
Homemade Creamy Banana and Pecan Ice Cream (Charlene Guidry Lacombe, Iota, LA)	11
Seafood Delight (Julie Guidry, Abbeville, LA)	11
French Fortresses in North America 1535-1763, Quebec, Montreal, Louisbourg and New Orleans (Rene Chartrand)	12
Sods, Soil, and Spades - The Acadians at Grand Pre and Their Dykeland Legacy (J. Sherman Bleakney)	12
Guédry-Labine & Petitpas Reunion - Bathurst, New Brunswick, August 16, 2009 (Marty Guidry)	18
The Archives of Canada (On the Web)	20
The Guédry-Labine Family Genealogical Database (On the Web)	20
Les Guidry d'Asteur (On the Web)	20
The Louisiana State Archives (On the Web)	20
Volume 7 No. 4 (Fall 2009)	
Guédry-Labine & Petitpas Reunion - Bathurst, New Brunswick, August 16, 2009 [Highlights and Photos] (Marty Guidry)	1
Girard Guidry - 2 Airmen Rescue Yank Overcome in Smokey Room	8
James Guidry - You'd Faint, Too	8
Joseph Guidry - Just Like Home	8
Robery G. Guidry - Mother's Day at Marbo-Guam	8
John Guidry - 1871 Census; Québec West, St. Pierre Ward, Québec, Canada	9
David Jeddry - WW II Draft Registration Card - 1942, Salmon River, Nova Scotia	9
Gilbert Labine - Winnipeg Free Press - Manitoba, Canada, June 2, 1936	9
Paul Labine - US Yearbook - Hancock Central High, Hancock, Michigan 1958	9
Baby Lima Beans and Tomato (Mary Guidry Dupont, Houma, LA)	10
Eggplant Fritters (Jack Guidry, Lafayette, LA)	10
Postcards from Acadia (Barbara LeBlanc)	11
A Travel in Time to Grand Pré (Michele Doucette)	11
Guédry-Labine & Petitpas Reunion - Louisiane Day-Espace Neuf, August 17-18, 2009 - Pokemouche, New Brunswick (Marty Guidry)	12
Les Guédry d'Asteur Merchandise (Cindy Herdt)	13
Volume 8 No. 1 (Winter 2010)	
Bernard Bugaret - An Acadian Pioneer (Marty Guidry)	2
Sherwin Jonas Guidry (Sheri Guidry Bergeron)	9
Bobby Charles (Robert Charles Guidry), Louisiana Songwriter Dies at 71	11
Theodule Guidry - Patent Application on a Baler (Allison Guidry)	15
Sausage Jambalaya (Charlene Lacombe, Jennings, LA)	19
Stuffed Bell Peppers (Maudry Guidry Viator, Abbeville, LA)	19
Dr. Leonard Charles Labine Turns 90 (Marty Guidry)	20
Ronald Guidry - Guidry Gets Gold (Boxing) - (Jeremy Theriot)	21
Rev. Felix Guedry - Pastor	23

TABLE OF CONTENTS INDEX TO "GENERATIONS" -
THE NEWSLETTER OF LES GUÉDRY ET PETITPAS D'ASTEUR
(Prepared by Cheryl Tholen; Updated by Martin Guidry)

TITLE	Page
Volume 8 No. 1 (Winter 2010) (Continued)	
Crossword Puzzle Clue - Evangeline	24
Abel Guidry - Special Refrigerator Cars	24
Sgt. Martin Guidry - The Soldiers Life	24
Dictionary of Louisiana French: As Spoken in Cajun, Creole and American Indian Communities (Sr. Editor - Albert Valdman)	25
La Verdure de Mirligueche - The Story of the Guidry dit Labine Family in North America (Mark Labine)	25
Albert Geddry - Honored (Marty Guidry)	26
The Drouin Collection - A Valuable Research Source (Marty Guidry)	28
Volume 8 No. 2 (Summer 2010)	
A Letter from Private Cyrille Trasimon Guidry père durng the Civil War (Marty Guidry)	2
Guidry's Have Leading Roles in Deepwater Horizon Oil Spill Response (Martin Guidry)	2
Ophelia Guidry Perry - Over a Century of Living and Still Going Strong (Cindy Luquette)	8
Roland Guidry and Dr. Jimmy Guidry - Guidry's Having Leading Role In Oil Spill Response (Marty Guidry)	11
American Roots (Mark Labine)	12
The Old-House Journal Compendium (Clem Labine and Carolyn Flaherty)	12
Cuban Black Beans (Dana Guidry, Lafayette, LA)	13
Fish Cakes (Simone Comeau Geddry, Westmount, Québec)	13
Guidry Family Honored at 2010 Acadian Memorial Festival (Marty Guidry)	14
Guédry Family Photos from the Acadian Memorial Festival, March 20, 2010, St. Martinville, LA (Allison Guidry)	18
Malvina Menard Labine (1893-1967) - Reeve of Rayside Township (Claudette Mancini - her granddaughter)	19
Sue Guidry - Frog Queen	22
Guidry's Cleaners - Owner, Danny Domingue	22
Mrs. A. Guedry. - Mrs. Celeste Long, aged 104, dies in New Orleans - Mother of Mrs. A. Guedry	23
Herman Guidry - War "Got InTheir Hair"	23
Sharon Guidry - Writes to "Hints from Heloise"	23
Volume 8 No. 3 (Fall 2010)	
And You Said Your Name Is What Or How Guédry Has Evolved into So Many Variants (Marty Guidry)	2
French, Cajun, Creole, Houma (Carl A. Brasseaux)	6
Voyages: A Maine Franco-American Reader (Nelson Madore)	6
The Louisiana Slave Database & The Louisiana Free Database and Slave Narratives (Marty Guidry)	7
Slave Narratives (Marty Guidry)	16
Broccoli Salad (Ron and Joanne Pitts, Toronto, Ontario)	25
Ray's Cajun Hot Brisket (Ray Guidry, Lafayette, LA)	25
Albert Guidry - Man Questioned in Farmer's Death	26
Remy Guidry - Jefferson Drug Store Owner	26
Guidry's Sea Food (Kerrville, TX)	26
Volume 9 No. 1 (Winter 2011)	
André Labine - Alpine Skiing and My 2010 Winter Olympics Experiences (André Labine)	2
The Acadians - The Historical Basis for Longfellow's Poem of Evangeline (George P. Bible)	9
Deportation of the Prince Edward Island Acadians (Earle Lockerby)	9
David Emery Guidry (Singer, Songwriter, Guitarist)	10
Oyster Soup (Jack Guidry, Lafayette, LA)	12
Persimmon Bread (Maudry Guidry Viator, Abbeville, LA)	12
Extant Acadian Records - Part I: Acadian Church Records [Pre-Deportation - 1613-1759] (Martin Guidry)	13
Miz Liz Gaidry - in 'Panic on the Pecos'	45
Elie Guidry - Market Hunter	45
TSgt. Harry Guidry - Happy Family on Garmisch Holiday	45
Volume 9 No. 2 (Summer 2011)	
Guédry-Labine & Petitpas Sixth Reunion - Cutoff, LA, October 8, 2011 (Marty Guidry)	2
Acadian Culture In Maine (The National Park Service - Online Book)	10
The Attakapas County (Harry Lewis Griffin)	10
Creole Stewed Corn (Suzie Dossat Russell, wife of Marvin Russell, New Orleans, LA)	11
Deep Delta Shrimp (Beverly Butaud Guidry, Abbeville, LA)	11
W. Gaidry - Lima Sales Manager, The Lima News, Lima, Ohio, December 31, 1953	12
Elzinia Guidry - Employees of Guidry Cleaners	12
Martin Guidry, Sr. - Civil War Veteran; Images of America, Rayne, Louisiana	12
Mr. and Mrs. Telismar Guidry - Golden Anniversary	12
Extant Acadian Records - Part II: Acadian Church Records [United States & Caribbean - 1755-1800] (Martin Guidry)	13
Volume 9 No. 3 (Fall 2011) [Labeled as Volume 9 No. 4]	
Guédry-Labine & Petitpas Sixth Reunion ReCap - Cut Off, LA, October 8, 2011 (Marty Guidry)	2
Circle of Distinction Certificate Presentation (2011 Inductees)	
Daniel Charles 'Chuck' Guidry; BGen Albert Louis Geddry; Sandra Perro Pettipas; Rita Labine; Ronald Ames Guidry; Daine Adair Gaidry	8
Guédry-Labine & Petitpas Booth at Fête de Famille -Lafayette, LA Cajundome, 13 October 2011 (Allison Guidry)	14
The Big Thicket Guidebook - Exploring the Backroads and History of Southeast Texas (Lorraine G. Bonney)	17

TABLE OF CONTENTS INDEX TO "GENERATIONS" -
THE NEWSLETTER OF LES GUÉDRY ET PETITPAS D'ASTEUR
(Prepared by Cheryl Tholen; Updated by Martin Guidry)

TITLE	Page
Volume 9 No. 3 (Fall 2011) (Continued) [Labeled as Volume 9 No. 4]	
Driving Mr. Yogi - Yogi Berra, Ron Guidry, Baseball's Greatest Gift (Harvey Araton)	17
Lowell R. Gaidry - Gaidry's Tabasco Pepper Sauce , New Orlean's, Louisiana	18
Oliver Guidri - Sunday Law Violated	18
Horace Guidry - Harrington's Murderer	18
Louis T. Guidry - Private Sale Ad	18
Marjorie Sue Guidry - Port Arthur News, Port Arthur, Texas	18
Raymond Guidry - Pharmacist, Port Arthur, Texas	18
Tarte a la Bouillie (Daniel 'Chuck' Guidry, Lacombe, LA)	19
Cajun Jambalaya - Stove Top Method (Roland Guidry, Cut Off, LA)	20
Cajun Jambalaya For A Crowd - In a Large Cast Iron Pot (Roland Guidry, Cut Off, LA)	20
Creole White Beans (Daniel "Chuck" Guidry, Lacombe, LA)	21
Homemade Pepper Vinegar (Daniel C. "Chuck" Guidry, Lacombe, LA)	22
Maque Choux (Wayne Simoneaux, Montegut, LA)	22
Red Beans and Rice (Wayne Simoneaux, Montegut, LA)	23
Volume 10 No. 1 (Spring 2012)	
A Labine "Lost" in British Columbia - Léon Labine and the Hudson's Bay Company (Martin Guidry)	3
Guédry & Petitpas Reunion - Van Buren, ME, 16 August 2014 (Marty Guidry)	6
Acadian Village Historical Site, Van Buren, Maine (Marty Guidry)	7
Cajun By Any Other Name: Recovering the Lost History of a Family-and a People (Marie Rundquist)	8
Revisiting Anne Marie (Marie Rundquist)	8
Band of Acadians (John Skelton)	9
Minnesota Farm Family Memories (Mark Labine)	9
St. Martinville - Mars 2010 - An Article on Acadian Festival in *LA LETTRE*, (G.M.Braud)	10
Grapevine Opry Starring Blackie Guidry - Grapevine, Texas	10
Ernest Guidry - Necrology	10
Evariste Guidry - His Wife Katie Perrin Died	10
H. N. Guidry - Fifth Death From Accident	10
Hester M. Guidry - The Skyline Cafe - Advertisement	10
Hilda Guidry - LaLa's Beauty Parlor Advertisement	10
Pierre L. Guidry. - Died at Home in Church Point, Louisiana	10
Captain Petitpas - Missing Vessel	10
Joseph P. Guidry - Skipper of Hitler's Yacht (Joe Carmichael)	11
Extant Acadian Records - Part III: Acadian Church Records [Québec, Ontario, British Columbia - 1755-1900] (Martin Guidry)	15
Aubergine (Eggplant) de la Louisiane avec Ecrevisse (Shrimp) (Janet Bienert Higgins, New Orleans, LA)	37
Cabbage Patch Stew (Carolyn Guidry Hilderbran, Uvalde, TX)	37
Volume 10 No. 2 (Summer 2012)	
First Known Record of the Guédry Family in North America (Martin Guidry)	2
Mark & Jean Guidry - Wheaton Antique Mall (Wheaton, IL)	3
Renée Guidry, M.A., BCBA - Behavioral Intervention Group (Baton Rouge, LA)	3
Lloyd & Cindy Jeddry - Jeddry's Auto Body Shop (St. Alphonse, Nova Scotia)	3
André Labine - Lubricants Marketing Consultants (Fernie, British Columbia)	3
The Mapmaker's Legacy - Ninteenth Century Maps of Nova Scotia (Joan Dawson)	4
Nova Scotia's Lost Highways - The Early Roads That Shaped The Province (Joan Dawson)	4
Eggplant Casserole (Jeanette Leger, Rayne, LA)	5
Pain Perdu (Lost Bread) (Jack Guidry, Lafayette, LA)	5
Gravestones of Original Acadian Deportees (Martin Guidry)	6
Ernest Guidry - Died after Extended Illness	14
Sidney Guidry - Death Notice, 1903, Boerne, Texas	14
Sosthene Guidry - Tragedy at a Dance	14
L. C. Guidry - Fournet & Guidry Reply to the Eastin Charges in St. Martin Parish	15
Louis Guidry - Train Kills Boy of 13	15
W. LaBean - Muskegon Chronicle, Muskegon, Michigan, June 13, 1916	15
Extant Acadian Records - Part IV: Acadian Church Records [Nova Scotia, NB, PEI, Newfoundland, St-Pierre-et-Miquelon] (Martin Guidry)	16
Volume 10 No. 3 (Fall 2012)	
Rita Labine - Announcement of Death (October 12, 2012 in Ottawa, Canada) (André Labine)	1
Dance Halls, Hostelries and The Guedry's (Marty Guidry)	2
Family of Charles Joseph Guedry & Marie Leontine Gaudet	7
Mickey J. Guidry, CFA - Branch Manager and Registered Principal (Baton Rouge, LA)	8
Nonc Jules Guidry and "Lachez-Les" - Authentic Cajun Music Band (Carencro, LA)	8
Circle of Distinction Certificate Presentation (2012 Inductees)	
Bernard L. Geddry; Vernon Paul Guidry; Gilbert Adélard Labine; Dr. Thomas Henry LaBean; George Henri Petitpas	9
Amy Guidry (Artist)	11
Guédry & Petitpas Reunion - Van Buren, ME, 16 August 2014 (Marty Guidry)	13
The Acadian Diaspora - An Eighteenth-Century History (Christopher Hodson)	16
Histoire des Acadiennes et Acadiens de La Louisiane (Zachary Richard, et al)	16

TABLE OF CONTENTS INDEX TO "GENERATIONS" -
THE NEWSLETTER OF LES GUÉDRY ET PETITPAS D'ASTEUR
(Prepared by Cheryl Tholen; Updated by Martin Guidry)

TITLE	Page
Volume 10 No. 3 (Fall 2012) (Continued)	
L. J. Guidry - State Officers of the Catholic Knights of America	17
John A. Geddry - Patrolman Finds Man Hurt Is His Father-in Law (The Boston Herald, Newburyport, Massachusetts, November 17, 1932)	18
Tom Geddry - Scouting Historical Award for Florence Bank Project (Omaha Evening World-Herald, Nebraska, September 13, 1963)	18
Guidry's Wine and Cheese (Nolan and Bobbie Guidry)	18
Lowell R. Gaidry - Gaidry's Tabasco Pepper Sauce, New Orlean's, Louisiana	19
Mama's Fish Court de Boullion (Lloyd J. Guidry, Waco, TX)	20
Orange Slice Cake (Jeanette Leger, Rayne, LA)	20
LeeAnn Raye Law (Cajun Fiddler) - Carrying On A Family Tradition (Written by her mother Christine Guidry Law)	21
Douglas Guidry, MAI - Certified General Real Estate Appraiser (Gloucester, MA)	22
Mark Guidry - Manager, Speech and Editorial Services, American Medical Services (Chicago, IL)	22
Volume 11 No. 1 (Spring 2013)	
Acadians in Madawaska - Their Journey and Struggle (Marty Guidry)	2
Hypolite Onizaphore Guidry & Corrine Sonnier Guidry Family	8
Guédry & Petitpas Reunion - Van Buren, ME, 16 August 2014 (Marty Guidry)	9
Josh Jeddry - Photography	12
R. Martin Guidry - DuPont Performance Elastomers	12
R. Martin Guidry - Exxon Chemicals	12
Billy Guidry - E Go Travel	12
Les Guidry and Luke Guidry - Guidry Painting	12
Rappie Pie (Vawn Jeddry, Edmonton, Alberta)	13
Zucchini Bread (Celeste Bancroft, East Hartford, CT)	13
Extant Acadian Records - Part V: Acadian Church Records [France, England, Caribbean, South America - 1755-1800] (Marty Guidry)	14
Acadian Hard Times: The Farm Security Administration in Maine's St. John Valley, 1940-1943 (C. Steward Doty)	38
The First Franco-Americans - New England Life Histories form the Federal Writers' Project (C. Stewart Doty)	38
Guédry & Petitpas Athletes - Professional (Baseball, Football, Ice Hockey, Racquetball, Golf, Rodeo, Fishing, Track & Field)	39
Miss Ethel L. Guedry - Medal Given Miss Guedry	43
Dr. Mark Guidry - Laser Built at LSU	43
Labine Bros. - Labine's Winchester Park Shoe Store - Advertisement	43
Frenchman Named Labine Who Keeps the Mountain Boys Saloon Shot	43
Labine's Winchester Park Shoe Store Advertisement	43
Charmaine Guidry - With Unbearable Sorrow	44
Dell Joseph Guidry - Boy Disappears After Scolding	44
Frank LaBine Now at Mineola Hospital	44
Volume 11 No. 2 (Summer 2013)	
Richard Guidry Honored Posthumously (Marty Guidry)	2
The New Acadie Project [Proget Nouvelle Acadie] (Marty Guidry)	4
Plaque Dedicated to the Acadians of Maryland (Martin Guidry)	6
Crab and Corn Bisque (Daniel C. "Chuck" Guidry, Lacombe, LA)	8
Persimmon Cake (Charlene Guidry Lacombe, Iota, LA)	8
Guédry & Petitpas Reunion - Van Buren, ME, 16 August 2014 (Marty Guidry)	9
Touring Acadian Madawaska - NE Maine, NW New Brunswick & SE Quebec (Congrès Mondial - 8-24 August 2014)	13
Home At Last: An Acadian Journey (Ollie Porche Voelker)	27
Tirailleurs: A History of the 4th Louisiana and The Acadians of Company H (Thomas H. Richey)	27
Guidry's Hardware Celebrating 80 Years	28
Dufossat Guidry - The Assumption Homicide	35
F. E. Guidry - Railroad News from All Around - Guidry Returns from Seeing Soldiers on the Border	35
L. J. Guedry Is Seeking Stolen Cash And Gems	36
Louis Guidry - Local Prep School Goes Against Springhill Today	36
Mr. and Mrs. David Labean - "Hose Joke" Is Fatal to Bay City Workman	36
Volume 11 No. 3 (Fall 2013)	
Guédry & Petitpas Reunion - Van Buren, ME - So What Is There To Do at the Congrès Mondial Acadien 2014? (Marty Guidry)	2
Albert A. Guidry & Marie Gaudin Family	8
The Scattered - Thirty Years of Exile; A Lifetime of Loss; The Triumph of a Simple Man (Richard Holledge)	10
Voici The Valley Cultureway [Audio Story and Guide of Upper St. John Valley] (Sheila Jans, Don Cyr & Daniel Picard)	10
The Henry Guidry Family of Vermilion Parish, Louisiana (Robert L. Choate)	11
Circle of Distinction Certificate Presentation (2013 Inductees)	
Myrtle LaBean Pletos, Richard James Guidry, Mark Labine, Robinson Joseph Guidry, Robert Charles Guidry, Earl V. Guidry, Jr.	13
The Modern Acadians - The Picturesque French-Canadian Squatters in Maine	16
Frumenity ("Worcester County - Maryland's Arcadia")	17
Pumpkin Spice Bread (Allie Guidry, Springfield, VA)	17
A Couple of Louisiana Artists (Marty Guidry)	18
Dick Guidry Being Inducted in Louisiana Political Hall of Fame (Marty Guidry)	19
Guédry & Petitpas Reunion - Van Buren, ME, 16 August 2014 (Marty Guidry)	20

TABLE OF CONTENTS INDEX TO "GENERATIONS" - THE NEWSLETTER OF LES GUÉDRY ET PETITPAS D'ASTEUR
(Prepared by Cheryl Tholen; Updated by Martin Guidry)

TITLE	Page
Volume 12 No. 1 (Spring 2014)	
The Grivois of Northeast Maine - Another Branch of the Guédry Family (Marty Guidry)	2
Guédry & Petitpas Reunion - Van Buren, ME, 16 August 2014 (Marty Guidry)	10
Percy Guidry's Hearth & Patio - (Keith Guidry)	16
Guidry & Company Real Estate	16
Christine Guidry Law - Acadian/Cajun Culture (Zachary, LA)	16
Noodle Pudding (Bernie & Barbara Geddry, Peoria, AZ)	17
Venison Tenderloin (Ray Guidry, Lafayette, LA)	17
The Acadians - In Search of A Homeland (James Laxer)	18
The French Canadian Heritage in New England (Gerard J. Brault)	18
Oak Island - An Acadian Tale (Mark Labine)	19
G. W. Baylor & Guedry - Real Estate and Insurance Agents	20
Guidry - One of New Orleans' Best-Drilled Gridiron Squads Whose Work Improves with Each Game	20
Eugene Labine - Harvesting 500 Acres	20
Beatrice A. Guidry & Earl J. Guidry - Work Completed at Bourg High School	21
Mrs. Horace Guidry - After Many Years	21
L. J. Guidry - State Officers of the Catholic Knights of America	21
Alfred A. Labine Marries Marie Catudal	21
Volume 12 No. 2 (Summer 2014)	
Acadian Genetic Diseases (Matin Guidry)	2
Ruth Guidry's Butter Cream Frosting (Charelene Guidry Lacombe, Jennings, LA)	12
Acadian Pea Soup (Bouchard Family Farms Cookbook) (Bouchard Family, Fort Kent, ME)	12
Ployes - Buckwheat Pancakes (Bouchard Family Farms Cookbook) (Bouchard Family, Fort Kent, ME)	12
Emelie Guidry (Singer)	13
French Acadian Cookbook: Keeping the Tradition Alive - Bouchard Family Farms ((Bouchard Family)	14
Pulp, Potatoes and Ployes - An Acadian Odyssey (Jules M. Seletz)	14
Guédry & Petitpas Reunion - Van Buren, ME, 16 August 2014 (Marty Guidry)	15
Mrs. Antoine Guidry (Hortense Broussard) - Succession	16
Homer Guidry - The Homer Guidry & Elizabeth Martin Family	16
Mareuse Guidry - Six Arrests Made in Mareuse Guidry Case	16
Alex Guidry - Pleasure Boat Trip to Vermilion Bay and Gulf Coast	17
David Guidry - Claim of 480 Superficial Arpents of Land	17
W. LaBean - Charged with Murder	17
Charles Leo Labine - Uranium Miner Labine Is Dead (Obituary)	17
Volume 12 No. 3 (Fall 2014)	
Guédry & Petitpas Reunion (6th) Recap - Van Buren, ME, 16 August 2014 (Marty Guidry)	2
Circle of Distinction Certificate Presentation (2014 Inductees)	
Leo Joseph Guedry, Jr.; Allison Lynn Guidry; Michael Wayne Guidry; Daryl LaBine; Roland "Clem" Labine, Jr.; Bishop Gérard Petitpas	7
5 Cup Salad (Maudry Guidry Viator, Abbeville, LA)	11
Old Fashioned Grilled Lobster Roll (Alain Bosse, "The Kilted Chef", Halifax, Nova Scotia)	11
DNA & Genealogy - A Brief Primer (Marty Guidry)	12
Acadie Then And Now - A People's History (Warren Perrin, Mary Perrin, Phil Comeau)	17
Two Homes Built By Exiled Acadians in Connecticut (Marty Guidry)	18
And Where Did You Say They Lived (Marty Guidry)	22
Marty R. Guidry. - New Eagle Scout	23
Mrs. Joe A. Guidry (Goldie Ann) - Death Struck Here	24
Olivier D. Guidry - Resigned As Justice of Peace in St. Landry Parish, LA	24
Summerall Guidry - Sunset Developers, Inc. Homebuilding Advertisement	24
Virgie Lea Guidry - Featured Speakers at CCD Conference	24
Benoit Guidry - Guidry Family Reunion at Benoit Guidry Home in Carlyss, LA in 1964	25
Florence M. Guidry - Valedictorian of Mercy Hospital Graduation Class in Nursing	25
Representative Richard Guidry - Inspects Tornado Damage in Lafourche Parish, LA	25
Widow Theodule Guidry (Celestine Touchet) - Lost Military Warrant	25
Volume 13 No. 1 (Winter 2015)	
Guédry & Petitpas Reunion - Henderson, LA, 10 October 2015 (Marty Guidry)	2
Milton F. Guidry & Summerall Guidry - Ligthning, Inc. Letterhead	5
Dancehalls and the Guédry's (An Update) (Marty Guidry)	6
Blueberry Cake (Bernie & Barbara Geddry, Peoria, AZ)	12
Rapure (Patricia LaBine Knodel, Calgary, Alberta, Canada)	12
Histoire de l'Acadie (Nicolas Landry & Nicole Lang)	13
The Town That Crawfish Built - A History of Henderson, Louisiana (Marjorie R. Esman)	13
Marie Clausimire Guildry dit Labine	14
Emery Louis Geddry - A Canadian Soldier Who Gave The Ultimate Sacrifice (World War II) (Marty Guidry)	15
Fred Guidry - Cajun Carving	23
Camille Guedry - Died At His Home in Ascension Parish, LA	24

TABLE OF CONTENTS INDEX TO "GENERATIONS" -
THE NEWSLETTER OF LES GUÉDRY ET PETITPAS D'ASTEUR
(Prepared by Cheryl Tholen; Updated by Martin Guidry)

TITLE	Page
Volume 13 No. 1 (Winter 2015) (Continued)	
Mr. and Mrs. Ambrose LaBine, et. al. - Wedding Anniversaries Observed by LaBines	24
Albin Petitpas - Recover Miner's Body Trapped in Cave-In	24
Thoma L. Petitpas - Completed Basic USAF Training at Lackland AFB, TX	24
Volume 13 No. 2 (Summer 2015)	
Update - Emery Louis Geddry: A Canadian Soldier Who Gave The Ultimate Sacrifice (World War II) (Marty Guidry)	3
Angel Guidry - 2015 Young Heroes Award	6
Guidry's Nursery (Parks, LA)	8
Guidry's Repair Shop - Owner, Harry Guidry (St. Martinville, LA)	8
Ronald Guidry - Talent Spotlight (Boxing)	9
Poet's Chicken Salad (Beverly Butaud Guidry, Abbeville, LA)	11
Peanut Butter Fudge (Jeanette Guidry Leger, Rayne, LA)	11
The Story of Nova Scotia Acadians Who Came to the Aid of Hurricane Rita Victims (Jude Avery)	12
A Tribute to Our Acadian Ancestors [Poems] (Jude Avery)	15
Charles Guidry - Erath's Guidry Has Overcome Obstacles To Be Successful Sugarcane Farmer (Abbeville Meridional, Abbeville, LA)	16
Evelyn Pettipas - Valley View Villa Senior Evelyn Pettipas Graduates At 93 (The News, New Glasgow, Nova Scotia)	17
The Petitpas of Acadia (L'Acadye) (Sandra Pettipas Perro)	18
Guédry & Petitpas Reunion - Henderson, LA, 10 October 2015 (Marty Guidry)	22
Death In l'Acadie - A Kesk8a Story (Sherrill Wark)	26
A Silver Lining From Acadie to Louisiana (Ollie Ann Porche Veolker)	26
Fontenot & Guidry Department Store & Fabric Shop (Breaux Bridge, LA)	27
Frank J. Guidry Oil Company - Crawfish Festival (Breaux Bridge, LA)	27
Henry J. Guidry, Jr. - Captain of Jerusalem Temple Arab Patrol	27
James O. LaBean. - Seeking Relative for Receiving Body	27
Henry Guidry - Purchases Half-Interest in Mr. C. P. Moss' Saloon And Restaurant	28
Bill Guidry's Electric Service et. al. (Listing of Guidry Businesses in 1959 Lafayette, LA City Directory)	28
Abraham LaBean - Rescued From Fishing Accident in Michigan	28
Volume 13 No. 3 (Fall 2015)	
Guédry & Petitpas Seventh Reunion Re-Cap - Henderson, LA, 10 October 2015 (Marty Guidry)	2
Circle of Distinction Certificate Presentation (2015 Inductees)	
Rebecca E. Boggess; Oran 'Doc' Guidry; Roland David Guidry; Roland J. Guidry; Clement ' Clem' Walter Labine; Leo F. Pettipas	7
Guidry Sisters Compete in International Science Fairs (Barry Guidry)	10
J. Alfred Jeddry of Meteghan, Nova Scotia, Receives French Military Recognition (Albert Geddry)	12
Acadians of Québec (Sandra Pettipas Perro)	14
Ginette Petitpas Taylor Takes the Moncton-Riverview-Dieppe Seat (Marty Guidry)	18
Philemone Guidry - Overseer of Michel Bernard Cantrelle Plantation (Marty Guidry)	19
Shepherd's Pie - The English Way (Jean Guidry, Naperville, IL)	25
Sweet Potato - Pecan Casserole (Carol Leger, Rayne, LA)	25
Clem Labine - Always A Dodger (Richard Elliott)	26
Mi'kmaq Treaties on Trial (William C. Wicken)	26
Joseph Guedry Found Dead in Room at Melrose House	27
Justice Mitchell Completes His Investigation as to the Cause of the Death of Joseph Guedry	27
William Guedry - Death of William Guedry	27
Elizabeth Ann Guedry Represents Auxiliary at State Convention	28
Guedry's Pharmacy - Advertisement	28
Fergus Guidry - Knocked in Head by Euphemon LeBlanc	28
Jules Guidry - Grandson Eli Completed the Diploma Business Course at Kentucky University	28
Volume 14 No. 1 (Winter 2016)	
Roman Antoine Guidry - Necrology	2
Early Analysis of the Guédry & Petitpas Families (Martin Guidry)	3
Blackberry Dumplings (Jack Guidry, Lafayette, LA)	13
Crawfish Dip (Jack Guidry, Lafayette, LA)	13
Minnesota Farm Family Memories (Mark Labine)	14
Pauli The Musical Pumpkin (Pamela O. Guidry)	14
Reyanne's Rainbow Swamp (Adina Guidry)	14
Lowell R. Gaidry - Gaidry's Tabasco Pepper Sauce, New Orlean's, Louisiana	15
Clem Labine and Jackie Robinson Keep Brooklyn Hopes Alive	15
Sgt. Raymond Edmond Petitpas - Warrant Officers, N.C.O.'s and Men Previously Reported Missing Now Reported Killed in Action	15
Stanley Petitpas - Eczema on Face and Arms for a Year. Healed by Cuticura - Testimonial	15
The Caliste Guidry Home for Sale	16
F. E. Guidry - General Merchandise and Plantation Supplies Advertisement	16
Fred Guidry and Louis Guidry - Planters Bank & Trust Company Advertisement	16
Olive LaBine - Girls Senior Board - 1929 Yearbook	16

TABLE OF CONTENTS INDEX TO "GENERATIONS" - THE NEWSLETTER OF LES GUÉDRY ET PETITPAS D'ASTEUR
(Prepared by Cheryl Tholen; Updated by Martin Guidry)

TITLE	Page
Volume 14 No. 2 (Summer 2016)	
Guédry, Hébert & Breaux Reunion - Maurice, LA, 25 June 2016 (Marty Guidry)	2
Should the Guédry Surname Really Be Melançon? - A DNA Genealogical Study (Mark Labine & Marty Guidry)	4
Why Did The Petitpas And Guédry Families Settle at Merliguèche? (Marty Guidry)	13
Meredith Guidry Competes Again at International Science Fair	16
Michel Labine of Northwest Territories Creates Beautiful Stained Glass in Northern Themes	16
Dr. Charles Guidry - 2016 Stars of Style Best Dressed Gala	17
Crawfish Cornbread (Jack Guidry, Lafayette, LA)	18
Fruit Salad Dressing (Jean Guidry, Naperville, IL)	18
Books & Websites on the Genealogy of the Guédry (Guidry, Labine, LaBean) & Petitpas Families	19
Les Acadiens Déportés Qui Acceptérent l'Offre de Murray (André-Carl Vachon)	21
They Spoke French (Mark Labine - Contributor)	21
The Acadian Deportations (Marty Guidry)	22
Glenn Guidry "Mr. Rock'n Piano" at the Ponderosa - Advertisement	30
Glynn Guidry And the Other Brothers at Hurley's Tavern - Advertisement	30
Mr. and Mrs. Jules Pierre Guidry - Couple Observes 50th Anniversary of Marriage Here	30
Allain Guedry - Orange Blossoms - Marriage of Allain Guedry, son of Joseph Guedry & Angeline Rodrigue, to Angelique Rodrigue	31
Caliste Guidry - A Wholesale Raid	31
F. E. Guidry - General Merchandise and Plantation Supplies Advertisement	31
Joseph Guidry - Songs by Joseph 'Frenchy' Guidry at Carnival and Entertainment - Advertisement	31
Volume 14 No. 3 (Fall 2016)	
Seeking the Roots of Art Guidry - A Louisiana Creole Genealogical Study (Art Guidry & Marty Guidry)	2
Historic Plaisance Rosenwald (Art Guidry)	14
Joanie Labine - Remember the Go-Go Dance? (Martin Guidry)	16
Circle of Distinction Certificate Presentation (2016 Inductees)	
Claude Guédry; Jules 'Nonc Jules' Guidry; Joseph Alfred Jeddry; André Robert Labine; Claude Petitpas; Colonel William J. Pettipas	17
Cyrille Trasimond's Jelly Roll (Cyrille Trasimond Guidry, Abbeville, LA)	21
Meat Pie a l'Acadienne (Simone Comeau Geddry, St. Benoni, Nova Scotia)	21
In the Beginning, There Was A Chapel (Mark Labine)	22
Teche - A History of Louisiana's Most Famous Bayou (Shane Bernard)	22
Miss Mae Guidry, Daughter of Jules Paul Guidry, Weds J. Nugent	23
Guidry's Louisiana Blue Rhythm Boys - Nick's Place - Advertisement	23
Guidry's Orchestra - Nick's Place - Advertisement (Two Ads)	23
Eugene Labine - Harvesting 500 Acres	23
Inez Guidry - Guidry Shot Three Times by His Brother-in-Law	24
Nolan, Billy and Ronald Guidry - Guidry Family in Golden Gloves	24
Rev. Robert Guidry - Presentation of Altar Cloths and Accessories	24
Aurore A. Labine, et. al. - One Opposes Nine in Fight Over Estate of Fred Labine	24
Volume 15 No. 1 (Spring 2017)	
Catherine Bugaret - Ancestral Mother of the Petitpas Family, Ancestral Grandmother of the Guédry Family (Martin Guidry)	2
Leo Pettipas - Discusses Yeti Pettipas from 2004 Atlantic Film Festival	10
City of Remembering - A History of Genealogy in New Orleans (Susan Tucker)	11
Ghosts of Good Times - Louisiana Dance Halls Past and Present (Philip Gould & Herman Fuselier)	11
Sour Cream Pound Cake (Anita Guidry, Church Point, LA)	12
Toasted Orzo Chicken Soup (Cindy Guidry Herdt, Wenatchee, WA)	12
J. A. Guedry - Fine Fish from Bayou Corne	13
Alcee Guidry - Guidry Company Brick Plant Has Baby Naming Contest	13
Mrs. Alcee Guidry - Invites Readers to See New Hats for Sale at Her Home	13
Eugene Guidry - Engaged to Marry Eugenie LeBlanc	13
Lois Anne Guidry - Engaged to Marry Walter Alvin Souther, Jr.	13
A. A. Gaidry. - From Oyster Cocktail to Roast Turkey at the Gem Café - Advertisement	14
A. A. Gaidry - Stores to Close at Earlier Hour	14
Howard Guidry - Boy Accidentally Shot by Chum in Jennings	14
Gil Labine - Labine Tabbed to Head Northwest LHIN Board	15
Volume 15 No. 2 (Summer 2017)	
John Leonce Guidry and Lillian Lefort Guidry of Galliano, LA - Ordinary People, Extraordinary Lives (Martin Guidry)	2
Eileen Avery and Sandra Perro Pettipas - Tor Bay Acadians Honor Roll Inductions	10
Ginette Petitpas Taylor & Stephen Poloz Unveil New Canadian Banknote	14
Claire Labine - Soap Opera Writer and Co-Creator of 'Ryan's Hope' Dies at 82 - November 11, 2016 (Sam Robertson)	15
Dr. Jay Labine - Chief Medical Officer at Priority Health	17
Nancy LaBine - CSCC's LaBine Receives Volunteer Award	18
Biggs and Guidry Typewriters Advertisement	20
Emile Guidry - Ripley's Believe or Not - His Hen Laid an Egg in a Cold Cream Jar	20
Mr. and Mrs. Johnny Guidry - Gave Food and Cash Shower to Alcide J. Smith Family Who Lost All in Hurricane Audrey	20
Pierre Guidry & Son Co. - Pre-Finished Plywood Advertisement	20

TABLE OF CONTENTS INDEX TO "GENERATIONS" -
THE NEWSLETTER OF LES GUÉDRY ET PETITPAS D'ASTEUR
(Prepared by Cheryl Tholen; Updated by Martin Guidry)

TITLE	Page
Volume 15 No. 2 (Summer 2017) (Continued)	
Raymond Dale Guidry - Suffered Injury When Case of Pop Fell And Cut Him	20
Family of Late Ignace Guidry & Azelie David Hold Reunion in 1976 at Chicot Park, LA	21
Charles LaBean And His Brother Gilbert A. LaBean Visit Hollywood with Their Families (Should be Labine)	21
James LaBine Gets U. S. Mail Contract	21
Acadian Legends, Folktales, and Songs from Prince Edward Island (Georges Arsenault)	22
The Forgotten Battle - A History of the Acadians of Canso/Chedabuctou (Mark Haynes)	22
Double 'J' Cajun Fried Catfish Strips (Guidry's Catfish)	23
Ice Cream Cake (Cindy Guidry Herdt, Wenatchee, WA)	23
Volume 15 No. 3 (Fall 2017)	
Hank Williams' *Jambalaya* and the Guidry Connection (Martin Guidry)	2
Turkey and Oyster Gumbo (Jack Guidry, Lafayette, LA)	5
One Generation at a Time - Biography of a Cajun and Creole Music Festival (Barry Jean Ancelet & Philip Gould)	6
Portraits of South Louisiana (Emile Waagenaar)	6
Guédry & Petitpas Eighth Reunion - Summerside, Prince Edward Island, 17 August 2019 (Marty Guidry)	7
Circle of Distinction Certificate Presentation (2017 Inductees)	
Fred G. Guidry; Dr. Jimmy N. Guidry; Seth Wayne Guidry; Leonard 'Leo' Gerald Labine; Marie Ginette Petitpas Taylor; Marguerite Petitpas	12
Guédry, Hébert & Breaux Reunion - Thibodaux, LA, 10 March 2018 (Marty Guidry)	15
Gaidry Gas and Oil Co. Recently Organized	16
Alexander Guidry Killed Hog That Was 7 Foot 2 Inches And Weighed 610 Pounds	16
L. R. Guidry - Transferring to Mexico	16
Clem Labine - Editor of the *Old-House Journal*	16
Audrey Guidry - Story "Vickie and the Elf" Written by Audrey Guidry, 9 Years Old	17
Charles Guidry - Is Not A Candidate for Commissary	17
Jules Guidry - Emancipation of Victorine Melancon, wife of Jules Guidry	17
Mrs. Jospeh LaBean - Thrown from Wagon and Injured While Returing from Daughter's Wedding	17
Cajun Musicians in the Family - An Early History (Martin Guidry)	18
Volume 16 No. 1 (Spring 2018)	
Guédry & Petitpas Eighth Reunion - Summerside, Prince Edward Island, 17 August 2019 (Marty Guidry)	2
Claude Guédry - Grandson of Claude Guédry and Marguerite Petitpas [Parents Found] (Martin Guidry)	6
Blackie Guidry - "The Singing Crawfish Man" (Shreveport, LA)	12
Blackie Guidry - Guidry Reaches for Stardom	12
Blackie Guidry - Concert at Centenary College's Gold Dome	12
Who Were the Parents of Maire-Josephe Guédry, Wife of Charles Boutin (Martin Guidry)	13
Gator - My Life in Pinstripes (Ron Guidry with Andrew Beaton)	17
Piau: Journey to the Promised Land (Bruce Murray)	17
Some Guédry's Held Captive in Boston in 1722-1723 (Martin Guidry)	18
Cheesy Ham and Grits Breakfast Casserole	21
Pain Perdu, Lost Bread or French Toast (Jck Guidry, Lafayette, LA)	21
Octave Gaidry - Attention Battalion; After Firing Prizes at Store of Mr. O. Gaidry	22
Allain Guedry - Orange Blossoms - Marriage of Allain Guedry, son of Joseph Guedry & Angeline Rodrigue, to Angelique Rodrigue	22
Miss Elodi Guedry - Wedding of Elodi Guedry and John H. Ayraud	22
Guidry Odorless Cleaners - Advertisement (Lancaster, OH)	22
Alfred Labine - Graduate of University of Michigan	23
Louis Labine - Proprietor of Labine Soda Shoppe in Wethersfield, CT	23
Mrs. Alfred Petitpas - Lend Helping Hand	23
Mrs. Eva Petitpas - Tomato Race Gets Down to Girth	23
Who Was the Husband of Hélène Guédry, Daughter of Augustin Guédry & Jeanne Hébert (Martin Guidry)	24
Volume 16 No. 2 (Summer 2018)	
The Early Guedry Family of Southeast Texas - An Update (Marty Guidry)	2
Greek Watermelon Salad with Feta and Mint (Cheryl Guidry Tyiska, Silver Spring, MD)	20
Slow Cooker Ravioli Lasagna (Michael Guidry, Torrance, CA)	20
Guédry & Petitpas Eighth Reunion - Summerside, Prince Edward Island, 17 August 2019 (Marty Guidry)	21
Pop' Guidry - Spry 'Bird-Loving' 'Pop' Guidry Adds Local Color to Orange	24
Walter 'Jake' Guidry - Announces He Has Purchased Whately's Barber Shop	24
Walter 'Jake' Guidry - Bore & Jake's Barber Shop Advertisement	24
Clem Labine and Jackie Robertson Photo	24
James LaBine Gets U. S. Mail Contract	24
The Acadian Refugees in France 1758-1785: The Impossible Reintegration (Jean François Mouhut)	25
Nuclear Deception: A Novel of Espionage & Treason Set in the 1970s (Bernard dit Grivois a.k.a. Bernard Geddry)	25

TABLE OF CONTENTS INDEX TO "GENERATIONS" -
THE NEWSLETTER OF LES GUÉDRY ET PETITPAS D'ASTEUR
(Prepared by Cheryl Tholen; Updated by Martin Guidry)

TITLE	Page
Volume 16 No. 3 (Fall 2018)	
Seeking Places Associated with the Guédry & Petitpas Families (Martin Guidry)	2
Guédry & Petitpas Reunion - Summerside, Prince Edward Island, 17 August 2019 (Martin Guidry)	7
Collared Greens with Pancetta	12
Seasoned Pork Chops	12
Circle of Distinction Certificate Presentation (2018 Inductees)	
ArthurLee Guidry; Elvord Floyd Guidry; Gregory Mark Guidry; James Ray Guidry; Tyler Sean Labine; Scott Pettipas	13
A Distinct Alien Race - The Untold Story of Franco-Americans (David Vermette)	17
Acadian Christmas Traditions (Georges Arsenault)	17
Pfc. Wilson M. Guidry - Reburial Rites Held for Kaplan Soldier	18
Clairville Guidry - A Tragedy at Raceland	18
Mrs. Jules Guidry - Died May 1, 1895 in Scott, Louisiana	18
Jean Pierre Guidry - Return from Airman Rites	19
Antoine Guidry - Abbeville Man Dies in Underwater Accident in Texas	19
Ralph Guidry, wife and family - Five Lives Lost As Storm Sweeps Louisiana Town	19
Fred Guidry - Guidry Has Emergency Operation at Hospital	19

Index by Topic

TOPICAL INDEX TO "GENERATIONS" -
THE NEWSLETTER OF LES GUÉDRY ET PETITPAS D'ASTEUR
(Prepared by Cheryl Tholen; Updated by Martin Guidry)

TITLE	Volume	Issue	Page	Year	Season
ACTORS / ACTRESSES					
Gaidry, Diane Adair (Actress and Producer)	6	2	10	2008	Summer
Labine, Kyle	4	2	21	2006	Summer
Labine, Tyler	4	2	22	2006	Summer
ARTISTS					
Guidry, Amy	10	3	11	2012	Fall
Guidry, Kelly	11	3	18	2013	Fall
Guidry, Michael	11	3	18	2013	Fall
ATHLETES					
Guédry & Petitpas Athletes - Professional (Baseball, Football, Ice Hockey, Racquetball, Golf, Rodeo, Fishing, Track & Field)	11	1	39	2013	Spring
Guedry, Phyllis Marie (Softball)	1	3	8	2003	Summer
Guidry, Carlette (Track & Field)	1	3	7	2003	Summer
Guidry, George T. (Golf)	2	1	8	2004	Winter
Guidry, Kevin Dale (Football)	1	1	6	2003	Winter
Guidry, Mark (Horseracing)	1	4	7	2003	Fall
Guidry, Michael (Golf)	2	1	8	2004	Winter
Guidry, Mickey (Football)	2	3	8	2004	Summer
Guidry, Mike (Raquetball)	1	2	8	2003	Spring
Guidry, Paul Michael (Football)	1	1	6	2003	Winter
Guidry, Ronald (Ron) Ames (Baseball)	1	1	5	2003	Winter
Guidry, Ronald (Boxing) - (Jeremy Theriot)	8	1	21	2010	Winter
Guidry, Ronald (Boxing)	13	2	9	2015	Summer
Guidry, Vernon A. (Rodeo Stockman)	2	1	8	2004	Winter
LaBean, Dennis (Fishing Guide)	2	1	8	2004	Winter
Labine, Clement (Clem) Walter (Baseball)	1	2	7	2003	Spring
Labine, Leo Gerald (Ice Hockey)	1	2	8	2003	Spring
ATTORNEYS / POLITICIANS					
Guidry, Judge Greg G. - Associate Justice - Louisiana Supreme Court	7	1	40	2009	Winter
Labine, Malvina Menard (1893-1967) - Reeve of Azilda, Ontario (Claudette Mancini - her granddaughter)	5	1	5	2007	Winter
Labine, Malvina Menard - The Woman Who Can Do Anything (Marty Guidry and André Labine)	5	3	5	2007	Fall
Labine, Malvina Menard (1893-1967) - Reeve of Rayside Township	8	2	19	2010	Summer
BON APPÉTIT - RECIPES					
5 Cup Salad (Maudry Guidry Viator, Abbeville, LA)	12	3	11	2014	Fall
Aubergine (Eggplant) de la Louisiane avec Ecrevisse (Shrimp) (Janet Bienert Higgins, New Orleans, LA)	10	1	37	2012	Spring
Baby Lima Beans and Tomato (Mary Guidry Dupont, Houma, LA)	7	4	10	2009	Fall
Banana Nut Bread (Maudry Guidry Viator, Abbeville, LA)	4	3	3	2006	Fall
Blackberry Dumplings (Jack Guidry, Lafayette, LA)	14	1	13	2016	Winter
Blueberry Cake (Bernie & Barbara Geddry, Peoria, AZ)	5	2	4	2007	Summer
Blueberry Cake (Bernie & Barbara Geddry, Peoria, AZ)	13	1	12	2015	Winter
Brisket (Maundry Guidry Viator, Abbeville, LA)	3	1	3	2005	Winter
Broccoli Salad (Ron and Joanne Pitts, Toronto, Ontario)	4	2	3	2006	Summer
Broccoli Salad (Ron and Joanne Pitts, Toronto, Ontario)	8	3	25	2010	Fall
Butter Cream Frosting, Ruth Guidry's (Charelene Guidry Lacombe, Jennings, LA)	12	2	12	2014	Summer
Cabbage Patch Stew (Carolyn Guidry Hilderbran, Uvalde, TX)	10	1	37	2012	Spring
Cajun Jambalaya - Stove Top Method (Roland Guidry, Cut Off, LA) [Labeled as Vol. 9 No. 4]	9	3	20	2011	Fall
Cajun Jambalaya For A Crowd - In a Large Cast Iron Pot (Roland Guidry, Cut Off, LA) [Labeled as Vol. 9 No. 4]	9	3	20	2011	Fall
Cheesy Ham and Grits Breakfast Casserole	16	1	21	2018	Spring
Chicken Fricot (Margaret Jeddry, Nahant, MA & Metegham, Nova Scotia)	7	2	10	2009	Spring
Chicken Salad, Poets (Beverly Butaud Guidry, Abbeville, LA)	13	2	11	2015	Summer
Collared Greens with Pancetta (Leona Guidry, Beaumont, TX)	16	3	12	2018	Fall
Crab and Corn Bisque (Daniel C. "Chuck" Guidry, Lacombe, LA)	11	2	8	2013	Summer
Crawfish Cornbread (Jack Guidry, Lafayette, LA)	14	2	18	2016	Summer
Crawfish Dip	14	1	13	2016	Winter
Crawfish Etouffee-Creole Style (Jack Guidry, Lafayette, LA)	6	2	6	2008	Summer
Creamy Pralines (Charlene Guidry Lacombe, Jennings, LA)	3	2	3	2005	Summer
Creole Stewed Corn (Suzie Dossat Russell, wife of Marvin Russell, New Orleans, LA)	9	2	11	2011	Summer
Creole White Beans (Daniel "Chuck" Guidry, Lacombe, LA) [Labeled as Vol. 9 No. 4]	9	3	21	2011	Fall
Cuban Black Beans (Dana Guidry, Lafayette, LA)	8	2	13	2010	Summer
Deep Delta Shrimp (Beverly Butaud Guidry, Abbeville, LA)	9	2	11	2011	Summer
Double 'J' Cajun Fried Catfish Strips (Guidry's Catfish)	15	2	23	2017	Summer
Eggplant Casserole (Jeanette Leger, Rayne, LA)	10	2	5	2012	Summer
Eggplant Fritters (Jack Guidry, Lafayette, LA)	7	4	10	2009	Fall
Fish Cakes (Simone Comeau Geddry, St. Benoni, Nova Scotia)	4	2	3	2006	Summer
Fish Cakes (Simone Comeau Geddry, Westmount, Québec)	8	2	13	2010	Summer
Frannie's Beer Bread (Charlene Guidry Lacombe, Jennings, LA)	7	1	15	2009	Winter

TOPICAL INDEX TO "GENERATIONS" -
THE NEWSLETTER OF LES GUÉDRY ET PETITPAS D'ASTEUR
(Prepared by Cheryl Tholen; Updated by Martin Guidry)

TITLE	Volume	Issue	Page	Year	Season
BON APPÉTIT - RECIPES (Continued)					
Fruit Salad Dressing (Jean Guidry, Naperville, IL)	14	2	18	2016	Summer
Frumenity ("Worcester County - Maryland's Arcadia")	11	3	17	2013	Fall
Greek Watermelon Salad with Feta and Mint (Cheryl Guidry Tyiska, Silver Spring, MD)	16	2	20	2018	Summer
HodgePodge (Susan Corkum-Greek, Lunenburg, Nova Scotia)	3	2	3	2005	Summer
Homemade Creamy Banana and Pecan Ice Cream (Charlene Guidry Lacombe, Iota, LA)	7	3	11	2009	Fall
Homemade Pepper Vinegar (Daniel C. "Chuck" Guidry, Lacombe, LA) [Labeled as Vol. 9 No. 4]	9	3	22	2011	Fall
Ice Cream Cake (Cindy Guidry Herdt, Wenatchee, WA)	15	2	23	2017	Summer
Iced Tea (Charlene Guidry Lacombe, Jennngs, LA)	4	1	3	2006	Winter
Jelly Roll, Cyrille Trasimond's (Cyrille Trasimond Guidry, Abbeville, LA)	14	3	21	2016	Fall
Lemonade (Marie-Claude Geddry, Gagetown, New Brunswick)	4	2	3	2006	Summer
Mama's Fish Court de Boullion (Lloyd J. Guidry, Waco, TX)	10	3	20	2012	Fall
Mama's Fricassee du Poulet (Loyd J. Guidry, Waco, TX)	3	3	3	2012	Fall
Maque Choux (Alice Matte Guidry, Lake Charles, LA)	3	3	3	2005	Fall
Maque Choux (Wayne Simoneaux, Montegut, LA) [Labeled as Vol. 9 No. 4]	9	3	22	2011	Fall
Meat Pie a l'Acadienne (Simone Comeau Geddry, St. Benoni, Nova Scotia)	14	3	21	2016	Fall
Myra's Scalloped Potatoes (Marie-Claude Geddry, Gagetown, New Brunswick)	3	1	3	2005	Winter
Navy Bean Soup (Allie Guidry, Springfield, VA)	4	3	3	2006	Fall
Noodle Pudding (Bernie & Barbara Geddry, Peoria, AZ)	12	1	17	2014	Spring
Lobster Roll, Old Fashioned Grilled (Alain Bosse, "The Kilted Chef", Halifax, Nova Scotia)	12	3	11	2014	Fall
Old Fashioned Crackling Cornbread (Charlene Guidry Lacombe, Iota, LA)	2	4	12	2004	Fall
Orange Slice Cake (Jeanette Leger, Rayne, LA)	10	3	20	2012	Fall
Oyster Soup (Jack Guidry, Lafayette, LA)	6	1	4	2008	Winter
Oyster Soup (Jack Guidry, Lafayette, LA)	9	1	12	2011	Winter
Pain Perdu (Lost Bread) (Jack Guidry, Lafayette, LA)	10	2	5	2012	Summer
Pain Perdu, Lost Bread or French Toast (Jck Guidry, Lafayette, LA)	16	1	21	2018	Spring
Pan Fried Haddock (Nathalie Geddry, Halifax, Nova Scotia)	2	4	12	2004	Fall
Pea Soup, Acadian (Bouchard Family Farms Cookbook) (Bouchard Family, Fort Kent, ME)	12	2	12	2014	Summer
Peanut Butter Fudge (Jeanette Guidry Leger, Rayne, LA)	13	2	11	2015	Summer
Persimmon Bread (Charlene Guidry Lacombe, Jennings, LA)	5	3	4	2007	Fall
Persimmon Bread (Maudry Guidry Viator, Abbeville, LA)	9	1	12	2011	Winter
Persimmon Cake (Charlene Guidry Lacombe, Iota, LA)	11	2	8	2013	Summer
Ployes - Buckwheat Pancakes (Bouchard Family Farms Cookbook) (Bouchard Family, Fort Kent, ME)	12	2	12	2014	Summer
Pork Chop-Squash Casserole (Carol Leger (Don)-Jeanette Leger, Rayne, LA)	6	3	6	2008	Fall
Pumpkin Spice Bread (Allie Guidry, Springfield, VA)	11	3	17	2013	Fall
Pumpkin Mousse (Jim Graham, Kemah, TX)	6	1	4	2008	Winter
Pumpkin Pie (Jim Graham, Kemah, TX)	6	3	6	2008	Fall
Rappie Pie (Vawn Jeddry, Edmonton, Alberta)	5	3	4	2007	Fall
Rappie Pie (Vawn Jeddry, Edmonton, Alberta)	11	1	13	2013	Spring
Rapure (Patricia LaBine Knodel, Calgary, Alberta, Canada)	13	1	12	2015	Spring
Ray's Cajun Hot Brisket (Ray Guidry, Lafayette, LA)	5	1	3	2007	Winter
Ray's Cajun Hot Brisket (Ray Guidry, Lafayette, LA)	8	3	25	2010	Fall
Red Beans and Rice (Wayne Simoneaux, Montegut, LA) [Labeled as Vol. 9 No. 4]	9	3	23	2011	Fall
Sausage Jambalaya (Charlene Lacombe, Jennings, LA)	8	1	19	2010	Winter
Seafood Casserole (Aurore Comeau, Comeauville, Nova Scotia)	5	2	4	2007	Summer
Seafood Delight (Julie Guidry, Abbeville, LA)	7	3	11	2009	Fall
Seasoned Pork Chops (Marvin Guidry, Naperville, IL)	16	3	12	2018	Fall
Shepherd's Pie - The English Way (Jean Guidry, Naperville, IL)	13	3	25	2015	Fall
Slow Cooker Ravioli Lasagna (Michael Guidry, Torrance, CA)	16	2	20	2018	Summer
Smothered Okra (Alice Matte Guidry, Lake Charles, LA)	7	2	10	2009	Spring
Sour Cream Pound Cake (Anita Guidry, Church Point, LA)	15	1	12	2017	Spring
Stuffed Bell Peppers (Maudry Guidry Viator, Abbeville, LA)	8	1	19	2010	Winter
Stuffed Catfish Fillets (Wayne Simoneaux, Montegut, LA)	3	2	3	2005	Summer
Stuffed Mirlitons (Jack Guidry, Lafayette, LA)	4	1	3	2006	Winter
Sweet Potato - Pecan Casserole (Carol Leger, Rayne, LA)	13	3	25	2015	Fall
Taco Beef Soup (Carolyn Guidry Hilderbran, Uvalde, TX)	7	1	15	2009	Winter
Tarte a la Bouillie (Daniel 'Chuck' Guidry, Lacombe, LA) [Labeled as Vol. 9 No. 4]	9	3	19	2011	Fall
Toasted Orzo Chicken Soup (Cindy Guidry Herdt, Wenatchee, WA)	15	1	12	2017	Spring
Turkey and Oyster Gumbo (Jack Guidry, Lafayette, LA)	15	3	5	2017	Fall
Venison Tenderloin (Ray Guidry, Lafayette, LA)	12	1	17	2014	Spring
Zucchini Bread (Celeste Bancroft, East Hartford, CT)	11	1	13	2013	Spring
BOOKS REVIEWED					
Acadia - A Novel (Alfred Silver)	2	4	15	2004	Fall
Acadian Awakenings - France & Acadie: Routes & Routes; International Links; An Acadian Family in Exile (William D. Gerrior)	2	3	13	2004	Summer
Acadian Christmas Traditions (Georges Arsenault)	16	3	17	2018	Fall
Acadian Culture In Maine (The National Park Service - Online Book)	9	2	10	2011	Summer
Acadian Diaspora, The - An Eighteenth-Century History (Christopher Hodson)	10	3	16	2012	Fall
Acadian Hard Times: The Farm Security Administration in Maine's St. John Valley, 1940-1943 (C Steward Doty)	11	1	38	2013	Spring
Acadian Heritage, My (Leonie Comeaux)	5	3	19	2007	Fall

TOPICAL INDEX TO "GENERATIONS" -
THE NEWSLETTER OF LES GUÉDRY ET PETITPAS D'ASTEUR
(Prepared by Cheryl Tholen; Updated by Martin Guidry)

TITLE	Volume	Issue	Page	Year	Season
BOOKS REVIEWED (Continued)					
Acadian Homecoming - 2004 Congrès Mondial Acadien (Clive Doucet)	3	3	9	2005	Fall
Acadian Legends, Folktales, and Songs from Prince Edward Island (Georges Arsenault)	2	3	14	2004	Summer
Acadian Legends, Folktales, and Songs from Prince Edward Island (Georges Arsenault)	15	2	22	2017	Summer
Acadian Lives in Cape Breton Island (Ronald Caplan with Rose Aucion Grace)	4	3	11	2006	Fall
Acadian Redemption - From Beausoleil Broussard to the Queen's Royal Proclamation (Warren A. Perrin)	4	2	13	2006	Summer
Acadian Refugees in France 1758-1785, The: The Impossible Reintegration (Jean François Mouhut)	16	2	25	2018	Summer
Acadian Root Baskets of Atlantic Canada (Joleen Gordon)	4	1	10	2006	Winter
Acadians of Nova Scotia: Past and Present (Sally Ross & Alphonse Deveau)	1	4	9	2003	Fall
Acadians - The Historical Basis for Longfellow's Poem of Evangeline (George P. Bible)	3	2	4	2005	Summer
Acadians - The Historical Basis for Longfellow's Poem of Evangeline (George P. Bible)	9	1	9	2011	Winter
Acadians, The - In Search of A Homeland (James Laxer)	12	1	18	2014	Spring
Acadie Then And Now - A People's History (Warren Perrin, Mary Perrin, Phil Comeau)	12	3	17	2014	Fall
Acadiens Déportés Qui Acceptèrent l'Offre de Murray, Les (André-Carl Vachon)	14	2	21	2016	Summer
Accordions, Fiddles, Two Step & Swing - A Cajun Music Reader (Ryan A. Brasseaux & Kevin S. Fontenot)	5	1	30	2007	Winter
American Roots (Mark Labine)	8	2	12	2010	Summer
Attakapas County, The (Harry Lewis Griffin)	9	2	10	2011	Summer
Band of Acadians (John Skelton)	10	1	9	2012	Spring
Battle of Baton Rouge - 1862 (W. A. Spedale)	1	3	9	2003	Summer
Bell Terre Acadie (A.K. Keller)	4	2	12	2006	Summer
Belle's Bayou Bounty (Belle Guidry)	3	1	4	2005	Winter
Belle's Country Cooking (Belle Guidry)	3	1	4	2005	Winter
Best of Everything: Mama's Creole Kitchen (Marilyn Goudeau Guidry)	3	1	4	2005	Winter
Big Thicket Guidebook - Exploring the Backroads and History of Southeast Texas (Lorraine G. Bonney) [Labeled as Vol. 9 No. 4]	9	3	17	2011	Fall
Books & Websites on the Genealogy of the Guédry (Guidry, Labine, LaBean) & Petitpas Families	14	2	19	2016	Summer
Bouchard Family Farms French Acadian Cookbook ((Bouchard Family)	12	2	14	2014	Summer
Bread and Respect: The Italians of Louisiana (A. V. Margavio & Jerome J. Salomone)	2	1	6	2004	Winter
Cajuns and Their Acadian Ancestors - A Young Reader's History (Shane K. Bernad)	6	2	17	2008	Summer
Cajun By Any Other Name: Recovering the Lost History of a Family-and a People (Marie Rundquist)	10	1	8	2012	Spring
Cajuns - Essays on Their History and Culture, The (Glenn R. Conrad)	1	1	7	2003	Winter
Cajuns: From Acadia to Louisiana, The (William Faulkner Rushton)	1	1	7	2003	Winter
Cajuns on the Bayous (Caroline Ramsey)	1	1	7	2003	Winter
Cajun Sketches from the Prairies of Southwest Louisiana (Lauren C. Post)	1	1	7	2003	Winter
Century of Acadian Culture: The Development of a Cajun Community: Erath 1899-1999 (General Curney J. Dronet)	2	1	6	2004	Winter
City of Remembering - A History of Genealogy in New Orleans (Susan Tucker)	15	1	11	2017	Spring
Civil War Soldiers (Reid Mitchell)	1	3	10	2003	Summer
Compendium of the Confederate Armies Louisiana (Stewart Sifakis)	1	3	9	2003	Summer
Confederate Nation: 1861-1865, The-The New American Nation Series (Emory M. Thomas)	1	3	10	2003	Summer
Crucible of Reconstruction -War, Radicalism and Race in Louisiana 1862-1877 (Ted Tunnell)	1	3	10	2003	Summer
Death In l'Acadie - A Keskéa Story (Sherrill Wark)	13	2	26	2015	Summer
Deportation of the Prince Edward Island Acadians (Earle Lockerby)	9	1	9	2011	Winter
Dictionary of Louisiana French: As Spoken in Cajun, Creole and American Indias Communities (Sr. Editor - Albert Valdman)	8	1	25	2010	Winter
Discovering New Brunswick (Marianne and H.A. Eiselt)	7	1	21	2009	Winter
Distinct Alien Race, A - The Untold Story of Franco-Americana (David Vermette)	16	3	17	2018	Fall
DNA & Genealogy (Colleen Fitzpatrick)	4	2	25	2006	Summer
Driving Mr. Yogi - Yogi Berra, Ron Guidry, Baseball's Greatest Gift (Harvey Araton) [Labeled as Vol. 9 No. 4]	9	3	17	2011	Fall
Encyclopedia of Cajun & Creole Cuisine (John D. Folse)	5	2	28	2007	Summer
First Franco-Americans, The - New England Life Histories form the Federal Writers' Project (C. Stewart Doty)	11	1	38	2013	Spring
Filbustiers de l'"Acadie - Coureurs des Mers, Les (Armand G. Robichaud)	7	2	14	2009	Spring
Fodor's Nova Scotia, New Brunswick, Prince Edward Island (Fodor's Gold Guides)	1	4	8	2003	Fall
Forensic Genealogy (Colleen Fitzpatrick)	4	2	25	2006	Summer
Forge in the Forest (Charles G.D. Roberts)	4	1	11	2006	Winter
Forgotten Battle, The - A History of the Acadians of Canso/Chedabuctou (Mark Haynes)	15	2	22	2017	Summer
Fortune & LaTour - The Civil War in Acadia (M. A. MacDonald)	2	4	14	2004	Fall
French, Cajun, Creole, Houma (Carl A. Brasseaux)	8	3	6	2010	Fall
From Migrant To Acadian (A North American Border People, 1604-1755) (N.E.S. Griffiths)	4	1	10	2006	Winter
French Canadian Heritage in New England, The (Gerard J. Brault)	12	1	18	2014	Spring
French Fortresses in North America 1535-1763, Quebec, Montreal, Louisbourg and New Orleans (Rene Chartrand)	7	3	12	2009	Summer
Genealogical Research in Nova Scotia (Terrence M. Punch)	2	3	11	2004	Summer
Gentlemen and Jesuits (Glory and Adventure in the Early Days of Acadia) (Elizabeth Jones)	2	3	11	2004	Summer
Ghosts of Good Times - Louisiana Dance Halls Past and Present (Philip Gould & Herman Fuselier)	15	1	11	2017	Spring
Great and Noble Scheme - The Tragic Story of the Expulsion of the French Acadians from their American Homeland (John Mack Faragher)	3	3	9	2005	Fall
Guédry-LaBine Genealogy	1	2	9	2003	Spring
Guédry, Guidry, Geddry, Jeddry; Guildry dit LaBine, LaBine and LaBean Family - Descendants of Claude Guédry and Marguerite Petitpas (Daryl LaBine)	1	2	9	2003	Spring
Guidry, Brady and Siblings - The Ancestors and Family History (Holly Newhouse-Guidry)	1	2	9	2003	Spring
Guidry's (Guédry's), The (Eunice Helen Barber)	1	2	9	2003	Spring
Guidry, The (Geneva Seymour)	1	2	9	2003	Spring
Guidry, Joseph Villere & Rosa Hollier - Ancestors of Family in Orange, Texas (Marshall Villeré Woolner)	1	2	9	2003	Spring
Guidry, John & Rosa LeJeune -Ancestors & Descendants (Roland Guidry)	1	2	9	2003	Spring
La Verdure de Mirligueche - The Story of the Guidry dit Labine Family in North America (Mark Labine)	8	1	25	2010	Winter

TOPICAL INDEX TO "GENERATIONS" -
THE NEWSLETTER OF LES GUÉDRY ET PETITPAS D'ASTEUR
(Prepared by Cheryl Tholen; Updated by Martin Guidry)

TITLE	Volume	Issue	Page	Year	Season
BOOKS REVIEWED (Continued)					
Guidry, Mark - Books featuring horseracing	6	1	14	2008	Winter
Ride of Their Lives - The Triumphs and Turmoil of Today's Top Jockeys (Lenny Shulman)	6	1	14	2008	Winter
The Original 2004 Thoroughbred Times Racing Almanac (The Staff of Thoroughbred Times)	6	1	14	2008	Winter
Guidry, Ron - Books featuring baseball	6	1	13	2008	Winter
Guidry (Ron Guidry & Peter Golenbock)	6	1	13	2008	Winter
Sports Hero Ron Guidry (Marshall Burchard)	6	1	13	2008	Winter
Ron Guidry Louisiana Lightning (Maury Allen)	6	1	13	2008	Winter
Louisiana's Athletes - The Top Twenty (Marty Mule with Bob Remy)	6	1	13	2008	Winter
Louisiana Sports Legends - The Men and Women of The Louisiana Sports Hall of Fame (Jerry Byrd)	6	1	13	2008	Winter
Louisianians All (Jeanne Frois)	6	1	13	2008	Winter
New York Yankees - Players in Pinstripes (Mark Vancil & Mark Mandrake)	6	1	13	2008	Winter
The New York Yankees - The Greatest Yankees Teams (Mark Vancil & Mark Mandrake)	6	1	13	2008	Winter
Gator - My Life in Pinstripes (Ron Guidry with Andrew Beaton)	16	1	17	2018	Spring
Guide to Louisiana Confederate Military Units 1861-1865 (Arthur W. Bergeron)	1	3	10	2003	Summer
Hear What You See Along Baie Sainte-Marie (Alexander C. Axent-Hilton)	2	4	13	2004	Fall
Histoire de l'Acadie (Nicolas Landry & Nicole Lang)	5	2	28	2007	Summer
Histoire de l'Acadie (Nicolas Landry & Nicole Lang)	13	1	13	2015	Winter
Histoire des Acadiennes et Acadiens de La Louisiane (Zachary Richard, et al)	10	3	16	2012	Fall
Historic LaHave River Valley (Sheila Chambers, Joan Dawson & Edith Wolter)	3	2	4	2005	Summer
Historic Yarmouth - Town & Country (Eric Ruff & Laura Bardley)	2	3	14	2004	Summer
History of Louisiana, The: From the Earliest Period (Francois-Xavier Martin)	4	1	11	2006	Winter
History of Port-Royal, Annapolis Royal, A 1605-1800 (Brenda Dunn)	5	1	31	2007	Winter
History of the Cajuns - From Ancient France to Nova Scotia to Louisiana to Colonial Texas (Alex Loya)	7	2	14	2009	Spring
History of the County of Lunenburg (1895) (M. B. DesBrisay)	2	3	12	2004	Summer
Home At Last: An Acadian Journey (Ollie Porche Voelker)	11	2	27	2013	Summer
In the Beginning, There Was A Chapel (Mark Labine)	14	3	22	2016	Fall
Island Acadians, The 1720-1980 (Georges Arsenault)	5	3	19	2007	Fall
Labine, Clem - Books featuring baseball	6	1	14	2008	Winter
Brooklyn Dodgers in Their Original Voices (Vince Scully)	6	1	14	2008	Winter
The Boys of Summer (Roger Kahn)	6	1	14	2008	Winter
When the Cheering Stops...Former Major Leaguers Talk About Their Game & Their Lives (Lee Heiman, Dave Weiner & Bill Gutman)	6	1	14	2008	Winter
"That Was Part of Baseball Then" - Interviews with 24 Former Major League Baseball Players, Coaches and Managers (Victor Debs, Jr.)	6	1	14	2008	Winter
Clem Labine - Always A Dodger (Richard Elliott)	13	3	26	2015	Fall
La Fleur du Rosier - Acadian Folksongs (Helen Creighton)	5	1	31	2007	Winter
La Verdure de Mirligueche (Mark Labine)	8	1	25	2010	Winter
Land of Disocrd Always, A - Acadia from Its Beginnings to the Expulsion of Its People, 1604-1755 (Charles D. Mahaffie, Jr.)	3	2	4	2005	Summer
Louisiana Families in Southeast Texas (1840s - 1940s) (Rev. Donald J. Hebert)	5	1	30	2007	Winter
Louisiana History: An Annotated Bibliography (Florence M Jumonville)	2	1	7	2004	Winter
Louisiana Indian Tales (Elizabeth Mooe & Alice Couvillon)	6	3	12	2008	Fall
Louisiana Purchase, The: An Historical and Geographical Encyclopedia (Rodriguez, Junius P.)	2	1	7	2004	Winter
Louisiana, Yesterday and Today: An Historical Guide to the State (John Wilds, Charles L. Dufour & Walter G. Cowan)	2	1	7	2004	Winter
Louisiana's German Coast - A History of St. Charles Parish (Harry E. Yoes III)	5	3	18	2007	Fall
Louisbourg The Phoenix Fortress (Photograhs-Chris Reardon; Text - A.J.B. Johnston)	4	2	12	2006	Summer
Lunenburg - Then and Now (Brian Cuthbertson)	2	4	14	2004	Fall
Man For Two Peoples - Pierre-Amand Landry (Della M. M. Stanley)	5	2	29	2007	Summer
Mapmaker's Legacy - Ninteenth Century Maps of Nova Scotia (Joan Dawson)	10	2	4	2012	Summer
Minnesota Farm Family Memories (Mark Labine)	10	1	9	2012	Spring
Minnesota Farm Family Memories (Mark Labine)	14	1	14	2016	Spring
Mississippi and the Making of A Nation, The (Stephen E. Ambrose)	5	3	18	2007	Fall
Mi'kmaq Treaties on Trial (William C. Wicken)	13	3	26	2015	Fall
Moon Handbooks Atlantic Canada: New Brunswick, PEI, Nova Scotia, Newfoundland and Labrador (3rd Edition) (Mark Morris, et. al.)	1	4	8	2003	Fall
New Brunswick Book of Everything (Edited by Martha Walls)	7	1	21	2009	Winter
Notes from Exile: On Being Acadian (Clive Doucet)	1	4	9	2003	Fall
Nova Scotia: A Colour Guidebook (Stephen Poole)	1	4	8	2003	Fall
Nova Scotia's Lost Highways - The Early Roads That Shaped The Province (Joan Dawson)	10	2	4	2012	Summer
Nuclear Deception (Bernard dit Grivois a.k.a. Bernard Geddry)	16	2	25	2018	Summer
Oak Island - An Acadian Tale (Mark Labine)	12	1	19	2014	Spring
Old-House Journal Compendium, The (Clem Labine and Carolyn Flaherty)	8	2	12	2010	Summer
Old Man Told Us, The - Excerpts from Micmac History - 1500-1950 (Ruth Holmes Whitehead)	6	3	12	2008	Fall
Olde St. John's - Stories from a Seaport City (Frank Galgay & Michael McCarthy)	4	3	11	2006	Fall
One Generation at a Time - Biography of a Cajun and Creole Music Festival (Barry Jean Ancelet & Philip Gould)	15	3	6	2017	Fall
Pauli The Musical Pumpkin (Pamela O. Guidry)	14	1	14	2016	Spring
People of the Bayou: Cajun Life in Lost American (Christopher Hallowell)	1	1	7	2003	Winter
Piau: Journey to the Promised Land (Bruce Murray)	16	1	17	2018	Spring
Politics of Nova Scotia 1710-1896 (J. Murray Beck)	2	3	13	2004	Summer
Portraits of Conflict, A Photographic History of Louisiana in the Civil War (Carl Moneyhon & Bobby Roberts)	1	3	9	2003	Summer
Portraits of South Louisiana (Emile Waagenaar)	15	3	6	2017	Fall
Port-Royal Habitation - The Story of the French and Mi'kmaq at Port-Royal (1604-1613) (W. P. Kerr)	3	3	9	2005	Fall
Postcards from Acadia (Barbara LeBlanc)	7	4	11	2009	Fall

TOPICAL INDEX TO "GENERATIONS" -
THE NEWSLETTER OF LES GUÉDRY ET PETITPAS D'ASTEUR
(Prepared by Cheryl Tholen; Updated by Martin Guidry)

TITLE	Volume	Issue	Page	Year	Season
BOOKS REVIEWED (Continued)					
Pulp, Potatoes and Ployes - An Acadian Odyssey (Jules M. Seletz)	12	2	14	2014	Summer
Reminiscences of Uncle Silas: A History of the 18th Louisiana Infantry Regiment (Silas T. Grisamore)	1	3	9	2003	Summer
Revisiting Anne Marie (Marie Rundquist)	10	1	8	2012	Spring
Reyanne's Rainbow Swamp (Adina Guidry)	14	1	14	2016	Winter
Scattered, The - Thirty Years of Exile; A Lifetime of Loss; The Triumph of a Simple Man (Richard Holledge)	11	3	10	2013	Fall
Siege of Fort Beauséjour 1755 The (Chris M. Hand)	7	2	13	2009	Spring
Shiloh to Stones River: The True Story of Private John H. Sullivan of the 16th Louisiana Regiment CSA (Travis L. Ayers)	1	3	9	2003	Summer
Silver Lining From Acadie to Louisiana, A (Ollie Ann Porche Voelker)	13	2	26	2015	Summer
Six Micmac Stories (Ruth Holmes Whitehead)	2	4	15	2004	Fall
Sods, Soil, and Spades - The Acadians at Grand Pre and Their Dykeland Legacy (J. Sherman Bleakney)	7	3	12	2009	Summer
Song For Acadia (Mary Alice Downie & George Rawlyk)	5	2	29	2007	Summer
Spanish in New Orleans and Louisiana (Jose de Montero Pedro, Marques de Casa Mena, Richard E. Chandler)	2	1	6	2004	Winter
Stir the Pot: The History of Cajun Cuisine (Marcelle Bienvenu, Carl Brasseaux, Ryan A. Brasseaux)	4	3	12	2006	Fall
Story of the 26th Louisiana Infantry, In the Service of The Confederate States (Winchester Hall)	1	3	9	2003	Summer
Talking Acadian: Communication, Work, and Culture (John Chetro-Szivos)	4	3	12	2006	Fall
Teche - A History of Louisiana's Most Famous Bayou (Shane Bernard)	14	3	22	2016	Fall
They Spoke French (Mark Labine - Contributor)	14	2	21	2016	Summer
Tirailleurs: A History of the 4th Louisiana and The Acadians of Company H (Thomas H. Richey)	11	2	27	2013	Summer
Town That Crawfish Built, The - A History of Henderson, Louisiana (Marjorie R. Esman)	13	1	13	2015	Winter
Tracking Doctor Lonecloud Showman to Legend Keeper (Ruth Holmes Whitehead)	2	3	12	2004	Summer
Travel in Time to Grand Pré, A (Michele Doucette)	7	4	11	2009	Fall
Truth about the Cajuns, The (Trent Angers)	1	1	7	2003	Winter
Two Beginnings - A Brief Acadian History (Deveau Alphonse Deveau)	4	2	13	2006	Summer
Unsettled Conquest, An: The British Campaign Against the Peoples of Acadia (Geoffrey Gilbert Plank)	1	4	9	2003	Fall
Unsettled Conquest, An: The British Campaign Against the Peoples of Acadia (Geoffrey Gilbert Plank)	7	2	13	2009	Spring
Voici The Valley Cultureway [Audio Story and Guide of Upper St. John Valley] (Sheila Jans, Don Cyr & Daniel Picard)	11	3	10	2013	Fall
Voyages: A Maine Franco-American Reader (Nelson Madore)	8	3	6	2010	Fall
Yankee Autumn in Acadiana: A Narrative of the Great Texas Overland Expedition through Southwestern Louisiana October-December 1863 (David C. Edmonds)	6	2	17	2008	Summer
Yoga Kitchen: Recipes from the Shoshoni Yoga Retreat (Faith Stone and Rachel Guidry)	3	1	4	2005	Winter
BUSINESS CARDS					
Guidry, Billy - E Go Travel	11	1	12	2013	Spring
Guidry, Blackie - "The Singing Crawfish Man" (Shreveport, LA)	16	1	12	2018	Spring
Guidry, Douglas, MAI - Certified General Real Estate Appraiser (Gloucester, MA)	10	3	22	2012	Fall
Guidry, Fred - Cajun Carving	13	1	23	2015	Winter
Guidry, Les and Luke Guidry - Guidry Painting	11	1	12	2013	Spring
Guidry, Mark & Jean - Wheaton Antique Mall (Wheaton, IL)	10	2	3	2012	Summer
Guidry, Mark - Manager, Speech and Editorial Services, American Medical Services (Chicago, IL)	10	3	22	2012	Fall
Guidry, Mickey J., CFA - Branch Manager and Registered Principal (Baton Rouge, LA)	10	3	8	2012	Fall
Guidry, Milton F. & Summerall Guidry - Ligthning, Inc. Letterhead	13	1	5	2015	Winter
Guidry, Nonc Jules and "Lachez-Les" - Authentic Cajun Music Band (Carencro, LA)	10	3	8	2012	Fall
Guidry, Percy's Hearth & Patio - (Keith Guidry)	12	1	16	2014	Spring
Guidry, Renee, M.A., BCBA - Behavioral Intervention Group (Baton Rouge, LA)	10	2	3	2012	Summer
Guidry, R. Martin - DuPont Performance Elastomers	11	1	12	2013	Spring
Guidry, R. Martin - Exxon Chemicals	11	1	12	2013	Spring
Guidry & Company Real Estate	12	1	16	2014	Spring
Jeddry, Josh - Photography	11	1	12	2013	Spring
Jeddry, Lloyd & Cindy - Jeddry's Auto Body Shop (St. Alphonse, Nova Scotia)	10	2	3	2012	Summer
Labine, Andre - Lubricants Marketing Consultants (Fernie, British Columbia)	10	2	3	2012	Summer
Law, Christine Guidry - Acadian/Cajun Culture (Zachary, LA)	12	1	16	2014	Spring
CIRCLE OF DISTINCTION					
Circle of Distinction Certificate Presentation (2011 Inductees) [Labeled as Vol. 9 No. 4] Daniel Charles 'Chuck' Guidry; BGen Albert Louis Geddry; Sandra Perro Pettipas; Rita Labine; Ronald Ames Guidry; Daine Adair Gaidry	9	3	8	2011	Fall
Circle of Distinction Certificate Presentation (2012 Inductees) Bernard L. Geddry; Vernon Paul Guidry; Gilbert Adélard Labine; Dr. Thomas Henry LaBean; George Henri Petitpas	10	3	9	2012	Fall
Circle of Distinction Certificate Presentation (2013 Inductees) Myrtle LaBean Pletos, Richard James Guidry, Mark Labine, Robinson Joseph Guidry, Robert Charles Guidry, Earl V. Guidry, Jr.	11	3	13	2013	Fall
Circle of Distinction Certificate Presentation (2014 Inductees) Leo Joseph Guedry, Jr.; Allison Lynn Guidry; Michael Wayne Guidry; Daryl LaBine; Roland "Clem" Labine, Jr.; Bishop Gérard Petitpas	12	3	7	2014	Fall
Circle of Distinction Certificate Presentation (2015 Inductees) Rebecca E. Boggess; Oran 'Doc' Guidry; Roland David Guidry; Roland J. Guidry; Clement 'Clem' Walter Labine; Leo F. Pettipas	13	3	7	2015	Fall
Circle of Distinction Certificate Presentation (2016 Inductees) Claude Guédry; Jules 'Nonc Jules' Guidry; Joseph Alfred Jeddry; André Robert Labine; Claude Petitpas; Colonel William J. Pettipas	14	3	17	2016	Fall
Circle of Distinction Certificate Presentation (2017 Inductees) Fred G. Guidry; Dr. Jimmy N. Guidry; Seth Wayne Guidry; Leonard 'Leo' Gerald Labine; Marie Ginette Petitpas Taylor, Marguerite Petitpas	15	3	12	2017	Fall
Circle of Distinction Certificate Presentation (2018 Inductees) Arthur Lee Guidry; Elvord Floyd Guidry; Gregory Mark Guidry; James Ray Guidry; Tyler Sean Labine; Scott Pettipas	16	3	13	2018	Fall

TOPICAL INDEX TO "GENERATIONS" -
THE NEWSLETTER OF LES GUÉDRY ET PETITPAS D'ASTEUR
(Prepared by Cheryl Tholen; Updated by Martin Guidry)

TITLE	Volume	Issue	Page	Year	Season
FAMILY HISTORY					
Acadian Deportations, The (Marty Guidry)	14	2	22	2016	Summer
Acadian Genetic Diseases (Matin Guidry)	12	2	2	2014	Summer
Acadian Village Historical Site, Van Buren, Maine (Marty Guidry)	10	1	7	2012	Spring
Acadians in Madawaska - Their Journey and Struggle (Marty Guidry)	11	1	2	2013	Spring
Acadians of Québec, The (Adrien Bergeron) with Short Genealogy Commentaries - France, Acadia, Quebec (Sandra Pettipas Perro)	6	1	2	2008	Winter
Acadians of Québec (Sandra Pettipas Perro)	13	3	14	2015	Fall
Arrival in New Orleans, 1768 (Marty Guidry)	7	2	17	2009	Spring
Bugaret, Bernard - An Acadian Pioneer (Marty Guidry)	8	1	2	2010	Winter
Bugaret, Catherine - Ancestral Mother of the Petitpas Family, Ancestral Grandmother of the Guédry Family (Martin Guidry)	15	1	2	2017	Spring
Cajun Musicians in the Family - An Early History (Martin Guidry)	15	3	18	2017	Fall
Cantrelle, Michel - Commandant of the First Acadian Coast (Marty Guidry)	7	3	2	2009	Summer
Claude Petitpas, Sr. and Catherine Bugart (parents of Maguerite and Claude Petitpas, Jr. (Sandra Pettipas Perro)	4	3	9	2006	Fall
Census of Acadians at Port Tobacco, Maryland Desiring to Go to France, 7 July 1763 (Marty Guidry)	7	2	15	2009	Spring
Commemoration of the Guédry-Labine-Petitpas Reunion of August 2004 (Marty Guidry)	4	2	10	2006	Summer
Dance Halls, Hostelries and The Guedry's (Marty Guidry)	10	3	2	2012	Fall
Dancehalls and the Guédry's (An Update) (Marty Guidry)	13	1	6	2015	Winter
Dedication of Plaque to Augustin Guédry and Marie Jonson - (Marty Guidry)	5	3	2	2007	Fall
Distribution of Land to the Acadians Settling at Fort San Luis de Natchez, February 1768 (Marty Guidry)	7	2	20	2009	Spring
DNA & Genealogy - A Brief Primer (Marty Guidry)	12	3	12	2014	Fall
Drouin Collection - A Valuable Research Source (Marty Guidry)	8	1	28	2010	Winter
Extant Acadian Records - Part I: Acadian Church Records [Pre-Deportation - 1613-1759] (Martin Guidry)	9	1	13	2011	Winter
Extant Acadian Records - Part II: Acadian Church Records [United States - 1755-1800] (Martin Guidry)	9	2	13	2011	Summer
Extant Acadian Records - Part III: Acadian Church Records [Québec, Ontario, British Columbia - 1755-1900] (Martin Guidry)	10	1	15	2012	Spring
Extant Acadian Records - Part IV: Acadian Church Records [Nova Scotia, NB, PEI, Newfoundland, St-Pierre-et-Miquelon] (Martin Guidry)	10	2	16	2012	Summer
Extant Acadian Records - Part V: Acadian Church Records [France, England, Caribbean, South America - 1755-1800] (Martin Guidry)	11	1	14	2013	Spring
Family Associations - An Oft-Overlooked Resource (Betty Jo Stockton)	1	1	8	2003	Winter
First Known Record of the Guédry Family in North America (Martin Guidry)	10	2	2	2012	Summer
Gravestones of Original Acadian Deportees (Martin Guidry)	10	2	6	2012	Summer
Grivois Family of Northeast Maine, The - Another Branch of the Guédry Family (Marty Guidry)	12	1	2	2014	Spring
Geddry, Emery Louis - A Canadian Soldier Who Gave The Ultimate Sacrifice (World War II) (Marty Guidry)	13	1	15	2015	Winter
Geddry, Emery Louis - A Canadian Soldier Who Gave The Ultimate Sacrifice (World War II) [An Update] (Marty Guidry)	13	2	3	2015	Summer
Guedry Family of Clare, Nova Scotia (Jeddry, Geddry), Ancestry of the (Marty Guidry)	1	3	3	2003	Summer
Guedry Family of Southeast Texas, Early (Marty Guidry)	1	2	2	2003	Spring
Guedry Family of Southeast Texas, Early - An Update (Marty Guidry)	16	2	2	2018	Summer
Guédry & Petitpas Families, Early Analysis of (Martin Guidry)	14	1	3	2016	Winter
Guédry, Antoine - An Intriguing Acadian (Marty Guidry)	6	1	5	2008	Winter
Guédry, Augustin - Hero of the Expulsion (Bernard L. Geddry)	2	4	11	2004	Fall
Guédry Crest (Marty Guidry)	6	3	7	2008	Fall
Guedry dit Laverdure, Claude & The Origins of the Guedry Family in North America (Marty Guidry)	2	3	2	2004	Summer
Guédry, Claude - Grandson of Claude Guédry & Marguerite Petitpas, Search for Father of (Marty Guidry)	4	2	14	2006	Summer
Guédry, Claude - Grandson of Claude Guédry and Marguerite Petitpas [Parents Found] (Martin Guidry)	16	1	6	2018	Spring
Guédry, Hélène, Daughter of Augustin Guédry & Jeanne Hébert - Who Was The Husband of (Martin Guidry)	16	1	24	2018	Spring
Guédry, Helene & Marie-Josephe, Exciting Find About - Twin Daughters of Augustin Guédry & Jeanne Hebert (Marty Guidry)	5	2	30	2007	Summer
Guédry, Jean-Baptiste, husband of Anne Magdeleine Dupuis - An Interesting Genealogical Puzzle: Using Land Records to Determine Parentage (Marty Guidry)	7	2	2	2009	Spring
Guédry, Joseph - Inventory of Estate (Marty Guidry)	7	2	21	2009	Spring
Guédry, Joseph and Acadian Card Money (Marty Guidry)	4	3	13	2006	Fall
Guédry, Marie-Josephe, Wife of Charles Boutin - Who Were the Parents of (Martin Guidry)	16	1	13	2018	Spring
Guédry-Labine Family and the World's First Atomic Bomb - Gilbert Labine (Marty Guidry)	1	1	2	2003	Winter
Guédry's Held Captive in Boston in 1722-1723, Some (Martin Guidry)	16	1	18	2018	Spring
Guedry's in Merligueche, The Last or The Labrador and Guedry Family (Marty Guidry)	1	4	3	2003	Fall
Guédry's - New Research Revealed Exiled to North Carolina (Marty Guidry)	7	1	12	2009	Winter
Guidrey, Joseph J. (Captain, USNR) - Saga of the USS YMS-378, June-July 1944 (as told to his daughter, Jo Ann Guidrey Aulick)	6	2	2	2008	Summer
Guidry (Guedry) Family of Vermilion, The (Velma Guidry Beauxis)	5	2	36	2007	Summer
Guidry, Art, Seeking the Roots of - A Louisiana Creole Genealogical Study (Art Guidry & Marty Guidry)	14	3	2	2016	Fall
Guidry, Cyrille Trasimon père, Private - A Letter Durng the Civil War (Marty Guidry)	8	2	2	2010	Summer
Guidry, Sr., Edwin Joseph (E.J.) and Leon Graugnard - Terre Haute (High Grounds) Plantation (Marty Guidry)	5	3	14	2007	Fall
Guidry, Emery J. - D-Day Landing and POW Experience of, from Cow Island, Louisiana (as told to his nephew Jeffrey Guidry)	6	3	2	2008	Fall
Guidry, John Leonce and Lillian Lefort Guidry of Galliano, LA - Ordinary People, Extraordinary Lives (Martin Guidry)	15	2	2	2017	Summer
Guidry, Mitchell, Rev. - Tours Italy and France (Father Mitchell Guidry)	4	1	12	2006	Winter
Guidry, Philemon - Overseer of Michel Bernard Cantrelle Plantation (Marty Guidry)	13	3	19	2015	Fall
Guidry, Theodule - Patent Application on a Baler (Allison Guidry)	8	1	15	2010	Winter
Guidry (Guédry) Family of Vermilion, The (Marty Guidry)	5	2	36	2007	Summer
Guildry dit Labine, Charles - Voyageur (Mark Labine)	7	1	3	2009	Winter
Guidry's Have Leading Roles in Deepwater Horizon Oil Spill Response (Martin Guidry)	8	2	2	2010	Summer
Hank Williams' *Jambalaya* and the Guidry Connection (Martin Guidry)	15	3	2	2017	Fall
Historic Plaisance Rosenwald (Art Guidry)	14	3	14	2016	Fall
LaBeans of Michigan - Another Branch of the Guédry Family (Marty Guidry)	2	2	4	2004	Spring

TOPICAL INDEX TO "GENERATIONS" -
THE NEWSLETTER OF LES GUÉDRY ET PETITPAS D'ASTEUR
(Prepared by Cheryl Tholen; Updated by Martin Guidry)

TITLE	Volume	Issue	Page	Year	Season
FAMILY HISTORY (Continued)					
Labine Hotel - Fort Coulonge, Québec, Canada (Marty Guidry)	7	2	11	2009	Spring
Labine, Léon & the Hudson's Bay Company - A Labine "Lost" in British Columbia (Martin Guidry)	10	1	3	2012	Spring
Labine, Malvina Menard (1893-1967) - Reeve of Azilda, Ontario (Claudette Mancini - her granddaughter)	5	1	5	2007	Winter
Labine, Malvina Menard (1893-1967) - Reeve of Azilda, Ontario (Claudette Mancini - her granddaughter)	8	2	19	2010	Summer
Labine, Malvina Menard - The Woman Who Can Do Anything (Marty Guidry and André Labine)	5	3	5	2007	Fall
Louisiana Slave Database, The & The Louisiana Free Database and Slave Narratives (Marty Guidry)	8	3	7	2010	Fall
L'Ouragan de la Cheniere Caminada de 1893 (The Hurricane of Cheniere Caminada of 1893) (Marty Guidry)	3	3	4	2005	Fall
Origins of the Guédry Family in Louisiana, 1765-1785 (Marty Guidry)	5	1	32	2007	Winter
Origins of the Guédry Family in Louisiana, 1765-1800 - Amended (Marty Guidry)	5	2	37	2007	Summer
Permit to Sail to New Orleans for the "Jane" - 2 March 1767 (Marty Guidry)	7	2	19	2009	Spring
Petitpas of Acadia (L'Acadye), The (Sandra Pettipas Perro)	13	2	18	2015	Summer
Plaque Dedicated to the Acadians of Maryland (Martin Guidry)	11	2	6	2013	Summer
Search for the Father of Claude Guedry, Grandson of Claude Guedry & Marguerite Petitpas (Marty Guidry)	4	2	14	2006	Summer
Seeking the Roots of Art Guidry - A Louisiana Creole Genealogical Study (Art Guidry & Marty Guidry)	14	3	2	2016	Fall
Seeking Places Associated with the Guédry and Petitpas Families (R. Martin Guidry)	16	3	2	2018	Fall
Seven Acadian Expeditions of 1785 (Marty Guidry)	2	2	8	2004	Spring
Should the Guédry Surname Really Be Melançon? - A DNA Genealogical Study (Mark Labine & Marty Guidry)	14	2	4	2016	Summer
Slave Narratives (Marty Guidry)	8	3	16	2010	Fall
Survival of a Family: The Migration of the Guedry Family during the 18th Century (Marty Guidry)	3	1	2	2005	Winter
Survival of a Family: The Family of Augustin Guedry & Jeanne Hebert (Marty Guidry)	3	2	1	2005	Summer
Survival of a Family: Update the Family of Augustin Guedry & Jeanne Hebert (Marty Guidry)	3	3	1	2005	Fall
Survival of a Family: The Family of Francoise Guedry & Jean LeJeune (Marty Guidry)	5	1	1	2007	Winter
Survival of a Family: The Family of Jean-Baptiste Guedry & Madeleine Mius d'Azy (Marty Guidry)	4	2	1	2006	Summer
Survival of a Family: The Family of Marie-Josephe Guedry and Philippe Doiron (Marty Guidry)	5	2	1	2007	Summer
Survival of a Family: The Family of Paul Guedry dit Jovial & Anne Mius d'Entemont d'Azit de Pobomcoup (Marty Guidry)	3	3	1	2005	Fall
Survival of a Family: The Family of Pierre Guedry dit Labine & Marguerite Brasseau (Marty Guidry)	4	1	1	2006	Winter
Survival of a Family: Update on Pierre Guedry dit Labine (Marty Guidry)	4	2	8	2006	Summer
Survival of a Family: The Remaining Sons of Claude Guedry and Marguerite Petitpas (Claude, Charles, Alexis, Claude and Joseph) (Marty Guidry)	4	3	1	2006	Fall
Tragedy for the Guedry Family - An Act of Piracy On The High Seas - Part 1 of 2 (Marty Guidry)	5	1	7	2007	Winter
Tragedy for the Guedry Family - An Act of Piracy On The High Seas - Part 2 of 2 (Marty Guidry)	5	2	8	2007	Summer
Trials of Five Persons for Piracy, Felony and Robbery - Part 1 of 2 (Marty Guidry)	5	1	9	2007	Winter
Trials of Five Persons for Piracy, Felony and Robbery - Part 2 of 2 (Marty Guidry)	5	2	12	2007	Summer
Two Homes Built By Exiled Acadians in Connecticut (Marty Guidry)	12	3	18	2014	Fall
Virgin of Mount Gédry - La Vierge du Mont Gédry (Bernard L. Geddry)	4	3	4	2006	Fall
Who Was The First Guedry in Louisiana? (Marty Guidry)	2	1	2	2004	Winter
Why Did The Petitpas And Guédry Families Settle at Merliguèche? (Marty Guidry)	14	2	13	2016	Summer
FAMILY PHOTO CORNER					
Albert A. Guidry & Marie Gaudin Family	11	3	8	2013	Fall
Charles Joseph Guedry & Marie Leontine Gaudet Family	10	3	7	2012	Fall
Hypolite Onizaphore Guidry & Corrine Sonnier Guidry Family	11	1	8	2013	Spring
Marie Clausimire Guildry dit Labine	13	1	14	2015	Winter
FAMILY STORIES					
"A Hard Day's Work" (A Poem by Marvin 'Mark' Guidry)	2	4	16	2004	Fall
"Reunion" (A Poem by Marvin 'Mark' Guidry)	3	1	3	2005	Winter
And Where Did You Say They Lived (Marty Guidry)	12	3	22	2014	Fall
And You Said Your Name Is What Or How Guédry Has Evolved into So Many Variants (Marty Guidry)	8	3	2	2010	Fall
Avery, Eileen & Sandra Perro Pettipas - Tor Bay Acadians Honor Roll Inductions	15	2	10	2017	Summer
Charles, Bobby (Robert Charles Guidry), Louisiana Songwriter, Dies at 71	8	1	11	2010	Winter
Clare- 2005 Festival Acadian de Clare (Al & Simone Geddry)	3	3	7	2005	Fall
Couple of Louisiana Artists, A - Michael Guidry & Kelly Guidry (Marty Guidry)	11	3	18	2013	Fall
Geddry, Albert - Honored (Marty Guidry)	8	1	26	2010	Winter
Guédry Family Honored at 2010 Acadian Memorial Festival (Marty Guidry)	8	2	14	2010	Summer
Guédry Family Photos from the Acadian Memorial Festival, March 20, 2010, St. Martinville, LA (Allison Guidry)	8	2	18	2010	Summer
Guidry, Angel - 2015 Young Heroes Award	13	2	6	2015	Summer
Guidry Lacombe, Charlene - Les Guédry d'Asteur Membership Chair Recognized Nationally (Marty Guidry)	7	1	2	2009	Winter
Guidry, Charles - Erath's Guidry Has Overcome Obstacles To Be Successful Sugarcane Farmer (Abbeville Meridional, Abbeville, LA)	13	2	16	2015	Summer
Guidry, Dr. Charles - 2016 Stars of Style Best Dressed Gala	14	2	17	2016	Summer
Guidry, Dick - Being Inducted in Louisiana Political Hall of Fame (Marty Guidry)	11	3	19	2013	Fall
Guidry, Henry Family of Vermilion Parish, Louisiana (Robert L. Choate)	11	3	11	2013	Fall
Guidry, Jeff - Freedom and Jeff (Marty Guidry)	6	2	12	2008	Summer
Guidry, Joseph P. - Skipper of Hitler's Yacht (Joe Carmichael)	10	1	11	2012	Spring
Guidry, Marvin "Mark" - "A Hard Day's Work" - Poem (Allison Guidry)	2	4	16	2004	Fall
Guidry, Marvin "Mark" - "Reunion" (Poem) (Allison Guidry)	3	1	3	2005	Winter
Guidry, Meredith, Competes Again at International Science Fair	14	2	16	2016	Summer
Guidry Perry, Ophelia - Over a Century of Living and Still Going Strong (Cindy Luquette)	8	2	8	2010	Summer
Guidry, Richard - Honored Posthumously (Marty Guidry)	11	2	2	2013	Summer

TOPICAL INDEX TO "GENERATIONS" -
THE NEWSLETTER OF LES GUÉDRY ET PETITPAS D'ASTEUR
(Prepared by Cheryl Tholen; Updated by Martin Guidry)

TITLE	Volume	Issue	Page	Year	Season
FAMILY STORIES (Continued)					
Guidry, Roland and Dr. Jimmy Guidry - Guidry's Lead In Oil Spill Response (Marty Guidry)	8	2	11	2010	Summer
Guidry, Roman Antoine - Necrology	14	1	2	2016	Winter
Guidry, Ronald - Talent Spotlight	13	2	9	2015	Summer
Guidry, Scott - Local Man Researches History of Lockport Church (Thad Angelloz & Marty Guidry)	6	2	7	2008	Summer
Guidry, Sherwin Jonas (Sheri Guidry Bergeron)	8	1	9	2010	Winter
Guidry, Summerall Martin - And How Did I Get That Name? (Marty Guidry)	6	3	10	2008	Fall
Guidry Sisters Compete in International Science Fairs (Barry Guidry)	13	3	10	2015	Fall
Guidry's Hardware Celebrating 80 Years	11	2	28	2013	Summer
How Guédry Has Evolved Into So Many Variants (Marty Guidry)	8	3	2	2010	Fall
Jeddry, J. Alfred - Meteghan, Nova Scotia, Receives French Military Recognition (Albert Geddry)	13	3	12	2015	Fall
Jedrey, Jim & Little Eddie Kelly - Vaudville Team (Bernard Geddry)	6	3	15	2008	Fall
Labine, André - Alpine Skiing and My 2010 Winter Olympics Experiences (André Labine)	9	1	2	2011	Winter
Labine, Claire - Soap Opera Writer and Co-Creator of 'Ryan's Hope' Dies at 82 - November 11, 2016 (Sam Robertson)	15	2	15	2017	Summer
Labine, Gil - Labine Tabbed to Head Northwest LHIN Board	15	1	15	2017	Spring
Labine, Dr. Jay - Chief Medical Officer at Priority Health	15	2	17	2017	Summer
Labine, Joanie - Remember the Go-Go Dance? (Martin Guidry)	14	3	16	2016	Fall
Labine, Leonard Charles Turns 90 (Marty Guidry)	8	1	20	2010	Winter
Labine, Michel - of Northwest Territories Creates Beautiful Stained Glass in Northern Themes	14	2	16	2016	Summer
LaBine, Nancy - CSCC's LaBine Receives Volunteer Award	15	2	18	2017	Summer
Labine, Ray - Dual Roles, His Job & His Lifelong Love (Marty Guidry)	7	2	5	2009	Spring
Labine, Rita - Announcement of Death (October 12, 2012 in Ottawa, Canada) (André Labine)	10	3	1	2012	Fall
Les Guédry d'Asteur Merchandise (Cindy Herdt)	7	4	13	2009	Fall
New Acadie Project, The (Marty Guidry)	11	2	4	2013	Summer
Petitpas Taylor, Ginette - Takes the Moncton-Riverview-Dieppe Seat (Marty Guidry)	13	3	18	2015	Fall
Petitpas Taylor, Ginette & Stephen Poloz Unveil New Canadian Banknote	15	2	14	2017	Summer
Pettipas, Evelyn - Valley View Villa Senior Evelyn Pettipas Graduates At 93 (The News, New Glasgow, Nova Scotia)	13	2	17	2015	Summer
Pettipas, Leo - Discusses Yeti Pettipas from 2004 Atlantic Film Festival	15	1	10	2017	Spring
Pettipas, Sandra Perro & Eileen Avery - Tor Bay Acadians Honor Roll Inductions	15	2	10	2017	Summer
St. Martinville - Mars 2010 - An Article on Acadian Festival in *LA LETTRE*, (G.M.Braud)	10	1	10	2012	Spring
Story of Nova Scotia Acadians Who Came to the Aid of Hurricane Rita Victims, The (Jude Avery)	13	2	12	2015	Summer
Touring Acadian Madawaska - NE Maine, NW New Brunswick & SE Quebec (Congrès Mondial - 8-24 August 2014)	11	2	13	2013	Summer
Tribute to Our Acadian Ancestors, A [Poems] (Jude Avery)	13	2	15	2015	Summer
GENEALOGY / HISTORY					
Guidry, Alcee	4	2	6	2006	Summer
Guidry, Archange	4	3	6	2006	Fall
Guidry, Clans	3	1	5	2005	Winter
Guidry, Marie Lucien	3	3	6	2005	Fall
Guidry, O.G.	4	1	6	2006	Winter
Guidry, Ozair	5	1	6	2007	Winter
HISTORICAL TIDBITS					
Acadians To Have Music At Reunion	7	3	9	2009	Summer
Crossword Puzzle Clue - Evangeline	8	1	24	2010	Winter
Gaidry Gas and Oil Co. - Recently Organized	15	3	16	2017	Fall
Gaidry, A. A. - From Oyster Cocktail to Roast Turkey at the Gem Café - Ad	15	1	14	2017	Spring
Gaidry, A. A. - Stores to Close at Earlier Hour	15	1	14	2017	Spring
Gaidry, Lowell R. - Gaidry's Tabasco Pepper Sauce, New Orlean's, Louisiana [Labeled as Vol. 9 No. 4]	9	3	18	2011	Fall
Gaidry, Lowell R. - Gaidry's Tabasco Pepper Sauce, New Orlean's, Louisiana	10	3	19	2012	Fall
Gaidry, Lowell R. - Gaidry's Tabasco Pepper Sauce, New Orlean's, Louisiana	14	1	15	2016	Winter
Gaidry, Miz Liz - in 'Panic on the Pecos'	9	1	45	2011	Winter
Gaidry, Octave - Attention Battalion; After Firing Prizes at Store of Mr. O. Gaidry	16	1	22	2018	Spring
Gaidry, W. - Lima Sales Manager, The Lima News, Lima, Ohio, December 31, 1953	9	2	12	2011	Summer
Geddry, John A. - Patrolman Finds Man Hurt Is His Father-in Law (The Boston Herald, Newburyport, Massachusetts, November 17, 1932)	10	3	18	2012	Fall
Geddry,Tom - Scouting Historical Award for Florence Bank Project (Omaha Evening World-Herald, Nebraska, September 13, 1963)	10	3	18	2012	Fall
Guedry - G. W. Baylor & Guedry Real Estate and Insurance Agents	12	1	20	2014	Spring
Guedry, A., Mrs. - Mrs. Celeste Long, aged 104, dies in New Orleans-Mother of Mrs.A. Guedry	8	2	23	2010	Summer
Guedry, Allain - Orange Blossoms - Marriage of Allain Guedry, son of Joseph Guedry & Angeline Rodrigue, to Angelique Rodrigue	14	2	31	2016	Summer
Guedry, Allain - Orange Blossoms - Marriage of Allain Guedry, son of Joseph Guedry & Angeline Rodrigue, to Angelique Rodrigue	16	1	22	2018	Spring
Guedry, Camille - Died At His Home in Ascension Parish, LA	13	1	24	2015	Winter
Guedry, Elizabeth Ann - Represents Auxiliary at State Convention	13	3	28	2015	Fall
Guedry, Elodi - Wedding of Elodi Guedry and John H. Ayraud	16	1	22	2018	Spring
Guedry, Ethel L, Miss. - Medal Given Miss Guedry	11	1	43	2013	Spring
Guedry, Felix, Rev. - Pastor	8	1	23	2010	Winter
Guedry, J. A. - Fine Fish from Bayou Corne	15	1	13	2017	Spring
Guedry, Joseph - Found Dead in Room at Melrose House	13	3	27	2015	Fall
Guedry, Joseph - Justice Mitchell Completes His Investigation as to the Cause of the Death of Joseph Guedry	13	3	27	2015	Fall
Guedry, L. J. Is Seeking Stolen Cash And Gems	11	2	36	2013	Summer

TOPICAL INDEX TO "GENERATIONS" - THE NEWSLETTER OF LES GUÉDRY ET PETITPAS D'ASTEUR
(Prepared by Cheryl Tholen; Updated by Martin Guidry)

TITLE		Volume	Issue	Page	Year	Season
HISTORICAL TIDBITS (Continued)						
Guedry, William - Death of William Guedry		13	3	27	2015	Fall
Guedry's Pharmacy - Advertisement		13	3	28	2015	Fall
Guidri, Oliver - Sunday Law Violated	[Labeled as Vol. 9 No. 4]	9	3	18	2011	Fall
Guidry - Biggs and Guidry Typewriters Advertisement		15	2	20	2017	Summer
Guidry - Fontenot & Guidry Department Store & Fabric Shop (Breaux Bridge, LA)		13	2	27	2015	Summer
Guidry - One of New Orleans' Best-Drilled Gridiron Squads Whose Work Improves with Each Game		12	1	20	2014	Spring
Guidry Family - Guidry Family in Golden Gloves		14	3	24	2016	Fall
Guidry Odorless Cleaners - Advertisement (Lancaster, OH)		16	1	22	2018	Spring
Guidry, Mr. - Scott Scrapings		7	1	18	2009	Winter
Guidry, A. A. - Guidry's Seafood Ad; Kerrville, Texas		6	3	9	2008	Fall
Guidry, Abel - Special Refrigerator Cars		8	1	24	2010	Winter
Guidry, Albert, Hon. - Citizens Meeting		6	1	34	2008	Winter
Guidry, Albert - Man Questioned in Farmer's Death		8	3	26	2010	Fall
Guidry, Alcee - Guidry Company Brick Plant Has Baby Naming Contest		15	1	13	2017	Spring
Guidry, Alcee, Mrs. - Invites Readers to See New Hats for Sale at Her Home		15	1	13	2017	Spring
Guidry, Alex - Pleasure Boat Trip to Vermilion Bay and Gulf Coast		12	2	17	2014	Summer
Guidry, Alexander - Killed Hog That Was 7 Foot 2 Inches And Weighed 610 Pounds		15	3	16	2017	Fall
Guidry, Antoine - Abbeville Man Dies in Underwater Accident in Texas		18	3	19	2018	Fall
Guidry, Mrs. Antoine (Hortense Broussard) - Succession		12	2	16	2014	Summer
Guidry, Aubrey - Back Home After Detention		7	2	9	2009	Spring
Guidry, Audrey - Story "Vickie and the Elf" Written by Audrey Guidry, 9 Years Old		15	3	17	2017	Fall
Guidry, Aymar - Ad for Order of Wood and Coal		7	1	18	2009	Winter
Guidry, Beatrice A. & Guidry, Earl J. - Work Completed at Bourg High School		12	1	21	2014	Spring
Guidry, Benoit - Guidry Family Reunion at Benoit Guidry Home in Carlyss, LA in 1964		12	3	25	2014	Fall
Guidry, Blackie - Grapevine Opry Starring - Grapevine, Texas		10	1	10	2012	Spring
Guidry, Blackie - Guidry Reaches for Stardom		16	1	12	2018	Spring
Guidry, Blackie - Concert at Centenary College's Gold Dome		16	1	12	2018	Spring
Guidry, Caliste - The Caliste Guidry Home for Sale		14	1	16	2016	Winter
Guidry, Caliste - A Wholesale Raid		14	2	31	2016	Summer
Guidry, Celestine Touchet (Mrs. Theodule Guidry) - Lost Military Warrant		12	3	25	2014	Fall
Guidry, Charles - Is Not A Candidate for Commissary		15	3	17	2017	Fall
Guidry, Charmaine - With Unbearable Sorrow		11	1	44	2013	Spring
Guidry, Clairville - A Tragedy at Raceland		18	3	18	2018	Fall
Guidry, David - Claim of 480 Superficial Arpents of Land		12	2	17	2014	Summer
Guidry, Dell Joseph - Boy Disappears After Scolding		11	1	44	2013	Spring
Guidry, Dufossat - The Assumption Homicide		11	2	35	2013	Summer
Guidry, Elie - Market Hunter		9	1	45	2011	Winter
Guidry, Elzinia - Employees of Guidry Cleaners		9	2	12	2011	Summer
Guidry, Emile - Ripley's Believe or Not - His Hen Laid an Egg in a Cold Cream Jar		15	2	20	2017	Summer
Guidry, Ernest - Necrology		10	1	10	2012	Spring
Guidry, Ernest - Died after Extended Illness		10	2	14	2012	Summer
Guidry, Ethel - Hadacol Helps Thousands of All Age Groups		7	1	18	2009	Winter
Guidry, Eugene - Engaged to Marry Eugenie LeBlanc		15	1	13	2017	Spring
Guidry, Evariste - His Wife Katie Perrin Died		10	1	10	2012	Spring
Guidry, F. E. - Railroad News from All Around - Guidry Returns from Seeing Soldiers on the Border		11	2	35	2013	Summer
Guidry, F. E. - General Merchandise and Plantation Supplies Advertisement		14	1	16	2016	Winter
Guidry, F. E. - General Merchandise and Plantation Supplies Advertisement		14	2	31	2016	Summer
Guidry, Felix - Claim Allowed		6	2	9	2008	Summer
Guidry, Felix - Shot Accidentally		6	2	9	2008	Summer
Guidry, Fergus - Knocked in Head by Euphemon LeBlanc		13	3	28	2015	Fall
Guidry, Florence M. - Valedictorian of Mercy Hospital Graduation Class in Nursing		12	3	25	2014	Fall
Guidry, Frank - Birds Make A Refuge From Farm Swampland		7	3	9	2009	Summer
Guidry, Frank J. Oil Company - Crawfish Festival (Breaux Bridge, LA)		13	2	27	2015	Summer
Guidry, Fred - Guidry Has Emergency Operation at Hospital		18	3	19	2018	Fall
Guidry, Fred & Louis - Planters Bank & Trust Company Advertisement		14	1	16	2016	Winter
Guidry, Girard - 2 Airmen Rescue Yank Overcome in Smokey Room		7	4	8	2009	Fall
Guidry, Glenn "Mr. Rock'n Piano" - at the Ponderosa - Advertisement		14	2	30	2016	Summer
Guidry, Glynn - And the Other Brothers at Hurley's Tavern - Advertisement		14	2	30	2016	Summer
Guidry, H. D., M.D. - Advertisement		6	2	8	2008	Summer
Guidry, H. D., M.D. - Advertisement		6	3	17	2008	Fall
Guidry, H. N. - Fifth Death From Accident		10	1	10	2012	Spring
Guidry, Harry - Happy Family on Garmisch Holiday		9	1	45	2011	Winter
Guidry, Henry - Purchases Half-Interest in Mr. C. P. Moss' Saloon And Restaurant		13	2	28	2015	Summer
Guidry, Henry J., Jr. - Captain of Jerusalem Temple Arab Patrol		13	2	27	2015	Summer
Guidry, Herman - War "Got In Their Hair"		8	2	23	2010	Summer
Guidry, Hester M. - The Skyline Cafe - Advertisement		10	1	10	2012	Spring
Guidry, Hilda - LaLa's Beauty Parlor Advertisement		10	1	10	2012	Spring
Guidry, Hilda and Isaure - Sisters are Injured When Train Hits Buggy		7	1	18	2009	Winter
Guidry, Homer - The Homer Guidry & Elizabeth Martin Family		12	2	16	2014	Summer

TOPICAL INDEX TO "GENERATIONS" -
THE NEWSLETTER OF LES GUÉDRY ET PETITPAS D'ASTEUR
(Prepared by Cheryl Tholen; Updated by Martin Guidry)

TITLE		Volume	Issue	Page	Year	Season
HISTORICAL TIDBITS (Continued)						
Guidry, Horace - Harrington's Murderer	[Labeled as Vol. 9 No. 4]	9	3	18	2011	Fall
Guidry, Horace, Mrs. - After Many Years		12	1	21	2014	Spring
Guidry, Howard - Boy Accidentally Shot by Chum in Jennings		15	1	14	2017	Spring
Guidry, Ignace - Family of Late Ignace Guidry & Azelie David Hold Reunion in 1976 at Chicot Park, LA		15	2	21	2017	Summer
Guidry, Inez - Guidry Shot Three Times by His Brother-in-Law		14	3	24	2016	Fall
Guidry, James - You'd Faint, Too		7	4	8	2009	Fall
Guidry, James Pierre - Return from Airman Rites		18	3	19	2018	Fall
Guidry, Jewel and Johnnie - Jewel's Lounge, Kerrville, Texas - Advertisement		6	3	18	2008	Fall
Guidry, Jeo A., Mrs. Joe, Goldie Ann - Death Struck Here		12	3	24	2014	Fall
Guidry, John - 1871 Census; Québec West, St. Pierre Ward, Québec, Canada		7	4	9	2009	Fall
Guidry, Johnny M/M - Gave Food and Cash Shower to Alcide J. Smith Family Who Lost All in Hurricane Audrey		15	2	20	2017	Summer
Guidry, Joseph - Just Like Home		7	4	8	2009	Fall
Guidry, Joseph - Songs by Joseph 'Frenchy' Guidry at Carnival and Entertainment - Advertisement		14	2	31	2016	Summer
Guidry, Jules - Short Note To Him		7	2	9	2009	Spring
Guidry, Jules - Grandson Eli Completed the Diploma Business Course at Kentucky University		13	3	28	2015	Fall
Guidry, Jules - Emancipation of Victorine Melancon, wife of Jules Guidry		15	3	17	2017	Fall
Guidry, M/M Jules Pierre - Couple Observes 50th Anniversary of Marriage Here		14	2	30	2016	Summer
Guidry, Mrs. Jules - Died on May 1st 1895		18	3	18	2018	Fall
Guidry, L. C. - Fournet & Guidry Reply to the Eastin Charges in St. Martin Parish		10	2	15	2012	Summer
Guidry, L. J. - State Officers of the Catholic Knights of America		10	3	17	2012	Fall
Guidry, L. J. - State Officers of the Catholic Knights of America		12	1	21	2014	Spring
Guidry, L. R. - Transferring to Mexico		15	3	16	2017	Fall
Guidry, Lois Anne - Engaged to Marry Walter Alvin Souther, Jr.		15	1	13	2017	Spring
Guidry, Louis - Train Kills Boy of 13		10	2	15	2012	Summer
Guidry, Louis - Local Prep School Goes Against Springhill Today		11	2	36	2013	Summer
Guidry, Louis T. - Private Sale Advertisement	[Labeled as Vol. 9 No. 4]	9	3	18	2011	Fall
Guidry, Mae - Daughter of Jules Paul Guidry, Weds J. Nugent		14	3	23	2016	Fall
Guidry, Mareuse - Six Arrests Made in Mareuse Guidry Case		12	2	16	2014	Summer
Guidry, Marjorie Sue - Port Arthur News, Port Arthur, Texas	[Labeled as Vol. 9 No. 4]	9	3	18	2011	Fall
Guidry, Mark, Dr. - Laser Built at LSU		11	1	43	2013	Spring
Guidry, Martin, Sgt - The Soldiers Life		8	1	24	2010	Winter
Guidry, Martin, Sr. - Civil War Veteran; Images of America, Rayne, Louisiana		9	2	12	2011	Summer
Guidry, Marty R. - New Eagle Scout		12	3	23	2014	Fall
Guidry, Mary Mae, Miss - 14th Surprise Birthday Party		7	1	18	2009	Winter
Guidry, Nolan, Billy & Ronald - Guidry Family in Golden Gloves		14	3	24	2016	Fall
Guidry, Oleus - Refugees from Coast Jam Inland Shelters		6	2	9	2008	Summer
Guidry, Olivier D. - Resigned As Justice of Peace in St. Landry Parish, LA		12	3	24	2014	Fall
Guidry, Pierre - Pierre Guidry & Son Co. - Pre-Finished Plywood Ad		15	2	20	2017	Summer
Guidry, Pierre L. - Died at Home in Church Point, Louisiana		10	1	10	2012	Spring
Guidry, 'Pop' - Spry 'Bird-Loving' 'Pop' Guidry Adds Local Color to Orange		16	2	24	2018	Summer
Guidry, Ralph and Family - Five Lives Lost as Storm Sweeps Louisiana Town		18	3	19	2018	Fall
Guidry, Raymond - Pharmacist, Port Arthur, Texas	[Labeled as Vol. 9 No. 4]	9	3	18	2011	Fall
Guidry, Raymond Dale - Suffered Injury When Case of Pop Fell And Cut Him		15	2	20	2017	Summer
Guidry, Remy - Jefferson Drug Store Owner		8	3	26	2010	Fall
Guidry, Representative Richard - Inspects Tornado Damage in Lafourche Parish, LA		12	3	25	2014	Fall
Guidry, Robert - Mother's Day at Marbo-Guam		7	4	8	2009	Fall
Guidry, Robert, Rev. - Presentation of Altar Cloths and Accessories		14	3	24	2016	Fall
Guidry, Sharon - Writes to "Hints from Heloise"		8	2	23	2010	Summer
Guidry, Sidney - Death Notice, 1903, Boerne, Texas		10	2	14	2012	Summer
Guidry, Sosthene - Tragedy at a Dance		10	2	14	2012	Summer
Guidry, Sue - Frog Queen		8	2	22	2010	Summer
Guidry, Summerall - Sunset Developers, Inc. Homebuilding Advertisement		12	3	24	2014	Fall
Guidry, Telismar - Golden Anniversary		9	2	12	2011	Summer
Guidry, Theodule, Widow (Celestine Touchet) - Lost Military Warrant		12	3	25	2014	Fall
Guidry, Virgie Lea - Featured Speakers at CCD Conference		12	3	24	2014	Fall
Guidry, Walter 'Jake' - Announces He Has Purchased Whately's Barber Shop		16	2	24	2018	Summer
Guidry, Walter 'Jake' - Bore & Jake's Barber Shop Advertisement		16	2	24	2018	Summer
Guidry, William - Baby Falls Three Stories, Uninjured		7	2	9	2009	Spring
Guidry, William - One of New Orleans' Best-Drilled Gridiron Squads Whose Work Improves with Each Game		12	1	20	2014	Spring
Guidry, Pfc. Wilson M. - Reburial Rites Held for Kaplan Soldier		16	3	18	2018	Fall
Guidry, Woody, Jr. - Skating Rink Dance Advertisement		6	2	9	2008	Summer
Guidry's Bill Electric Service et. al. (Listing of Guidry Businesses in 1959 Lafayette, LA City Directory)		13	2	28	2015	Summer
Guidry's Cleaners - Owner, Danny Domingue		8	2	22	2010	Summer
Guidry's Louisiana Blue Rhythm Boys - Nick's Place - Advertisement		14	3	23	2016	Fall
Guidry's Nursery (Parks, LA)		13	2	8	2015	Summer
Guidry's Orchestra - Nick's Place - Advertisement (Two Ads)		14	3	23	2016	Fall
Guidry's Repair Shop - Owner, Harry Guidry (St. Martinville, LA)		13	2	8	2015	Summer
Guidry's Sea Food (Kerrville, TX)		8	3	26	2010	Fall

TOPICAL INDEX TO "GENERATIONS" -
THE NEWSLETTER OF LES GUÉDRY ET PETITPAS D'ASTEUR
(Prepared by Cheryl Tholen; Updated by Martin Guidry)

TITLE	Volume	Issue	Page	Year	Season
HISTORICAL TIDBITS (Continued)					
Guidry's Wine and Cheese (Nolan and Bobbie Guidry)	10	3	18	2012	Fall
Jeddry, David - WW II Draft Registration Card - 1942, Salmon River, Nova Scotia	7	4	9	2009	Fall
Jeddry, John - Murdered in St. Alphonse	5	2	11	2007	Summer
LaBean, Abraham - Rescued From Fishing Accident in Michigan	13	2	28	2015	Summer
LaBean, Charles - And His Brother Gilbert A. LaBean Visit Hollywood with Their Families (Should be Labine)	15	2	21	2017	Summer
LaBean, David - "Hose Joke" Is Fatal to Bay City Workman	11	2	36	2013	Summer
LaBean, Gilbert - And His Brother Charles LaBean Visit Hollywood with Their Families (Should be Labine)	15	2	21	2017	Summer
LaBean, James O. - Seeking Relative for Receiving Body	13	2	27	2015	Summer
LaBean, Joseph, Mrs. - Thrown from Wagon and Injured While Returning from Daughter's Wedding	15	3	17	2017	Fall
LaBean, W. - Muskegon Chronicle, Muskegon, Michigan, June 13, 1916	10	2	15	2012	Summer
LaBean, W. - Charged with Murder	12	2	17	2014	Summer
Labine - Frenchman Named Labine - Man Shot	11	1	43	2013	Spring
Labine, Alfred - Graduate of University of Michigan	16	1	23	2018	Spring
Labine, Alfred A. - Marries Marie Catudal	12	1	21	2014	Spring
LaBine, M/M Ambrose, et. al. - Wedding Anniversaries Observed by LaBines	13	1	24	2015	Winter
Labine, Aurore A. et. al. - One Opposes Nine in Fight Over Estate	14	3	24	2016	Fall
Labine, Charles Leo - Uranium Miner Labine Is Dead (Obituary)	12	2	17	2014	Summer
Labine, Clem - Keep Brooklyn Hopes Alive	14	1	15	2016	Winter
Labine, Clem and Jackie Robertson - Photo	16	2	24	2018	Summer
Labine's Winchester Park Shoe Store Advertisement	11	1	43	2013	Spring
Labine, Clem - Editor of the *Old-House Journal*	15	3	16	2017	Fall
Labine, Eugene - Harvesting 500 Acres	14	3	23	2016	Fall
Labine, Eugene - Harvesting 500 Acres	12	1	20	2014	Spring
LaBine, Frank - Frank LaBine Now at Mineola Hospital	11	1	44	2013	Spring
Labine, Fred - One Opposes Nine in Fight Over Estate	14	3	24	2016	Fall
Labine, Gilbert - Winnipeg Free Press - Manitoba, Canada, June 2, 1936	7	4	9	2009	Fall
Labine, Hormidas G. - Husband Is Absolute Boss	7	2	9	2009	Spring
LaBine, James - James LaBine Gets U. S. Mail Contract	15	2	21	2017	Summer
LaBine, James - James LaBine Gets U. S. Mail Contract	16	2	24	2018	Summer
Labine, Louis - Proprietor of Labine Soda Shoppe in Wethersfield, CT	16	1	23	2018	Spring
LaBine, Olive - Girls Senior Board - 1929 Yearbook	14	1	16	2016	Winter
Labine, Paul - US Yearbook - Hancock Central High, Hancock, Michigan 1958	7	4	9	2009	Fall
Labine's Winchester Park Shoe Store	11	1	43	2013	Spring
Longfellow Memorial for Evangeline Park at Grand Pré	7	3	10	2009	Summer
Modern Acadians, The - The Picturesque French-Canadian Squatters in Maine	11	3	16	2013	Fall
Mystery Shrouds Fate of Pennsylvania's "Cajuns"	7	3	9	2009	Summer
Petitpas, Albin - Recover Miner's Body Trapped in Cave-In	13	1	24	2015	Winter
Petitpas, Alfred, Mrs. - Lend Helping Hand	16	1	23	2018	Spring
Petitpas, Captain - Missing Vessel	10	1	10	2012	Spring
Petitpas, Eva - Tomato Race Gets Down to Girth	16	1	23	2018	Spring
Petitpas, Raymond Edmond, Sgt. - Warrant Officers, N.C.O.'s and Men Previously Reported Missing Now Reported Killed in Action	14	2	15	2016	Winter
Petitpas, Stanley - Eczema on Face and Arms for a Year. Healed by Cuticura - Testimonial	14	1	15	2016	Winter
Petitpas, Thomas L. - Completed Basic USAF Training at Lackland AFB, TX	13	1	24	2015	Winter
"Petitpas Restaurant" - About Town	6	3	9	2008	Fall
MEET OUR MEMBERS					
Guidry, Daniel Charles "Chuck"	1	4	1	2003	Fall
Guidry, Jack Anthony	2	1	1	2004	Winter
Guidry, Michael G. C.	1	2	1	2003	Spring
Guidry, Richard Martin "Marty"	1	1	1	2003	Winter
Herdt, Cynthia Kay Guidry	1	3	1	2003	Summer
MUSICIANS					
Geddry, Nathalie (Acadian Singer)	3	1	2	2005	Winter
Guidry, David Emery (Singer, Songwriter, Guitarist)	9	1	10	2011	Winter
Guidry, Emelie (Singer)	12	2	13	2014	Summer
Guidry, Frank (Guitar, Singer)	4	3	15	2006	Fall
Guidry, Gregory M. "Greg" (Singer and Songwriter)	2	3	10	2004	Summer
Guidry, Jules "Nonc Jules" (Cajun Band Leader and Musician)	2	2	6	2004	Spring
Guidry, Michael & Barbara Hall (The Enablers)	1	2	6	2003	Spring
Guidry, Michael & Barbara Hall (The Enablers)	3	1	2	2005	Winter
Guidry, Oran "Doc" (Cajun Fiddler)	2	3	9	2004	Summer
Guidry, Robert "Bobby" Charles - Louisiana Songwriter Dies at 71	8	1	11	2010	Winter
Guidry, Ron "Black" (The Cajun Man)	3	2	2	2005	Summer
Guidry, Sidney (Guitarist, Vocalist, Songwriter)	2	2	7	2004	Spring
Guidry, Wes (Rock Disk Jockey)	2	2	7	2004	Spring
Jeddry, Randy (Disk Jockey)	2	2	7	2004	Spring
LaBine, Laura Jane (Singer & Songwriter)	4	1	15	2006	Winter
Law, LeeAnn Raye (Cajun Fiddler) - Carrying On A Family Tradition (Written by her mother Christine Guidry Law)	10	3	21	2012	Fall

TOPICAL INDEX TO "GENERATIONS" -
THE NEWSLETTER OF LES GUÉDRY ET PETITPAS D'ASTEUR
(Prepared by Cheryl Tholen; Updated by Martin Guidry)

TITLE	Volume	Issue	Page	Year	Season
ON THE WEB					
Acadian-Cajun Genealogy & History (Tim Hebert)	4	3	8	2006	Fall
Acadians in Gray	1	3	10	2003	Summer
Acadians in Gray (Steven A. Cormier)	5	1	27	2007	Winter
Acadians in Gray (Steven A. Cormier)	4	3	8	2006	Fall
Archives of Canada	7	2	28	2009	Spring
Archives of Canada	7	3	20	2009	Summer
Archives Nationales (French National Archives)	5	1	27	2007	Winter
Cajuns, The - Genealogy, History and Culture (Stanley LeBlanc)	4	3	8	2006	Fall
Civil War in Louisiana	1	3	10	2003	Summer
Eighteeth Louisiana Infantry Regiment	1	3	10	2003	Summer
Forensic Genealogy & DNA & Genealogy (Colleen Fitzpatrick)	4	2	25	2006	Summer
Guédry-Labine Family Genealogical Database	6	3	19	2008	Fall
Guédry-Labine Family Genealogical Database	7	1	43	2009	Winter
Guédry-Labine Family Genealogical Database	7	2	28	2009	Spring
Guédry-Labine Family Genealogical Database	7	3	20	2009	Summer
La Ferme Musée Acadienne	5	1	27	2007	Winter
Les Guidry d'Asteur	6	3	19	2008	Fall
Les Guidry d'Asteur	7	1	43	2009	Winter
Les Guidry d'Asteur	7	2	28	2009	Spring
Les Guidry d'Asteur	7	3	20	2009	Summer
Library & Archives - Canada	6	1	9	2008	Winter
Library & Archives - Canada	6	2	14	2008	Summer
Louisiana Military Units	1	3	10	2003	Summer
Louisiana Slave Database & The Louisiana Free Database and Slave Narratives (Marty Guidry)	8	3	7	2010	Fall
Louisiana State Archives	5	2	9	2007	Summer
Louisiana State Archives	5	3	17	2007	Fall
Louisiana State Archives	6	1	9	2008	Winter
Louisiana State Archives	6	2	14	2008	Summer
Louisiana State Archives	6	3	19	2008	Fall
Louisiana State Archives	7	1	43	2009	Winter
Louisiana State Archives	7	2	28	2009	Spring
Louisiana State Archives	7	3	20	2009	Summer
National Archives	5	1	27	2007	Winter
National Archives	5	2	9	2007	Summer
National Archives	5	3	17	2007	Fall
National Archives	6	1	9	2008	Winter
National Archives	6	2	14	2008	Summer
National Archives of Quebec	5	2	9	2007	Summer
National Archives of Quebec	5	3	17	2007	Fall
Seventh Louisiana Cavalry	1	3	10	2003	Summer
REUNIONS					
Guédry-Labine & Petitpas Reunion - Clare & Lunenburg, Nova Scotia, August 5 & 7, 2004 (Marty Guidry)	1	1	8	2003	Winter
Guédry-Labine & Petitpas Reunion - Clare & Lunenburg, Nova Scotia, August 5 & 7, 2004 (Marty Guidry)	1	2	10	2003	Spring
Guédry-Labine & Petitpas Reunion - Clare & Lunenburg, Nova Scotia, August 5 & 7, 2004 (Marty Guidry)	1	3	11	2003	Summer
Guédry-Labine & Petitpas Reunion - Clare & Lunenburg, Nova Scotia, August 5 & 7, 2004 (Marty Guidry)	1	4	10	2003	Fall
Guédry-Labine & Petitpas Reunion - Clare & Lunenburg, Nova Scotia, August 5 & 7, 2004 (Marty Guidry)	2	1	9	2004	Winter
Guédry-Labine & Petitpas Reunion - Clare & Lunenburg, Nova Scotia, August 5 & 7, 2004 (Marty Guidry)	2	2	1,11	2004	Spring
Guédry-Labine & Petitpas Reunion - Clare & Lunenburg, Nova Scotia, August 5 & 7, 2004 (Marty Guidry)	2	3	15	2004	Summer
Guédry-Labine & Petitpas Tour - Clare Region, Nova Scotia, August 4, 2004 (Marty Guidry)	2	4	2	2004	Fall
Guédry-Labine & Petitpas Tour - Clare Region Photo Gallery - August 4, 2004 (Marty Guidry)	2	4	7	2004	Fall
Guédry-Labine & Petitpas Reunion - Meteghan, Nova Scotia, August 5, 2004 (Marty Guidry)	2	4	5	2004	Fall
Guédry-Labine & Petitpas Reunion - Lunenburg Nova Scotia, August 7, 2004 (Marty Guidry)	3	1	1	2005	Winter
Guédry-Labine & Petitpas Tour - Lunenburg Area, August 8, 2004 (Marty Guidry)	3	1	1	2005	Winter
Guédry-Labine & Petitpas Mini-Reunion - Acadian Village at Lafayette, LA, October 13, 2007 (Marty Guidry)	5	1	40	2007	Winter
Guédry-Labine & Petitpas Mini-Reunion - Acadian Village at Lafayette, LA, October 13, 2007 (Marty Guidry)	5	2	45	2007	Summer
Guédry-Labine & Petitpas Mini-Reunion - Acadian Village at Lafayette, LA, October 13, 2007 (Marty Guidry)	5	3	11	2007	Fall
Guédry-Labine & Petitpas Reunion - Bathurst, New Brunswick, August 16, 2009 (Marty Guidry)	6	1	10	2008	Winter
Guédry-Labine & Petitpas Reunion - Bathurst, New Brunswick, August 16, 2009 (Marty Guidry)	6	2	15	2008	Summer
Guédry-Labine & Petitpas Reunion - Bathurst, New Brunswick, August 16, 2009 (Marty Guidry)	6	3	20	2008	Fall
Guédry-Labine & Petitpas Reunion - Bathurst, New Brunswick, August 16, 2009 (Marty Guidry)	7	1	41	2009	Winter
Guédry-Labine & Petitpas Reunion - Bathurst, New Brunswick, August 16, 2009 (Marty Guidry)	7	2	26	2009	Spring
Guédry-Labine & Petitpas Reunion - Bathurst, New Brunswick, August 16, 2009 (Marty Guidry)	7	3	18	2009	Summer
Guédry-Labine & Petitpas Reunion - Bathurst, New Brunswick, August 16, 2009 [Highlights and Photos] (Marty Guidry)	7	4	1	2009	Fall
Guédry-Labine & Petitpas Reunion - Louisiane Day-Espace Neuf, August 17-18, 2009 - Pokemouche, New Brunswick (Marty Guidry)	7	4	12	2009	Fall
Guédry-Labine & Petitpas Sixth Reunion - Cutoff, LA, October 8, 2011 (Marty Guidry)	9	2	2	2011	Summer
Guédry-Labine & Petitpas Sixth Reunion ReCap - Cut Off, LA, October 8, 2011 (Marty Guidry) [Labeled as Vol. 9 No. 4]	9	3	2	2011	Fall
Guédry-Labine & Petitpas Booth at Fête de Famille -Lafayette, LA Cajundome, 13 October 2011 (Allison Guidry) [Labeled as Vol. 9 No. 4]	9	3	14	2011	Fall
Guédry & Petitpas Reunion - Van Buren, ME, 16 August 2014 (Marty Guidry)	10	1	6	2012	Spring

TOPICAL INDEX TO "GENERATIONS" -
THE NEWSLETTER OF LES GUÉDRY ET PETITPAS D'ASTEUR
(Prepared by Cheryl Tholen; Updated by Martin Guidry)

TITLE	Volume	Issue	Page	Year	Season
REUNIONS (Continued)					
Guédry & Petitpas Reunion - Van Buren, ME, 16 August 2014 (Marty Guidry)	10	3	13	2012	Fall
Guédry & Petitpas Reunion - Van Buren, ME, 16 August 2014 (Marty Guidry)	11	1	9	2013	Spring
Guédry & Petitpas Reunion - Van Buren, ME, 16 August 2014 (Marty Guidry)	11	2	9	2013	Summer
Guédry & Petitpas Reunion - Van Buren, ME - So What Is There To Do at the Congrès Mondial Acadien 2014? (Marty Guidry)	11	3	2	2013	Fall
Guédry & Petitpas Reunion - Van Buren, ME, 16 August 2014 (Marty Guidry)	11	3	20	2013	Fall
Guédry & Petitpas Reunion - Van Buren, ME, 16 August 2014 (Marty Guidry)	12	1	10	2014	Spring
Guédry & Petitpas Reunion - Van Buren, ME, 16 August 2014 (Marty Guidry)	12	2	15	2014	Summer
Guédry & Petitpas Reunion (6th) ReCap - Van Buren, ME, 16 August 2014 (Marty Guidry)	12	3	2	2014	Fall
Guédry & Petitpas Reunion - Henderson, LA, 10 October 2015 (Marty Guidry)	13	1	2	2015	Winter
Guédry & Petitpas Reunion - Henderson, LA, 10 October 2015 (Marty Guidry)	13	2	22	2015	Summer
Guédry & Petitpas Seventh Reunion Re-Cap - Henderson, LA, 10 October 2015 (Marty Guidry)	13	3	2	2015	Fall
Guédry, Hébert & Breaux Reunion - Maurice, LA, 25 June 2016 (Marty Guidry)	14	2	2	2016	Summer
Guédry, Hébert & Breaux Reunion - Thibodaux, LA, 10 March 2018 (Marty Guidry)	15	3	15	2017	Fall
Guédry & Petitpas Eighth Reunion - Summerside, Prince Edward Island, 17 August 2019 (Marty Guidry)	15	3	7	2017	Fall
Guédry & Petitpas Eighth Reunion - Summerside, Prince Edward Island, 17 August 2019 (Marty Guidry)	16	1	2	2018	Spring
Guédry & Petitpas Eighth Reunion - Summerside, Prince Edward Island, 17 August 2019 (Marty Guidry)	16	2	21	2018	Summer
Guédry & Petitpas Eighth Reunion - Summerside, Prince Edward Island, 17 August 2019 (Marty Guidry)	16	3	8	2018	Fall

Fall, 2007

Volume 5, Issue 3

Les Guidry d'Asteur

GENERATIONS

IN THIS ISSUE

Dedication of Plaque to Augustin Guedry & Marie Jonson (Aug. 2007) — 2

Bon Appetit - Recipes from the Guedry-Labine Family Cookbook — 4

Genealogy/History: The Woman Who Could Do Anything - Malvina Menard Labine — 5

Guidry Mini-Reunion, Oct. 13, 2007, Highlights — 11

The Guidry's of St. John The Baptist Parish, LA — 13

Book Nook — 18

This issue of "GENERATIONS" contains several interesting articles about the Guedry-Labine family. A truly extraordinary woman, Malvina Labine captured the hearts and votes of the townspeople of Azilda, Ontario to become its reeve. On the opposite end of the continent Edwin Guidry, Sr. and his descendents have had a similar impact on a small rural parish of Louisiana. Their lives hightlight the strengths and accomplishments of our Guedry-Labine family.

The Woman Who Can Do Anything-Malvina Menard Labine

In the Winter 2007 edition of "Generations" Claudette Mancini shared with us the inspiring story of her grandmother Malvina Menard Labine. Upon reading Claudette's story, Andre Labine, also a grandchild of Malvina, remembered a 1959 article in Maclean's Magazine about "The Woman Who Can Do Anything". Truly Malvina Labine did do everything – rising from near poverty after her husband's untimely death to become reeve (mayor) of Azilda, Ontario. Her story is truly one of courage in the face of troubled times - a woman with a huge heart and the will to better the lives of her people. The story of Malvina Menard Labine is one of an ordinary woman doing extraordinary things.

Article on page 5

The Guidry's of St. John The Baptist Parish, LA

Just west of New Orleans, St. John the Baptist Parish is often overlooked as one travels to Baton Rouge. St. John, however, lies on the German Coast of the Mississippi River and has a rich history. First settled in the early 1700's by German immigrants and later by Acadians moving southeastward, St. John was plantation country – with large homes and sugar cane as the main crop. And among the largest cane planters of St. John Parish were Leon Graugnard and his son-in-law Edwin Joseph Guidry, Sr. As he matured in the sugar cane business, E. J. Guidry gained increasing responsibility in the operations of the family business - eventually assuming full ownership and management of Terre Haute Plantation. His significant contributions to St. John Parish during the twentieth century are widely recognized. Today his descendants are leading the parish into the twenty-first century.

Article on page 13

DEDICATION OF PLAQUE TO AUGUSTIN GUEDRY AND MARIE JONSON by Marty Guidry

Sunday afternoon, August 12, 2007 at 4:00 pm approximately 100 Guédry descendants met near the cemetery of St. Alphonse Catholic Church in St. Alphonse, Nova Scotia to dedicate a memorial plaque honoring Augustin Guédry and his wife Marie Jonson – founders in 1787 of Chéticamp on St. Mary's Bay in Nova Scotia. This community is known now as St. Alphonse.

Today the numerous descendents of Augustin and Marie are settled principally in St. Alphonse and nearby Meteghan although small numbers can be found throughout Nova Scotia and in the New England states. Few today are called Guédry as the learned priests and scribes of yesteryear transformed the name to Jeddry, Jedry, Jeddrie, Jeddrey, Geddry, Gedry, Gidry, Guidry and other similar phonetic spellings.

As Master of Ceremonies, Albert Geddry of Meteghan welcomed everyone to the ceremonies and then briefly discussed the life of Augustin Guédry, a grandson of Claude Guédry and Marguerite Petitpas and the youngest son of Pierre Guédry and Marguerite Brasseau. Born in 1740 in Acadia, Augustin was only fifteen years old when the Acadian deportations began in 1755. Through cunning, good luck and skill he evaded the British and was not deported – the only Guédry not deported. Helped by the friendly Mi'kmaq, he survived near Merligueche (today Lunenburg) until 1763 when the Treaty of Paris ended the deportations and allowed some Acadians to return to the 'new' Nova Scotia. Augustin emerged from hiding in 1764 and settled at Hobb's Hill near Gilbert's Cove in Digby County where he fished and farmed, married and began a family. As the new English settlers began to encroach near his land, he became uncomfortable and yearned to "escape" the British once again. With all his belongings in a boat he left Hobb's Hill in 1787 for a more isolated area. Making landfall at Bear Cove, he settled about a mile from the seashore near today's St. Alphonse

There he and Marie began anew their life of fishing and farming while raising their growing family. From his humble home near Bear Cove the community of Chéticamp grew as his children matured and had families of their own and as new settlers moved into the area. In 1826 Augustin died near Chéticamp at the age of eighty-six years.

An Acadian with a close connection to the Guédry family through his wife Aurore Geddry, Senator Gerald Comeau described the rich cultural heritage of the Acadians - developed over the past two hundred years. He emphasized the pride that all feel today in being Acadian.

Martin Guidry of Louisiana, representing Les Guidry d'Asteur, thanked the communities of St. Alphonse and Meteghan for welcoming our family to their communities in 2004 during our Guédry-Labine and Petitpas Reunion. Here began the genesis of this plaque and ceremony. Folks attending the Reunion felt a special connection to our cousins in the St. Mary's Bay area and wanted to 'leave behind' a special remembrance of our good times here. Working together with our counterparts in St. Alphonse and Meteghan, we developed the concept of a plaque honoring Augustin Guédry and Marie

Jonson. With funding from Les Guidry d'Asteur and the hard work of several folks from St. Alphonse and Meteghan the plaque was completed – letting us appropriately honor the founders of Chéticamp (St. Alphonse) and commemorate our 2004 Guédry-Labine and Petitpas Reunion.

Bernard (Bernie) Geddry of Arizona, the closest living relative to Augustin Guédry, related several interesting stories about Augustin and his family. Of particular interest to the attendees was Bernie describing his visit to Meteghan in the 1970's when he first learned of his Acadian heritage and his seeing Philippe Geddry's home for the first time. Philippe was Augustin's son and Bernie's great great grandfather. Bernie crawled under the house and observed rough axe markings on the beams – perhaps cut by Philippe or Augustin. The home still stands on Highway 1 between St. Alphonse and Meteghan.

Adding a very special touch to the ceremony was Father Paul Belliveau, pastor of St. Bernard Catholic Church in St. Bernard. Father Belliveau stressed that the hardy spirit and religious strength of Augustin Guédry and the other Acadians returning to Nova Scotia after 1763 played a major role in the survival and the growth of the Acadian communities in Nova Scotia.

With the ceremony concluding Father Abeni d'Entremont, pastor of St. Alphonse Catholic Church led everyone in singing "Ave Maris Stella"- the Acadian national anthem.

Afterwards all walked across Highway 1 to the parish hall to enjoy a nice bowl of chicken fricot and other treats prepared by the parishioners of St. Alphonse. Visiting with our Acadian cousins over a bowl of fricot culminated a wonderful afternoon honoring our ancestors Augustin Guédry and Marie Jonson.

L-Albert Geddry

Above-Bernie Geddry, R-Father Belliveau, Below-Attendees

BON APPETIT - Recipes from The Guedry-Labine Cookbook

RAPPIE PIE - *Vawn Jeddry Alberta, Canada*

One large chicken/rabbit (some people even use clams or beef)
15-20 lbs. of potatoes
Salt and pepper
3 large onions diced

2 large diced onions (additional)

Cook meat until tender with salt/pepper and 3 large diced onions, remove meat from water and save water. Grate about 10 pounds potatoes, squeeze the water from potatoes (a juicer works nicely for this). Put a cup at a time of the boiling water from the meat into the grated potatoes and stir fast (this cooks the potatoes). Put the 2 large diced onions, uncooked, into the potatoes and stir, then put meat into the potatoes and stir, salt and pepper to taste. Place in a buttered roast pan to 2 inches from top. (Optional to put a few slices of bacon or salt pork on top to give it that nice crust)

Put in oven at 350 F for about 3 hours, then 400 F for approx. 1 hour to get the nice crust. Enjoy.

There is an old saying that the English put butter on their Rappie Pie and the French put molasses on top when cooked, and that was to distinguished the difference between the two.

I got this recipe from a Belliveau woman in New Brunswick, CA.
- Vawn Jeddry

PERSIMMON CAKE - *From Charlene Guidry Lacombe, Jennings, LA*

3 cups flour
2 cups sugar
1 tsp. soda
1 tsp. salt
1 1/2 cups of persimmon pulp
1 cup oil
3 eggs
1 teaspoon cinnamon
1 cup pecans

Mix together everything and pour in greased bundt pan or two loaf pans. Bake at 350 F for 35 minutes, check with toothpick or knife to make sure it's done.

At 65, after bearing 20 children, "Grannie" Labine is reeve of a flourishing Ontario township. This doesn't country eaters, dig ditches and run a farm. They call her

The woman who can do anything

With reeve-like dignity, Malvina Labine strides through her bailiwick near Sudbury. Her election ousted the former principal of a school where she'd once been janitor.

For her houseful of hearty young eaters, Mme. Labine buys bread 400 loaves at a time and stores it in her freezer.

By Dorothy Sangster
PHOTOGRAPHS BY HORST EHRICHT

December 2, 1958, found the nickel-mining city of Sudbury, in northern Ontario, in the paralyzing grip of a strike. Christmas was coming but nobody had any money. Almost eight thousand miners had been idle for more than two months and settlement seemed as far off as ever. In desperation, a motorcade of a hundred and fifty cars was heading for Toronto, where union spokesmen would discuss the critical situation with Premier Leslie Frost.

Yet the most eye-catching item on page one of the Sudbury Star that day had nothing to do with the strike. It was a large picture of a sixty-five-year-old French-Canadian grandmother named Malvina Labine, who had just been elected reeve of adjacent Rayside Township.

"Widow Scores Upset," the caption said, and there she sat, looking as if there was nothing odd in a grey-haired farm woman with only grade-school education defeating the forty-one-year-old incumbent reeve, who had once been principal of the school where she had worked as janitor.

If Malvina Labine was not overly surprised by her victory, neither was anybody else up her way, where she is often referred to as The Woman Who Can Do Anything. Since her husband died eighteen years ago, she has looked after sixteen children, successfully run a farm and market garden, kept a dairy herd, dug ditches, built two houses, taken an active role in church affairs, cared for a dozen foster children, and cooked sit-down dinners for as many as six hundred people at a time. Last November, when she announced her intention to run for reeve, her admirers figured she was as good as in.

One morning not long after her election victory, I taxied eight miles out of Sudbury to interview Madame Labine in Azilda, the hamlet where she lives. Her house was the square brick one on a raised foundation, right next to the Catholic church. The door was opened by the new reeve herself, who greeted me in English (a language she'd learned in childhood from her English-speaking cousins) and suggested I make myself comfortable on the chesterfield while

surprise her constituents, who've watched her build houses, cook for 600

Township affairs are conducted by telephone, while 15-year-old foster daughter Gloria waits by Grannie's rocker.

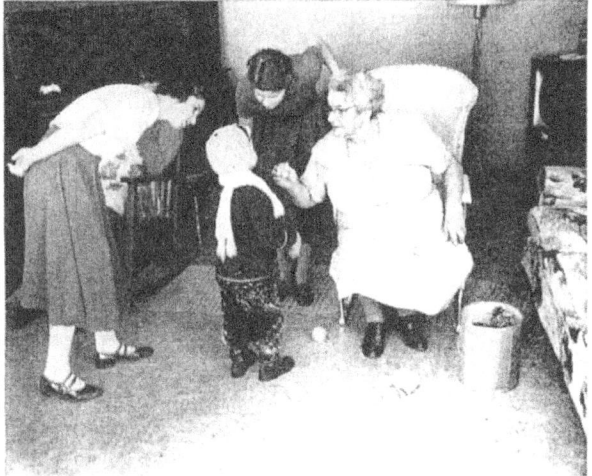

From a parlor chair, she dispenses love, justice, first aid. Ron, youngest foster child, has a cut lip

Family affairs are conduced after a hearty lunch. "Growing children must eat well," says Mme Labine

The new reeve is never too busy for a moment's play.

she lowered herself into a rocking chair and reached for her knitting.

"Everybody calls me Grannie," she said.

In a corner of the big living room a little boy with soft brown eyes, too young to go to school, was playing with some tin soldiers. This was the youngest of the eight foster children (some sent to her privately, some by the Children's Aid Society) currently being boarded in the Labine household. In the adjoining kitchen, Madame's unmarried daughter Germaine was busy at the stove, for the other children would soon be home for lunch.

As I took in the scrubbed kitchen floor and the blue oilcloth on the table, Grannie Labine gave me the first clue to her character. She is a plain woman and likes plain things.

"The more you have, the more you have to look after," is her philosophy.

She told me, "Back in 1913 I bought myself a nice muskrat coat for sixty-nine dollars and getting out of the buggy at Mass one Sunday I tripped and fell in the mud. I guess it served me right for my vanity. Now I'm not so vain about my appearance. I don't envy anybody their fancy clothes and twenty-dollar hats. I have a neck like a turkey and I weigh two hundred and twenty pounds. I could live for quite a while on my fat, so if I have a few cents it's better if I give them to the poor."

According to what I'd already heard, that is exactly what she does. If anyone's sick, Grannie Labine's in there helping, if anybody needs something, she brings it. When the miner who rented a farmhouse she owns went on strike and couldn't pay his rent, she told him to forget it until he was working again. As the strike persisted and townsfolk began to suffer, she quietly despatched cases of canned goods, children's shoes, strained baby food.

One of her daughters had told me, "Mother never buys anything for herself." But Madame Labine scoffed. "Nonsense! Just last summer I paid a hundred and sixty dollars for some stainless-steel pots for my banquets! You know I make banquets? From Palm Sunday to October I catered for sixteen affairs. The one on Palm Sunday was a sit-down dinner for six hundred people in aid of the church in Chelmsford. I bought fourteen turkeys and ninety pounds of ham for that one. **continued on page 54**

The woman who can do anything continued from page 19

"When her husband was in the lumber camps, she was a farmer. One year she made $1,240."

and carrots and corn and peas, and we made homemade beans, and bought ice-cream roll for dessert. The women in the parish cooked the turkeys and I spent a whole day slicing them. Then I prepared two banquets for the church in Espanola, and three ordination dinners, and a picnic for my own church, and twice in the summer I catered for wedding banquets three days in a row."

The telephone rang and she excused herself to answer it. One of her friends, it appeared, was ready to buy half a calf if she would buy the other half.

Back in her rocking chair again, Madame Labine gave me character clue No. 2: She is a good provider and fortunate are her foster children.

She was saying, "Last winter I bought a five-hundred-and-twenty-six-pound cow and some pork and it was gone in seven months. We have two hundred and thirty pounds of veal in my big freezer right now. I buy a hundred pounds of beans at one time, and twenty pounds of shortening, and thirty pounds of peanut butter, and a dozen cases of corn and tomato juice and tomato soup (I make my own pea soup) and four hundred loaves of bread. I fill the freezer with bread and sell the remaining loaves to my neighbors at three for twenty-nine cents, the same price they cost me. The children drink four quarts of milk a day. Their favorite foods are spaghetti and cabbage rolls and home-baked beans with a chunk of fat pork in them for flavor. It's important that growing children should eat well."

Even as she spoke, seven healthy-looking youngsters trooped in the side door, removed their snowy overcoats, washed their hands at the sink, nodded a polite hello in our direction, and jostled into place at the table, where Germaine was ladling out a rich beef stew.

Listening to their chatter, Madame Labine said thoughtfully, "I don't know what gets into people to give their children away. I wouldn't have done that. Germaine and I never leave these children alone. They're good children, and we're willing to work hard to see they don't go astray."

A queen and her family

According to those who know her best, Malvina Menard has always worked hard. She was thirteen when she left home to work as a nursemaid in Sudbury and nineteen when she married a young blacksmith named Joseph Labine. They settled down in a small shack on a few acres of flat farmland, twelve miles from Azilda, in Rayside County. In the next twenty-nine years she gave birth to twenty babies. Four died in their infancy. Six sons (Romeo, Gerrard, Robert, Leo-Paul, Raymond and Bernard) and ten daughters (Yvonne, Germaine, Lucienne, Aline, Laurette, Lorraine, Adrienne, Jeanne, Thérèse and Claire) still survive.

Too many children? She never thought so.

"When I went to Mass on Sunday with all of them walking behind me, I felt like a queen," she says.

She didn't have a queen's life. During six months of the year when her husband was off in the lumber camps, she was the family farmer. Each spring, she sowed a garden of one acre that she could hoe herself. One year she made $1,240 profit from its produce. She milked cows, baked bread, lugged buckets of water up the hill, heated them in big boilers on a wood stove and gave every child a Saturday-night bath. Twice a week in summer she climbed out of bed at 3 a.m. and worked in the cucumber patch till dawn, an old oat bag tied around her waist. (When it was full, by her reckoning, it was a bushel.) Then she piled fruit and vegetables and eggs into her rickety old truck and headed for the Sudbury market. Whoever arrived first got the best vendor's stall, next to the butcher. She always arrived first.

Joseph Labine was a good man, but cautious. For years he saved lumber to

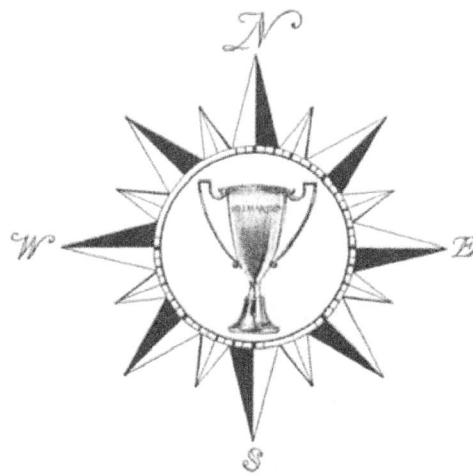

all points point to the fine points of **HILLMANSHIP!**

HILLMAN MINX SEDAN
price p.o.e. $1,925.

Trim, nimble and powerful—that's the new 1959 HILLMAN. With a larger engine for improved power and acceleration, here is *performance*—best in its class! There's stunning, clean-line styling with Hillman. Deeper, cushiony seating *comfort*, unitary construction and ball-joint suspension smooths any road. Wherever you go, you'll get poised big-car ride and Hillman's famous up to 35-miles-per-gallon *economy*. Discover for yourself *all* the fine points of Hillmanship. Test-drive the new 1959 Hillman at your dealer's today! There are over 200 of them across Canada, supplying parts and service from coast to coast.

HILLMAN FOR '59

ROOTES MOTORS (CANADA) LIMITED • *ROOTES PRODUCTS:* HILLMAN • SUNBEAM • HUMBER

build a house, but then he decided to build a barn for his eight horses and cows instead. The house would come next, he promised.

That was how things stood one morning in 1941 when he set off for the market. Madame Labine stayed home that day with her new baby (as she puts it in her colorful English, "When you have your twentieth child you don't come out of bed like a cork pops out of water!"). Her friend, Madame Sara Trothier, recalls bumping into Joseph Labine as he emerged from the market cafeteria at noon. He was a big, jovial man who weighed two hundred and eighty-six pounds and enjoyed his food. He told Madame Trothier, "Well, if I die today at least I had a good meal!" Two hours later he dropped dead of a heart attack.

Malvina Labine thus became a widow at forty-seven, with nine children under sixteen to support, and nothing but debts. The shack was so old that snow came in the windows. The children crowded around the stove hoping to warm themselves for the long march to school, but what heat the stove gave out the draughts along the floor dissipated.

Another woman might have called it quits, but not Madame Labine. She traded five of the horses as down payment on a tractor and scrapped the old jalopy with the dangerous brakes for a new truck, payments to be carried by her three oldest sons who had just found work in the mines.

Then she turned her attention to the house.

Her daughter Laurette recalls the day her mother called the family together and told them, "Tomorrow I'm bringing the stuff to market and I'm going to see Monsieur Labarge (the lumber dealer). Watch for me when I come back. If I've made a deal, I'll toot the horn and that means we'll tear down the old house and build a new one."

"We waited and we heard the horn," Laurette says. "Fifteen minutes later the chimney was down. I still don't know how it was done."

Madame Labine was determined to have a good basement, so the boys got explosives and blasted away enough rocky terrain to build a cement foundation. The school board gave permission for the three oldest girls to stay home and help their mother build the house. A carpenter brother-in-law donated services and advice for fifty-five days at five dollars a day, but it was Malvina Labine who directed operations and did most of the heavy work, sawing lumber, hoisting two-by-fours, pounding in nails, laying hardwood floors.

The only time she slipped up was when she put hot lime instead of hydrated lime in the shavings for insulation, with the result that when it rained the house caught fire. Her son Gerrard, now a garage owner in Sudbury, says, "We were all sleeping in the grain shed and I had to take the alarm clock to bed with me and wake up every hour to make sure the house wasn't on fire. One morning I didn't wake up until 10 o'clock, and five men with fire hoses were fighting the flames. We had to take the boards off and let the lime out."

By the end of September, they had moved into the house, but it wasn't until late November that they got the brick siding on. Since they had no more money, the house stayed unfinished inside until the following summer, when the whole family picked potatoes for their neighbors and spent their wages on paint. Then, as the girls crack-filled the Gyproc and enameled the four upstairs bedrooms, Madame Labine rolled up her sleeves and skilfully papered the downstairs. The only job beyond her was the construction of an outdoor steambath where the children could scrub up after a day in the fields. A Scandinavian workman built her one for seventy-five dollars.

Now that she was a widow, she worked harder than ever. She pressed hay, threshed grain, picked potatoes, hoed her one-acre garden, cooked meals, sewed, and knitted warm winter clothes. Once she and Germaine earned fifty-five dollars helping workmen install a heavy culvert, and when a janitor was needed for the new school Madame Labine applied and got the job.

"It wasn't human the work my mother did!" marvels her daughter Adrienne.

From DTC the Right Product — at the Right Time

School days are the best days. And today's are made even better than those we knew, thanks to the increasing range of products from Dominion Tar & Chemical subsidiary companies. SIPOREX precast cellular concrete building slabs, for instance, form an economical insulating floor and ceiling that absorb noise, aid concentration of teacher and pupils ... while text books printed on fine papers from Howard Smith Paper Mills give faithful reproduction and reading ease. These and other DTC products, meet in the modern classroom and make their contribution to better education.

ANSWERING THE CHALLENGE of supplying the right product at the right time is typical of DTC and its operating subsidiaries. These subsidiaries are continually solving problems—supplying new answers, new products, for home, farm and industry. The result? A widely diversified list of products that benefits everyone—customers, shareholders and employees.

SIPOREX Limited
Precast Haydite Limited
Murray-Brantford Limited
Cooksville-Laprairie Brick Limited
Canada Creosoting Company, Limited

DOMINION TAR & CHEMICAL COMPANY, LIMITED

Sifto Salt Limited
Javex Company Limited
NO-CO-RODE Company Limited
Howard Smith Paper Mills, Limited
Chemical Developments of Canada Limited

Changing your address?

Be sure to notify us at least six weeks in advance, otherwise you will likely miss copies. Give us both old and new addresses — attach one of your present address labels if convenient.

Write to:
Subscription Dept., Maclean's Magazine, 481 University Ave., Toronto 2, Ontario.

P.S. Your postmaster also needs your new address. Fill out a Post Office change-of-address card.

She knew a spot where succulent raspberries grew, and she'd pick them at night and start selling at dawn. By 9 a.m. they'd be gone, and Leo-Paul would be despatched home to the berry patch where his sisters were gathering a second load. One summer they made two hundred dollars on black currants alone.

When it came to training her children, Madame Labine enforced strict rules. The young Labines were expected to attend church, pray devoutly, make themselves useful, help one another, and do what they were told without argument.

If a child carelessly tore his clothes, he was made to sit down and mend them. If he misbehaved, he was punished at once. She discouraged her sons from smoking, but when she discovered them in the barn passing around cigarettes she invited them into the house. Her daughters were brought up to believe that smoking and drinking were for men only.

"I'm lucky in my children," Madame Labine says. "All my daughters are good girls, and my married sons, thank God, are crazy about their wives."

Her children recall that she never showed favoritism. When eleven of them married in seven years she gave each one the same send-off: a big celebration with turkey and vegetables and pickles and pies and ice cream. After an early nuptial Mass the wedding party would return to the big farmhouse for breakfast, then off to the photographer's for the wedding portraits, then home again for another bite to eat, and then the long afternoon filled with dancing and joking and singing, leading up to the big dinner laid out on the best tablecloth and centred by the towering bride's cake. With mother at the piano and Leo-Paul or Gerrard on violin, and Jeanne on guitar, and Romeo on clarinet or sax —for they were all natural musicians and had accumulated an assortment of second-hand instruments over the years —they had no need to hire an orchestra.

Almost before she realized it, all her children except Germaine and young Bernard were married and gone. The big farmhouse seemed empty and meaningless. That's when she decided to take in foster children.

Daniel Feeny, executive director of the Sudbury Children's Aid Society, says "This is a family-loving community and plenty of middle-aged women apply for foster children when their own families are grown up and married."

What made Madame Labine's case unusual was that she applied for four at once. Two months after her youngest daughter's wedding she had installed a family of two brothers and two sisters in her home; six months after that she had found room for four others. It was almost like having her own children back again.

Over the years, the Children's Aid Society has had the best of relations with Madame Labine, whom they regard as a warm, understanding person with a lot of common sense. A case worker who has known her for ten years says, "She got around thirty dollars a month for each child in her care, but she was never in it for the money. Whenever I had a problem child I thought immediately of her. She was a real grandmother type, the kind that gives kids little bits of dough when she bakes. I remember when one troubled little boy confided that he'd never gone fishing, she bought him a fine new rod and delegated one of the older lads to take him down to the creek. When a little girl set her heart on a winter coat that cost more than the budget provided, she chipped in four dollars from her own purse. She kept in touch with their teachers, and checked on their homework, and Saturdays she'd pack them into the truck and take them to a Bingo or a church picnic. Sunday morning saw

IN THE NEXT ISSUE

Quebec editor Ken Lefolii blends his colorful prose with some striking full-color photographs to tell the story of

MOUNT ROYAL'S VALIANT STAND AGAINST PROGRESS

How one of our best-known and best-loved landmarks has withstood the invasions of time and traffic—though it splits our biggest city up the middle

ON THE NEWSSTANDS
MARCH 17

them all lined up for Communion. It's considerable training for a Catholic child to live in her home."

The Church has always loomed large in Grannie Labine's life. On its behalf, she has sold raffle tickets, organized bazaars, arranged Bingo games, cooked innumerable dinners. For six years she was president of the local Catholic women's organization, and she spearheaded the drive for funds for a new rectory.

The only time her children ever saw her cry was when one daughter wrote home that she was marrying a Protestant. Finally Madame Labine dried her tears and decided to leave it to the Blessed Virgin, to whom she has great devotion. She organized the whole family in a round of prayers and novenas, and after a year they received word that the son-in-law had become a convert!

For years, Madame Labine's dearest wish has been to go to Rome and see the Pope. Last spring, she had saved up $2,200, but she decided to pay off the mortgage on her house in Azilda instead. "I felt more comfortable that way," she explains.

Until last November, she had no political aspirations, although she had spent all her life in Azilda and was thoroughly acquainted with township affairs.

She throws clean dirt

To realize what she stepped into, it is necessary to know something of Rayside, a township of thirty-six square miles, northwest of Sudbury, of which Azilda is the hub. Ten years ago a farming community, today Rayside is practically a suburb of the city. In six years its population has jumped from 1,460 to 3,790, and its interests are reflected in such Sudbury Star news stories as: Azilda Passes Curfew Law for Children, Wild Fowl Sanctuary Considered for Azilda, Dog Sled Derby Coming to Azilda, St. Jean Baptiste Day Celebrated with 25 Floats in Azilda, Volunteers raise $15,000 for New Azilda School, Fire Brigade Organized for Azilda, and Principal of Bilingual School in Azilda Denies English Pupils Taught Prayers in French.

Over this colorful community, until Grannie Labine came along, presided Tyne Castonguay, onetime school principal who has lately devoted his talents to running a patent-medicine business.

When she was asked to run against Castonguay for reeve, Madame Labine thought it was a huge joke. But, after consideration, she consented.

"Some people throw an awful lot of dirt at other people when they get into politics. Some day they'll get it all back on their own heads, but it won't be from me. I intend to fight a clean fight," she told her cheering supporters.

Nevertheless, dirt—good clean dirt, that is—played its part in her campaign. Culverts and ditches are important issues in the country, and last year Grannie Labine built her own culvert and braced it with muck from the smelters at Copper Cliff at fourteen dollars a load. When people stopped to stare and ask "Why are you doing this hard work yourself?" she told them characteristically, "I am doing it myself so I will know how to do it." Later, a road gang widened Azilda ditches and propped up her displaced culvert with light dusty sand at five dollars a load. Grannie Labine was furious. "Muck costs more, but it stays where you put it," she told reporters, and at least one newspaper story was headed, More Muck in Ditches if Azilda Widow Wins.

Election night found Madame Labine setting out sandwiches and cakes and doughnuts and coffee in the town hall for campaign workers of both sides, at her own expense. "Win or lose, I'll have a party," she had sworn. An unprecedented turnout of women voters swung the tide her way on the last poll and when the defeated Castonguay shook her hand and told the press "Madame Labine is a fine lady whom I've always admired" she learned she was the new reeve by a majority of sixty-eight votes.

An hour later, in line with French-Canadian custom, bonfires were burning in front of the homes of the defeated candidates for council. The biggest blaze of all illuminated the front of Tyne Castonguay's Patent Medicine and Confectionery Store.

Now that she's reeve, Malvina Labine has her work cut out for her. There are trees and flowers to be planted in the civic centre, gravel to go on the shore of a nearby swimming hole, amalgamation with neighboring townships to discuss, roads to improve and, above all, people to be helped.

How she'll do it remains to be seen. Her admirers have no doubts.

Dan Fenny of the Children's Aid Society says, "She'll be more concerned about people than about the budget" and Philippe Lefèbvre, the butcher who worked alongside her at the market for thirty-six years, says, "She's going to be the best reeve Rayside ever had." Townspeople testify to her honesty and good intentions. But the supreme accolade comes from her son Gerrard.

"Mama can do anything," he says proudly. "I predict she'll improve the whole township and take the taxes down too." ★

Traditions *that live*

Strong and honourable traditions provide the foundation of firm training in leadership expressed today in the motto of the three Canadian Services Colleges: Truth—Duty—Valour.

Allied to the prestige of the past is advanced education at university level given by these colleges to the officer-cadets of Canada's armed forces. Carefully selected high school graduates are trained for challenging professional careers as officers in the Navy, Army or Air Force, for the responsibility of holding the Queen's Commission.

to serve the **Future**

The closing date for acceptance into the 1959 fall classes is July 1, 1959. For full information on entry requirements write:

R.O.T.P. SELECTION BOARD,
DEPARTMENT OF NATIONAL DEFENCE,
OTTAWA, ONT.

GUEDRY-LABINE & PETITPAS MINI-REUNION
ACADIAN VILLAGE AT LAFAYETTE, LA by Marty Guidry

On Saturday, October 13, 2007 approximately fifty Guidry and Petitpas cousins from Louisiana and Texas gathered at the old Stutes Store in Acadian Village, Lafayette, LA to renew friendships, meet new relatives and share our family history.

On arriving at 10:00 am each person grabbed a cup of Louisiana coffee and began studying the several displays setup by various family members. Among the displays were two computers displaying Guidry genealogy, a large map describing the worldwide dispersion of the

Guidry family during the period 1755-1800, several volumes honoring our Guidry-Labine ancestors who have served in their country's military, copies of published articles and old documents about the Guedry-Labine and Petitpas families and two superb photographic displays of the Guidry family.

Within a few minutes several small groups were seen at various tables poring over family genealogy and discussing their mutual history. Some blanks were filled in, lots of questions asked and contacts made to continue their mutual work on the family.

Others ventured outside to see the extensive Guidry agricultural equipment on permanent display at Acadian Village. Les Guidry d'Asteur member John Guidry of Metairie, LA loaned the agricultural implements of his father to Acadian Village for the enjoyment of all visiting the area. John's father used this equipment for many years on his Church Point, LA farm. During the Mini-Reunion John and his son Lance described the implements and their uses to all visiting the very informative display.

At noon po-boy fixings were spread on the buffet table along with various soft drinks and cookies. It wasn't long before someone discovered the spread and a line formed. After filling our plates, we all enjoyed a pleasant meal together – discussing our family as recorded music by Guidry and Labine musicians filled the air.

John Guidry demonstrating family farm equipment on loan to the Acadian Village.

GUEDRY-LABINE & PETITPAS MINI-REUNION ACADIAN VILLAGE AT LAFAYETTE, LA - *continued*

After lunch folks continued discussing their genealogy with family members, viewing the interesting displays and enjoying the old homes and buildings of Acadian Village. One person even discovered an old death certificate of Lessin Guidry hanging on the wall of one of the historic Acadian Village homes. And on view in the old Stutes Store was an authentic Acadian diatonic accordion built by Paul Guidry of Carencro, LA.

Of particular interest to attendees was the boyhood home of Dudley LeBlanc, Louisiana state senator, early Acadian historian and inventor of the elixir Hadacol. Items in the home included a history of Hadacol with examples of this historic cure-all and an extensive collection of early Cajun music. Also, catching the eye of many was the Aurelie Bernard House which contained several large paintings by Robert Dafford describing the dispersion of the Acadians around the world and their arrival in Louisiana.

Chuck Guidry discussing genealogy with attendees

John Guidry & family members enjoying lunch

As the four o'clock hour approached, cousins said their good-byes, exchanged contact information and departed Acadian Village with new information, new friends and great memories.

Attendees viewing displays on the Guidry family

Whoever said "Seek and Ye Shall Find" was NOT a genealogist!

PRECIOUS GEMS FROM FADED MEMORIES:
A PICTORIAL HISTORY OF ST. JOHN THE BAPTIST PARISH

BY
GERALD J. KELLER Ph.D.
LISA KELLER-WATSON
DARROCH WATSON

LEON GRAUGNARD FAMILY (Left to Right) Leon Graugnard, son Emile, dtr. Marie (Nancy), dtr. Eva, Mrs. Leon Graugnard, son Fernand Adam. Both sons are in uniform of Jefferson College, Convent.

TERRE HAUTE (High Grounds) PLANTATION
LEON GRAUGNARD AND
EDWIN JOSEPH (E.J.) GUIDRY, SR.
Plantation Owner and Dairyman

A pioneer in the sugar industry, Leon Graugnard was one of the Barcelonnet Valley men who settled in St. John the Baptist Parish. One of seven children of Jean Joseph Graugnard and Angelique Caire, Leon Graugnard was born on February 1, 1855 in the tiny Alpine village of Faucon, France. At the age of 16, Leon Graugnard came to America and went to work on the sugar cane plantation of Jean Teissier, an earlier arrival from the Barcelonnette Valley. Soon, Mr. Auguste Servell, another native of France established in St. James Parish encouraged young Leon to better himself by starting in business as a peddler and advanced Leon Graugnard enough money to begin his enterprise with the purchase of two mules, a cart, and a stock of merchandise. He sold fabrics and other sewing essentials and was very successful in this venture.

Within five years, in 1876, he was able to form a general merchandise partnership with Firmin Maurin, under the firm name of Maurin and Graugnard. The business thrived and in 1880 the business expanded and was moved to a new location in lower Reserve.

On April 19, 1882, at the St. Louis Cathedral in New Orleans, Leon Graugnard married Marie Eve Bacas, a daughter of Anatole Joseph Bacas and Marie Madeline Celeste Conrad. Of the six children born to this couple, three died in infancy. A fourth child, a son died one month following his 19th birthday. Only two children, son Emile and daughter Eve, lived to maturity. Eve was educated at St. Joseph's Academy in New Orleans and would marry Edwin Joseph (E.J.) Guidry, Sr. on September 22, 1914. Emile married Azelie Eleonore Breaud on February 6, 1922 and would raise seven children. The son of Philemon Guidry III and Marie Adele Porrier, E. J. Guidry Sr. was born in St. James, Louisiana on September 4, 1890. He was educated at Jefferson College in Convent, Louisiana. The Guidrys had twelve children—Sister Celeste, Inez, Edwin, Jr., Marion, Leon, James, Manual, Lionel, Albert, Francis, John, and Theresa. In 1913, E.J. Guidry, Sr. went to work for the New Orleans and Great Northern Railroad near Tylertown, Mississippi.

Wedding Picture of Edwin J. Guidry, Sr. and Eve Graugnard

In 1892, after twelve years in the general merchandise business with Firmin Maurin, Leon Graugnard sold his interest to his partner and established the Four Seasons Store on the upper end of St. John's east bank. The following year, on January 27, 1893, Leon Graugnard bought the 785 acre Glencoe Plantation from Mrs. Felicie Perilloux Reine and Mr. Paul N. Bossier for $11,000. He cultivated red sugar cane on 275 acres of the property until April 4, 1901 when he sold Glencoe to a representative of the Lyon Lumber Company for $14,500. The Lyon Lumber Company operation, as well as a large portion of the town, which later became Garyville, were situated on the land which was once Glencoe. After the sale of Glencoe, the Graugnard family moved to New Orleans, where Leon Graugnard, along with Firmin Reynaud had an interest in the Clerc Wholesale Grocery. When the business proved unsatisfactory, both partners disposed of their interest in 1904.

Meanwhile Leon Graugnard purchased river front land from the San Francisco Plantation and the Doherty Family. On this land, he built a large general merchandise store and a house a short distance down-river from the San Francisco Plantation House. In later years, the house and store were painted dark green and became known as "The Englade Store and House." The Englade Family were long-time occupants of the property until it was sold to the Inger Oil Company, predecessor of Marathon Petroleum Company.

On February 3, 1905, the Firmin Reynaud-Leon Graugnard partnership bought Terre Haute Plantation

Mrs. Leon Graugnard (Marie Eve Bacas)

from Catherine Davis Trenton, widow of John Cofield and wife of James Webster. The purchase price was $100,000. In 1910, the partnership also bought the 600 acres Lilly Plantation in Convent, Louisiana. Sugar cane was grown on both plantations and the larger Terre Haute sugar mill ground not only the sugar cane from Terre Haute and Lilly, but also cane grown by surrounding sugar cane farms. Graugnard's son-in-law, E.J. Guidry, Sr. returned to St. John the Baptist Parish in 1915 and became the overseer at the Lilly Plantation sugar cane operation in Convent. As on other plantations of the era, workers had cabins and were paid in tokens, which were redeemed in the community store located on the plantation.

In 1922, the Reynaud family sold their undivided half interest in Terre Haute Plantation to Leon Graugnard in

Plantation Worker Houses on Terre Haute Plantation

exchange for full interest in Lilly Plantation plus $65,000. The Guidrys moved from Lilly to the Terre Haute Plantation where Mr. Guidry would assume co-responsibility for operation of the plantation, and Leon Guidry, Jr. would be the first Guidry child to be born after the Guidrys had moved to the Terre Haute plantation.

Following his wife's death in 1929, Leon Graugnard had two marble statues of St. Peter imported from Italy and inscribed in his wife's memory. One statue was place on the exterior of St. Peter Church and the other on St. Peter School, where they remain until this day. The Guidrys and Graugnards and others were very instrumental in working with Monsignor Eyraud in getting a Catholic school for the community—St. Peter School. Sixty-seven years after leaving his homeland thousands of miles away, Leon Graugnard, the little Shepard from Faucon in the Barcolonnette Valley of France died at the age of 83 on December 26, 1938. He was laid to rest in the family tomb in St. Peter Cemetery in Reserve.

By 1944, E.J. Guidry and his wife, Eva Graunard Guidry had assumed full ownership and management of the Terre Haute Plantation. Besides the sugar cane operation and operation of the Terre Haute Company Store, E.J. Guidry, Sr. also managed the Sunnyside Dairy on the property from 1930 through World War II. The dairy had 65 cows and delivered milk throughout Reserve from the plantation to Our Lady of Grace. Milk was sold for eight cents at the plantation store and was sold for ten cents on home deliveries. Milk was also delivered to LaPlace, Norco, and Good Hope. Guidry utilized captured German soldiers to assist with cane cultivation and cutting during World War II. E.J. Guidry, Sr. was an active member of St. Peter's Council No. 3436, Knights of Columbus and frequently attended the laymen's retreat at Manresa House in Convent.

Through the years, the Guidry family has made major contributions to St. John Parish.

Wedding Picture of Francis Guidry and Gertrude Rome

All were active members of the St. Peter Church and St. Peter School. Following the death of E.J. Guidry, Sr. on December 6, 1949, two of his sons continued the sugar cane growing operation of the plantation--Edwin Guidry,

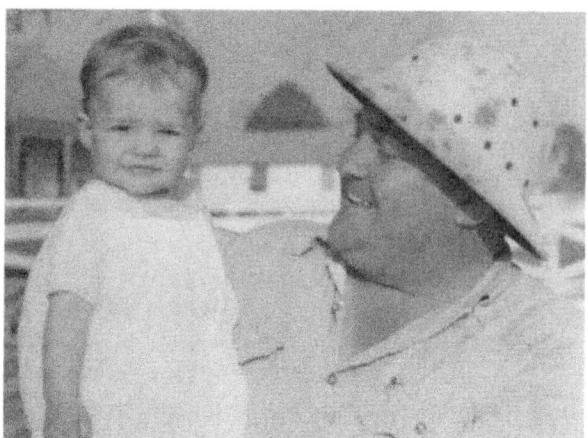
Edwin J. "Fils" Guidry, Jr. and daughter, Claire

Jr. and Francis Guidry. Francis Guidry would marry Gertrude Rome and they had ten children—Michelle, Francis, Jr., E.J. Guidry, III, Steven, David, Chris, Greg, Fran, Barry, and Leon Guidry. Francis also served on the St. Peter School Board and was elected to the St. John the Baptist Parish (Public) School Board.

In 1973, Marathon Petroleum Company assumed possession of the refining operation on the former Terre Haute land, and Cargill purchased 622 acres from Terre Haute's remaining acreage for the construction of their grain elevator in Reserve. To meet the region's growing industrial needs, the Guidrys started Highlanders Fabrication, a maintenance and pipe fabrication company in Reserve.

A third generation of Guidrys have continued their business enterprises in St. John the Baptist Parish into this early part of the 21st century. Steven Guidry manages Guidry Industries, a tree cutting, lawn service grass cutting operation. The brothers also formed Gen-G Corporation, a real estate and land development company. Chris Guidry served as an aid to U.S. Representative Clyde C. Holloway and worked with Parish President Nickie Monica as his chief administrative officer. Currently, Chris Guidry manages Guidry Associates, LLC. Commander Greg Guidry is a graduate of the U.S. Naval Academy and is an aviator on the aircraft carrier, U.S. John C. Stennis.

CARAQUET-*Capitale de l'Acadie*

For information on travel accommodations, events and attractions visit: http://www.ville.caraquet.nb.ca/

Caraquet is situated on the shore of the Chaleur Bay in the Acadian Penisula, its name is derived from the Micmac term for 'meeting of two rivers'. The Caraquet River and Riviere du Nord flow into the bay west of the town.

Caraquet was first settled in 1757 after Acadians, led by Alexis Landry, moved there after being expelled from southern New Brunswick and Nova Scotia in the Expulsion of the Acadians. The original town site is now called Sainte-Anne-du-Bocage. Land was officially granted for the town in 1774.

The town still calls itself the unofficial capital of Acadia, and as such hosts the annual Acadian Festival in August.

The National Archives of Quebec

This is the official website for the Quebec National Archives. It provides an excellent overview of the archival collection and some virtual expositions. There are no images of original records at this time.

http://www.townshipsheritage.com/Eng/Articles/Research/archives.html

The National Archives

This is the official website for the U. S. National Archives. The site primarily describes the holdings of the U. S. National Archives. Click on the Genealogists/Family Historians button for an overview of genealogical holdings. There are also a publications store and an online ordering service for records. Images of original records are found under the Access to Archival Databases (AAD) button.

http://www.archives.gov/

The Louisiana State Archives

This is the official website for the Louisiana State Archives. It provides a very nice overview of the archival holdings and services. Although there are no images of original documents at this time, there is a very nice index to Confederate Pension Applications with numerous Guidry records. Click on Research Library under Sections of Organization, then Confederate Pension Applications to the left of the top photograph, then Search the Database.

http://www.sos.louisiana.gov/archives/archives/archives-index.htm

Book Nook

LOUISIANA'S GERMAN COAST
A History of St. Charles Parish by Harry E. Yoes III

St. Charles Parish was one of the earliest settlements in Louisiana when French plantations began around 1719. Shortly thereafter, German settlers destined to settle in Arkansas as part of John Law's Louisiana concession were persuaded to settle in the parish, located two parishes upriver on the Mississippi from New Orleans. The Germans eventually expanded to the Second German Coast, which was later to be called St. John Parish.

These early German planters largely fed New Orleans during the 1700s and were a large part in the Rebellion of 1768 to overthrow Spanish rule. Later, in 1811, the largest slave insurrection in the United States ended in St. Charles Parish. Three of its most famous plantations still standing are Destrehan, Ormond and Home Place, the former two opened to visitors. Later the parish became the site of numerous oil and chemical refineries and is one of the most industrialized parishes in Louisiana.

`The book **Louisiana's German Coast: A History of St. Charles Parish** is an update of **A History of St. Charles Parish to 1973** written by the same author, Henry E. "Gene" Yoes III, a former associate editor of the St. Charles Herald which was founded by ex Governor Michael Hahn in 1873.

Stephen E. Ambrose, renowned author of **Undaunted Courage**, historian Douglas G. Brinkley, author of *The Unfinished Presidency,* and award-winning National Geographic photographer Sam Abell traveled the entire length of the Mississippi—from its mouth at Delacroix Island, Louisiana, to its source at Itasca, Minnesota—to bring readers the full, rich history of America's great river. In 11 chapters, each covering a length of the river, readers will witness the early explorations of DeSoto and the momentous signing of the Louisiana Purchase; they will meet Jim Bowie, Ulysses S. Grant, and Robert Johnson; they will relive the Civil War and the Great Flood, the Underground Railroad and the Trail of Tears; and they will discover the immense impact of the Mississippi on American arts, from the birth of the Blues to the literature of Mark Twain and T.S. Eliot.

To expand the book's visual dimension, each chapter of **The Mississippi And The Making Of A Nation** is illustrated with period paintings, lithographs, artifacts, and maps, and features unique photographic essays by Sam Abell.

THE MISSISSIPPI * AND THE MAKING OF A NATION By Stephen E. Ambrose

The result is a lively, comprehensive, and beautiful work that panoramically explores and celebrates the American icon that is the Mighty Mississippi as it celebrates America itself.

Book Nook — continued

THE ISLAND ACADIANS 1720-1980
By Georges Arsenault

The Island Acadians is a history of the Acadians on Prince Edward Island and their importance not only within their own community and province, but also regionally and nationally.

In five chapters: Under the French Regime, the First Century After Expulsion, Period of Transition, Successful Initiatives and Post-War Period, this historical book traces the early Acadians of Prince Edward Island from the community's founding through the 1980's. It is a valuable resource for anyone with roots to Canada or PEI.

The Island Acadians is a work of cultural preservation - breaking new ground in establishing the importance of the PEI Acadians.

MY ACADIAN HERITAGE *By Leonie Comeau*

In **My Acadian Heritage**, the author, Leonie Comeau Poirier, vividly describes, with many amusing anecdotes, life in earlier years in St. Mary's Bay, Nova Scotia, an Acadian community. While the old ways have largely disappeared, the spirit of the Acadians is enduring and is seen in their attitude, language, and distinctive cuisine. Poirier gets to the heart of their very spirit.

Les Guidry d'Asteur

Share your ideas for the Newsletter

Contact:

**Marty Guidry
6139 North Shore Drive
Baton Rouge, LA 70817**

**225-755-1915
guidryrm@cox.net**

'GENERATIONS' newsletter is now in its fifth year. We hope to provide our readers with an interesting, informative and entertaining newsletter. Your input is always welcome and we look forward to another year of sharing family history and news with you.

The Guedry-Labine Family Newsletter, GENERATIONS, serves as a focal point for family members to share and learn about us. To submit your ideas, articles or comments, please contact:

Allie Guidry
txguidry2000@yahoo.com

Marty Guidry
guidryrm@cox.net

Les Guidry d'Asteur Officers and Committees

OFFICERS:
President - Martin Guidry (LA)
Vice-President - Warren Guidry (TX)
Secretary - Billy Harrell Guidry (LA)
Treasurer - Daniel "Chuck" Guidry (LA)

COMMITTEES:
Website - Becky Boggess (IA) - Chairperson
    Annie Grignon-Labine (QU) - Translator
    Elaine Clement (LA) - Translator
    Martin Guidry (LA)*
Genealogy - Daryl LaBine (FL/ON) - Chairperson
    Bernard Geddry (AZ)
    Mark Labine (MN)
    Daniel "Chuck" Guidry (LA)
    Martin Guidry (LA)*
Finance - Cheryl Guidry Tyiska (MD) - Chairperson
    Paul Labine (IL)
    Marshall Woolner (OR)
    Gloria Parrent (TX)
    Chuck Guidry (LA)*

Membership - Charlene Guidry Lacombe (LA) - Chairperson

    Gayle Guidry (LA) - Special Projects
    Warren Guidry (TX)*
Sales - Cindy Guidry Herdt (WA) - Chairperson
    Wayne Simoneaux (LA)
    Billy Harrell Guidry (LA)*
Publicity - Elaine Clement (LA) - Chairperson
    Margaret Jeddry (MA)
    Warren Guidry (LA)*

Newsletter - Allie Guidry Hardee (VA)
    Rachel Hardee (VA)
    Lindsey Hardee (VA)

CAFA Board Member - Jeanette Guidry Leger (LA)

Les Guidry d'Asteur
Membership Application
(Formulaire d'adhésion)

Name (Nom) _____
             Last (Nom de famille)   First (Prénom)   Middle (Deuxième prénom)

Spouse (Épouse) _____
             Maiden (Nom de jeune fille)   First (Prénom)   Middle (Deuxième prénom)

Children (Enfants) _____

Address (Adresse) _____
             Street (Rue)

_____
City (Ville)   State (État/Province)   Zip Code (Code postal)   (Pays)

Telephone (Téléphone) _____

Fax (Numéro de télécopieur) _____

E-mail Address (Courriel) _____

Hobbies or Special Talent _____
(Passe-temps ou talent particulier)

Type of Membership (Type de cotisation):

   _____   Individual (Individuelle) $ 6.00 U.S. Dollars (Dollars américains)

   _____   Family (Familiale) $10.00 U.S. Dollars (Dollars américains)

Benefactor Levels (Niveaux de bienfaiteur):

   _____   dit Jovial Level $50.00 U.S. Dollars (Dollars américains)

   _____   dit Labine Level $100.00 U. S. Dollars (Dollars américains)

   _____   dit Grivois Level $500.00 U. S. Dollars (Dollars américains)

Please return form and payment to: Make check payable to: *Les Guidry d'Asteur, Inc.*
(Retournez le formulaire et le paiement à:)   (Libellez le chèque à: *Les Guidry d'Asteur, Inc.*)

Les Guidry d'Asteur, Inc.
Charlene Guidry Lacombe
Membership Chair
141 Lesim Lane
Jennings, LA 70546

WINTER 2008

Volume 6, Issue 1

Les Guidry d'Asteur

GENERATIONS

IN THIS ISSUE

The Acadians of Quebec by Adrien Bergeron and Sandra Perro	2
Bon Appetit - Recipes from the Guedry-Labine Family Cookbook	4
Genealogy/History: Antoine Guedry-An Intriguing Acadian	5
CMA 2009- Reunion Update and Travel Accommodations	10
Book Nook	13
1806 Lawsuit - Louis Chauvin vs. Antoine Geudry	18

....

CMA 2009

As we begin our sixth year of "*GENERATIONS*", we have another outstanding issue that reveals new aspects of our Guedry-Labine and Petitpas family history, serves up outstanding recipes for our cooks and diners, highlights some interesting books that you may want to read and updates us on our upcoming Reunion.

Member Sandra Perro presents an outstanding article on Claude Petitpas - providing a rare look into the life of one of our founding ancestors in Acadia during the seventeenth century. Don't miss the copy of the original 1684 document authored by Claude Petitpas that contains his signature.

Antoine Guedry, born in Acadia, deported to France and resettled in Louisiana, led an intriguing life - leaving us with many unanswered questions. And spend a moment reading the copy of the original lawsuit against Antoine by Louis Chauvin – providing a peak into the life of an Acadian family in early nineteenth century New Orleans.

Have you ever wondered if our family had famous athletes? We sure have. Look at the Book Nook for several books on three of these Guedry-Labine athletes – Ron Guidry, pitcher for the New York Yankees from 1976-1989 and Cy Young Award winner; Clem Labine, pitcher for the Brooklyn Dodgers,

Los Angeles Dodgers and New York Mets in the 1950's and 1960's and Mark Guidry, one of the most successful horseracing jockeys today.

As an aside, Clem Labine was the first true relief pitcher in major league baseball.

Hungry? How about a bowl of Oyster Soup and for dessert a dish of delicious Pumpkin Mouse? And don't forget to glance at "On the Web" for some great websites to aid your research.

Thinking of joining your cousins for the 2009 Guedry-Labine & Petitpas Reunion? The planning has begun. Read about when and where the Reunion will be, where you can get accommodations and the history of the Acadian Peninsula in New Brunswick.

The Acadians of Quebec by Adrien Bergeron, s.s.s.
Short Genealogy Commentaries: France, Acadia, Quebec 1625 - 1925

Obtained from Société de Généalogie de Lanaudière, Joliette, Quebec
by
Sandra (Pettipas) Perro, 2006
Translated by Edward Ulysee Pellerin, 2007
(both are descendants of Claude Petitpas and originally from Nova Scotia)
[Boldface comments by Sandra Perro]

In the history of Acadia, if anyone should be remembered for promoting his name and his country it is certainly Claude Petitpas because he relentlessly and boldly wandered the lands of New France as well as New England.

Also many Madelinots (inhabitants of les Îles-de-la-Magdeleine) and Acadians from Quebec's North Shore will find it particularly interesting to familiarize themselves with the exploits of this tireless voyageur and the families of Charles de Menou d'Aulnay, of des De Villebon, of d'Iberville, of Bonnaventure and many others. The testimonies on his behalf are prominent: « *la Collection de manuscripts relatifs à la Nouvelle-France* » alone mentions more than nine detailed accounts and strong evidence beginning in 1692. However there is an even older document which mentions his name; it originates in "*la généalogie manuscrite de la famille de Menou,*" **[The Genealogical Manuscript of the Menou Family]** which brings us to the 15th century and leads us to the Motin genealogy wherein is recorded in 1638 the marriage of Charles de Menou and Jeanne Motin who arrived in Acadia on the famous ship, *Le Saint-Jehan*.

It is precisely in this genealogical manuscript of the Motin family that we find that which follows: *Extract of baptism September 21, 1639 Pt R1 (Port Royal) stating that Marie, daughter of Sieur Charles de Menou, Esquire ... lieutenant- general for the King of the coast of Acadie, New France, was baptized at 4 o'clock in the evening of the day that she was born at 1:00 p.m. Wednesday September 21 and that she was consecrated to the Blessed Virgin by Claude Petitpas and Mr. Boudrot, first syndicates of Port Royal.* In addition to this honourable citation, it is extremely interesting for Petitpas descendants to note that our ancestor Claude was present in Acadia even before 1639 because on this date he was already a deputy syndicate of Port Royal.

[**It is thought by many that the Petitpas referred to above was syndicate, Claude Petitpas Sr., Sieur de la Fleur, father of Marguerite (Petitpas) Guédry. However others question this assumption noting that the Petitpas in question may have been a relative rather than Claude Sr. himself who was born in 1624 and would have only been 15 years old in 1639.**]

However let us reflect on the year 1692 where in "*Isles des Monts Déserts Nov 9th*" an edict appears in favour of Sieurs Saint-Aubin and Petitpas" : (*Col. des Man., II p.92). Regarding the requistion that we have made on behalf of Sieurs Saint-Aubin and Petitpas, residents of Acadia, it gives us great pleasure, given the services which they have rendered to the King, i.e., they have remitted in the hands of the French two soldiers who had fled from Canada and had taken letters to the English who were coming to seize Sieur de St Castinet to deliver him to the English.*

The Acadians of Quebec - Continued

*This is after they [**Saint-Aubin and Petitpas**] had left behind families who were at present prisoners detained in Boston where they had actually come to give us advice as to the plans of the English toward Canada and to give us account of the state of affairs of New England, this information having been burned and destroyed by the said English. Seeing them now hardly able to exist, we find it necessary to repay these inhabitants, having no funds to satisfy their extraordinary expenses.*

With the good wishes and in concert with Sieurs d'Hyberville and Bonnaventure, Captain and Lieutenant of a light frigate, at present moored at Isles des Monts Deserts, ordered the clerk (treasurer) of the gentlemen of Acadia to remit to said persons five hundred and fifty-four pounds, French money, from company coffers, to be distributed to said Saint Aubin and Petitpas, in payment for the important service that they rendered to Canada and promising to said clerk that he would be discharged and that it will please the court not to impede and order the payment. Signed at Isles des Monts Deserts this ninth day of November, 1692. Le C. de Villebon, D'Hyberville, Bonnaventure.

Three pages further the same official manuscript presents us with a memorandum on the abduction of Sieur de Saint-Castin. It clearly states that Villebon, d'Iberville and Bonnaventure thought it necessary for this service to give 554 pounds to these two inhabitants deprived of everything and to provide them with means to liberate their wives and family from the hands of the English in consideration for their loyalty.

[The Petitpas mentioned above refers to Jacques Petitpas, son of Claude Sr., and brother of Marguerite (Petitpas) Guédry. Saint-Aubin was the maiden name of Jacques wife, Genevieve. The Saint-Aubin involved with Jacques is either his father-in-law or brother-in-law.]

In 1693 (ibidem p.109) a letter appears from the Minister of France to Count de Frontenac dated February 14 wherein it is stated, *You will have learned that the advice that you have given us with regard to New England's attack on Quebec next Spring by the people of New England has been confirmed by said Petitpas and Saint-Aubain and in such detail that there is no doubt"* . . . *In 1698 (ibidem II/307) in a secret message in a letter from M. de Bonaventure to the Minister we learn "that an English caiche [**possibly a curse**] has been made towards the Petitpas name at Nasiscaud- abouet in the region of Pentagouët to the effect that the Indians have told them that the English have made the threat at Cap St. Tambre* . . .

Here let us overlook all the rest so that we may deal with more recent dates and facts, beginning in the year 1752 with 'la tournée d'inspection' [**census**] of Sieur de Roque where we find a number of Petitpas families from the Acadian peninsula, "refugees on Isle Saint-Jean" [**Prince Edward Island**]: they are, at Port Toulouse, [**St. Peter's, Cape Breton**] "Judieth Petitpas, 60 years of age, native of Port Royal, widow of Marc La Soude, living with two of her sons [**Judith is a niece of Marguerite Guédry, i.e., the daughter**

Continued on page 6

BON APPETIT - Recipes from The Guedry-Labine Cookbook

OYSTER SOUP
Jack Guidry-Lafayette

1 cup (2 sticks) melted butter
1 cup chopped onions
1 cup chopped celery
1/2-cup chopped bell pepper
1/4-cup (2 tablespoons) diced garlic
1/2- cup finely diced pork tasso, andouille or spicy sausage
1 cup all purpose flour
6 cups chicken stock (if using boullion add a few more cubes)
4 cups oyster liquid
1 pint heavy whipping cream (has a richer flavor than milk)
4-6 dozen medium to small oysters
1/2-cup sliced fresh green onions (about 3/4" long)
1/2-cup chopped fresh parsley
Salt, white and black pepper to taste

This is a favorite winter dish when the oysters are fresh and salty down in South Louisiana.

In a 2-gallon soup pot, on a medium fire, melt butter and add onions, celery, bell pepper and garlic. Saute for about 10 minutes (don't brown them). Add tasso and stir. Sprinkle flour stirring constantly until well blended (do not scorch).

Add chicken stock a cup at a time, stirring constantly, keeping the mixture hot (you don't want everything to cool down too much). Do the same with the oyster liquor.

Bring to a boil then reduce heat to a simmer (no more boiling) and cook for 30 minutes. Add heavy whipping cream, oysters, green onions, parsley and pepper. Don't add salt yet. Cook for another 20 minutes stirring occasionally. Remove a little to cool and taste. Add salt and/or pepper accordingly. The oysters and liquor may be salty enough not to have to add salt.

PUMPKIN MOUSSE
Jim Graham-Kemah, Texas

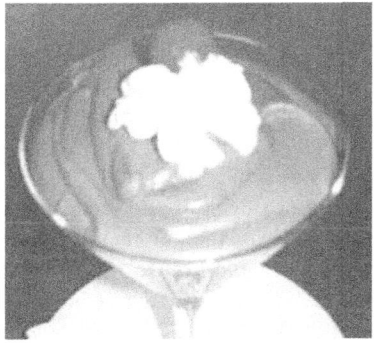

15 oz. canned pumpkin
1 oz. fat-free sugar-free instant vanilla pudding & pie filling mix
1/4-cup 1% low-fat milk
8 oz. Cool Whip Lite Whipped Topping

Instructions:

Mix pumpkin, pudding and milk together. Fold in Cool Whip.

Refrigerate. Can be served in individual serving dishes or perhaps in a graham-cracker pie crust. You can top with a dab of the Cool Whip before serving.

ANTOINE GUEDRY-AN INTRIQUING ACADIAN
By Marty Guidry

Antoine Guedry, the second child of Charles Guedry and Adelaide Madeleine Hebert, arrived in New Orleans, Louisiana from Nantes, France between 1775 and 1780. What brought Antoine to Louisiana at least five years before the vast majority of French Acadians arrived in 1785? Did he visit Louisiana as a seaman aboard a French vessel and remain when his ship left for the return voyage? What was the lure of New Orleans? Intriguing questions - however, only tidbits of his interesting life emerge from the records.

Born about 1754 on Ile Royale after his parents fled their Acadian home in August 1751 to escape English persecution[1], Antoine Guedry and his family were deported from their home at La Pointe-a-la-Jeunese, Ile Royale (today Grand Narrows, Cape Breton Island) on the ship du Supply in early 1759. They arrived at St. Malo, France on 9 March 1759. Shortly after arriving in France, Charles Guedry settled his family at the small village of Bonnaban, France[2].

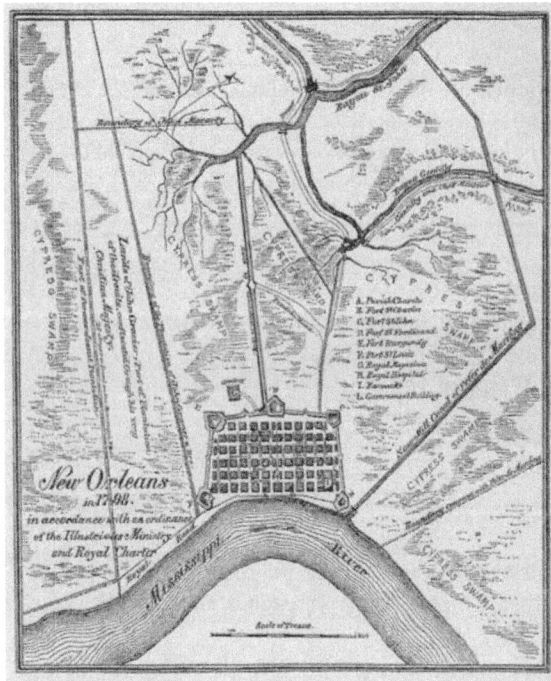

Here on 23 April 1760 Antoine's mother Adelaide Madeleine Hebert died leaving her husband Charles and her children Marie Madeleine Braud (daughter by her first husband), Antoine Guedry, Marguerite Guedry and Anne Laurence Guedry[2].

Needing help to raise his family, Charles remarried shortly after Madeleine Hebert's death. On 13 January 1761 he wed Agnes Bourg at St. Suliac, France[2]. Shortly thereafter the family moved to LaGouesniere, France and remained there until 1763 where Charles and Agnes had a son Pierre-Jean. In 1763 Charles relocated his family to St. Servan, France. Here four sons were born: Joseph Hippolite, Jean-Pierre, Jacques-Servais and Theodore-Felix[2]. For a brief period from 1773-1775 Charles Guedry and his family resettled in Chatellerault, France where Charles joined 1500 other Acadian refugees in the agricultural experiment of Marquis Perusse des Cars. Encountering sterile soil in the Poitou region, the Acadians experienced two crop failures and quickly abandoned the experiment. On 15 November 1775 Charles and his family left Chatellerault in the Second Convoy for Nantes, France. The son Antoine, age 22, was listed as "absent" on the manifest[3]. The family resettled at Saint-Similien, Hauts Paves near Saint-Donatien at Coudray[4]. Shortly after arriving near Nantes, Theodore-Felix Guedry died on 22 January 1776[2,5-6].

At some point during the next five years Antoine Guedry, the eldest son of the family, left France and settled in New Orleans, LA. We'll discuss his life shortly.

On 11 June 1785 Charles Guedry, his daughter Anne Laurence and sons Joseph, Jean and Jacques departed France on the ship Le Beaumont and arrived in New Orleans on 19 August 1785[7-11]. On arriving in Louisiana, the family eventually dispersed to various settlements including East Baton Rouge Parish, Ascension Parish and Point Coupee Parish. Also, on the Le Beaumont were Pierre-Jean Guedry and Louise-Julienne Blandin, the son and new daughter-in-law of Charles Guedry[7-11].

Continued on page 11

The Acadians of Quebec - *Continued*

of Marguerite's brother, Claude Jr., and his 1st wife Marie-Thérèse, a Mi'kmaq]; Jacques Petitpas, coastal fisherman married to Françoise Breault **[Jacques is a nephew of Marguerite Guédry, i.e., the son of Marguerite's brother, Claude Jr., and his 2nd wife, Françoise Lavergne whose descendants settled in the Tracadie, Nova Scotia area)**; Jean Petitpas coastal fisherman married to Françoise Monthory; **[Jean a.k.a. Jean Baptiste, is a nephew of Marguerite Guédry, son of her brother, Claude Jr., and his 2nd wife, Françoise Lavergne]**. Then at Baie-de-l'Ardoise **[Cape Breton]** Joseph Petitpas, fisherman married to Anne Lafargue; Magdeleine Coste, widow of Barthelémy Petitpas: **[Barthelémy is a nephew of Marguerite Guédry, i.e., the son of Marguerite's brother, Claude Jr., and his 1st wife Marie-Thérèse]** and lastly Louis (Benjamin) Petitpas married to Magdeleine Poujet: these latest families are situated on Île de la Sainte-Famille, near Port Toulouse.

[Louis (Benjamin) is a nephew of Marguerite Guédry, i.e., the son of Marguerite's brother, Claude Jr., and his 2nd wife, Françoise Breault. It was Louis' close association with Fr. Maillard, a French priest whom the English both feared and revered because of his ability to amicably control the Mi'kmaq, that Claude Jr.'s family was able to avoid deportation to Louisiana unlike the family of Claude's sister, Marguerite Guédry, and to eventually resettle in the Tracadie and Larry's River areas of Nova Scotia.]

In regard to the last person mentioned, and this is not too pleasant to relate, Abbé C.J. d'Entremont wrote a six page article published in "les Cahiers de la S.H.A. de Moncton, vol. 7, no.1, pp.14ss entitled "The First Naturalized American Acadian in 1781."

The author, citing the opinion of M. Roland J. Auger, Minister of Cultural Affairs of Quebec, suggests there is - *in the United States at present, a population of at least one million residents of which one or the other of their ancestors was of Acadian descent* - let us not forget incidentally that Louisiana, consisting of many Acadian refugees, was not part of the Union until 1812 and consequently cannot be included in the count - the author himself who is Acadian/American believes that the first Acadian to become a naturalized American citizen was named Louis-Benjamin Petitpas in 1781. He writes that he was from Chezzetcook, Nova Scotia. For some time he conducted business between Halifax and Boston with his ship. One must add his name to those Acadians who fought in the Army of Independence because he fought in the American Expeditionary Forces on July 1st 1782 against Lunenburg, Nova Scotia. **[This is the same Louis-Benjamin as mentioned above, i.e., a nephew of Marguerite Guédry.]**

Insofar as to the conclusions of the aforementioned article, it would seem to me difficult to endorse them totally. However this is not the place to discuss one's opinion. Alone, from the rest and of the same points of view, this document is sufficient to prove that in Quebec, for example, next door to old Acadia so dear to our hearts, there are more than a million and a half Acadians who by their culture, their language and their conviction have remained faithful to their mother country, maintaining an integral part of its traditions.

The Acadians of Quebec - *Continued*

That said, let us return to the two principal acado-québécois Petitpas - those from Îles-de-la Magdeleine and of the North Shore **[Québec]**. It is said that François, son of Guillaume and of Angélique Sceaux, was the first by that name to land on the Islands in 1804, coming from Miquelon; one year later, on September 16, he married Anne Boudrot at Havre-Aubert. It is however at Havre-aux-Maisons that they appear to have established their home. [**Miquelon is a small island located off the coast of Newfoundland and today, along with neighbouring St. Pierre, is France's only remaining possession in North America. Havre-Aubert and Havre-aux-Maisons are both part of the archipelago of Îles-de-la-Magdeleine, i.e., the Magdalen Islands, belonging to the province of Québec, but located in the Gulf of Saint Lawrence just north of Prince Edward Island**]

However, shortly thereafter, if I am not mistaken, two of the four sons of François à Guillaume migrated towards the North Shore **[Québec]** via Pointe-aux-Esquimaux **[Eskimos Point]**: Francois II married Marie-Barbe Cormier and Lazare married Marie Lapierre: the latter hailing from Cap-aux-Meules **[part of Îles-de-la-Magdeleine]** and reaching Blanc-Sablon in 1854 **[east of northern Quebec and off the southern coast of Labrador]**. These facts were found in the precious Journal of Placide Vigneau having left on May 27th or 28th, 1857, from Havre-aux-Maisons **[part of Îles-de-la-Magdeleine]** aboard the schooner of Firmin Boudreau accompanied by the families of Raphaël Boudreau, Benjamin Landry, Louis Cormier and Joseph Boudreau. It is worthy to note that Vigneau always spelled his name 'Petit-Pas': if logic had anything to do with it, he would have had perfect

Fort Anne National Historic Site

reason to do so. But who can say if in fact this was the proper spelling of this very prominent name. [**In a copy of a document signed by Claude Petitpas Sr. in 1684 in the capacity of clerk at Port Royal, Acadia, and which I, Sandra Perro, have in my possession, Claude also spelled his name "petit pas" meaning 'little step' or one who treds or walks with a quick, light step.**] *See next page.*

And now what would you say if we ended these 'Short Commentaries' as we could or should have started: quoting from the first Acadian census of 1671: *CLAUDE PETITPAS laboureur (plowman) 45 years of age, his wife, Catherine Bagard (Bugaret) 33 years of age. Their seven children: Bernard 12 years old, Marguerite 10 years old [**she later married Claude Guédry**], Claude 8 years old, Jehan 7 years old, Jacque 5 years old, Marie 2 ½ years old, and Elisabeth 1 year old. Their 20 cattle and 12 sheep and their 30 acres of cultivated land.* Nothing can be more reliably authentic than that.

Our most treasured heirlooms are our sweet family memories

The Acadians of Quebec - Continued

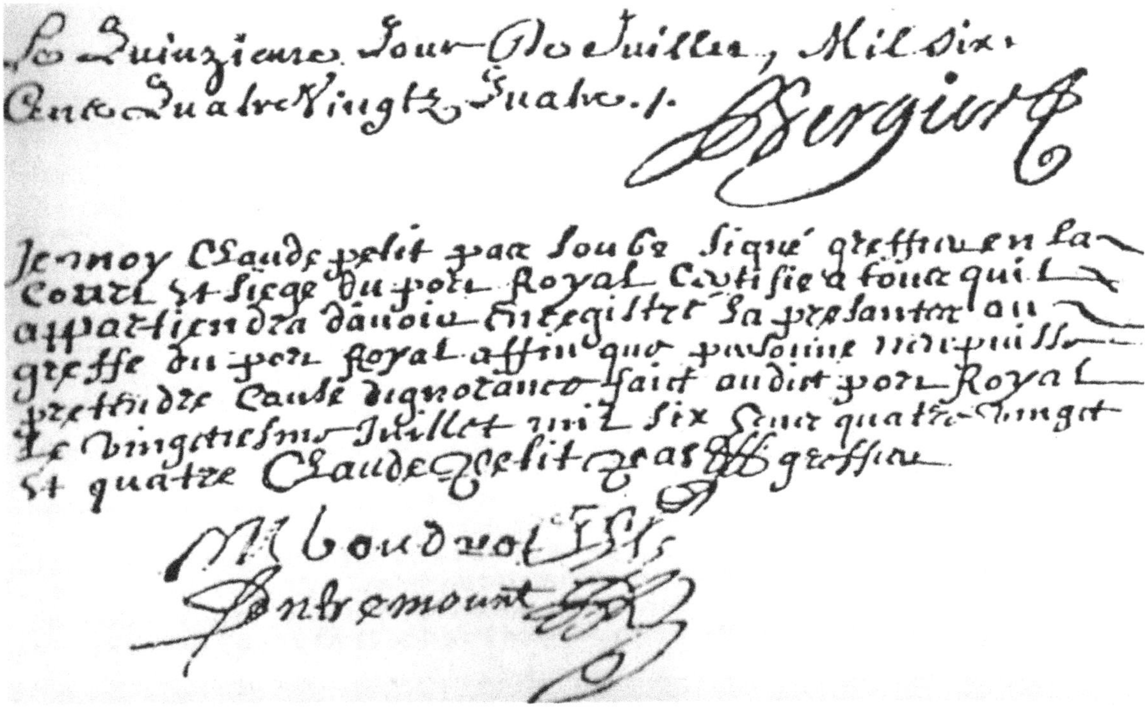

Le Quinzieme Jour de Juillet, Mil six Cent Quatre Vingts Quatre

                                    B Sergiurt

Je moy Claude petit pas sous signé greffier en la cour et siege du port Royal certifie a tout qui appertiendra d'avoir enregistré se presenter au greffe du port Royal affin que personne n'en puisse pretendre cause dignorance fait au dit port Royal Le vingtieme Juillet mil six cent quatre vingt et quatre   Claude petit pas   greffier

        M boudrot
        Dentremont

The Fifteenth Day of July, One Thousand Six Hundred Eighty-four

                                    B. Sergiurt

I Claude petit pas undersigned clerk of the court and seat of Port Royal certify to all who appertain to have registered to appear at the clerk's office at Port Royal so that nobody can plead ignorance made at the said Port Royal the twentieth of July one thousand six hundred eighty-four   Claude petit pas clerk of the court

        M boudrot
        Dentremont

ON THE WEB

Library & Archives - Canada

This is the official website for the Library & Archives of Canada. In French & English. Canada's national collection of books, historical documents, government records, photos, films, maps, music and much more.

http://collectionscanada.gc.ca

The National Archives

This is the official website for the U. S. National Archives. The site primarily describes the holdings of the U. S. National Archives. Click on the Genealogists/Family Historians button for an overview of genealogical holdings. There are also a publications store and an online ordering service for records. Images of original records are found under the Access to Archival Databases (AAD) button.

http://www.archives.gov/

The Louisiana State Archives

This is the official website for the Louisiana State Archives. It provides a very nice overview of the archival holdings and services. Although there are no images of original documents at this time, there is a very nice index to Confederate Pension Applications with numerous Guidry records. Click on Research Library under Sections of Organization, then Confederate Pension Applications to the left of the top photograph, then Search the Database.

http://www.sos.louisiana.gov/archives/archives/archives-index.htm

Beautiful Bathurst, New Brunswick, CA

THE 2009 GUEDRY-LABINE & PETITPAS REUNION

Although August 2009 is a long way off, as we begin planning our 2009 Guedry-Labine & Petitpas Reunion, it seems to be just around the corner.

Congres Mondial Acadien (CMA) for 2009 will be held on the Acadian Peninsula in New Brunswick from 7 August - 23 August 2009. CMA activities will be centered around Caraquet, New Brunswick. You can click on this website to keep up with the events planned for the 2009 CMA.

http://www.cma2009.ca/

We are having our Guedry-Labine & Petitpas Reunion on Sunday, 16 August 2009 in the Conference Center of Danny's Inn in Bereford, New Brunswick. Beresford is just five miles north of Bathurst, New Brunswick and Danny's Inn is on Highway 134 just south of Beresford. Bathurst has a rich Acadian history that we'll explore in the coming months.

Although plans for our Reunion are being developed at this time, we will have an all-day Reunion beginning about 8:30 am and lasting until 5:00 pm with an excellent full buffet dinner at Danny's Inn about noon. More to come later on the agenda, entertainment and other activities.

Unlike Nova Scotia in 2004 where family reunions and CMA activities occurred over the entire province, in 2009 all reunions and CMA activities will occur in the Acadian Peninsula. Bathurst is at the southern end of the Peninsula and Caraquet is near the northern edge. The driving distance between Bathurst and Caraquet is only 41 miles (66 kilometers).

As is true throughout the Acadian Peninsula, accommodations in the Bathurst area are limited. To see the major motels and hotels in the Bathurst area, click on the website link below, go to "Visitors Information" in the left column and click on "Accommodations". This website also has a lot of information on the history of Bathurst as well as interesting sites to explore.

http://www.bathurst.ca/english/home/index.cfm?id=156

The 2009 CMA website has an excellent page on accommodations within the Acadian Peninsula. Visit it by clicking on this link:

http://www.cma2009.ca/?page=hebergement&start=0

The official New Brunswick Tourism Website is at the link below. You can learn about interesting locations, sites and activities at this website. By clicking on the word "Guides" in the left column of the page, you can order a free 2008 Experience New Brunswick Vacation Planner" which is excellent.

http://www.tourismnewbrunswick.ca/en-CA/GeoLanding_US?source=other

In the near future we will let everyone know how to register for the 2009 Guedry-Labine & Petitpas Reunion. We'll also send out memos periodically as our agenda is developed and our plans become firm. It's time to begin planning your trip to New Brunswick in August 2009 and attending the 2009 Guedry-Labine & Petitpas Reunion. It will be a fun time to meet your cousins, learn about our family and experience the wonderful Acadian culture of New Brunswick.

New Brunswick Accommodations - CMA 2009

The Guidry-Labine family reunion is scheduled to take place August 16, 2009, in the town of Bathurst, not far from Caraquet. Here are a few more links for accomodations in those areas. We'll add more details about our reunion in the next few months.

BATHURST - http://www.bathurst.ca/english/home/

Authentique Bed & Breakfast Enjoy our 4 star B&B in a heritage home of the 20's with 'Arts & Craft's influences, conveniently located in the heart of Bathurst. You are welcome to relax in a cozy atmosphere with personalized service. Spacious rooms with very comfortable beds, cable TV, DVD, MP3, wireless internet, work desk and telephone. Each room has a private bathroom. Breakfast 'A la Carte' will be served in our elegant dining room.

Comfort Inn Bathurst Conveniently located on St. Peter Avenue. Close to shopping and offices. 35 person meeting room available.

John's Motel Our rooms have a full bath and shower, color television with cable, and most importantly comfortable beds! We also boast a swimming pool and an area for picnics. We also have in-room coffee.

Sea'scape Cottage This is our fully equipped beach house located on the beautiful Bay of Chaleur in Bathurst, New Brunswick. Select the virtual tour button to have a closer look.

CARAQUET - http://www.ville.caraquet.nb.ca/

Hotel Paulin "The Pearl of Baie des Chaleurs", Caraquet. Internationally acclaimed, seaside hotel and country inn, c.1891, rich in Acadian history. Luxurious waterfront suites, French country rooms, licensed fine dining, golf and spa packages. Hotel Paulin has the charm, elegance and inn keeping spirit of the 19th century. It offers intimate surroundings with old-world French village charm. It has been written up by the New York Times, Montreal Gazette, Fodor's and Frommer's, La Presse, Paris Match Magazine, Micheline Guide, France's Le Routard. The cuisine is innovative, upscale, inspired by local fresh foods with a Sommelier wine pairing menu.

La Maison Touristique Dugas House built by one of the first Acadian architects (1926). 10 minute walk through wooded area to private beach. Close to the Acadian Peninsula tourist attractions.

Motel Colibri 12 rooms smoking and non-smoking. 2 double beds. Telephone, cable television, air conditioning. Free outside pool. Continental breakfast.

Super 8 Motel 50 guest rooms including 18 junior suites and 1 Jacuzzi suite - Rooms with balconies overlooking the Acadian Coast and Le Carrefour de la Mer (Crossroads of the Sea) - Swimming pool with three-story 80 foot waterpark and kiddie pool - Whirlpool - Complimentary continental breakfast

Antoine Guedry-*Continued*

They settled in Pointe Coupee Parish.

Marie-Victoire Guedry, the eldest child of Charles Guedry, married Jean-Charles Boudrot in 1780 in Nantes. On 20 June 1785 they departed Nantes on the St. Remi with Henriette Boudrot (Marguerite Victoire's step-daughter) and their three children. They disembarked at New Orleans on 9 September 1785[12-15]. Jean-Charles Boudrot settled his family in Ascension Parish.

[See "Generations", Volume 4 No. 1 for a more complete discussion of Charles Guedry and his family.] http://freepages.genealogy.rootsweb.com/~guedrylabinefamily/winter2006newsletter.pdf

After arriving in Louisiana in the 1770's or early 1780, Antoine Guedry married Marie-Josephe Hebert, daughter of Paul Hebert and Marguerite Meansou, on 31 July 1780 in New Orleans, Louisiana. Marie-Josephe Hebert, a native of Grand-Pre, Acadia, was the widow of Augustin Moreno, a merchant in New Orleans[16-17].

On the 29th of November 1782 Antoine and Marie-Josephe had a daughter Marie Emilie Guedry, who was baptized in New Orleans on 9 March 1783[18-19]. A son, Antoine Eusebe Guedry, was baptized by the couple in February, 1786[20-21]; however, shortly thereafter, sadness struck the family with the death of a three year old son whom they buried in New Orleans on 17 July 1787. His name remains unknown[20,22].

On the 19th of August 1785 Antoine Guedry's father and five of his siblings arrived in New Orleans from France on the ship Le Beaumont. Surely Antoine went to the docks to meet his family and visited with them during their brief stay in New Orleans. It is not known what, if any, contact he had with his family after they moved to the Ascension, Baton Rouge and Pointe Coupee areas. A month later on 9 September 1785 his sister Marguerite Victoire Guedry, her husband and children arrived in New Orleans on the St. Remi. Again Antoine certainly greeted them on their arrival and visited with them while they awaited transport to their new home in Ascension Parish. Despite his family coming to Louisiana and settling along the Mississippi River above New Orleans, Antoine Guedry never left New Orleans to join his family. Again Antoine certainly greeted them on their arrival and visited with them while they awaited transport to their new home in Ascension Parish. Despite his family coming to Louisiana and settling along the Mississippi River above New Orleans, Antoine Guedry never left New Orleans to join his family.

Antoine Guedry apparently was a laborer in New Orleans for on 20 June 1788 he submitted a bill to the Spanish government for repairing twenty-one bridges that had been burned during the fire of 21 March 1788[23-24]. Likewise, on 24 October 1788 he presented a bill for expenses and personal labor incurred in fencing the new Catholic cemetery[25-26].

When, in June 1798 Joseph Dosite Babin of Iberville requested a dispensation of consanguinity to marry Marguerite Hebert, he presented several witnesses to testify that he and his fiancé were related in the third degree, that he had courted Marguerite for one year and that her parents were very poor. Antoine Guedry, one of the witnesses, testified on 9 July 1798 that Joseph Dosite Babin was unmarried, had not promised to marry anyone other than Marguerite Hebert and that no other impediment to marriage existed except that they were related in the third degree. In this document Antoine signed his name as Antoine Guedry[27-28].

The 1805 New Orleans City Directory lists Antoine Guedry living at 50 Rue de Conti (Conti Street) in the Vieux Carre (French Quarter) of New Orleans[29-30].

During 1804 Antoine evidently incurred debt that he refused to repay. On 14 June 1806 Louis Chauvin of New Orleans sued Antoine Guedry in the Orleans County Court for the Territory of Orleans for the sum

Continued on page 14

BOOK NOOK

This issue of the *BOOK NOOK* highlights just a few of the very talented Guidry-Labine family athletes. We will feature many more here in future issues.

RON GUIDRY

RON GUIDRY

1. Guidry by Ron Guidry and Peter Golenbock (Prentice-Hall, Inc., Englewood Cliffs, NJ, 1980) [Hardcover]

2. Sports Hero Ron Guidry by Marshall Burchard (G. P. Putnam's Sons, New York, NY, 1981) [Hardcover]

3. Ron Guidry Louisiana Lightning by Maury Allen (Harvey House, Publishers, New York, NY, 1979) [Hardcover]

4. Louisiana's Athletes – The Top Twenty by Marty Mule with Bob Remy (Pelican Publishing Company, Gretna, LA, 1981) [Hardcover; Chapter on Ron Guidry]

5. Louisiana's Athletes – The Top Twenty by Marty Mule with Bob Remy (Pelican Publishing Company, Gretna, LA, 1981) [Hardcover; Chapter on Ron Guidry]

6. Louisiana Sports Legends – The Men and Women of the Louisiana Sports Hall of Fame by Jerry Byrd (Northwestern State University Press, Natchitoches, LA, 1992) [Soft cover; Chapter on Ron Guidry]

7. Louisianians All by Jeanne Frois (Pelican Publishing Company, Gretna, LA, 1992) [Hardcover; Chapter on Ron Guidry]

8. New York Yankees – Players in Pinstripes by Mark Vancil and Mark Mandrake (Random House Publishing Group, New York, NY, 2004) [Hardcover; Chapter on Ron Guidry]

9. The New York Yankees – The Greatest Yankees Teams by Mark Vancil and Mark Mandrake (Random House Publishing Group, New York, NY, 2004) [Hardcover; Chapter on Ron Guidry plus other short discussions of him]

BOOK NOOK – *continued*

CLEM LABINE

CLEM LABINE
PITCHER—LOS ANGELES DODGERS

1. **Brooklyn Dodgers in Their Original Voices** by Vince Scully (Spear Printing Company, Inc., Washingtonville, NY, 1998) [Soft cover & CD; Major chapter on Clem Labine]

2. **The Boys of Summer** by Roger Kahn (Harper & Row, Publishers, New York, NY, 1971) [Hardcover & Soft cover; Significant discussion on Clem Labine]

3. **When the Cheering Stops…Former Major Leaguers Talk About Their Game & Their Lives** by Lee Heiman, Dave Weiner & Bill Gutman (Macmillan Publishing Company, New York, NY, 1990) [Hardcover; Chapter on Clem Labine]

4. **"That Was Part of Baseball Then" – Interviews with 24 Former Major League Babeball Players, Coaches and Managers** by Victor Debs, Jr. (McFarland & Company, Inc., Publishers, Jefferson, NC, 2002) [Soft cover; Chapter on Clem Labine]

MARK GUIDRY

1. **Ride of Their Lives – The Triumphs and Turmoil of Today's Top Jockeys** by Lenny Shulman (Eclipse Press, Lexington, KY, 2002) [Hardcover; Chapter on Mark Guidry, horseracing jockey

2. **The Original 2004 Thoroughbred Times Racing Almanac** by The Staff of Thoroughbred Times (Thoroughbred Times Company, Inc., Lexington, KY, 2003) [Soft back; Mentions Mark Guidry]

Antoine Guedry-*Continued*

$499 due to a debt from 5 June 1804. In the Petition to the Court Mr. Chauvin stated that he repeatedly asked Antoine Guedry to repay his indebtedness, but that Mr. Guedry refused to do so. The thirteen items of debt listed in the Petition included a cord and a half of firewood, sixty bottles of wine and wages for the work of Mr. Chauvin's four slaves. The Court requested that Antoine Guedry respond to Louis Chauvin's Petition; however, no response or decision is included in the record[31-32].

On 10 October 1805 Marie Emelie Guedry, daughter of Antoine Guedry and Marie-Josephe Hebert, married Jacques Armitage in New Orleans. Jacques was the son of Jacques Armitage and Abigail Loyal of New York. He was born in New York; however, by 1805 he lived in New Orleans[33-34]. On his wedding day at the age of 32 and in the presence of many New Orleanians, Jacques Armitage was baptized into the Catholic faith[33,35]. Within a year the young couple had a son Antoine James Armitage, born in New Orleans on 6 August 1806 and baptized at St. Louis Catholic Cathedral on 24 November 1806. His godparents were Antoine Guedry, his grandfather, and Augustine Hebert[33,36].

Born in Acadia, deported to France and resettled in Louisiana, Antoine Guedry died in New Orleans in April 1809 at the age of 54. He was buried in the Catholic cemetery there on 21 April 1809[37-38].

The questions remain unanswered – how did Antoine Guedry arrive in New Orleans and why did he come and stay. It seems romantic to surmise that he was a seaman on a merchant ship from the port at Nantes, France and came to New Orleans on a routine merchant trip. Here he met a beautiful young Acadian girl, fell in love and did not rejoin his crew for the return journey. We do know that he was a seaman and that he married an Acadian girl living in New Orleans; however, the records lend no other evidence of how he came or why he stayed in New Orleans. Equally interesting is why he remained in New Orleans after his family arrived in 1785. At this time he had been married only five years and had two small children. Surely he could have moved up the Mississippi River and resettled with them. Did the Spanish government prevent it or did he simply prefer to remain in New Orleans? Did he and his family visit each other in the ensuing years or were they isolated from each other? Again the record is silent. Perhaps one day documents will surface that will answer some of these questions. In the interim the life of Antoine Guedry highlights another aspect of the impact of the deportation on the lives of the Acadian people.

References

1. Canadian Archives; Report Concerning Canadian Archives for the Year 1905 in Three Volumes – Volume II (Sessional Paper No. 18) – "Tour of Inspection Made by the Sieur de la Roque, Census, 1752" (S. E. Dawson, Printer to the King's Most Excellent Majesty; Ottawa, Ontario, Canada, 1906), Appendix A Part I pp. 38, 40-41.

2. Robichaux, Albert J.; The Acadian Exiles in Saint-Malo 1758-1785 (Hebert Publications; Eunice, LA, 1981), pp. 376-378.

3. Rieder, Milton P. Jr. and Rieder, Norma Gaudet; The Acadians in France 1762-1776, Volume I (Milton P. Rieder Jr. and Norma Gaudet Rieder; Metairie, LA, 1967), pp. 62, 104.

4. Braud, Gerard-Marc; Les Acadiens en France – Nantes et Paimboeuf 1775-1785 Approche Genealogique (Quest Editions; Nantes, France, 1999), p. 129.

References –*Antoine Guiery*

5. Robichaux, Albert J.; The Acadian Exiles in Nantes, 1775-1785 (Albert J. Robichaux Jr.; Harvey, LA, 1978), p. 74.

6. Braud, Gerard-Marc; op. cit., p. 130.

7. Braud, Gerard-Marc; Les Acadiens a Nantes au 18eme Siecle Depart Pour la Louisiane (Association Regionale de l'Ouest des Amities Acadiennes; Nantes, France, 1999), p. 12.

8. Rieder, Milton P. Jr. and Rieder, Norma Gaudet; The Crew and Passenger Registration Lists of the Seven Acadian Expeditions of 1785 (Milton P. Rieder Jr. and Norma Gaudet Rieder; Metairie, LA, 1965), p. 30.

9. Hebert, Rev. Donald J.; Acadian Families in Exile – 1785 and (Part Two) Exiled Acadians – An Index (Hebert Publications; Rayne, LA, 1995), pp. 36-37.

10. Winzerling, Oscar William; Acadian Odyssey (Louisiana State University Press; Baton Rouge, LA, 1955), p. 202

11. Archivo General de Indias, "Papeles Procedentes de Cuba (P.P.C.)" (Seville, Spain) Legajo 576, folios 134-135.

12. Braud, Gerard-Marc; Les Acadiens a Nantes au 18eme Siecle Depart Pour la Louisiane (Association Regionale de l'Ouest des Amities Acadiennes; Nantes, France, 1999), p. 17.

13. Rieder, Milton P. Jr. and Rieder, Norma Gaudet; The Crew and Passenger Registration Lists of the Seven Acadian Expeditions of 1785 (Milton P. Rieder Jr. and Norma Gaudet Rieder; Metairie, LA, 1965), p. 39.

14. Hebert, Rev. Donald J.; Acadian Families in Exile – 1785 and (Part Two) Exiled Acadians – An Index (Hebert Publications; Rayne, LA, 1995), pp. 46-47.

15. Archivo General de Indias, "Papeles Procedentes de Cuba (P.P.C.)" (Seville, Spain) Legajo 576, folio 141.

16. Woods, Rev. Earl C. and Nolan, Dr. Charles E.; Sacremental Records of the Roman Catholic Church of the Archdioceses of New Orleans (Archdiocese of New Orleans; New Orleans, LA, 1987-2004), v. 3 pp. 151, 163, 218.

17. St. Louis Catholic Cathedral, Archives of the Archdiocese of New Orleans, Orleans Parish, Louisiana, Department of Historical Records (1100 Chartres Street, New Orleans, LA 70116-2596), St. Louis Marriage Book 4 (1777-1784), p. 87 and St. Louis Baptismal Book 7 (1772-1776), pp. 17, 50.

18. Woods, Rev. Earl C. and Nolan, Dr. Charles E.; op. cit., v. 3 p. 151.

19. St. Louis Catholic Cathedral, op. cit., St. Louis Baptismal Book 9 (1777-1786), p. 278.

20. Woods, Rev. Earl C. and Nolan, Dr. Charles E.; op. cit., v. 4 p. 155.

21. St. Louis Catholic Cathedral, op. cit., St. Louis Baptismal Book 9 (1777-1786), p. 397.

22. St. Louis Catholic Cathedral, op. cit., St. Louis Funeral Book 2 (1784-1793), p. 10.

23. Index to the Acts and Deliberations of the Cabildo, Work Projects Administration (WPA) Project No. 665-64-3-112.

24. http://nutrias.org/~nopl/inv/digest/digest63.htm

25. Index to the Acts and Deliberations of the Cabildo, Work Projects Administration (WPA) Project No. 665-64-3-112. (August, 1939). Book 3, Volume II, p. 67.

References –*Antoine Guedry*

26. http://archives.nd.edu/calendar/17980709.htm

27. University of Notre Dame Archives (UNDA) (Notre Dame, Indiana 46556); Archdiocese of New Orleans (La.) Collection 1576-1897 (ANO); Gift of Francis Janssens, Archbishop of New Orleans in the 1890's. Calendar (1798/07/09).

28. http://archives.nd.edu/calendar/17980709.htm

29. Thompson, Charles L.; New Orleans in 1805. A Directory and A Census, Together with Resolutions Authorizing Same Now Printed for the First Time from the Original Manuscript (Pelican Gallery; New Orleans, LA, 1936). (Facsimile).

30. Vinson, Judith and Fitzpatrick, Colleen; "1805 New Orleans City Directory" Louisiana Genealogical Register (Louisiana Genealogical and Historical Society; Baton Rouge, LA), Volume 54, No. 3 (September 2007), pp. 254.

31. Orleans County Court, Territory of Orleans, Civil Suit No. 348 (1806). New Orleans Public Library, Louisiana Division/City Archives and Special Collections.

32. http://louisdl.louislibraries.org/cdm4/document.php?CISOROOT=/lapur&CISOPTR=3900&REC=8

33. Woods, Rev. Earl C. and Nolan, Dr. Charles E.; op. cit., v. 8 pp. 9, 162.

34. St. Marie Catholic Church, Archives of the Archdiocese of New Orleans, Orleans Parish, Louisiana, Department of Historical Records (1100 Chartres Street, New Orleans, LA 70116-2596), St. Marie Marriage Book 1 (1805-1837), p. 12.

35. St. Marie Catholic Church, ibid., St. Marie Baptismal Book 1 (1805-1838), p. 4.

36. St. Louis Catholic Cathedral, op. cit., St. Louis Baptismal Book 20 (1806-1809), p. 37.

37. Woods, Rev. Earl C. and Nolan, Dr. Charles E.; op. cit., v. 9 p. 170.

Looking into the past to enrich our future

Below appears a copy of the original documents of the 1806 lawsuit against Antoine Guedry by Louis Chauvin. The list of debts is quite interesting and provides an insight into the lives of Antoine Guedry and his family. Why did Antoine Guedry have to borrow so much over a relatively short time? Did he come upon hard times suddenly? If so, what caused this major change in his life? And why could he not repay the debts? It seems he needed help in almost every phase of his life.

A transcription and translation of the documents follows the copy of the original. A few words are not decipherable and are indicated by a blank line.

Antoine Guedry 1806 Lawsuit

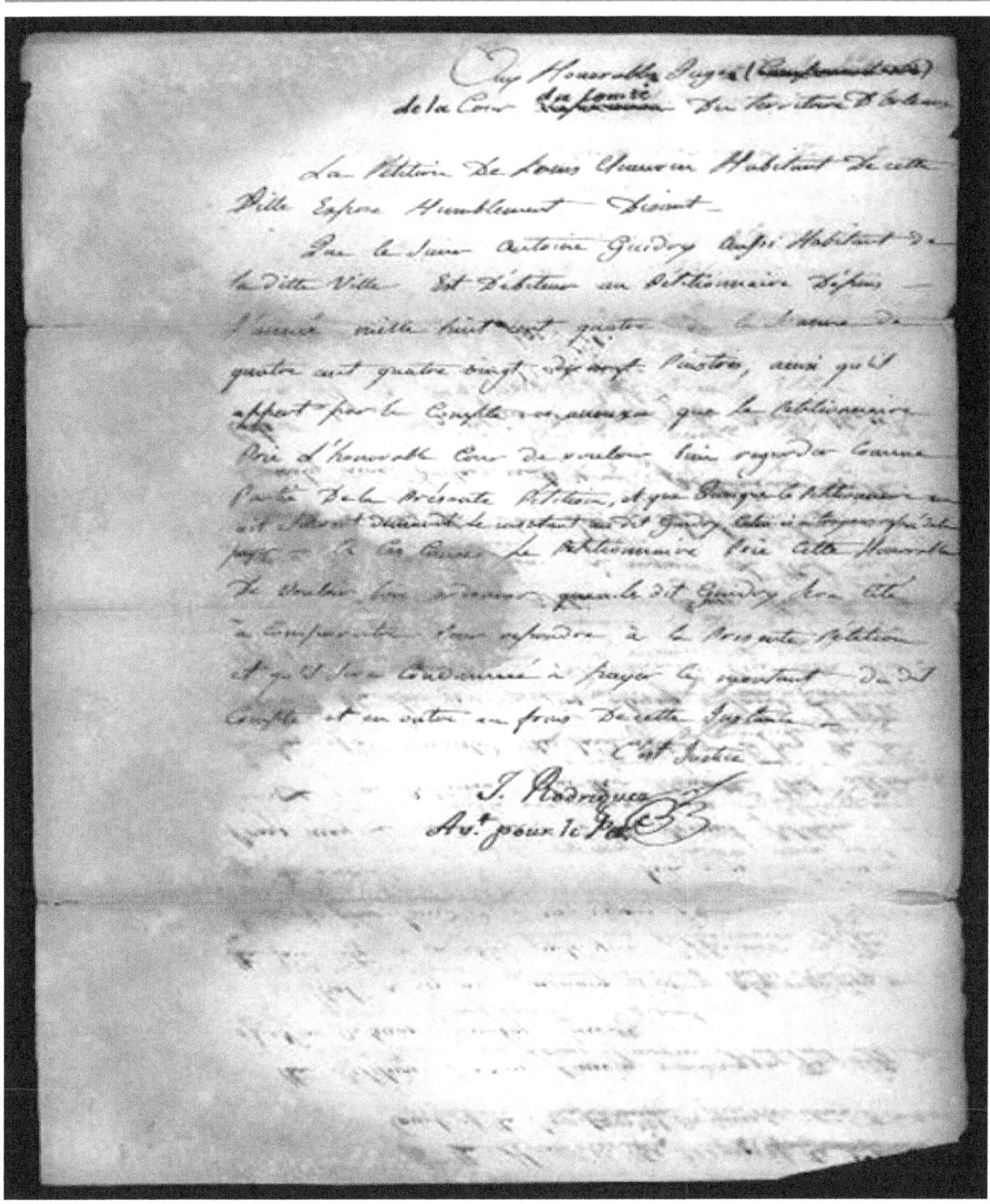

Antoine Guedry 1806 Lawsuit

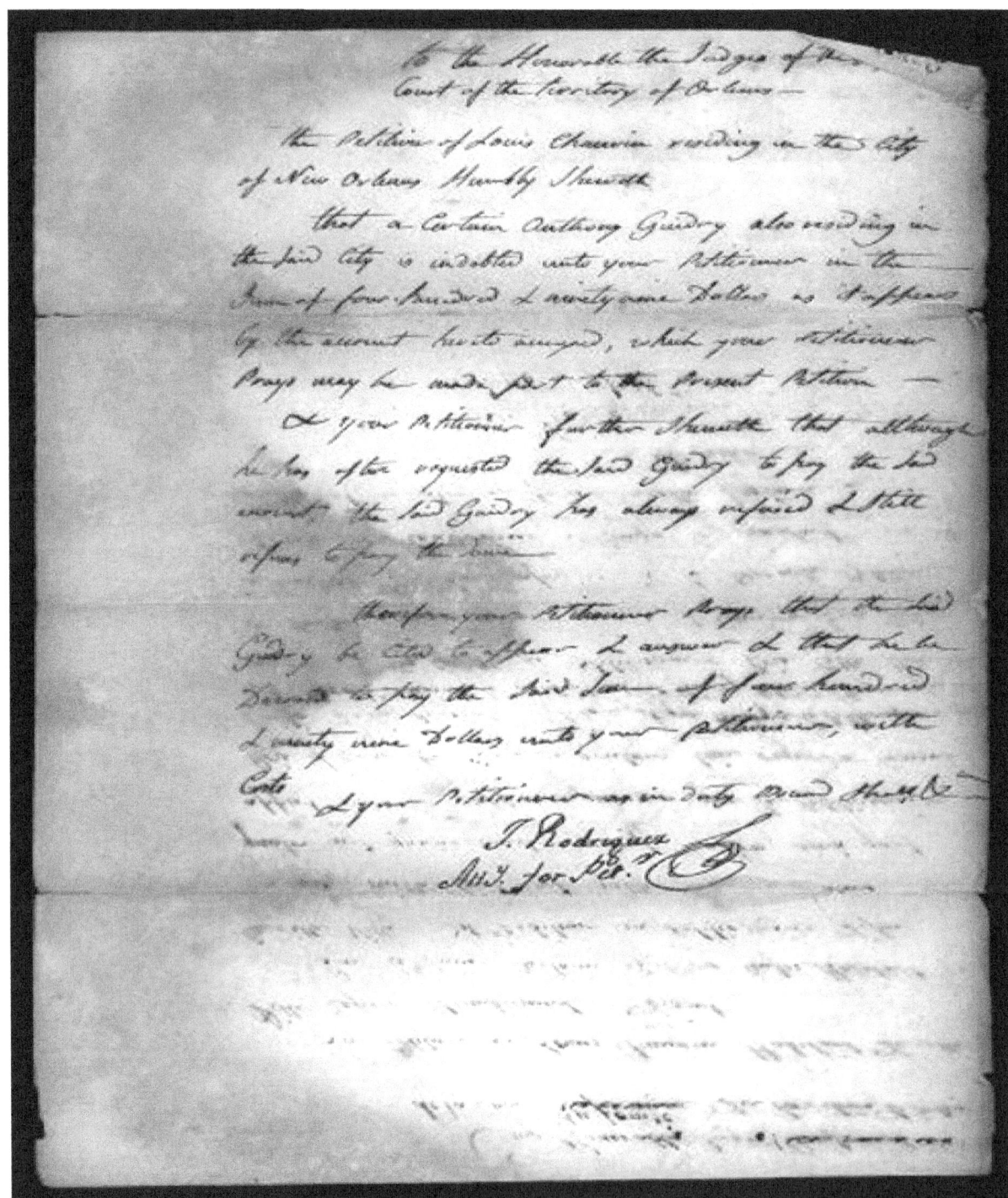

Antoine Guedry 1806 Lawsuit

Antoine Guedry 1806 Lawsuit

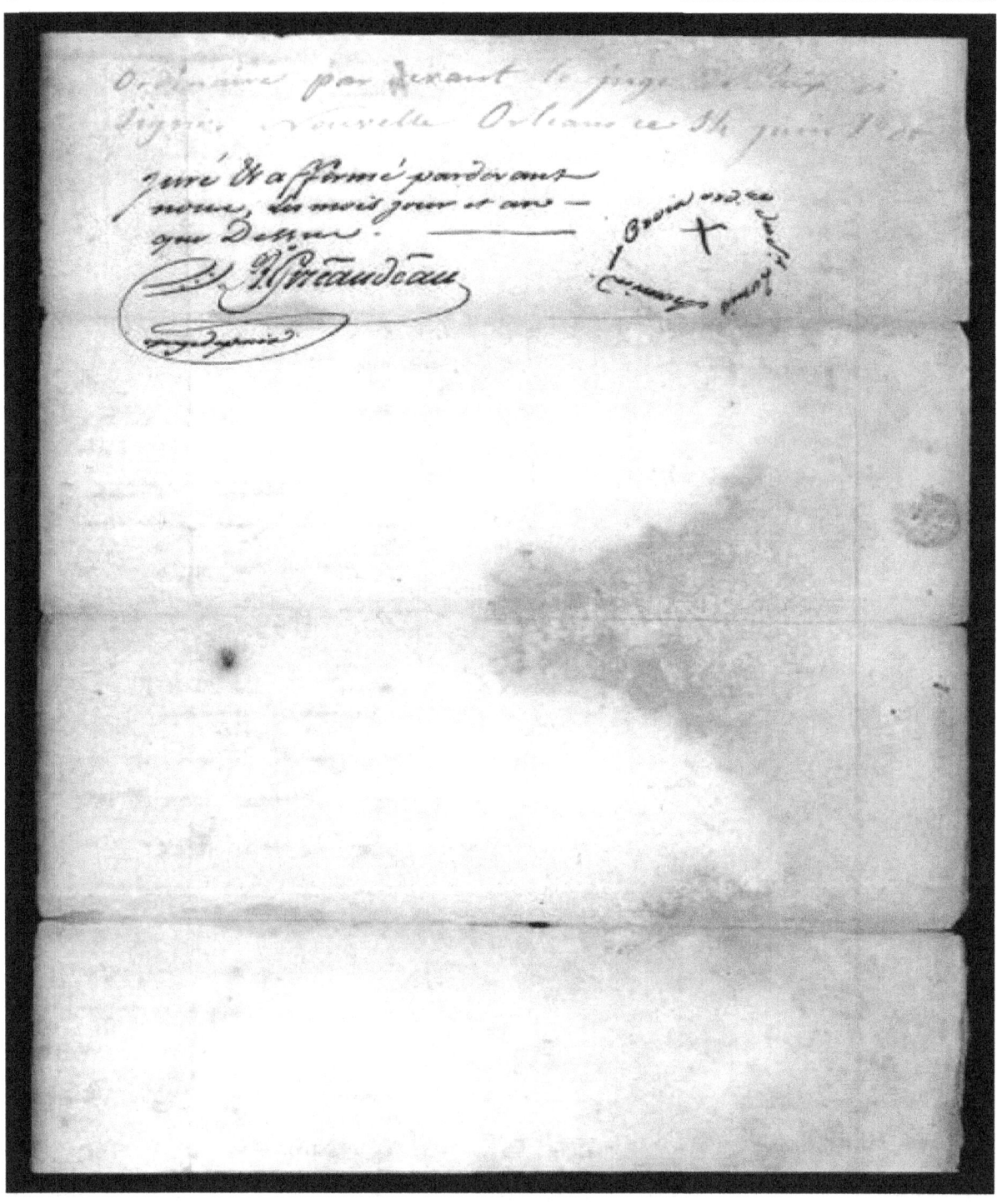

Antoine Guedry 1806 Lawsuit

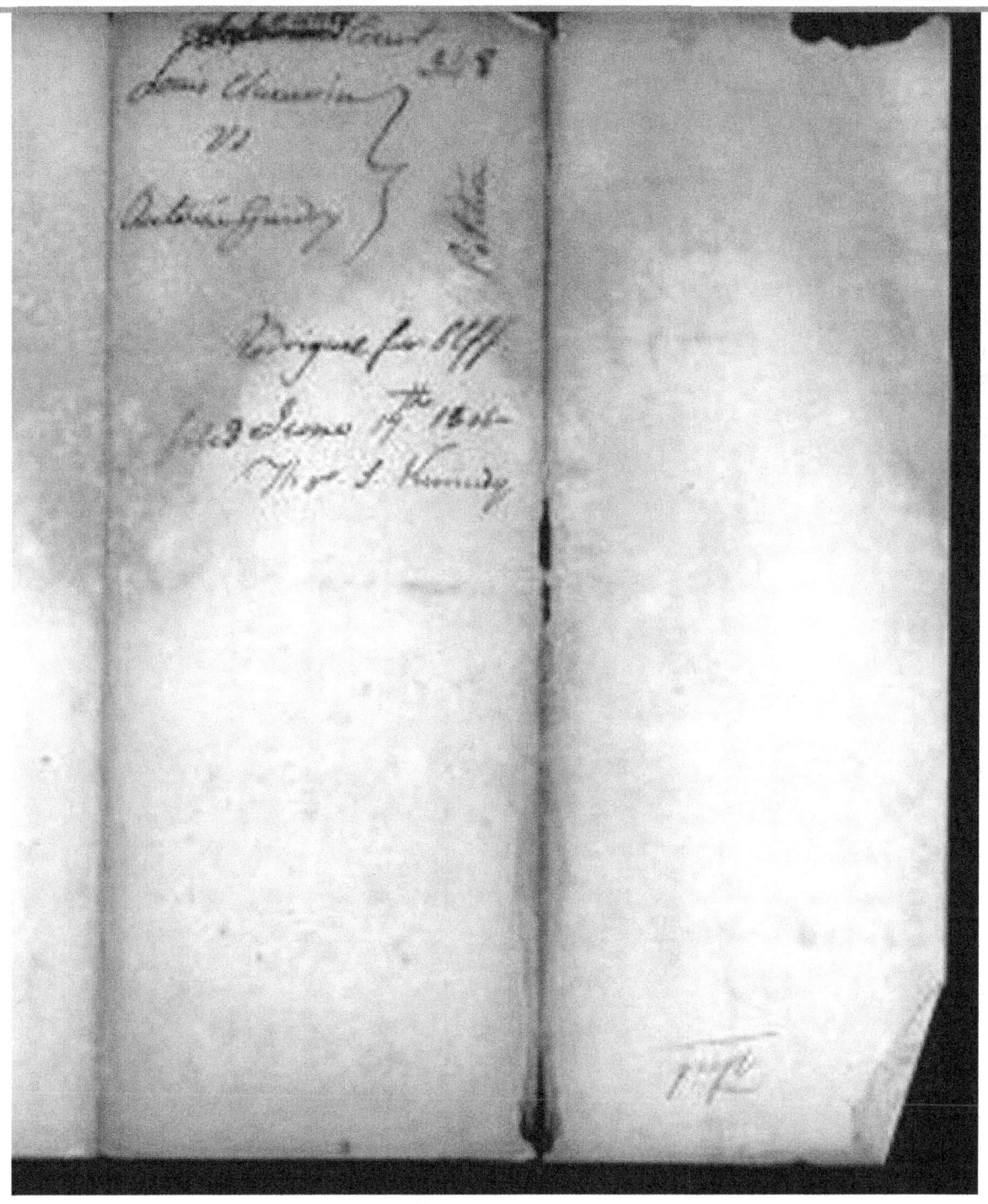

Antoine Guedry 1806 Lawsuit

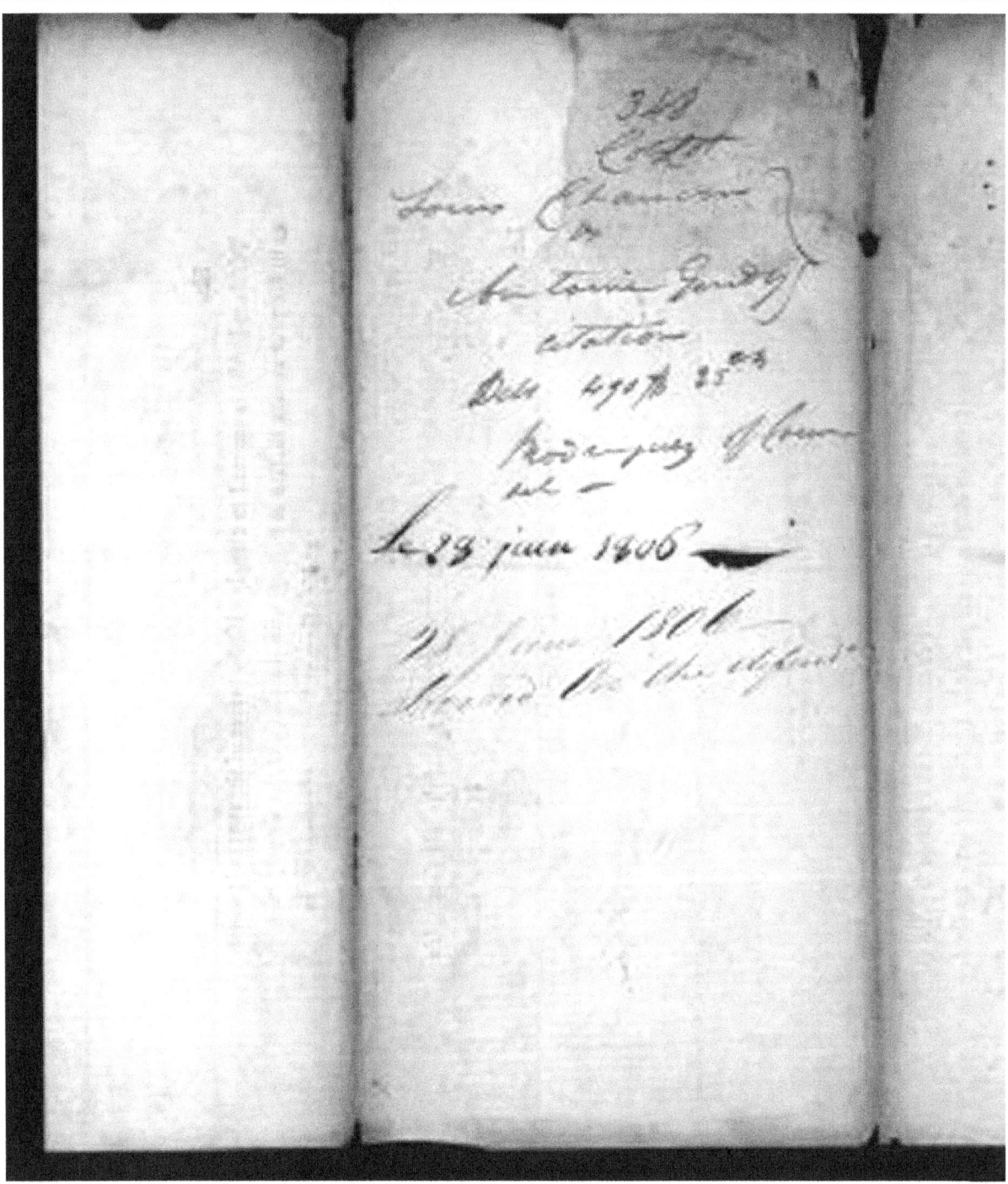

Antoine Guedry 1806 Lawsuit

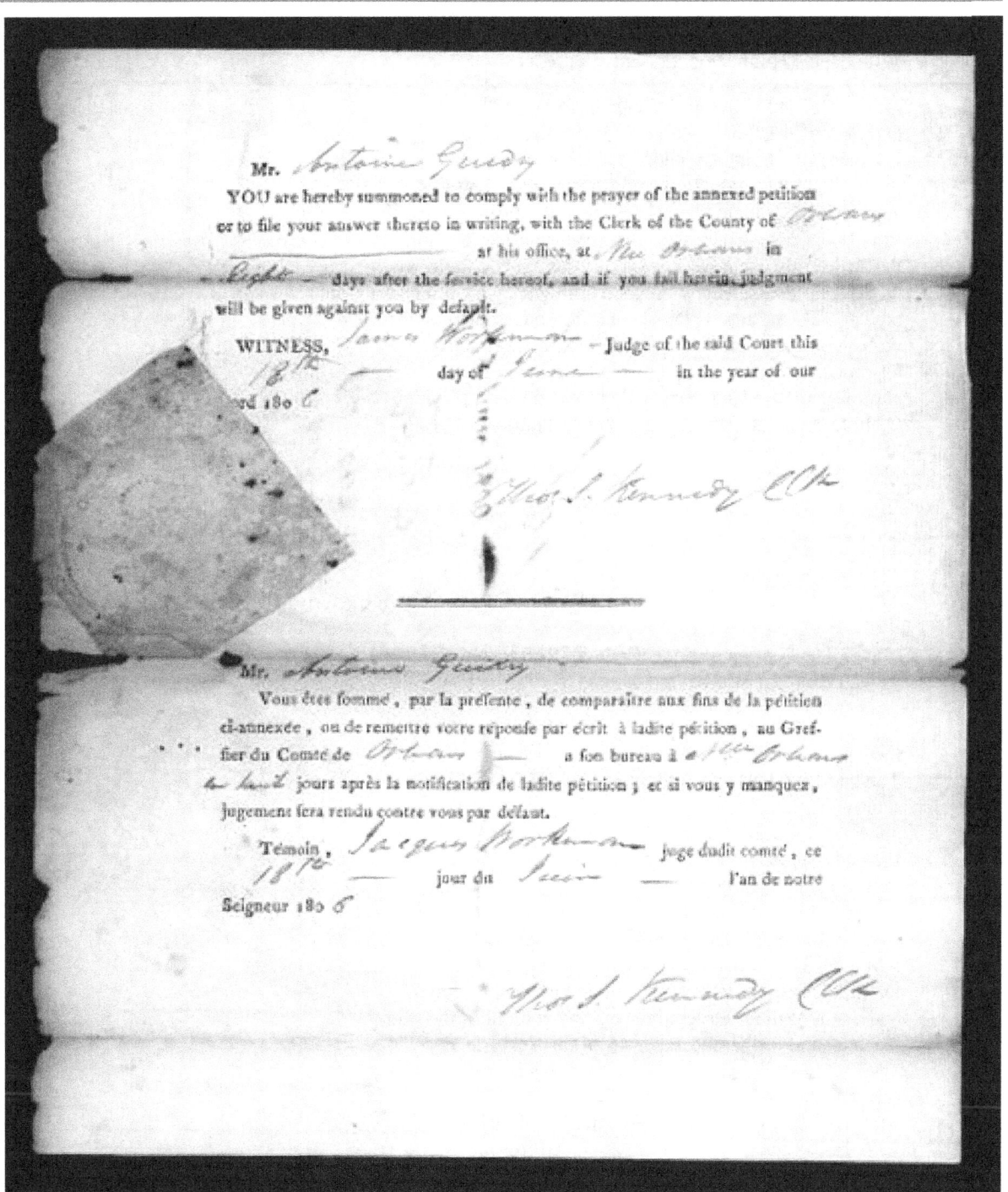

                    Au Honorable Juge
              de la Cour du Comté du territoire d'Orleans

      La Pétition de Louis Chauvin Habitant de cette
Ville Espere Humblement disant –

      Que le Sieur Antoine Guedry Aussi Habitant de
la ditte Ville Est débiteur au Pétitionnaire dépuis –
L'année mille huit cent quatre de la Somme de
quatre cent quatre vingt dix neuf Piastres, ainsi qu'il
appert par le Compte ici annexe que le Petitionnaire
Prie d'honorable Court de vouloir bien regarder Comme
Partie de la Présente Petition, et que dassigne le Petitionnaire
ait Souvent demandé le montant au dit Guidry Celui-ci a toujours refusé de la
payer – A Ces Cause le Petitionnaire Prie Cette Honorable
de Vouloir bien ordonner que la dit Guidry Sera Cité
à Comparaître Pour refondre à la Presente Pétition
et qu'il Sera Ordonné à payer Ce montant du dit
Compte et en outre au frais de cette Justamie -
              C'est Justice -

                (signed) T. Rodriquez
                  Av^t pour le Pet^e

TRANSLATION   To the Honorable Judge
                        of the Court of the County of the territory of Orleans

      The Petition of Louis Chauvin Resident of this
Town Humbly Trusts saying –

      That Mr. Antoine Guedry Also Resident of
the said Town Is in debt to the Petitioner from –
The year one thousand eight hundred four for the Sum of
four hundred ninety nine Piastres, as it
appears by the statement attached here which the Petitioner
Prays that the honorable Court will consider this As
Part of the Present Petition and, as cited the Petitioner
has often requested the amount from the said Guidry, he has always refused to
pay it – Thereunto The Petitioner Prays that the Honorable
will indeed order that the said Guidry will be cited
to Appear in order to correct upon the Present Petition
and the he Will Be Ordered to pay that amount of the said
Account and further the expenses of this Just friend –
                  This is Justice –

                (signed) T. Rodriquez
                  Att^y for the Pet^r

to the Honorable the Judge of the _____
Court of the territory of Orleans –

the Petition of Louis Chauvin residing in the City
of New Orleans Humbly Sheweth

that a Certain Anthony Guidry also residing in
the fair City is indebted unto your Petitioner in the
Sum of four hundred & ninety nine Dollars as it appears
by the account hereto annexed, which your Petitioner
Prays may be made part to the Present Petition –

& your Petitioner further sheweth that although
he has often requested the said Guidry to pay the said
amount, the said Guidry has always refused & still
refuses to pay the Sum

therefore your Petitioner Prays that the Said
Guidry be Cited to appear & answer & that he be
decreed to pay the said Sum of four hundred
& ninety nine Dollars unto your Petitioner, with
Costs

& your Petitioner as in duty bound shall etc.

(signed) T. Rodriquez
Att^y for Pet^r

Doit au^s Antoine Guédry à Mr Louis Chauvin depuis
le 5 juin 1804

	p^s	E^s
<u>Savoir</u>		
Pour pension à une piastres par jour pendant Quarante Cinq jour.	45	
Pour fourniture de Beur et frommage pour son maisonné	6	
Pour quatre Escalins de Lait tous les jour pendant un mois et demie pour sa maisoné	37	4
Pour une Corde et demie de Bois de Chaufage	6	
Pour Blanchissage	6	
Pour journé de mon Cabriolet pendant un mois et demie à six piastres par jour	270	
Pour journé de mes quatres Esclaves pendant douze jours a quatres Escalins chaque	36	
Pour journé de _____ Eislomme à une piaster et quatre escalins par jour	18	
Pour mes journée	13	4
Pour trois Barils Mais à une piastres et quatre Es	4	4
Pour dix piastres que je lui ait prêté pour payer Son testament à Mr Broutin	10	
Pour une piastres prêté pour arangé sa moutre	1	
Pour faire sa Banquete mois et mon negre	6	6
Pour soixante Bouteilles de Vin de Caisses à 4 Escalins le Bouteilles	<u>30</u>	
Total	<u>490 p^s 2</u>	

    Je declare sous serment que la Somme de
montre m'est due par le dit Sieur Antoiine Gudry.
Sauf erreur, et qu'elle ne ma pas été payé jus'que
aujour d'huy, en foi de quoi je fait ma marque

Ordinaire par devant le juge de Paix ici
signe   Nouvelle Orleans ce 14 juin 1804

Juré & affirmé pardevant
nous, Les mois jour et an –
que Dessus ----------   Bovia ord^e de
                                                                    +
  (signed)   L. B. Gireaudeau   Sr Louis Chauvin

TRANSLATION

Owed by Antoine Guédry to Mr. Louis Chauvin since 5 June 1804

	p^s	E^s
Namely		
For rent at one piastre per day during Forty Five days	45	
For supplies of Butter and cheese for his household	6	
For four Escalins of milk each day during a month and a half for his family	37	4
For a Cord and a half of Firewood	6	
For whitewashing	6	
For daily use of my carriage during a month and a half at six piastres per day	270	
For wages of my four Slaves during twelve days at four Escalins each	36	
For wages of _____ Eislomme at one piaster and four escalins per day	18	
For my wages	13	
For three Kegs Corn at one piaster and four Es	4	4
For ten piastres that I have lent him in order to pay for his will to Mr. Broutin	10	
For one piaster lent in order to settle his grinding	1	
To make his Boardwalk myself and my Negro	6	6
For sixty Bottles of Wine with Cases at 4 Escalins the Bottle	30	
Total	490 p^s 2	

I declare under oath that the Sum shown by me is due by the said Mr. Antoine Guidry. Without error, and that it has not been paid to me even to today, in testimony whereof I make my Ordinary mark

in front of the justice of the Peace here
signed,   New Orleans the 14 June 1804

Sworn & affirmed before
us, The month day and year -
as Above ---------   Ord^y Mark of
                                                                              +
   (signed) B. Gireaudeau   Mr Louis Chauvin

County Court

Louis Chauvin | 348
|
vs |
| Petition
Antoine Guidry |

Rodrigues for Plff

Filed June 17th 1806 –

Thos S. Kennedy

Filed

348

Court

Louis Chauvin |
 |
vs |
 |
Antoine Guedry |

citation

Debt 490 $ 25^{csc}

Rodriguez   of Counsel –

Le 28 juin 1806 –

28 June 1808
Served On the defend^t

Mr. Antoine Guidry

  YOU are hereby summoned to comply with the prayer of the annexed petition or to file your answer thereto in writing, with the Clerk of the County of Orleans ---------------------- at his office, at New Orleans in Eight days after the service hereof, and if you fail herein judgement will be given against you by default.

  WITNESS, James Workman - Judge of the said Court this 18th - day of June in the year of our Lord 1806

                Thos S. Kennedy Clk

===========================

Mr. Antoine Guidry

  Vous êtes fommé, par la présente, de comparaître aux fins de la petition ci-annexée, ou de remettre votre réponse par écrit `à ladite petition, au Greffier du Comté de Orleans - a son bureau à N^au Orleans en huit jours après la notification de ladite petition; et si vous y manquez, jugement sera rendu contre vous par défant.

  Témoin, Jacques Workman juge dudit comté, ce 18th - jour du Juin l'an de notre Seigneur 1806

                Thos S. Kennedy Clk

Genealogists live in the past lane

DUES REMINDER

A new year has begun - and, yes, it's the dreaded dues reminder. Attached is a membership application for renewing your membership in Les Guedry d'Asteur. Our dues are very reasonable at $6.00 for individuals and $10 for a family.

So, you say, why renew? We get everything free - the website, the newsletter, the email notices, etc. You're absolutely right - we want everyone interested in our family to have full access to all that we offer. So it is all free. But by joining and paying your dues, you provide us with the financial resources to do so much more. Your dues are why we could have a Mini-Reunion for the family in October 2007 and finance the plaque of Augustin Guedry and Marie Jeanson that we dedicated in St. Alphonse, Nova Scotia in August 2007. Your dues are why we could place Guedry and Labine genealogical books in various libraries throughout the United States and Canada so our family researchers would have access to these excellent reference books published in very limited quantities. These are just a few of the projects that we have done as a family because your dues provided the financial resources.

So take a moment, complete the Membership Application, enclose a check and send it to the address on the Application. It will help all of us do so much more for the family. And, if you would like to join at one of the Benefactor Levels, it would let us do even more.

RIGHT: From *The Lafayette Advertiser*, Lafayette, Louisiana, Saturday Morning, Sept. 9, 1899.

CITIZENS MEETING.

About sixty representatives citizens of all the wards of the parish met last Saturday morning at 11 o'clock at Falk's Hall.

Being present by a special invitation we noticed among those present, men who stands high both in character and integrity in each one of their respective wards.

Hon. Albert Guidry, of Carencro, a gentleman of high standing and ex-member of the Legislature was called to the chair and Mr. Albert Trahan, of Scott, was appointed secretary.

HON. ALBERT GUIDRY.
PRESIDENT OF THE MEETING.

Mr. Guidry has been a member of the Police Jury of St. Landry Parish during 14 consecutive years, eight of which he has been president. He has been a member of the Legislature from St. Landry parish. Mr. Guidry is now residing in Carencro where he conducts a mercantile business. He is very popular and liked by every one that knows him.

Les Guidry d'Asteur

Share your ideas for the Newsletter

Contact:

**Marty Guidry
6139 North Shore Drive
Baton Rouge, LA 70817**

**225-755-1915
guidryrm@cox.net**

'GENERATIONS' newsletter is now in its sixth year. We hope to provide our readers with an interesting, informative and entertaining newsletter. Your input is always welcome and we look forward to another year of sharing family history and news with you.

The Guedry-Labine Family Newsletter, GENERATIONS, serves as a focal point for family members to share and learn about us. To submit your ideas, articles or comments, please contact:

Allie Guidry
txguidry2000@yahoo.com

Marty Guidry
guidryrm@cox.net

Les Guidry d'Asteur Officers and Committees

OFFICERS:
President - Martin Guidry (LA)
Vice-President - Warren Guidry (TX)
Secretary - Billy Harrell Guidry (LA)
Treasurer - Daniel "Chuck" Guidry (LA)

COMMITTEES:
Website - Becky Boggess (IA) - Chairperson
    Annie Grignon-Labine (QU) - Translator
    Elaine Clement (LA) - Translator
    Martin Guidry (LA)*

Genealogy - Daryl LaBine (FL/ON) - Chairperson
    Bernard Geddry (AZ)
    Mark Labine (MN)
    Daniel "Chuck" Guidry (LA)
    Martin Guidry (LA)*

Finance - Cheryl Guidry Tyiska (MD) - Chairperson
    Paul Labine (IL)
    Marshall Woolner (OR)
    Gloria Parrent (TX)
    Chuck Guidry (LA)*

Membership - Charlene Guidry Lacombe (LA) - Chairperson
    Gayle Guidry (LA) - Special Projects
    Warren Guidry (TX)*

Sales - Cindy Guidry Herdt (WA) - Chairperson
    Wayne Simoneaux (LA)
    Billy Harrell Guidry (LA)*

Publicity - Elaine Clement (LA) - Chairperson
    Margaret Jeddry (MA)
    Warren Guidry (LA)*

Newsletter - Allie Guidry Hardee (VA)
    Rachel Hardee (VA)
    Lindsey Hardee (OH)

CAFA Board Member - Jeanette Guidry Leger (LA)

SUMMER 2008

Volume 6, Issue 2

Les Guidry d'Asteur

GENERATIONS

IN THIS ISSUE

The Saga of the   2
USS YMS-378 by
Joseph Guidrey, as
told to Jo Ann
Guidrey Aulick

Bon Appetit -   6
Recipes from the
Guedry-Labine
Family Cookbook

Scott Guidry-   7
History of Lockport
Church

Family Talent-   10
Diane Adair
Gaidry

Jeff Guidry &   12
Freedom

Book Nook   17

CMA 2009

In this Summer, 2008 issue of "Generations" you'll find a variety of excellent articles about our Guédry family. I believe you'll find them informative, interesting and entertaining.

It is rare that we find a first-person account of World War II as soldiers that returned from that War often remained silent about their experiences – even to their family. As with Joseph Guidrey, they often did not relate their experiences to anyone, even family, until shortly before their death. It is thus a special privilege for us to present "Saga of the USS YMS-378 June-July 1944". Here a true hero of WWII – U.S. Navy Lt. Joseph J. Guidrey - relates his role in the D-Day invasions. And what a role it was. Listen closely as you read and you'll feel the fear and the pride of this 28-year old naval officer as he is thrust suddenly into the role of Squadron Commander and charged with clearing the sea lanes just prior to Allied landings on Normandy. He knows success of the mission is the only alternative as the lives of thousands of young soldiers depend on his squadron providing safe access to the landing beaches. And succeed he does. A truly inspiring story of one of our own, Lt. Joseph Guidrey, faced with adversity and a difficult task, did what so many of our soldiers did in that War – he found innovative solutions to difficult problems, took command and succeeded in his mission.

In this issue you'll also find an interesting story about young Scott Guidry of Lockport, LA who recently compiled a history of the Catholic church at Lockport, LA. He then developed a very nice display of his work which can be seen at the public library in Lockport. And don't miss the article on Diane Gaidry, an actress in independent films and on the stage who is garnering a number of awards and honors. A truly inspiring story is that of Jeff Guidry at the Sarvey Wildlife Center (Arlington, WA) and his successful struggle to save an injured Bald Eagle "Freedom". The bond that developed between them is truly amazing. And for those of us that want to eat a truly Cajun meal and then relax, visit Bon Appetit and the Book Nook. You won't be disappointed.

Now – settle in a comfortable chair, get some munchies and enjoy this issue of "Generations".

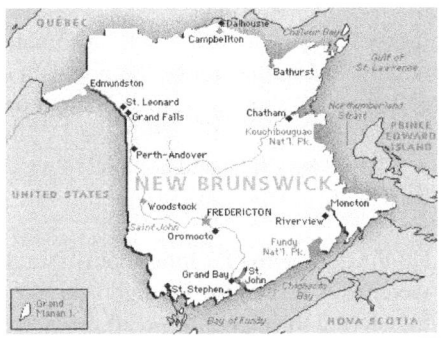

The Saga of the USS YMS-378
June-July 1944
(as recalled 50 years later)
By
Captain Joseph J. Guidrey, USNR
As told to his daughter, Jo Ann Guidrey Aulick

I was a Lieutenant and the C.O. of the minesweeper USS YMS-378 operating out of Plymouth, England since early May 1944. The first official information about "Operation Overlord", the code name for the Normandy Invasion, was given to me and 10 other C.O.'s of minesweepers at a meeting aboard a cruiser anchored in Plymouth Harbor on 2 June 1944. At this meeting we were informed the 11 ships had just become Squadron Y of the Assault Force "U" under a Squadron Commander who would ride one of the ships along with his staff.

The mission of Squadron Y was:

1. **Sweep and buoy the channel for the amphibious landing craft from a point 10 miles at sea to a point 2 miles offshore starting at 6 hours before "H".**

2. **Sweep and buoy the fire support channel for the bombarding ships from the west end of Omaha Beach through the west end of Utah Beach at a distance of about 1 mile offshore.**

3. **Sweep areas around the Troops Transports.**

It was vital that the mission be accomplished thoroughly and on time for the bombarding ships to soften up the shore guns before the troops landed. We were scheduled to start Phase 1 of the mission at 12:30 AM 5 June and complete Phases 1 and 2 by 6:30 AM-which was "H" hour.

On the afternoon of 2 June about 100 infantrymen were place aboard for the night and then were transferred to amphibious craft the next morning.

We were told this was to get as many personnel as possible off the shore and out of communication. Later in the evening a chaplain came on board for a brief time to say Mass and to bless the ship and all on board. Almost all attended the open air service.

The squadron set sail for Normandy late in the evening of 3 June and proceeded slowly along the English coast. The seas were very rough with high winds and waves of 20 feet. We sailed in complete silence - no running lights, no radio transmission, no radar, no sonar. Also, no sleep for anyone as the ship tossed and rolled and the use of the overhead "grab rails" were essential to remaining in one place.

We were off the Isle of Wight in the mid-morning of 4 June and heading directly for Utah Beach 70 miles away when we received orders to return to Plymouth. It would have been almost impossible for us to carry out the mission properly with the seas running so high.

On our return to base — as we approached the anti-submarine nets guarding Plymouth Harbor we received another message, which directed the squadron to turn around and carry out the original mission — only 24 hours later. I had been looking forward to a good night's sleep for myself and the crew but it was not to be.

It was now about 1 AM on 5 June. The sea and wind was calming and this improving continued throughout the night so that by morning the waves were about 10 feet high — which was tolerable for ships our size.

The Saga of the USS YMS-378

At 9 PM 5 June we were 40 miles off the French coast when I received a blinker light message from the Squadron Commander directing me to take over the command of the squadron because the electronic navigating equipment on board the ship he was riding was not working properly. Similar equipment on my ship was working perfectly and we always knew our location within 50 yards. However there was a problem in that my ship had only its regular wartime complement of officers and men and not the extra staff for navigating and signaling which was riding on the original command ship.

Minesweepers work in groups or squadrons and sweep abreast or in echelon formation so there will be no gaps in the swept area. Maintaining proper position and speed in the formation requires constant communication between the leading ship and the others and minesweepers have their own radio wavelength for this purpose. But tonight we were under radio silence and all directions concerning type and length of sweep gear, course and speed changes and location of buoy drops and various other instructions had to be passed via blinker light — and we had only 2 signalmen.

I assumed command about 9 PM and 40 miles from the French Coast, moved to the front of the squadron and notified the other 10 ships of the change by blinker. It was dark, lonely and scary out there. There were no other ships in sight. Our only company was the bombers returning from their raids which were flying so low that their vibrations reflected off the ship. The squadron was at battle stations at all times but we had no way to be certain the bombers were friendly. I ordered all ships to hold fire and it turned out to be the right decision. If the bombers had been hostile there probably would have been no swept channels for the landing craft and combatant ships in the Utah Beach area.

Thirty minutes after midnight on 6 June we arrived at the starting point for the first phase of the mission which was to sweep and buoy the assault channel in to 2 miles offshore. The formation was 9 ships abreast and 2 ships dropping buoys. This phase was completed without incident. At 2:30 AM we re-formed in a starboard echelon formation to sweep and buoy the fire support channel (phase 2) for the destroyers which were to follow an hour or so later.

Again we were alone, silent and wondering when we would be discovered and fired at. I had been on the flying bridge for the past 18 hours along with an officer of the deck and the signalmen while communicating with the navigator from below as to location and course changes.

This channel was to be 3/4 mile wide starting at the west end of Omaha Beach and extending about 15 miles along Utah Beach to its very end. Also distinctive lighted buoys with radar reflectors were to be dropped every 1/2 mile on each side of the channel. To accomplish this we had 6 ships sweeping, 2 ships laying buoys and 3 spare ships ready to replace any ship for any reason. As we started the sweep I could see the surf breaking on Utah Beach and I still wondered when the shore guns would open up. A minesweeper is a ship that can eliminate mines that can sink a combatant ship but cannot defend itself against shore guns or hostile combatant ships.

Our course took us between the Isles St. Marcouf - an enemy fortification lying 4 miles offshore and Utah Beach. The island was burning brightly probably from earlier bombings. We sailed by this fortification about 1/2 mile inshore with no problem but with lots of apprehension.

Dawn broke about 5 AM when we were within a few miles of the end of phase 2, and the shore guns opened up. They soon straddled the squadron.

The Saga of the USS YMS-378

We proceeded out to sea to commence phase 3 of our mission. Communication silence had been ended at day break, when the shore guns had opened up, which enabled us to sweep faster and more efficiently. The remainder of 6 June was spent sweeping the transport areas and we anchored about 9 PM for a much needed rest before our next mission.

During the night of 6-7 June 3 additional minesweepers arrived so now we had 14 ships and the group was divided into 2 squadrons of 7 ships each. I was appointed Squadron Commander of Squadron Y-1 and had 6 of the ships that were with me the previous night. We conducted sweeps in various areas of Omaha and Utah Beaches for some 15 hours each day searching for not only moored mines, but also magnetic and acoustic mines. Squadron Y-1 exploded some 150 mines in the next 6 days.

On 12 June, my 28th birthday, while opening up a merchant ship channel 1 mile off the Cotentin Peninsula we encountered fire from the shore and I ordered all ships to "proceed independently". The guns concentrated on the USS YMS-378 for some reason and we suffered enough damage, but no casualties, that the Flotilla Commander ordered us back to Plymouth for repairs.

Upon our return to Normandy on 20 June I received orders to take Squadron Y-1 and a squadron of British minesweepers to sweep a channel from the Bay of the Seine to Cherbourg. Two destroyers would follow us as escorts. After some 15 miles we encountered shore fire which forced us to run to sea. The destroyers finally silenced the guns with one of them suffering severe damage. The 2 squadrons of minesweepers returned to anchorage but early the next morning returned to sweep to Cherbourg with 2 different destroyers as escorts.

On 30 July Squadron Y-1 was sweeping a new channel for merchant ships in the Utah Beach area near St. Vaast. We were sweeping for magnetic and acoustic mines. USS YMS-378 and USS YMS-304 were sweeping in tandem. About 9 AM a mine exploded under YMS-304 and 2 others exploded close by YMS-378. YMS-304 started sinking immediately, and was gone within 5 minutes. YMS-378 lost all electrical power and one main engine and was taking on water. With the one remaining engine and manual steering we were able to rescue many of the crew of our sister ship. Other ships came alongside and took off the rescued personnel and put their gasoline-driven "handybillies" on board which enabled us to keep USS YMS-378 afloat long enough for us to run it aground on the beach. Repair crews arrived within the hour to patch the leaks, which principally were the sea chests which had been blown out, and the ship was refloated on the next high tide.

The Flotilla Commander decided Squadron Y-1 could use a few days R+R so the remaining 5 operating ships left for the Plymouth Navy Yard immediately with the USS YMS-378 under tow of 2 other minesweepers. The going was slow since the towed ship was drawing 9 feet of water — 3 feet more than usual — but fortunately the seas were calm and we arrived at Plymouth on 3 August with the ship still floating.

The hull and all engine room equipment was "surveyed" (declared worthless) but all equipment on the main deck and above, especially the electronic equipment, was saved for replacement on other ships. I was flown back within the week to report to the Navy Department Washington for further assignment.

I was the C.O. of the USS YMS-378 at its commissioning at the Brooklyn Navy Yard in September 1943 and at its de-commissioning at Plymouth Navy Yard in September 1944. It was a good ship manned by officers and men who were able to take on the additional duties and responsibilities of Commanding

The Saga of the USS YMS-378

the Squadron which led the invasion of Normandy, six hours before "H" hour on 6 June 1944. We did nothing heroic — just successfully carried out a dangerous task.

I was awarded the Bronze Star medal with Combat "V" for my efforts.

                                  Joseph J. Guidrey, Capt. USNR
                                  1 June 1994

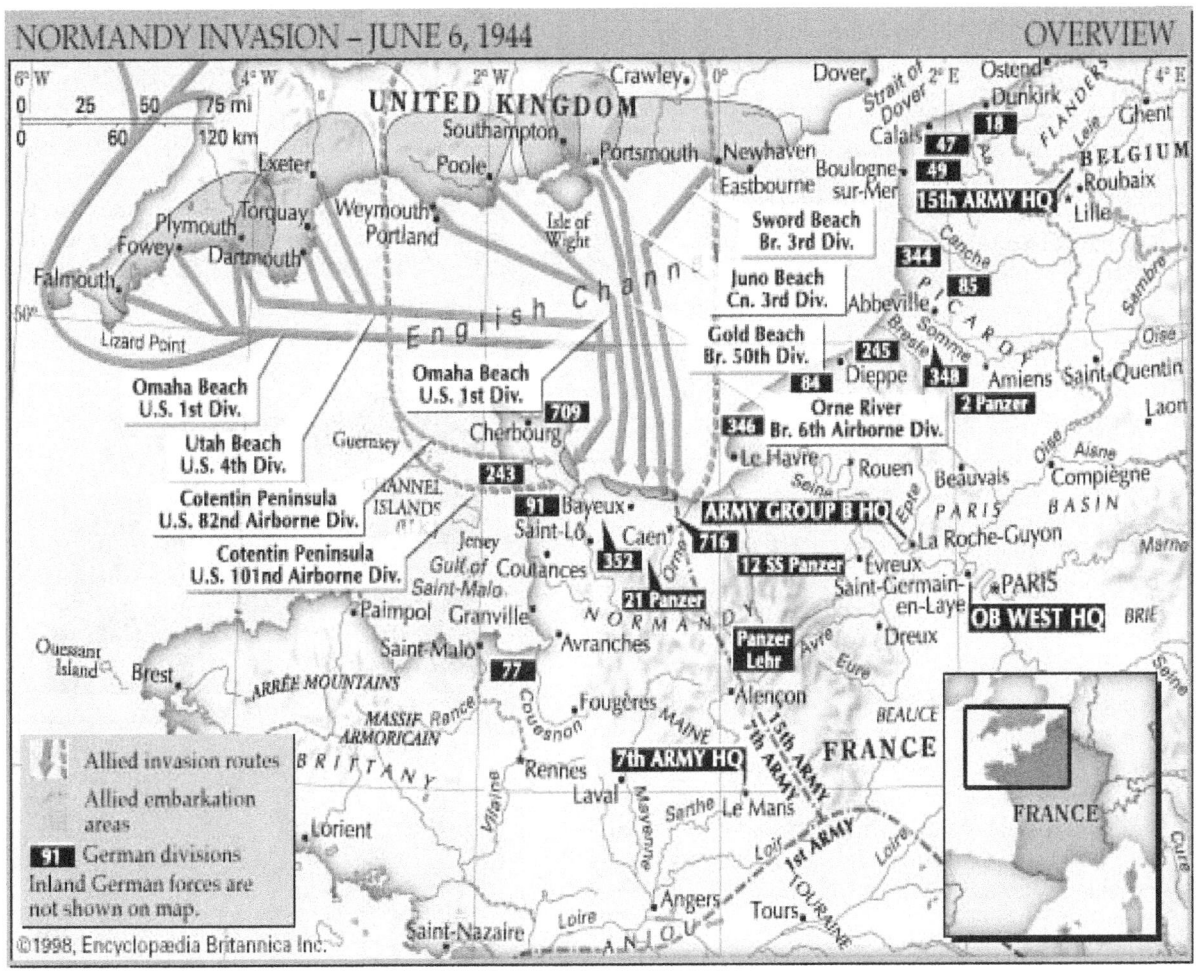

BON APPETIT - Recipes from The Guedry-Labine Cookbook

CRAWFISH ETOUFFEE-CREOLE STYLE
Jack Guidry-Lafayette, LA

1-1/2 to 2 lbs. crawfish tails with fat
  (from a crawfish boil)
2 tbs. bacon grease
2 tbs. flour
2 sticks butter or margarine
2 large onions, chopped
1/2 bell pepper, chopped
3 stalks celery, chopped
1 small (8 oz.) can tomato sauce
2 tbs. minced garlic
3 bay leaves
3/4 cup green onions, chopped
1/2 cup fresh parsley, chopped
1 tsp. creole seasoning
1 tsp. sugar
Salt and pepper to taste
Cooked rice

I noted that the crawfish tails were from a crawfish boil because they will already have seasoning in them, so be careful with what you add. If you have store bought crawfish you can season them with a tsp. of liquid seafood boil and a little cayenne pepper and let them sit in the icebox a few hours.

On the side, in a non-stick pan, scorch the tomato sauce using a few teaspoons of oil by cooking on a medium fire until most of the water is cooked out and it appears to be frying.

Add garlic and bay leaves to roux mix and continue to cook another ten minutes or so. Add crawfish and scorched tomato sauce. Let it come back up to heat. Add green onions, parsley, creole seasoning and sugar. Cook another ten minutes and taste to see what seasoning you need to add. Add water to desired thickness (thick stew-like) and continue to simmer for about 30 minutes. Remove bay leaves before serving.

Serve over cooked rice.

Crawfish Etouffee-Creole Style

Make a blond roux (very light brown) using bacon grease and flour. Add the butter, let it melt, then add the onions, bell pepper and celery. Cook on the medium heat for about 30 minutes stirring every few minutes (don't let it burn).

Local Man Researches History of Lockport Church

By Thad Angelloz
Staff Writer

*"The Courier" Newspaper (Houma, LA)
Published: Friday, May 9, 2008*

LOCKPORT -- While his classmates are busy celebrating the end of finals week, Scott Guidry's work continues.

The 21-year-old Nicholls State University student didn't even have the time to give himself a high-five for successfully navigating through another semester, because he's putting the finishing touches on a religious display that's heading to the Lockport Branch Library.

The special display, which includes write-ups and various artifacts, explores the vast history of Holy Savior Catholic Church in Lockport. It will be housed at the library, 518 Sixth St., Lockport, beginning Monday.

Guidry said the display would remain up for about a month. The exhibit is free and open to the public.

"My entire family dating back many years was born and raised in Lockport," Guidry said. "I had two grandparents who were mayor's of the town. I guess my passion for this grew out of my profound interest in learning more about the church all of us attended."

Guidry said he's been researching the topic for two years.

Along with locating old church statues, Guidry has discovered 130-year-old baptismal certificates written entirely in French.

"The archive center for the diocese in Thibodaux has been very helpful," Guidry said. "They've allowed me to spend as much time as necessary to locate documents and items related to the church's history.

Through asking longtime parishoners of the church questions, Guidry's been able to piece together information that he thinks gives a fairly accurate account of the church's history.

His grandmother, Antoinette Robichaux, also has provided invaluable support.

"She was there when they moved to the third church in 1953," Guidry said. "At that time, someone from the church ordered everything be tossed out. Luckily, she was able to retrieve numerous items."

Robichaux said she couldn't be any prouder of her grandson.

"What he's doing is truly a gift to everyone who ever went to Holy Savior," she said. "He's one of those types of guys that does whatever he puts his mind too. It's amazing what he's been able to uncover through his research. I can't wait to see what happens next."

Robichaux thinks her late-husband, Alfred, who served as mayor of Lockport for 20 years, had the biggest impact on Guidry's current work.

"He always talks about him," the 80-year-old said. "Whenever I ask where he found out how to do something, he tells me that ëgramps' showed him."

According to Guidry, Holy Savior Church took shape in 1870.

The original building was eventually destroyed after the Hurricane of 1915 ravaged the town.

"They built another church in 1953," Guidry said. "Throughout the years many church artifacts were misplaced or lost."

Local Man Researches History of Lockport Church

While Guidry has recovered some of them through hard work and dedication, many items remain missing.

"It's a process of tracking down leads and being persistent," Guidry said. "My goal is to recover as many things as possible."

After he graduates with his general-management degree from Nicholls, Guidry thinks he might write a book about the church one day.

"If I can make the time to do it it's something I definitely want to do," he said.

While he's made many interesting discoveries, one of the most fascinating is the three bells located in the church's main tower.

"When someone told me that three bells named Eugene, Emile and Laurent were up there I had to see it for myself," Guidry said. "Even though they don't ring them today, they are indeed up there. To know that three bells that are 92 years old are in that tower is amazing."

The process has been a labor of love for Guidry.

"Finding out about the stories of our ancestors is interesting," Guidry said. "When you look at it this really is the history of a community that's interweaved with the church."

H. D. GUIDRY, M. D.
OFFERS his professional services to the citizens of Vermilionville and vicinity.
Office on Lafayette Street, near the Convent.
April 2d. 1870—1y.

IN THE NEWS-HISTORICAL NEWS TIDBITS

SHOT ACCIDENTALLY.—Last Friday the 10th inst., at about 2 o'clock, A. M., Felix Guidry, eldest son of Mr. Alex. Guidry, was shot and severely wounded in the left arm and side by the accidental discharge of a gun, and we learn the particulars as follows: his father's sheep were being chased by dogs and as he was leaving the house with a gun to stop them, the accidental discharge took place with the result above stated. Though severe the wounds are not dangerous, and, by the last report, the sufferer was doing as well as could be expected.

Felix Guidry articles from The Lafayette Advertiser Lafayette, LA

Claim Allowed.

Lafayette, La., Feb. 18, 1904. This is to certify that I, Felix Guidry Admr. of the succession of Louisia Breaux, my deceased mother, put in the hands of Judge H. L. Monier, my claim vs. the U. S. Government for stores and commissary supplies taken by the Federal troops during the war of 1861-65. That this day, been awarded by the Court of claims of Washington D. C. the full sum of $7,780.00 in payment of said claim.

FELIX GUIDRY.

Woody Guidry, Jr. ad-Victoria Advocate, 1953, TX

DANCE

At Skating Rink

Port Lavaca, Texas

Thursday, November 19

8 to 12 p.m.

HENRY BUSSE AND ORCHESTRA

featuring

Woody Guidry, Jr.

VOCALIST

Sponsored by Knights of Columbus

Oleus Guidry-Port Arthur News-1974

Refugees from coast jam inland shelters

RACELAND, La. (UPI) — Oleus Guidry shook his head in an evacuation center and mourned the almost certain loss of his home and shrimping trawler with Hurricane Carmen fast approaching.

"I'm afraid when it hits we're not going to have anything left," said Guidry, a native of the salt marshes close to the Gulf of Mexico.

"If I lost that boat, it's going to be the third boat I lost in the bayou.

"It's the hardest thing you can do —to sit here two or three days only to go home and find nothing left." Guidry and his wife, both elderly and ill, lost everything they owned in Hurricane Hilda in 1964.

Thousands of coastal Louisiana residents fleeing Hurricane Carmen jammed inland schools and other public buildings Saturday to ride out the storm.

While children played and ran in the rain, ignoring the storm's approach, their parents listened to emergency radio reports and prayed.

There were 378 people in the Raceland Junior High School, 250 at Raceland Upper Elementary, 200 at Raceland Lower Elementary and 350 at Lockport Junior High.

Jerry Cox, an offshore oil rig worker, returned from the Gulf to his Grand Isle trailer home Friday afternoon only long enough to gather together his wife, Mary Jane, and two children and leave.

"I don't think the trailer will make it," sobbed Mrs. Cox. "We took as much as we could and got out. We were heading for New Orleans when our car broke down and he had to hitch a ride to Raceland."

Cecelia Boyd of Raceland listened to the hurricane warnings, boarded up her shanty, and moved down the road to the Lockport Junior High.

"I didn't feel safe in that old house where I was living," she said. "I knew that shanty couldn't stand that much wind, so I left."

Genealogy is not a fatal-but it is a grave disease

ACTRESS - DIANE ADAIR GAIDRY

Actress and Producer [1964 -]

A highly acclaimed veteran of film, television, stage and commercial productions, Diane Gaidry works diligently with other actors and actresses to develop the full creative potential of the independent film. Born on 11 October 1964 at Ellsworth AFB, South Dakota to Tom Gaidry and Barbara Carr, Diane moved as a youth to San Jose, California and then to Buffalo, New York where her interest in acting flourished.

While still in high school, she launched her professional career as an actress in local theatre productions. In 1986 she earned a Bachelor of Fine Arts degree from the New York University Tisch School of the Arts. In 1994 she received a Masters Degree in Psychology from the University of Santa Monica. Until recently Diane lived in Los Angeles, CA, but is now considering a move to New York as her career blossoms.

Her first major professional role was as Shawn Love, wife of Beach Boy Dennis Wilson, in the TV drama "Summer Dreams: The Story of the Beach Boys" (1990 ABC Movie of the Week). In 1991 she appeared in the television science fiction film "Frankenstein: The College Years" in which she played a friend. Following these initial roles, she was in the 1995 NBC TV drama "Ed McBain's 87th Precinct: Lightning" as Annie and in an episode NBC's "Medium".

Diane's first role in independent films was in 1986 in the feature film "The Stupid Years" shown at the Berlin Film Festival about a hipster coming of age. In 1998 she played a party girl in the short comedy "The Shy and the Naked, a story of love and obsession among artists and mathematicians and also was in the short film "Love Without Socks".

In 2001 she appeared as Greta in "Egg" and as Lucy in the full-length drama "America So Beautiful" - set during the Iranian hostage crisis. Diane co-produced and starred as Ellie Moore in the 2002 feature-length movie "The Dogwalker".

More recent credits include Diane as Maya in "Birth of an Industry" (2004), as the waitress in "The Act" (2004), as Angela, the call girl in Transaction" (2005) and as Petite in "Need" (2005). She starred in the award-winning movie "Loving Annabelle" (2006) as the Catholic school poetry teacher Simone Bradley who falls in love with her student Annabelle. For this role she won the 2006 Best Actress Award at the Los Angeles Outfest. Also in 2006 she was Beverly in the film "Concerned Lady for America".

In the Fall of 2006 Diane returned to her hometown of Buffalo to play Mary Tyrone in the Irish Classical Theatre Company's stage production of "Long Day's Journey Into Night". In 2008 at the same theater she completed a run of "Charley's Aunt" in which she played Dona Lucia.

In 1993 Diane Gaidry and Jacques Thelemaque co-founded Filmmakers Alliance (FA). From a grassroots collective of eight independent filmmakers, FA has grown into an important independent filmmaking resource with over 400 members. FA helps and supports young filmmakers

DIANE ADAIR GAIDRY

by providing them equipment as cameras, lights and shooting locations. Diane was the Executive Director of FA and oversaw Programming and Distribution. Several FA films in which she starred have won awards including Best Short Comedy at Cinquest 2001 and Best Short at Methodfest 2001 for "Egg", Best First Feature Film at Cinequest for "The Dogwalker", which also played at the Los Angeles Film Festival and the Prix du Grand Jury (the top honors) at the 2006 Clermont-Ferrand Film Festival in France for "Transaction". The Clermont-Ferrand Film Festival is rated worldwide as most prestigious short film festival.

Diane Gaidry is a superb, talented actress with a strong background in theater, television and independent films. With her outstanding talents and kind, appealing personality, she will continue to win wide acclaim as an actress and producer.

Genealogy of Diane Adair Gaidry

Diane Adair Gaidry
|
Tom Gaidry - Barbara Carr
|
Joseph Wilfred Gaidry Jr. - Ruth Taylor
|
Joseph Wilfred Guidry - Lillian W.
|
Adolphe Juacint Guidry - Marie Eve Aglae Cadiere
|
Pierre Eugene Guidry – Marie Elise Charpentier
|
Jean Pierre Guidry – Marie Anne (Marianne) Daspit
|
Pierre Janvier Guédry – Marie Josephe Lebert
|
Claude Guédry – Anne LeJeune dit Briard
|
(Uncertain as to Identity – Guédry) – (Wife)
|
Claude Guédry – Marguerite Petitpas

Freedom and Jeff

Freedom and I have been together 10 years this summer. She came in as a baby in 1998 with two broken wings. Her left wing doesn't open all the way even after surgery, it was broken in 4 places. She's my baby.

Jeff Guidry

When Freedom came in she could not stand. Both wings were broken, her left wing in 4 places. She was emaciated and covered in lice. We made the decision to give her a chance at life, so I took her to the vet's office. From then on, I was always around her. We had her in a huge dog carrier with the top off, and it was loaded up with shredded newspaper for her to lay in. I used to sit and talk to her, urging her to live, to fight; and she would lay there looking at me with those big brown eyes. We also had to tube feed her for weeks.

This went on for 4-6 weeks, and by then she still couldn't stand. It got to the point where the decision was made to euthanize her if she couldn't stand in a week. You know you don't want to cross that line between torture and rehab, and it looked like death was winning. She was going to be put down that Friday, and I was supposed to come in on that Thursday afternoon. I didn't want to go to the center that Thursday, because I couldn't bear the thought of her being euthanized; but I went anyway, and when I walked in everyone was grinning from ear to ear. I went immediately back to her dowl cage; and there she was, standing on her own, a big beautiful eagle. She was ready to live. I was just about in tears by then. That was a very good day.

Freedom & Jeff Guidry

We knew she could never fly, so the director asked me to glove train her. I got her used to the glove, and then to jesses, and we started doing education programs for schools in western Washington. We wound up in the newspapers, radio (believe it or not) and some TV. Miracle Pets even did a show about us. In the spring of 2000, I was diagnosed with Non-Hodgkins Lymphoma. I had stage 3, which is not good (one major organ plus everywhere), so I wound up doing 8 months of chemo. Lost the hair - the whole bit. I missed a lot of work. When I felt good enough, I would go to Sarvey and take Freedom out for walks. Freedom would also come to me in my dreams and help me fight the cancer. This happened time and time again.

Fast forward to November 2000, the day after Thanksgiving, I went in for my last checkup. I was told that if the cancer was not all gone after 8 rounds of chemo, then my last option was a stem cell transplant. Anyway, they did the tests; and I had to come back Monday for the results. I went in Monday, and I was told that all the cancer was gone. Yahoo! So the first thing I did was get up to Sarvey and take the big girl out for a walk. It was misty and cold. I went to her flight cage and jessed her up, and we went out front to the top of the hill. I hadn't said a word to Freedom, but somehow she knew. She looked at me and wrapped both her wings around me to where I could feel them pressing in on my back

Freedom and Jeff

(I was engulfed in eagle wings), and she touched my nose with her beak and stared into my eyes, and we just stood there like that for I don't know how long. That was a magic moment. We have been soul mates ever since she came in. This is a very special bird.

On a side note: I have had people who were sick come up to us when we are out, and Freedom has some kind of hold on them. I once had a guy who was terminal come up to us and I let him hold her. His knees just about buckled and he swore he could feel her power coarse through his body. I have so many stories like that.

I never forget the honor I have of being so close to such a magnificent spirit as Freedom's. Hope you enjoy this.

Jeff

Jeff Guidry and Freedom are at Sarvey Wildlife Center

DUES REMINDER

Attached is a membership application for renewing your membership in Les Guedry d'Asteur. Our dues are very reasonable at $6.00 for individuals and $10 for a family.

By joining and paying your dues, you provide us with the financial resources to participate in many projects, one being the CMA 2009 reunion in Bathurst, New Brunswick.

Please take a moment, complete the Membership Application, enclose a check and send it to the address on the Application. It will help all of us do so much for the family. And, if you would like to join at one of the Benefactor Levels, it would let us do even more.

Library & Archives - Canada

This is the official website for the Library & Archives of Canada. In French & English. Canada's national collection of books, historical documents, government records, photos, films, maps, music and much more.

http://collectionscanada.gc.ca

The National Archives

This is the official website for the U. S. National Archives. The site primarily describes the holdings of the U. S. National Archives. Click on the Genealogists/Family Historians button for an overview of genealogical holdings. There are also a publications store and an online ordering service for records. Images of original records are found under the Access to Archival Databases (AAD) button.

http://www.archives.gov/

The Louisiana State Archives

This is the official website for the Louisiana State Archives. It provides a very nice overview of the archival holdings and services. Although there are no images of original documents at this time, there is a very nice index to Confederate Pension Applications with numerous Guidry records. Click on Research Library under Sections of Organization, then Confederate Pension Applications to the left of the top photograph, then Search the Database.

http://www.sos.louisiana.gov/archives/archives/archives-index.htm

Beautiful Bathurst, New Brunswick, CA

THE 2009 GUEDRY-LABINE & PETITPAS REUNION

Congres Mondial Acadien (CMA) for 2009 will be held on the Acadian Peninsula in New Brunswick from 7 August - 23 August 2009. CMA activities will be centered around Caraquet, New Brunswick. You can click on this website to keep up with the events planned for the 2009 CMA.

http://www.cma2009.ca/

We are having our Guedry-Labine & Petitpas Reunion on Sunday, 16 August 2009 in the Conference Center of Danny's Inn in Bereford, New Brunswick. Beresford is just five miles north of Bathurst, New Brunswick and Danny's Inn is on Highway 134 just south of Beresford. Bathurst has a rich Acadian history that we'll explore in the coming months.

We will begin about 8:30 am and have activities until 5:00 pm. More on the agenda, activities and displays is forthcoming and will include formal sessions with music, presentations, etc. as well as time to mingle and get to know your cousins.

There will be a superb buffet lunch. It'll be a Hot & Cold Dinner Buffet that includes roast beef smothered in peppercorn gravy, sweet & sour meat balls, lasagna, chicken wings, potato casserole, coleslaw, tossed green salad, carrot salad, rolls, carrot cake, cherry cheesecake, fresh fruit salad, coffee and tea.

In the next two months we'll send out registration information. It is not too early to secure lodging. The website below contains a number of motels, hotels and bed & breakfasts in the Bathurst area.

http://www.bathurst.ca/english/home/index.cfm?id=156

The 2009 CMA website has an excellent page on accommodations within the Acadian Peninsula. Visit it by clicking on this link:

http://www.cma2009.ca/?page=hebergement&start=0

The official New Brunswick Tourism Website is at the link below. You can learn about interesting locations, sites and activities at this website. By clicking on the word "Guides" in the left column of the page, you can order a free 2008 Experience New Brunswick Vacation Planner" which is excellent.

http://www.tourismnewbrunswick.ca/en-CA/GeoLanding_US?source=other

In the near future we will let everyone know how to register for the 2009 Guedry-Labine & Petitpas Reunion. We'll also send out memos periodically as our agenda is developed and our plans become firm. It's time to begin planning your trip to New Brunswick in August 2009 and attending the 2009 Guedry-Labine & Petitpas Reunion. It will be a fun time to meet your cousins, learn about our family and experience the wonderful Acadian culture of New Brunswick.

New Brunswick Accommodations - CMA 2009

The Guidry-Labine family reunion is scheduled to take place August 16, 2009, in the town of Bathurst, not far from Caraquet. Here are a few more links for accomodations in those areas. We'll add more details about our reunion in the next few months.

BATHURST - http://www.bathurst.ca/english/home/

Authentique Bed & Breakfast Enjoy our 4 star B&B in a heritage home of the 20's with 'Arts & Craft's influences, conveniently located in the heart of Bathurst. You are welcome to relax in a cozy atmosphere with personalized service. Spacious rooms with very comfortable beds, cable TV, DVD, MP3, wireless internet, work desk and telephone. Each room has a private bathroom. Breakfast 'A la Carte' will be served in our elegant dining room.

Comfort Inn Bathurst Conveniently located on St. Peter Avenue. Close to shopping and offices. 35 person meeting room available.

John's Motel Our rooms have a full bath and shower, color television with cable, and most importantly comfortable beds! We also boast a swimming pool and an area for picnics. We also have in-room coffee.

Sea'scape Cottage This is our fully equipped beach house located on the beautiful Bay of Chaleur in Bathurst, New Brunswick. Select the virtual tour button to have a closer look.

CARAQUET - http://www.ville.caraquet.nb.ca/

Hotel Paulin "The Pearl of Baie des Chaleurs", Caraquet. Internationally acclaimed, seaside hotel and country inn, c.1891, rich in Acadian history. Luxurious waterfront suites, French country rooms, licensed fine dining, golf and spa packages. Hotel Paulin has the charm, elegance and inn keeping spirit of the 19th century. It offers intimate surroundings with old-world French village charm. It has been written up by the New York Times, Montreal Gazette, Fodor's and Frommer's, La Presse , Paris Match Magazine, Micheline Guide, France's Le Routard. The cuisine is innovative, upscale, inspired by local fresh foods with a Sommelier wine pairing menu.

La Maison Touristique Dugas House built by one of the first Acadian architects (1926). 10 minute walk through wooded area to private beach. Close to the Acadian Peninsula tourist attractions.

Motel Colibri 12 rooms smoking and non-smoking. 2 double beds. Telephone, cable television, air conditioning. Free outside pool. Continental breakfast.

Super 8 Motel 50 guest rooms including 18 junior suites and 1 Jacuzzi suite - Rooms with balconies overlooking the Acadian Coast and Le Carrefour de la Mer (Crossroads of the Sea) - Swimming pool with three-story 80 foot waterpark and kiddie pool - Whirlpool - Complimentary continental breakfast

BOOK NOOK

Yankee Autumn in Acadiana: A Narrative of the Great Texas Overland Expedition through Southwestern Louisiana October-December 1863

By David C. Edmonds

This narrative of the Great Texas Overland Expedition is storytelling at its finest. The author formerly resided in the area, and his attention to detail and treasure trove of sources are evident in his retelling of this tragic tale for the citizens of this area, caught between the two warring sides and preyed upon by not only regular troops but lawless bands of "jayhawkers" as well. This book is a must-own for those interested in the Civil War in Louisiana, the war in the Trans-Mississippi, and how citizens in the path of conflict can sometimes be made to suffer, innocent though they may be". The term "narrative" is a fitting one for David C. Edmonds' Yankee Autumn in Acadiana. This book is at its heart a story of the suffering of the population of southwestern Louisiana along Bayou Teche.

Cajuns and Their Acadian Ancestors-A Young Reader's History by Shane K. Bernard

In *The Cajuns*, Shane K. Bernard relates the story of how one of America's most distinctive ethnic groups, the Acadians, or Cajuns, of South Louisiana, made the transformation from a close-knit people retaining the strong cultural ties of their heritage to a group that has become assimilated into the mainstream of American society. Bernard maintains that for much of their history the Cajuns were looked down upon, derided as "backward, ignorant, and un-American". They spoke a separate language and lived a life-style that emphasized isolation and separation from traditional American culture.

Bernard has done an excellent job in treating this neglected aspect of Cajun history. His sources include a wide variety of both primary and secondary works. His chapters on the influences of World War II and of the atomic age on the Cajuns are fine interpretations. He also gives full credit to the important roles played by women and blacks in the region.

Les Guidry d'Asteur

Share your ideas for the Newsletter

Contact:

**Marty Guidry
6139 North Shore Drive
Baton Rouge, LA 70817**

**225-755-1915
guidryrm@cox.net**

'GENERATIONS' newsletter is now in its sixth year. We hope to provide our readers with an interesting, informative and entertaining newsletter. Your input is always welcome and we look forward to another year of sharing family history and news with you.

The Guedry-Labine Family Newsletter, GENERATIONS, serves as a focal point for family members to share and learn about us. To submit your ideas, articles or comments, please contact:

Allie Guidry
txguidry2000@yahoo.com

Marty Guidry
guidryrm@cox.net

Les Guidry d'Asteur Officers and Committees

OFFICERS:
President - Martin Guidry (LA)
Vice-President - Warren Guidry (TX)
Secretary - Billy Harrell Guidry (LA)
Treasurer - Daniel "Chuck" Guidry (LA)

COMMITTEES:
Website - Becky Boggess (IA) - Chairperson
    Annie Grignon-Labine (QU) - Translator
    Elaine Clement (LA) - Translator
    Martin Guidry (LA)*

Genealogy - Daryl LaBine (FL/ON) - Chairperson
    Bernard Geddry (AZ)
    Mark Labine (MN)
    Daniel "Chuck" Guidry (LA)
    Martin Guidry (LA)*

Finance - Cheryl Guidry Tyiska (MD) - Chairperson
    Paul Labine (IL)
    Marshall Woolner (OR)
    Gloria Parrent (TX)
    Chuck Guidry (LA)*

Membership - Charlene Guidry Lacombe (LA) - Chairperson
    Gayle Guidry (LA) - Special Projects
    Warren Guidry (TX)*

Sales - Cindy Guidry Herdt (WA) - Chairperson
    Wayne Simoneaux (LA)
    Billy Harrell Guidry (LA)*

Publicity - Elaine Clement (LA) - Chairperson
    Margaret Jeddry (MA)
    Warren Guidry (LA)*

Newsletter - Allie Guidry Hardee (VA)
    Rachel Hardee (VA)
    Lindsey Hardee (OH)
    Martin Guidry

CAFA Board Member - Jeanette Guidry Leger (LA)

FALL 2008

Volume 6, Issue 3

Les Guidry d'Asteur

GENERATIONS

IN THIS ISSUE

The D-Day Landing and POW Experience of Emery J. Guidry (from Jeffrey Guidry) — 2

Bon Appetit - Recipes from the Guedry-Labine Family Cookbook — 6

The Guedry Crest by Marty Guidry — 7

'And How Did I Get That Name' - Summerall Martin Guidry by Marty Guidry — 10

Book Nook — 12

The Vaudeville Team of Jim Jedry & Little Eddie Kelly by Bernie Geddry — 15

CMA 2009

IN THIS ISSUE *from Marty Guidry*

As we end the sixth year of publishing "Generations", Allie Guidry presents another superb issue of our newsletter with several interesting and informative articles about our Guédry-Labine family. Jeffrey Guidry from Crowley, LA relates the experiences of his uncle Emery J. Guidry of Cow Island, LA (now that's an intriguing name in itself) during the Battle of the Bulge and as a POW of the Germans. This story has an interesting twist that occurs many years after the end of WWII.

With Thanksgiving just around the corner peruse the taste-tempting fall recipes in 'Bon Appetit' and then head for the kitchen. As you enjoy that pumpkin pie, learn the meaning of all those symbols and colors on our new Guédry Crest and how they tell the unique story of our family history – a history we can all be proud to have.

Ever wonder how some of those strange first names we occasionally see came about. We've dug back and uncovered how Summerall Martin Guidry got his unique first name.

Need some reading during the holidays? The 'Book Nook' has two excellent book reviews on the Native Americans of Nova Scotia and those of Louisiana.

The Guédry-Labine family is quite diverse, encompassing many interesting occupations and avocations. James Geddry was no exception. Working at the Watertown Arsenal in Massachusetts by day, James Geddry became Jim Jedry is his second job – a ventriloquist with his sidekick Eddie Kelly. Bernard Geddry brings to life his uncle's passion for entertaining folks with his remarkable Vent dolls. Working at the Watertown Arsenal in Massachusetts by day, James Geddry became Jim Jedry is his second job – a ventriloquist with his sidekick Eddie Kelly. Bernard Geddry brings to life his uncle's passion for entertaining folks with his remarkable Vent dolls.

And don't forget to register for our upcoming Reunion at Bathurst, New Brunswick on August 16, 2009. We have booked the Conference Center at Danny's Inn. We'll have an opening French Mass at a local church in Bathurst and then all meet at Danny's Inn for a day of fellowship and exciting activities. We are beginning to finalize the agenda with a mixture of French music, interesting presentations, a wonderful buffet meal at noon, family-related items for sale, lots of time to mingle with cousins and a moving closing ceremony. Oh, watch your wallets and purses as I've heard we may have a magician visiting us during the Reunion.

The D-Day Landing and POW Experience of Emery J. Guidry from Cow Island, LA (as told to his nephew Jeffrey Guidry)

The following information was given to me over the years that I lived & worked with Uncle Emery and the many nights he spent at our home.

When Emery J. Guidry enlisted in the Army, his father (Malcolm Guidry) had to sign for him since all of his brothers were already in the service and he was the only remaining son on the farm. Grandpa Malcolm told him it was a dumb thing to do and he was going to get himself killed in a foreign country. But he said I can't stay home and not help out like my brothers! My Dad (Kerney Guidry) was in the Army in the Phillipines, Malcolm Jr. (Malcolm Guidry Jr.) was in England with the Air Force, Vern (Vern Guidry) was in the Army in California and Harry (Harry Guidry) was in the Army in Oklahoma.

Uncle Emery said on D-Day that he was all too happy to get off that darn boat and head to land even if he got killed! They landed at Utah Beach, walked ashore and never had a shot fired at them, He could hear a lot of firing down the beach in the distance, but it was three days before someone shot in his direction -- a machine gun was firing from behind a hedgerow and he fired back, but does not remember hitting anything except trees and dirt flying from around the position.

His unit moved up towards Cherbourg and he said the Germans were fleeing because they were trapped! There were a lot of firefights and Uncle Emery thinks he did kill some Germans, but there was so much firing and Germans falling everywhere that he could not remember actually shooting and seeing someone go down from his fire.

After Cherbourg they walked south for months, but he did not remember the names of any towns or places. He knew his unit never got close to Paris.

The next thing Uncle Emery remembered is that they were in the woods in Luxembourg in December, 1944 and it was the coldest place he had ever been. He was sent up front as a forward observer (two men to a foxhole with binoculars). They had been there about two weeks when one night it went wild! Artillery fire was falling all around their foxhole and German tanks were coming out of the woods behind them. He said it looked like at least 100 tanks headed right towards them. His foxhole buddy said "I better look and report back to HQ". He stuck his head out of the foxhole, was shot right through the head and dropped back into the hole. Uncle Emery said "I got as low as I could in that hole". A few minutes later a German stuck his gun into the hole and said "raus" (get out!). Would you believe that at the time I was thinking Poppa was right; I was going to get killed in a foreign country! I was scared out of my skin and knew that guy was going to blow my head off, but he lined me and about ten other observers up and started marching us back towards the German lines.

About an hour before the attack a friend (Winston Foreman) from Kaplan was in one of the foxholes and he yelled for me to go get coffee for the other guys. When I got back, I went to foxhole #1 to bring them coffee (my foxhole was #3) and that's when the shelling started. An 88mm round hit right in my old foxhole (#3)! Winston took off for HQ as soon as the shelling started and he reported me dead since he thought I was in my old foxhole (#3). The War Department sent my wife Willie Mae & Poppa (Malcolm Guidry) a letter saying I was killed in action!

The German guard walked us about four hours through their lines. There were Germans and tanks everywhere you looked, but he kept us walking until daylight. Then he stopped and we fell

The D-Day Landing and POW Experience of Emery J. Guidry

asleep in a forest until dark. This went on for days. One night, while we were walking, a German patrol did not see our guard and started shooting at us. I got hit in the left hip and the buttock and two other guys were shot dead before the guard finally got the Germans to quit shooting. I was hurting terribly, but not bleeding that much so the guard put a crude bandage on me and told me to keep walking. We finally got to a prison camp somewhere in Germany and an American doctor patched me up best he could. I had been running a high fever for about a week and infection had set into the wounds. We were all starving as the guard gave us a can of potted meat to share among the eight of us. I was down to 118 lbs from 160 lbs a few weeks earlier! I was in such bad shape at the prison camp that I did not know if it was day or night or how long we stayed there -- maybe a week at the most. When we arrived at the camp, all the prisoners came out to see what was going on.

A big guy with black curly hair hollered at me "Guidry, Where you from? " I said "Cow Island, Louisiana". He said "I am from Lyons Point, Louisiana. And I will take care of you". He got my name from the nametag on the fatigue uniform that I was wearing, but he had a prison suit so I never got his name. That night the big guy brought us some potato peelings soup which tasted great! It was dark and he had snuck into our barracks so we had to whisper. I was so bad off and never thought to ask him his name and really couldn't tell what he looked like in the dark. But that guy sure saved my life! The U. S. Air Force started dropping bombs on the camp and probably killed more POW's than Germans so our old guard decided it was time to move on.

AN ASIDE - JEFF'S UNLIKELY STORY ABOUT THIS INCIDENT

Jeff Guidry (Emery Guidry's nephew) worked for Allstate Insurance Company in Crowley, LA and he had a customer by the name of Julius Lamperez who lived in Crowley. He was a famous Cajun musician who went by the stage name of "Pappa Cario" (the King of Diamonds). Pappa would come to my office every month and he would start telling me music and war stories. He said he was a prisoner of war for two years in Germany and talked about how bad it was. Or he would tell me he played the Louisiana Hayride in Shreveport with Elvis Presley, Farron Young and George Jones and how he was the best steel guitar player EVER! I really thought most of it was lies, but, after he died, the Morning Advocate newspaper in Baton Rouge, LA listed his playing history and sure enough he played background steel guitar for all those singers.

One day out of the blue he says"Guidry, Where you from?" I said "Kaplan, but I was born in Cow Island". He said "I met a Guidry from Cow Island when I was in the prison camp, but I don't know what his first name was". He said "I saw his name on his field jacket the day they brought them in and I asked him where he was from. He said Cow Island and I told him I was from Lyon's Point". I was a cook and took care of my Louisiana boys. That first night I brought him some potato peelings soup because he was in really bad shape.

I could not believe what I was hearing!

I picked up the phone and called Uncle Emery and said I want you to talk to somebody you met many years ago. I handed the phone to Pappa and, as they talked, Pappa started crying and he kept saying "I ain't no hero" and to come see him in Crowley or at his nightclub in Houston. They talked for about 30 minutes and, when they hung up, Pappa gave me the phone back and said " That sure was the fellow from the prison camp, but when you see him you tell him that I ain't no hero, but I am one hell of a steel guitar player!"

Pappa died about two months later at the age of 81. He and Emery never got to see each other.

The D-Day Landing and POW Experience of Emery J. Guidry

EMERY'S STORY CONTINUES

When we left the prison camp, we now had about 15 guys with that one guard and we started walking at night and sleeping in train tunnels during the day. It wasn't long before we could hear our artillery shells falling all around us and our planes were overhead all day. Some of the guys started working on the guard - telling him to give up because, when the Americans caught up to us, it would be better for him to be our prisoner. After two or three days the German guard could see we were right and he handed us his gun and told us where our frontlines were. We walked about 3-4 hours before we ran into some Americans from the Big Red One (U. S. 1st Infantry Division). They called HQ and told them to send an ambulance as there were a couple of us in really bad shape. One of the medics gave me a cigarette and a morphine shot. My legs were numb and still infected and I was in pain the whole time. Boy, when he gave me that shot of morphine, I thought I had died and gone to heaven. I passed out and the next thing I remember was waking up in a hospital somewhere in France. I don't remember anything during that time - guess they kept me full of morphine until I got to the hospital. When I woke up, the first thing I noticed was the ceiling fan and I looked down at clean white sheets! The bad part was hearing all the guys that were really bad off crying and yelling. I tried to get out of the bed, but I couldn't move. I thought I must be paralyzed, but a nurse came by and said I was fine. They had strapped me to the bed to keep me from moving since they had removed the three bullets from my back. Boy, was I relieved! About two weeks later they brought me to the front office and gave me a telephone to call home. I had the operator call the little grocery store in Cow Island (as my family had no phone). The old man at the store was so excited; he keep asking me if it was really me because they told him I was dead! I assured him I was alive and that I would call back in two days at 2:00 pm their time and asked him to get my wife and Dad there.

When I finally talked to them, Pop (Malcolm Guidry) spoke only French and one of the French nurses said "Is that a local call?" I explained and she could not believe it. I did not know how long it would be before they shipped me home so I told everyone to hang in there cause "This old boy is coming home". It took about two months of rehabilitation before I could fully walk again and another month to put me on a boat back to the States. When we finally landed in New York, I was sent to another hospital for a complete checkup and was diagnosed as 30% disabled and that I would get a monthly check of $32 for the rest of my life with free medical care. I thought "Wow! I am fixed for life. I am going to send that money directly to the bank and that's gonna be my retirement."

(Uncle Emery was re-evaluated ten years later and upgraded to 63% disabled. He received about $1200-1800 per month until he died.)

THE CONCLUSION

Emery (or EJ as he was called) worked as a bartender in Sulphur, LA for a couple of years after returning home then got a job building the large Citgo refinery in Lake Charles, LA. After it was completed, he was offered a job in the laboratory at Jefferson Chemical Company in Port Neches, Texas where he worked for 43 years before he retired.

He and his wife Willa Mae had three children. She worked at a fabric shop and after 26 years of marriage she left him for another man. He was devastated. About a year later he met Jene who was his perfect mate. They married shortly thereafter and she took care of him like a king. She died about twenty years after their marriage. He then married an former schoolmate from Cow Island. She was with him until the end. Uncle Emery died in 1999 at the age of 76.

THE D-DAY LANDING AND POW EXPERIENCE OF EMERY J. GUIDRY

Emery J. Guidry

Born: 23 May 1923 at Cow Island, LA

Inducted into U. S. Army: 9 April 1942

Discharged from U. S. Army: 13 December 1945

Served in 1st Army, 101st Infantry Division, Company A

Landed at Utah Beach on D-Day (6 June 1944)

Captured in Ardennes Forest during the Battle of the Bulge

Held as a POW for eight months

Medals: Silver Star, Purple Heart, Croix de Guerre, and others

Utah Beach, June 6, 1944

Genealogy of Emery J. Guidry

Emery J. Guidry
|
Malcolm Guidry – Blanche Guidry
|
Duessard Guidry – Marguerite Idolie Hargrave
|
Edmond Guidry – Marie Aurelia Dartes
|
Francois Guidry – Celeste Dartes
|
Jean-Baptiste Guedry – Marguerite Lebert
|
Claude Guedry – Anne LeJeune
|
(Unknown) Guedry
{possibly Augustin Guedry & Jeanne Hebert or Paul Guedry & Anne Mius]
|
Cladue Guedry – Marguerite Petitpas

[Note: Jeffrey Guidry is the son of Kerney Guidry & Mable Hebert. Kerney Guidry is the brother of Emery J. Guidry]

BON APPETIT - Recipes from The Guedry-Labine Cookbook

PORK CHOP-SQUASH CASSEROLE
From Carol Leger (Don) - Jeanette Leger-Rayne, LA

6-8 yellow squash
6 center cut pork chops
1 stick oleo
1/2 C chopped celery
3/4 C chopped onion
1/2 C chopped bell pepper
1 jalapeno pepper chopped (optional)
2 cans cream of mushroom soup
1 box cornbread Stove Top stuffing

Boil sliced squash until tender, drain well and set aside. Brown pork chops - set aside. Sauté celery, onions, bell pepper and jalapeno in oleo. Add soup and mix well. Combine this mixture with cornbread stuffing mix (include seasoning in box). Fold in squash. Pour mixture into an oblong baking pan sprayed with Pam. Place pork chops and stuffing mix with Tex-Joy steak seasoning, garlic and red/black pepper to taste.

Serves 6

During the past few years we have used recipes from the Guedry-Labine Cookbook for our Bon Appetit section of the newsletter. We welcome recipes from all readers. If you missed the opportunity to contribute to the cookbook in 2004, you can still submit a favorite family recipe for us to share and enjoy. See the last page of this issue for e-mail addresses for either Marty Guidry or Allie Guidry. We look forward to trying out your entry.

PUMPKIN PIE

Thanks to *Jim Graham of Kemah, TX* for this lighter, healthier recipe for Pumpkin Pie. It sounds delicious.

15 oz. canned pumpkin
1/4 C Egg Beaters Frozen Egg Substitute
12 oz. fat-free evaporated milk
2 tsp. pumpkin pie spice
1 tsp. ground cinnamon
2 tsp. vanilla extract
1 3/4 C Splenda-No Calorie Sweetener

Mix all the above ingredients. Pour into a glass pie pan, sprayed with Pam. Bake for 15 minutes at 400 deg. F then lower temperature to 325 deg. F and cook an additional 45 minutes.

THE GUÉDRY CREST
By Marty Guidry

The Guédry Crest of Les Guidry d'Asteur briefly tells the story of our Guédry-Labine family – both its cultural values and its unique history from its French origins, its settlement at Merigueche and life with the Mi'kmaq people, its struggle through the years of exile and finally its survival and expansion throughout North America and Western Europe. Below is an explanation of the colors and symbols of our crest. It tells an impelling story of our family's strength, growth and survival against insurmountable odds.

The Guédry Crest is the official crest of Les Guédry d'Asteur and all of its members. Each of us can use the crest on clothing, stationary, hats, plaques, pens, etc. When using the Guédry crest for your personal use, feel free to substitute your surname (that is, your variation of the Guédry surname as Labine, Guildry, Jeddry, Geddry, etc.) on the crest.

The Guédry Crest represents all descendants of Claude Guédry and Marguerite Petitpas. Over the years our Guédry name has undergone many changes and today exists in over forty variations as shown below. It is not possible to show all the variations of the Guédry surname on a single crest. Current research strongly indicates that Guédry was the surname used by Claude Guédry - the first known Guédry in North America; therefore, the Guédry Crest uses this surname. This Guédry surname is symbolic of all variations that have occurred since Claude Guédry and Marguerite Petitpas first settled in Acadia.

Several other "Guédry" crests can be found on the internet and through commercial vendors. None of these crests have an historic or any other connection to Claude Guédry or the Guedry family. Of the several other "Guédry" crests researched on the internet and from several commercial vendors, it was determined that each of these crests was developed for commercial sale and did not have any specific connection to the Guédry family.

The colors and symbols on these crests are not related to the Guédry family in any way.

On Friday, 15 August 2008, the National Day of the Acadians, the Guédry Crest was unveiled on the Plaza of the Acadian Memorial. The Guédry Crest is one of approximately thirty crests of Acadian families displayed in the Plaza of the Acadian Memorial in St. Martinville, Louisiana. Each of the crests are artistically done in ceramic on the Plaza. It is an honor for our family to have its crest displayed at the Acadian Memorial – a truly unique memorial visited by people from throughout North America and the world.

SPECIAL THANKS
Thanks to member Lindsey Hardee of *Design to the Rescue* for taking the rough drawing of the Guédry Crest Committee, recommending improvements and professionally designing the final Guédry Crest. She has given all of us a wonderful crest of which we truly can be proud. The innovative services and solutions of *Design to the Rescue* can be seen at:
http://www.designtotherescue.com/

THE GUÉDRY CREST - THE STORY OF OUR FAMILY

The Guédry Crest tells the story of the Guédry family from its French origins through the struggle of its exile and eventually its resettlement throughout North America and Europe. It is the crest of the Guédry family in all of its name variations.

Each item and color on the crest has special significance. Below is an explanation of the colors and components of the Guédry crest as they tell the story of the Guédry family.

ESCUTCHEON – The field of the escutcheon (shield) is divided into two parts: the chief (broad band across the top) and the field per quarterly with simple cross charge.

CHIEF – The chief is divided into three sections per pale (vertical lines) of blue, white and red tinctures (colors). Blue, white and red are the colors of the Acadian flag. These colors, the same as the Tricolor of the French flag, signify the French origins of the Acadians and the Guédry family.

BLUE represents the personal color of the Holy Virgin Mary – the patron saint of the Acadians. It also signifies loyalty and truthfulness – traits the Guédry family exhibited throughout their lives in Acadie and during the bleakness of deportation.

WHITE represents peace. In Acadie our Guédry forefathers remained neutral between the English and French, striving for peaceful lives. Even while being deported, they maintained their peaceful demeanor.

RED represents fortitude – the strength of mind that enabled our Guédry ancestors to endure the almost unbearable treatment by the English and emerge a stronger people.

The YELLOW STAR symbolizes Our Lady of the Assumption (the Virgin Mary), the patron saint of the Acadians.

The CREEL (fish basket) symbolizes the unique relationship between the Guédry family of Merligueche and the Mi'kmaq nation. The Mi'kmaq taught their Guédry neighbors how to survive the harsh Merligueche environment using the bounty of the land and the sea.

The FIDDLE symbolizes the unique culture of the Guédry family - their music, their food, their faith, their joie de vivre. Although their culture has evolved and changed through the generations and where they may live, it has remained uniquely theirs. An old musical instrument, the fiddle has remained a constant of this culture wherever the music is played: in old Acadie, in Louisiana, in Nova Scotia, on Prince Edward Island, in New Brunswick or in France.

CHARGES – The four symbols in the quarterly fields represent the evolution of the Guédry family from the days of Old Acadie to today. The silver tincture of two fields represents the neutrality and peace that our ancestors strove to maintain during their two hundred years in Acadie. The blue tincture of two fields represents loyalty and truthfulness – qualities exhibited by our Guédry forefathers through much adversity.

The FLEUR-DE-LIS symbolizes the French origin of Claude Guédry, the North American forefather of our family. The GOLD color symbolizes the generosity of our ancestors toward others – striving for better lives for all.

The COAST-PILOT (boat) represents the early life of the Guédry family in North America. Settled near the Mi'kmaq at Merligueche, the Guédry's were excellent coasting pilots – plying the waters between Merligueche and Ile Royale.

Continued on page 11

IN THE NEWS-HISTORICAL NEWS TIDBITS

By Judy Ross

If you're interested in a literary pilgrimage — or if your mission is purely gastronomic — sooner or later you must find your way to "Petitpas Restaurant" on West 29th Street, where the poet Yeats was accustomed to hold convivial sway over the clientele. A painting of the poet and his artistic salon, dining perhaps at the very table you may occupy, hangs importantly close to proprietor Nick Petitpas' excellent French kitchen.

Here in one of New York's oldest restaurants, diners-out can combine all the advantages of fine food, really low tariffs (complete dinners start at $1.85) and an atmosphere that is unique even in our cosmopolitan city. You would never choose Petitpas for an evening's relaxation from a mere look at its unpretentious front in a shabby commercial district on 29th Street. But once you have descended the stairway ("petitpas" means "little steps" in French) you find yourself in a warm and cheerful atmosphere. Yes, there's a fireplace, and the traditional checkered table-cloths to make you right at home. Brick inside walls are decorated with twining vines and even in winter a few artificial flowers set a merry tone. The menu boasts all the familiar French delights from Coq Au Vin to Sweetbreads. We recommend the frog's legs to the venturesome.

Still on the track of French cuisine, but too busy to travel downtown, we might mention the Café Brittany on 56th Street near 9th Avenue. A little knowledge of the French tongue will help you manage your order; the waitresses seem to be fresh from "la belle France." They will recommend their onion soup with deserved pride — and you can follow this with "escargots" (snails served with a tangy garlic sauce — a typical native delicacy served in only a few authentic spots around this city), brains with a caper garnish or the old French favorite, coq au vin (chicken in red wine sauce). For a really festive touch, red or white table wine here sells for 20 cents the glass and other liquors are similarly priced. Vermouth cassise makes an exotic apertif, if you hanker for that authentic atmosphere.

Barnard Bulletin-(New York, New York) Feb. 19, 1953

Guidry's Seafood Invites Public To Tuesday Open House

A. A. GUIDRY

Borrowing a well-known slogan, A. A. Guidry, Kerrville's newest businessman, adds pertinent changes and promises that when fresher and better seafood is found, Guidry's will offer it to Hill Country patrons.

For the city's newest business firm—Guidry's Seafood—is open at 814 Main Street, and offers a full line of fresh seafood, "Direct from the wharf-side to you." Mr. and Mrs. A. A. Guidry have chosen Kerrville for their permanent family home, coming here from Beaumont where Mr. Guidry has been in the seafood market business and operates his own shrimp boats off the coast. Besides Mr. and Mrs. Guidry are three children, A. A. Jr. (Bubba), age 5; Ronnie, 1, and Zelma Katherine, 6. The family belong to the Catholic Church.

Insuring the finest and freshest seafood obtainable, Mr. Guidry will operate his own trucks from the coast to Kerrville. Shrimp and oysters will be a house specialty.

Mr. and Mrs. Guidry cordially invite the general public to inspect their place of business and attend their open house next Tuesday, December 21, at 814 Main Street.

The Kerrville Times, Kerrville, TX-1955

AND HOW DID I GET THAT NAME? SUMMERALL MARTIN GUIDRY by Marty Guidry

Summerall Martin Guidry

Most of us have common given names – a name our parents liked, the name of a saint with a quality that our parents hoped we would have, the name of a grandparent, etc. Occasionally, parents give their child an unusual name – a name that separates him from his peers. The source is often lost as the years pass by.

My Dad's name was Summerall Martin Guidry. Martin was the middle name of his father Emmanuel Martin Guidry and has been passed down to me and to my grandson. But Summerall as a given name is quite rare – possibly unique. How did Dad's parents decide on Summerall – a name that my Dad was called throughout his life.

As World War I heated up in Europe and young men in the United States lined up to serve their county, my grandfather Emmanuel Martin Guidry volunteered to enlist in the U. S. Army and joined the recently-formed 1st Infantry Division – the Big Red One.

Shortly he shipped overseas and fought in trenches against the Germans in France during 1917 and 1918. Injured twice, he recovered in French hospitals and returned to the front lines where he was cited for bravery by both the French and the American governments.

The Commander of the First Division during World War I was a veteran of the Spanish-American War, the Philippine Insurrection and the China Relief Expedition. Born in 1867 in Florida, Charles Pelot Summerall graduated from Porter Military Academy in South Carolina in 1885 and then attended the U.S. Military Academy from which he graduated in 1892. He then began a lifelong career in the U. S. Army and was promoted to Brigadier General in 1917 and Major General in 1918.

My grandfather served as an Aide to General Summerall during the latter part of WWI and admired the leadership of his commander. He maintained a friendship with General Summerall after the War. When my Dad was born in 1922, he named his son Summerall after his former Commander.

Many people would have resented such an odd first name as Summerall, but my Dad used this name throughout his life. After all, no one ever forgot his name or confused him with another person.

My grandfather died as a young man in 1932 – partially because of being gassed twice by the Germans in World War I. His friend General Summerall did not forget his namesake, my Dad.

In April 1942 with the U.S. having just entered World War II, my father was a senior at Southwestern Louisiana Institute (today the University of Louisiana at Lafayette) in Lafayette, Louisiana. Again young men, driven by patriotism, volunteered for military service. My Dad quit college two months before graduating, enlisted in the U.S. Army and requested service in the 1st Infantry Division. There were no positions available in the Big Red One and he was assigned to the 27th Infantry

AND HOW DID I GET THAT NAME? SUMMERALL MARTIN GUIDRY

Division. He fought with honor against the Japanese in the Pacific battles at Einewetok, Saipan and Okinawa ending his war service with the Occupation of Japan. General Summerall never forgot the young soldier named after him. Periodically during the war he would send Dad a small gift and always endorsed it "To my namesake with all good wishes, C P Summerall, Major General, Chief of Staff". I often wonder if any other young soldiers received such a package from the States. It must have been quite a morale lifter for Dad as he sat in a foxhole or ate his rations during a lull in the fighting.

General Summerall served as Chief of Staff of the U.S. Army from 1926 through 1930 when he retired from the U. S. Army after 38 years of distinguished military service. During World War II, when he remembered fondly a young man fighting in the middle of the Pacific Ocean, he was President of the Citadel in Charleston, South Carolina – a position he held for 22 years. Today the Citadel's award-winning demonstration team Summerall's Rifles honors General Summerall.

And now you know why my Dad was so proud of his name Summerall and treasured it throughout his life.

General Summerall

BOOK NOOK

THE OLD MAN TOLD US- Excerpts from Micmac History 1500-1950 by Ruth Holmes Whitehead

The Mi'kmaq people have been living in what is now Atlantic Canada for two thousand years or more, yet written history has largely ignored them, presenting them merely as a homogeneous mass or as statistics.

Renowned Mi'kmaq specialist Ruth Holmes Whitehead, former staff ethnologist and assistant curator in history at the Nova Scotia Museum, tries to redress that omission by restoring to the collective memory a true sense of the Mi'kmaq people.

In this rich collection, oral and written Mi'kmaq accounts are juxtaposed with contemporary European perceptions of native peoples, as documented in letters, journals, court cases, and much more. Above all, *The Old Man Told Us* is a historical jigsaw puzzle, a display of fragments in which one can capture moments in the lives of particular people. It is a book of excerpts from what little documentation has survived over the centuries.

LOUISIANA INDIAN TALES
By Elizabeth Moore & Alice Couvillon

Louisiana Indian Tales vividly recreates the struggles and triumphs of the state's first inhabitants. Dating back to 10,000 B.C. when the Paleo-Indians occupied the area and huge woolly mammoths and mastodons roamed the land, these poignant stories are based on archaeological evidence and historical knowledge traced through modern-day findings.

As archaeologist Dr. Ben Dominique and his young friends Richard and Rob soon discover while on an expedition in the first story, Louisiana is a state rich in Indian culture. Together the trio unearth the proud, industrious, and resourceful life-styles of the many cultures that contributed to this state's fascinating history. The tales in this collection for young readers focus on many tribes from around the state-the Tchefuncte, Choctaw, Chitimacha, Caddo, Houma, and Bayougoula.

THE GUEDRY CREST - THE STORY OF OUR FAMILY, Cont'd. from page 8

The weather-beaten OAK TREE symbolizes the difficult days of deportation for our Guédry ancestors and their survival through it. It represents the strength of our family as they were uprooted and exiled, separated from mother and father, brother and sister, cousin and friend; spread throughout the world. They endured the hardships, the persecution and the oppression; they survived and they spread their roots firm and deep. The BLACK color denotes the grief experienced during the dark days of exile.

The GLOBE symbolizes the worldwide breadth of our family today – throughout the United States, Canada, the Caribbean, Europe and even the Southern Hemisphere. Because of the firm, deep roots laid by our Guédry ancestors, we are truly a global family today tied closely together by the strong beliefs, characteristics and traits of our forefathers and passed along to us – generation by generation.

GOLD CROSS – The cross quartering the field symbolizes the strong Christian faith of our Guédry forefathers – the faith that helped them survive the early days of Acadie, endure the difficult years of deportation and overcome the struggle for survival afterwards to build the strong family that we are today. The gold tincture represents the generosity of our forefathers throughout their lives – a cornerstone of their faith.

MOTTO – The motto "Dieu, Famille, Acadien" translates to "God, Family, Acadian" – the guiding lights that have held our Guédry family together for over three hundred years and will continue to serve us well in the future.

The Guedry family crest as it appears at the Acadian Memorial in St. Martinville, LA

The Acadian Memorial, St. Martinville, LA.

THE GUÉDRY CREST - THE STORY OF OUR FAMILY

The Guédry crest represents all direct descendants of Claude Guédry and Marguerite Petitpas. The Guédry name has many variations in spelling today. All variations are represented by the Guédry crest. These variations include:

Guédry	Gaidry	Jeddrie
Guedry	Gaidrie	Jeddry
Guedrie	Gaidry	Jederie
Guedris		Jedrey
	Geddrie	Jedrie
Guidry	Geddry	Jedry
Gudiry	Gedree	
Guidery	Gedrie	Labeen
Guidrey	Gedry	Labene
Guidrie		Labine
Guiddry	Gettry	LaBine
Guiddery		
Guiddery	Gidrie	LaBean
Guiedri	Gidry	LaBeau
Guiedry		Labeau
Guildrie		Lledre
Guildry		
		Yedri
Guitry		

Heraldic Crests, done in mosaic, line the sidewalk before the cross and around the Eternal Flame in the Meditation Garden at the Acadian Memorial in St. Martinville, LA.

The GEUDRY family crest was installed and recognized on August 15, 2008.

The Vaudville Team of Jim Jedrey & Little Eddie Kelly
By Bernard Geddry

Many old timers (like me) remember the Ed Sullivan Show, a mainstay of network TV in the 50s and 60s. Everybody watched that show. One of the mainstays was the heavily accented and quite hilarious ventriloquist, Senor Wences. He was the one who popularized the technique of putting a pair of eyes on his index finger, hanging hair or putting ears on top of his closed fist, and painting lips on the outside of his index finger and thumb. This was supposed to make you believe the hand was alive and doing the talking rather than the tight-lipped Senor Wences. It worked. When his finger and thumb moved up and down the illusion became a reality…and it made you laugh.

Well, I'm looking at one of those sets of eyes right now as I write this article but they never belonged to the Senor. They belonged to one of his best friends, fellow ventriloquist Jim Jedrey whose team of Jim Jedrey and Little Eddie Kelly entertained New Englanders for two decades. Who knows who came up with the idea first.

Jim, or Jimmy Geddry as he was known offstage, never made it to the "Sullivan" show like his buddy Wences but he did make a lot of folks laugh just the same. He made me laugh. He was my favorite uncle.

He used the stage name Jedrey because the Nova Scotia Geddrys and their close New England cousins pronounce our family name with a soft "G" so it sounds like a "J". He wanted to make sure his public would pronounce his name the way he did so he adjusted the spelling accordingly.

Jimmy was born on October 4th, 1906 in Cambridge, Massachusetts. He was the eleventh of twelve children born to an Acadian father and an Irish mother. Jimmy's dad was Jean Adrien Geddry, a great grandson of Augustin Guedry, the founder of St. Alphonse, Nova Scotia, the person in whose honor the family recently dedicated a plaque. His Acadian genealogy is James Geddry; Jean Adrien Geddry/Mary Powers; Evariste Geddry/Francoise Saulnier; Philippe Geddry/Angelique Therriau; Augustin Guedry/Marie Jeanson; Pierre Guedry/Marguerite Brasseau; Claude Guedry/Marguerite Petipas.

The Vaudeville Team of Jim Jedrey & Little Eddie Kelly

Jimmy's parents imbued him with values that would guide him for the rest of his life. They were determined that their children would escape the poverty of the early twentieth century and the depression that followed. Their endeavor was successful. One of the children became Superintendent (CEO) of the Watertown Arsenal, where big naval guns were designed and built for the great behemoths of WWII. Others became machinists, tool makers and small business owners. A grandson became a successful columnist on the sports page of the Boston Globe. Jimmy wanted to make people happy. He became a ventriloquist.

It all started because he was curious. Though he had only an eighth grade education, common in the early 20th century, he taught himself many things by reading books. He learned to read music and play the piano as a teenager. Somehow, he learned to play the saxophone too and actually played professionally in a 1920's "Jazz" band. Along the way, he came across a book on ventriloquism and it fascinated him. The book taught him how to talk without moving his lips. He was hooked for life. All he needed was a "Vent" doll.

He started by removing the head of his older sister's discarded baby doll and "modifying" it so its lower jaw could move, thereby simulating speech while he was doing the talking. That wasn't satisfactory for very long, so he saved his pennies until he could afford a better doll, one that was designed and built for "beginner" ventriloquists. By the time he was done, he had a collection of six Vent dolls, some quite elaborate.

The first doll on the floor, on the left, is the one that belonged to his sister. The one on the far right, sitting on the couch is the most functional . Besides the standard movable lower jaw and rotatable head, Eddie Kelly II has movable eyes, eyelids, and eyebrows. He required a great deal of skill to control and was quite convincing.

Jimmy Geddry's Vent Doll Collection

Inside Eddie's body is a pole attached to his head. His body has an opening in the back where the ventriloquist's hand fits in and grasps the pole. Manipulating it moves Eddie's head back and forth or up and down. Four metal rings are tied to cords that lead to Eddie's head through holes or "venues" in the pole. Each ring controls one of the head's functions by inserting a finger and pulling (or releasing). A skilled ventriloquist would put his hand inside the doll's body, grasp the pole and simultaneously insert four of his fingers into the rings. Imagine being able to orchestrate all this while speaking and telling jokes, rotating Eddie's head so he looks at either the performer or the audience, moving his eyes and even winking at appropriate times, and raising or lowering his eyebrows to indicate emotional responses like surprise or concern. Jimmy Geddry was able to do just that. Unbelievable!

A Ventriloquist Museum says Eddie Kelly II is a twin for Paul Winchell's "Jerry Mahoney" of 50s and 60s fame. In the picture above, the doll sitting on the pint-sized rocker is the original Eddie Kelly, the doll Jimmy used for most of his performances.

The Vaudville Team of Jim Jedrey & Little Eddie Kelly

On the couch is Rosie, Eddie's chic girlfriend, Willie, his African American doll, and Eddie Kelly II. In the front row are Jimmy's "starter" doll, and a miscellaneous head (with her pole stuck in a vase) which Jimmy used for reasons known only to him.

Three of the heads, Eddie Kelly, Eddie Kelly II and Rosie, were made by the most famous Vent Doll creator of the 20th century, Frank Marshall. Marshall was famous because he was the artist who carved "Charlie McCarthy" and most of his pals.

One last comment on the name "Eddie Kelly". It was chosen because it can be said without moving the lips. Try it yourself. Open your lips about a half inch and concentrate on keeping your lips still. Then say, Eddie Kelly, Eddie Kelly. It's easy! You are now a Ventriloquist!

There was more to Jimmy Geddry's life than ventriloquism. He was also an expert machinist and parts inspector. He was employed by his brother at the Watertown Arsenal in Massachusetts when he wasn't on tour with Eddie Kelly.

Marshall carving a Vent Doll head

He used to brag that he was so good at his job that it was kept waiting for him when he came back from a tour. Of course, his brother *was* the "big boss".

Jimmy was also an expert stock-picker and had moderate success in "the market" after the crash of 1929. He claimed he purchased small amounts of crippled blue chip stocks each week with a dollar from his salary. He must have done something right as he was able to retire to Arizona at the "young" age of fifty-seven, an unusual feat in the 1960s.

In 1939, Jimmy married his beautiful blond companion Florence Yannis. While on tour, they came into contact with many famous performers of the 40s and 50s, including Edgar Bergen. For those readers who never heard of Edgar Bergen, he was Candice Bergen's father and the Ventriloquist behind "Charlie McCarthy" and "Mortimer Snerd". If you don't know who Candice Bergen is…congratulations, you might live until the 22nd century. It was on one of those tours that they met and became close friends of Senor Wences.

Jimmy and Florence also traveled extensively throughout the Caribbean and Cuba. They never had children but stayed together in a loving relationship until Florence's death in 1997. Jimmy died in 2002, on Saint Patrick's Day at the age of ninety-five.

Bernard Geddry, Jimmy's nephew, and his wife Barbara, his best friends, took care of Jimmy in his last years and now lovingly care for his collection of Vent Dolls and Vaudeville memorabilia.

H. D. GUIDRY, M. D.

OFFERS his professional services to the citizens of Vermilionville and vicinity.

Office on Lafayette Street, near the Convent.

April 2d. 1870—1y.

DUES REMINDER

Attached is a membership application for renewing your membership in Les Guedry d'Asteur. Our dues are very reasonable at $6.00 for individuals and $10 for a family.

By joining and paying your dues, you provide us with the financial resources to participate in many projects, one being the CMA 2009 reunion in Bathurst, New Brunswick.

Please take a moment, complete the Membership Application, enclose a check and send it to the address on the Application. It will help all of us do so much for the family. And, if you would like to join at one of the Benefactor Levels, it would let us do even more.

The Kerrville Times (Kerrville, Texas), June 9, 1955

Les Guidry d'Asteur

http://freepages.genealogy.rootsweb.ancestry.com/~guedrylabinefamily/

The Guedry-Labine Family Genealogical Database
Developed by the Les Guidry d'Asteur, Inc. Genealogy Committee

http://freepages.genealogy.rootsweb.ancestry.com/~guidryrm/Guedry-Labine/

The Louisiana State Archives

This is the official website for the Louisiana State Archives. It provides a very nice overview of the archival holdings and services. Although there are no images of original documents at this time, there is a very nice index to Confederate Pension Applications with numerous Guidry records. Click on Research Library under Sections of Organization, then Confederate Pension Applications to the left of the top photograph, then Search the Database.

http://www.sos.louisiana.gov/archives/archives/archives-index.htm

Covered Bridges of New Brunswick, CA

Becaguimec River

Trout Creek No. 5

Magnetic Hill Covered Bridge

Point Wolfe

Forty Five River No. 1

Digdeguash River No. 4

THE 2009 GUEDRY-LABINE & PETITPAS REUNION

Congres Mondial Acadien (CMA) for 2009 will be held on the Acadian Peninsula in New Brunswick from 7 August - 23 August 2009. CMA activities will be centered around Caraquet, New Brunswick. You can click on this website to keep up with the events planned for the 2009 CMA.

http://www.cma2009.ca/

We are having our Guedry-Labine & Petitpas Reunion on Sunday, 16 August 2009 in the Conference Center of Danny's Inn in Bereford, New Brunswick. Beresford is just five miles north of Bathurst, New Brunswick and Danny's Inn is on Highway 134 just south of Beresford. Bathurst has a rich Acadian history that we'll explore in the coming months.

We will begin about 8:30 am and have activities until 5:00 pm. More on the agenda, activities and displays is forthcoming and will include formal sessions with music, presentations, etc. as well as time to mingle and get to know your cousins.

There will be a superb buffet lunch. It'll be a Hot & Cold Dinner Buffet that includes roast beef smothered in peppercorn gravy, sweet & sour meat balls, lasagna, chicken wings, potato casserole, coleslaw, tossed green salad, carrot salad, rolls, carrot cake, cherry cheesecake, fresh fruit salad, coffee and tea.

Registration information was sent out in August to those on our distribution list. A copy of the registration form will be attached to the next few issues of this newsletter. It is not too early to secure lodging. The website below contains a number of motels, hotels and bed & breakfasts in the Bathurst area.

http://www.bathurst.ca

The 2009 CMA website has an excellent page on accommodations within the Acadian Peninsula. Visit it by clicking on this link:

http://www.cma2009.ca

The official New Brunswick Tourism Website is at the link below. You can learn about interesting locations, sites and activities at this website. By clicking on the word "Guides" in the left column of the page, you can order a free 2008 Experience New Brunswick Vacation Planner" which is excellent.

http://www.tourismnewbrunswick.ca/en-CA/GeoLanding_US?source=other

New Brunswick Accommodations - CMA 2009

The Guidry-Labine family reunion is scheduled to take place August 16, 2009, in the town of Bathurst, not far from Caraquet. Here are a few more links for accommodations in those areas. We'll add more details about our reunion in the next few months.

BATHURST - http://www.bathurst.ca/english/home/

Authentique Bed & Breakfast Enjoy our 4 star B&B in a heritage home of the 20's with 'Arts & Craft's influences, conveniently located in the heart of Bathurst. You are welcome to relax in a cozy atmosphere with personalized service. Spacious rooms with very comfortable beds, cable TV, DVD, MP3, wireless internet, work desk and telephone. Each room has a private bathroom. Breakfast 'A la Carte' will be served in our elegant dining room.

Comfort Inn Bathurst Conveniently located on St. Peter Avenue. Close to shopping and offices. 35 person meeting room available.

John's Motel Our rooms have a full bath and shower, color television with cable, and most importantly comfortable beds! We also boast a swimming pool and an area for picnics. We also have in-room coffee.

Sea'scape Cottage This is our fully equipped beach house located on the beautiful Bay of Chaleur in Bathurst, New Brunswick. Select the virtual tour button to have a closer look.

CARAQUET - http://www.ville.caraquet.nb.ca/

Hotel Paulin "The Pearl of Baie des Chaleurs", Caraquet. Internationally acclaimed, seaside hotel and country inn, c.1891, rich in Acadian history. Luxurious waterfront suites, French country rooms, licensed fine dining, golf and spa packages. Hotel Paulin has the charm, elegance and inn keeping spirit of the 19th century. It offers intimate surroundings with old-world French village charm. It has been written up by the New York Times, Montreal Gazette, Fodor's and Frommer's, La Presse , Paris Match Magazine, Micheline Guide, France's Le Routard. The cuisine is innovative, upscale, inspired by local fresh foods with a Sommelier wine pairing menu.

La Maison Touristique Dugas House built by one of the first Acadian architects (1926). 10 minute walk through wooded area to private beach. Close to the Acadian Peninsula tourist attractions.

Motel Colibri 12 rooms smoking and non-smoking. 2 double beds. Telephone, cable television, air conditioning. Free outside pool. Continental breakfast.

Super 8 Motel 50 guest rooms including 18 junior suites and 1 Jacuzzi suite - Rooms with balconies overlooking the Acadian Coast and Le Carrefour de la Mer (Crossroads of the Sea) - Swimming pool with three-story 80 foot water park and kiddie pool - Whirlpool - Complimentary continental breakfast

Les Guidry d'Asteur

Share your ideas for the Newsletter

Contact:

**Marty Guidry
6139 North Shore Drive
Baton Rouge, LA 70817

225-755-1915
guidryrm@cox.net**

'GENERATIONS' newsletter is now in its sixth year. We hope to provide our readers with an interesting, informative and entertaining newsletter. Your input is always welcome and we look forward to another year of sharing family history and news with you.

The Guedry-Labine Family Newsletter, GENERATIONS, serves as a focal point for family members to share and learn about us. To submit your ideas, articles or comments, please contact:

Allie Guidry
txguidry2000@yahoo.com

Marty Guidry
guidryrm@cox.net

Les Guidry d'Asteur Officers and Committees

OFFICERS:
President - Martin Guidry (LA)
Vice-President - Elaine Clement (LA)
Secretary - Billy Harrell Guidry (LA)
Treasurer - Daniel "Chuck" Guidry (LA)

COMMITTEES:
Website - Becky Boggess (IA) - Chairperson
    Annie Grignon-Labine (QU) - Translator
    Elaine Clement (LA) - Translator
    Martin Guidry (LA)*

Genealogy - Daryl LaBine (FL/ON) - Chairperson
    Bernard Geddry (AZ)
    Mark Labine (MN)
    Daniel "Chuck" Guidry (LA)
    Martin Guidry (LA)*

Finance - Cheryl Guidry Tyiska (MD) - Chairperson
    Paul Labine (IL)
    Marshall Woolner (OR)
    Gloria Parrent (TX)
    Chuck Guidry (LA)*

Membership - Charlene Guidry Lacombe (LA) - Chairperson
    Gayle Guidry (LA) - Special Projects
    Warren Guidry (TX)*

Sales - Cindy Guidry Herdt (WA) - Chairperson
    Wayne Simoneaux (LA)
    Billy Harrell Guidry (LA)*

Publicity - Elaine Clement (LA) - Chairperson
    Margaret Jeddry (MA)
    Warren Guidry (LA)*

Newsletter - Allie Guidry Hardee (VA)
    Rachel Hardee (VA)
    Lindsey Hardee (OH)
    Martin Guidry

CAFA Board Member - Jeanette Guidry Leger (LA)

Les Guidry d'Asteur
REGISTRATION for 2009 REUNION
(L'enregistrement pour 2009 Réunion)

Name (Nom) _____
                  Last (Nom de famille)   First (Prénom)   Middle (Deuxième prénom)

Spouse (Épouse) _____
                 Maiden (Nom de jeune fille) First (Prénom) Middle (Deuxième prénom)

Children (Enfants) _____
                 First Names of Children (Prénoms de enfants)

Address (Adresse) _____
                 Street (Rue)

                   _____
                 City (Ville)   State (État/Province) Zip Code (Code postal) (Pays)

Telephone (Téléphone) _____

Fax (Numéro de télécopieur) _____

E-mail Address (Courriel) _____

Number of People Attending (Le numéro de Gens qui assistent) _____

No. of Buffet Meals at Reunion (A l'intention de Manger des Repas à la Réunion) _____
(Buffet meal will cost $20-$25 per person / Le repas de buffet coûtera $20-$25 par la personne)

Registration: Includes Reunion & 2009 Membership in *Les Guidry d'Asteur* /
   L'enregistrement: Inclut la Réunion & 2009 Sociétariat dans *Les Guidry d'Asteur*)

<u>Family -Parents and Children under 22</u> (Famille - Les parents et les Enfants sous 22):

    _____ $40.00 Dollars (Canadian dollars for Canadian payments; U. S. dollars for U. S. payments)
    (Dollars canadiens pour les paiements Canadiens; Dollars américains pour les paiements américains)

<u>Individual (Individuelle)</u>:

    _____ $20.00 Dollars (Canadian dollars for Canadian payments; U. S. dollars for U. S. payments)
    (Dollars canadiens pour les paiements Canadiens; Dollars américains pour les paiements américains)

Please return form and payment to: Make check payable to: *Les Guidry d'Asteur, Inc.*
(Retournez le formulaire et le paiement à:) (Libellez le chèque à: *Les Guidry d'Asteur, Inc.*)

Les Guidry d'Asteur, Inc.
Martin Guidry, President
6139 North Shore Drive
Baton Rouge, LA 70817

WINTER 2009

Volume 7, Issue 1

Les Guédry d'Asteur

GENERATIONS

IN THIS ISSUE

Charlene Lacombe Guidry-Recognized Nationally — 2

Charles Guildry dit Labine-Voyageur- by Mark Labine — 3

Guédry's Exiled to North Carolina-by Marty Guidry — 12

Bon Appetit - Recipes from the Guédry-Labine Family Cookbook — 15

Book Nook — 21

Geneaology/ Biography: Judge Greg G. Guidry — 40

With a new year upon us and our 2009 Reunion approaching quickly, this issue of "Generations" offers a mix of informative historical articles, a look ahead to our reunion in August and some great food and books to enjoy in the interim. We open this issue of "Generations" highlighting one of our members, Charlene Guidry Lacombe, of LA who recently received national honors for service to her community.

Mark Labine of MN then takes us to the late eighteenth century in the Canadian north country, the land of his great great great grandfather Charles Guildry dit Labine. Here we experience the legendary life of the voyageur in the thriving Canadian fur trade business.

Through diligent work, researchers recently pieced together another puzzle of the Guédry family when they discovered that a small group of 50 Acadians deported to North Carolina in early 1756 were almost all members of the Augustin Guédry family. Learn how, by piecing together information from seemingly unrelated sources, researchers were able to reconstruct the long-lost manifest list of the sloop Providence that transported these most unfortunate Acadians from their Acadian homeland to the marshes of North Carolina.

Rest a moment, take Bon Appetit to the kitchen and cook up some delicious Taco Beef Soup and Beer Bread to enjoy by the fireplace on a cold, late winter evening while glancing through one of the superb New Brunswick books reviewed in the Book Nook.

Don't get caught off guard by the very quick approach of our Guédry-Labine & Petitpas Reunion being held at Danny's Inn in Bathurst, New Brunswick on Sunday, 16 August 2009. Get all the details including agenda, housing, dining, transportation and other information near the back of this issue of "Generations". Several folks have already sent in their registration forms and are ready to have a great time meeting their cousins and enjoying the music, dance, presentations, exhibits and food at the reunion. Don't miss out on the great experience of Congrés Mondial Acadien and our Guédry-Labine & Petitpas Reunion. There is so much to do and experience with your cousins. We encourage you to register NOW for the reunion so we can better plan our day together and ensure everyone has a great experience. Right now, before you forget, pull out the Registration Form from the back of this newsletter, complete it and send it along with the registration fee to the address listed. If you later find you cannot attend, we will refund your registration fee per your request. We look forward to visiting with everyone in Bathurst this August.

We are planning a new feature in "Generations" for our members who own businesses. Each issue we will feature brief "business card" type ads of member-owned businesses. If you are a member and have your own business, send a copy of your business card or a brief ad to Allie Guidry, our editor, or Marty Guidry and we will include your business in upcoming issues of "Generations". You can send it by email or by regular mail. The appropriate addresses are listed in the back of this issue of "Generations".

CHARLENE GUIDRY LACOMBE, LES GUIDRY D'ASTEUR MEMBERSHIP CHAIR, RECOGNIZED NATIONALLY

Charlene Guidry Lacombe, Regent of Acadia Chapter, Daughters of the American Revolution and Chairman of the Louisiana Society Daughters of the American Revolution State Veterans, and Alma Brunson Reed, Acadia Chapter Public Relations Committee Chairman and State Chairman of Community Service Awards for the Louisiana Society Daughters of the American Revolution, recently co-authored the book 2007 Pictorial Directory of Acadia Parish Patriots. This book presents short biographies of many Acadia Parish, LA veterans.

The main program of the 4th Annual Veterans Day Program by the Acadia Chapter, Louisiana Society Daughters of the American Revolution held at the Rice Theatre in Crowley, LA on November 11, 2007 was a discussion of the Pictorial Directory by Charlene and Alma. Over 300 persons attended this program. Throughout the year preceding this Veterans Day Program, Charlene coordinated with seven area newspapers to feature stories on Acadia Parish veterans and their personal wartime experiences.

This superb 2007 Veterans Day program by the Acadia Chapter garnered an Outstanding Louisiana Chapter Award for a Community Event. The Acadia Chapter then won the Outstanding Regional Award in its seven-state region and the Outstanding National Award for the United States.

The 2007 Pictorial Directory of Acadia Parish Patriots presents a historical account of 196 men and women from Acadia Parish, LA who have served in the United States military. For each veteran the Pictorial Directory features family information, date and place of birth, date and place of marriage, date of death if deceased, spouse, children, parents and siblings. Additionally, the book includes a photograph of each veteran and his/her military history, awards and citations.

On July 10, 2008 Charlene and Alma represented the Acadia Chapter and the State of Louisiana at the National Award ceremony in Washington, D. C.. Presenting the National Award to Charlene and Alma was Karon Jarrard, National Chairman of Public Relations and Media Committee for the National Society of the Daughters of the American Revolution. We salute Charlene for her superb work as Regent of the Acadia Chapter and for garnering these outstanding state, regional and national awards for the Acadia Chapter.

Committed to honoring our nation's veterans, Charlene is also a member of Bugles Across America, an organization providing buglers for military funerals and functions. Charlene has played for military funerals and functions for more than 40 years and is active in local and state activities.

A few 2007 Pictorial Directory of Acadia Parish Patriots books are available for purchase. The cost is $30.00, shipping included. If you wish to purchase a book, please contact Charlene at:

Charlene Guidry Lacombe
226 Bulldog Lane
Iota, LA 70543

Or email at charleneguidry@hotmail.com

Charles Guildry dit Labine -Voyageur[1]

Painting of Voyageurs by Mary Hopkins

I am the Great Great Great Great Grandson of Jean Charles Guidry dit Labine (hereinafter referred to as Charles Guidry dit Labine). Charles lived in St. Jacques Quebec, which is located just to the northeast of Montreal. He was born in Boston, Massachusetts in the year 1760 to **Jean Augustin Baptiste Guidry dit Labine dit Labrador** and Marguerite Picotte. His father had been deported from Acadia in the year 1755 and ended up as a refugee in Boston, Mass. Jean's first wife, Helen Benoit, died sometime after 1753 (probably during the deportation) and Jean and Charles's mother Marguerite Picotte began living together in Boston in a common law marriage and began having children. They were not married in Boston because there was no Catholic Priest there. They had their common law marriage blessed in L'Assomption, Quebec in 1766 after they arrived there as refugees. It was at that time that the baptism of Jean Charles Guidry dit Labine was also validated.

Charles grew up in a farm located near a small parish called St. Jacques L'Achigan. His father had purchased the land in 1767 after spending the winter at the church in L'Assomption, Quebec. Since his parents were Acadian refugees, it cannot be expected that Jean Charles's family had much wealth. It was probably important that he find a way to earn his way as soon as possible. Fortunately, for those willing and strong enough, there were good cash paying jobs available at that time working in the fur trade industry as Voyageurs.

---

[1] Written by Mark Labine, Arden Hills, MN

Old Church in St. Jacques, Quebec

Family chart showing lineage of Jean Charles Guidry dit Labine and Mark Labine, the author of this story.

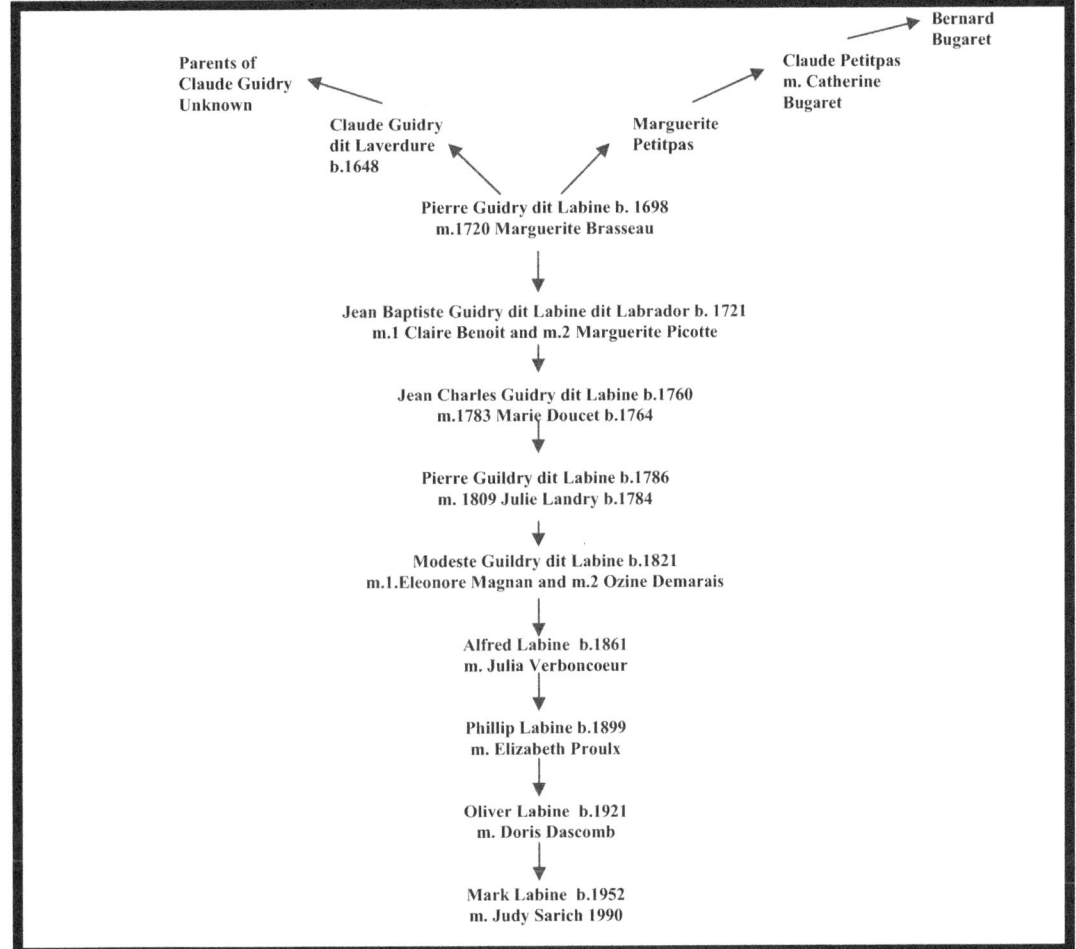

Voyageurs were the crews hired to man the canoes that carried trade goods and supplies to "rendezvous posts" (example: Grand Portage) where goods and supplies were exchanged for furs.

The fur trade was big business in New France and there was much money to be made in it. In early years the fur trade business was wide open and many early settlers risked the perils of traveling through Indian country to seek out Native trappers to trade with. These *coureurs des bois* were not looked upon favourably by Montreal authorities or royal officials. By 1681, the French authorities realized the traders had to be controlled so that the industry might remain profitable. There were simply too many *coureurs des bois* and the fur supply was flooding the market. They therefore legitimized and limited the numbers of coureurs des bois by establishing a system that used permits (*congés*). This legitimization created a "second-generation" coureur des bois: the **voyageur**, which literally means "traveller". This name change came as a result of a need for the legitimate fur traders to distance themselves from the unlicensed ones. **Voyageurs therefore, held a permit or were allied with a Montreal merchant who had one**.

Over time, Voyageurs came to be known as those men who did the hard labor required to trade furs. The voyageurs were highly valued employees of trading companies, such as the North West Company (NWC) and the Hudson's Bay Company (HBC). In 1779, Charles Guidry dit Labine signed on to work for the North West Company. We also know that at least three of Charles' brothers signed Voyageur contracts and were hired to work for the Northwest Company.

Today, the voyageurs are legendary, especially in French Canada and also in Minnesota. They are folk heroes celebrated in folklore and music. The reality of their lives was that being a Voyageur was hard work. For example, they had to be able to carry two 90 pound bundles of fur over portages. More suffered from strangulated hernias than any other injury.

Voyageurs who only paddled between Montreal and Grand Portage were known as "mangeurs de lard" (pork eaters) because of their diet, much of which consisted of salt pork. This is considered to be a derogatory term. Those who overwintered and ate "off the land" (mainly fish, pemmican and Rubaboo) were called "hommes du nord" (northern men) or "hivernants" (winterers).

Voyageurs were expected to work 14 hours per day and paddle at a rate of 55 strokes per minute. Few could swim. Many drowned in rapids or in storms while crossing lakes[2]. Portages and routes were often indicated by lob trees, or trees that had their branches cut off just below the top of the tree.

---

[2] Charles Guidry dit Labine's brother Marin (Mauthurin) died in the rapids at Lachine, Quebec.

Northwest Company Coat of Arms

Copies of Charles Guidry and his three brother's contracts or "engagements" are in the Quebec Archives reports for the years 1943-44 and 1946-47. I have a copy of a Voyageur contract signed by Charles Guidry dit Labine on April 20, 1779, on St. Paul Street in old Montreal, right behind the Notre Dame Cathedral. This contract provided that Charles Guidry would go by canoe to Michilimackinac and Lake Superior to secure furs for the Northwest Company. The literal translation of the "engagement" was as follows:

*"Before the Notary of the town and District of Montreal, in the province of tower Canada, there resident, the undersigned, Charles Guidry, of the parish of St., Jacques, who of his own free will has engaged and engages himself by these present to Messrs. McTavish and Frobisher, to this agreeing and accepting, at their first command to leave this town in the position of **voyageur mileau** in one of their canoes to make the voyage, as much going up to Michilimackinac as for coming down, to go and come and to take good and due care during the voyage, and in the said place of the Merchandise, Edibles, Furs, Utensils and of all the things necessary for the trip; to serve, obey and execute faithfully all that the said McTavish and Frobisher or any of their agents may command that is lawful and honest; to make their profit, avoid damage to them, warn them of it if it comes to his knowledge, and generally all that a good "engage" must and is obliged to perform; without being able to make any private agreement, neither to absent himself from or to quit the said service, under the penalties imposed by the law, and to lose his wages. This Engagement thus made, for and providing the sum of **two hundred and forty livre or old shillings** of this province, which they promise themselves to give and pay to the said "engage" one month after his return to this town, and on his departure a simple ordinary*

kit. Charles Guidry recognizes that he has received in advance on account of the said wages four piastres³."

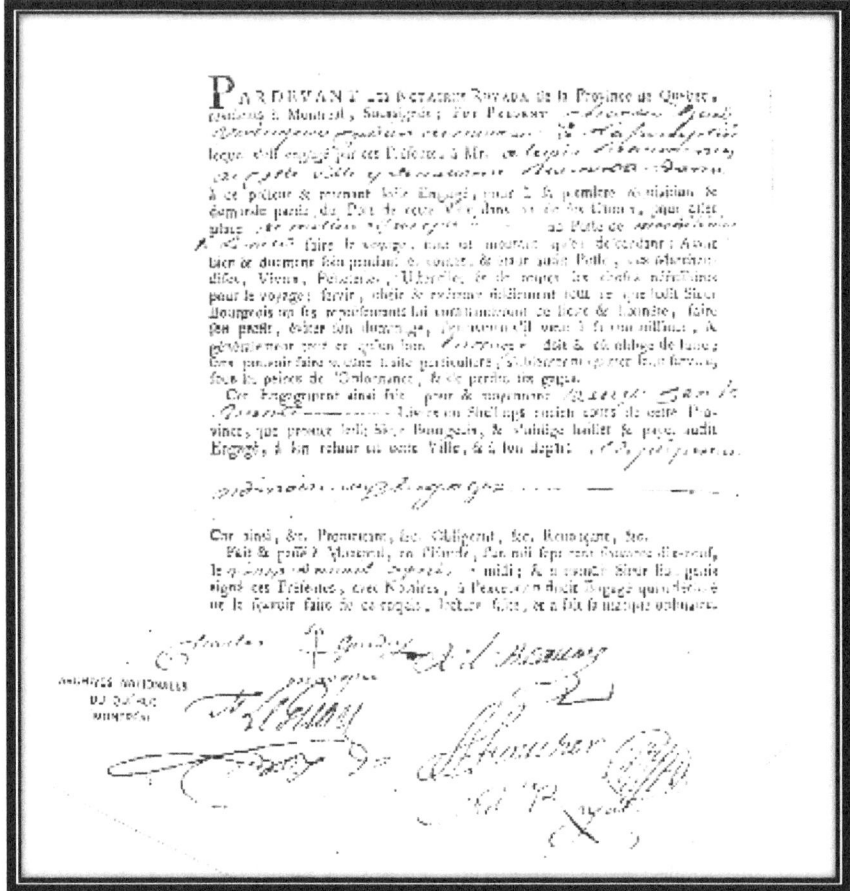

Copy of 1779 Charles Guidry Voyageur Contract (*unfortunately copy is hard to read*)

There are several interesting things to note about the Voyageur contract signed by Charles Guidry dit Labine in 1779.

- **First -** he was only 19 years old.

- **Second -** the contract is filed under the name "Guidry" and not "Labine". The family of Jean Baptiste continued to use the name Guidry or Guildry in their formal legal documents until at least 1879. The church records use the name Guildry in the entries I have read rather than Guidry. My Great Grandfather Modeste Labine signed a Mortgage

---

³ Piastres was a word used for "dollar" so 4 piastres would equal four dollars.

in 1870 using the signature "Modeste Guildry". Sometime after that the name Guidry disappears and only Labine is used. It appears from these records that the family was called Labine but they used Guidry or Guildry on their legal documents.

- **Third -** Charles could not sign his name and simply left an X where his signature would have been.

- **Fourth -** Charles was signed up to be a Voyageur Mileau or a middle canoeman and paid 240 livres. The more experienced Voyageurs were in the front and back of the canoe, with the middle men less experienced. More experienced Voyageurs would be paid 400 livres or even more.

- **Fifth -** Charles got paid 240 livres or old shillings (shilling ancient) for his work. According to Wikopedia, livres were printed and used by the French Republic until 1794. In 1795 the Franc was introduced and livres were not longer printed or made. This same article says that in 1795 the Livre was worth about 4 dollars American or 2.5 pounds English. Webster's New World Dictionary says that the Livre at the time it was discontinued in 1795 was worth about the same as an English pound. There is a website called www.measuringworth.com which provides a table to try to measure the worth of money between different time periods. According to this website's calculator, 240 livres or old shillings in 1779 would be worth $15,078.00 pounds in 2007 using the average earnings index. Other calculators I used show the earnings to be even higher. Trying to equate the actual value of money in 1779 compared to today is difficult but I believe it is a fair statement to say that the amount of money earned by Charles Guidry dit Labine as a Voyageur was a good wage and it must have been a sought after job by young French Canadian men in the province at the time.

- **Sixth -** The Voyageur contracts are said to number around 35,000. The University of Ottowa is setting up a database that will consolidate the information found in more than 35,000 notarized contracts signed by the voyageurs between 1755 and 1870 in the Montréal-Trois-Rivières corridor. Copies of these contracts are also available in the Quebec Archives.

Charles signed a contract to take a canoe from Montreal to Fort Michilimackinac and back. These canoes would depart in April or May from above Lachine Rapids in Montreal and paddle up the St. Lawrence River to the Ottawa River, up the Ottawa River to the Mattawa River, through Lake Nippissing, down the French River to Lake Huron, around Lake Huron to Sault St. Marie and then either on through Lake Superior to Fort William in Thunder Bay or down to Fort Michilimackinac. At Fort William in mid July there would be a rendezvous where the furs from the interior would be exchanged for the goods being brought from Montreal. The "mangeurs de lard" or summer Voyageurs would then head back to Montreal with the furs and the "hivernants" would take the goods and head back into the interior.

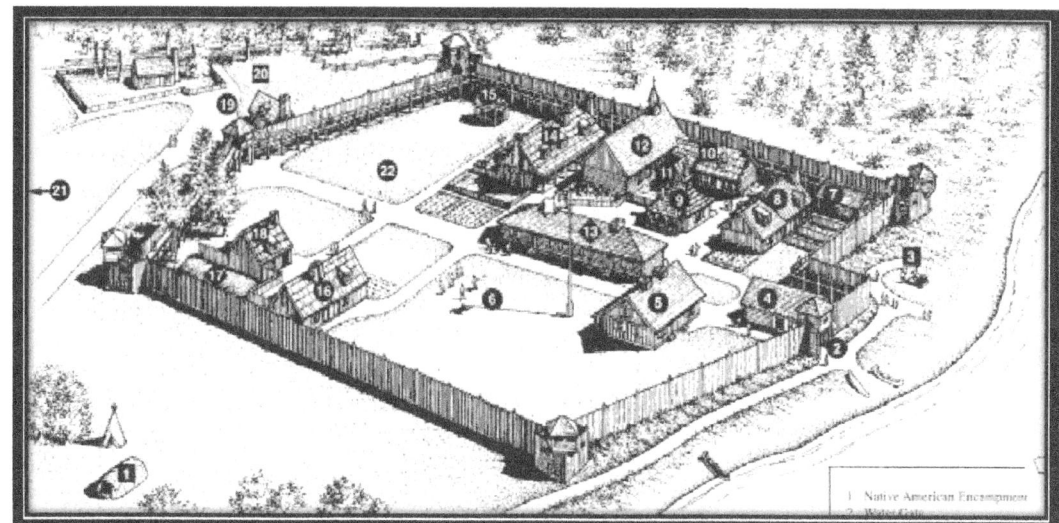
Fort Michilimackinac

We don't know how long Charles was a voyageur, although we know he eventually settled down on his Father's farm in St. Jacques. He married Marie Doucet in 1783 at the age of 22 and began his family shortly thereafter, so it would be a good guess that he was a voyageur for only a few years.

Charles's older brothers Joseph and Mathurin or Marin also signed voyageur contracts with the Northwest Company. Joseph (b.1759) signed a contract on May 14, 1779. Joseph bought lot number 318 from Germain Landry in 1780 and he raised his family in St. Jacques so I assume he was not a Voyageur long. Marin (his mother was Helen Benoit) was a Voyageur until 1784 when he drowned at the rapids of Lachine near Montreal. These rapids were long and dangerous and at times were deadly.

Picture of Lachine Rapids near Montreal, Canada

Olivier (b.1765) and Jean Baptiste Jr. (b.1768) appear to have been voyageurs for a longer period. It is believed Olivier was a voyageur until he was in his late twenties. He married when he was 28 years old in the year 1793 and settled down in Louisiana. On his birth certificate his father is listed as Augustin Guidry from Canada. I believe this refers to Jean Baptiste Guidry dit Labrador dit Labine. When Jean Baptiste's son Joseph married in Quebec in 1783 Jean Baptiste is shown with the middle name Augustin. It is said that Olivier made the trip from Montreal to New Orleans by canoe to find his distant relatives. After arriving in Louisiana, Olivier farmed along the Mermenou in Louisiana, married Felicite Aucoin and had a son Pierre who had the nickname "Canada".

Jean Baptiste Jr., (b.1768) we know, spent many years as a voyageur. He was, a "hivernant" (winterer). Jean Baptiste was also called a Northwester, or one of those who crossed the Grand Portage in Northern Minnesota on their way to the Red River settlement near Lake Winnipeg and traveled other routes beyond. In fact, we know that on January 14, 1800, Jean Baptiste, Jr. signed an "engagement" with the Northwest Company to go to the Red River Settlement. Shortly after that he married Josette Vincent (October, 1801), who was the third woman he would have children with. The first one, we know was an Indian woman. Their child was Jean Baptiste III, a Metis.

Charles Guidry dit Labine lived out his life in St. Jacques Quebec. His son Pierre took over his farm and then his grandson Modeste. It appears from maps and historical documents that they continued to sign their names "Guidry" or "Guildry" but called themselves "Labine". The Guidry or Guildry name disappeared, however, around the time that my ancestors came to the United States. My Great Grandfather, Alfred, simply uses the name Labine on his Homestead certificate when he acquired farmland in Minnesota.

The Voyageur legacy lives strong in Minnesota, where many place names and historical sites celebrate the history of the Voyageurs. A fur trading post museum exists in Pine City,

Minnesota celebrating the lives of the Voyageurs. At Fort William, Ontario, which is just north of the Minnesota Border, exists one of the largest living history attractions in North America, devoted to re-creating the days of the North West Company and the Canadian fur trade. Fort William Historical Park is recognized as one of the Top Ten Attractions in Canada and one of the world's most impressive historic sites.

Located on Lake Superior, Fort William became the key midway transshipment point for voyageurs ("winterers") paddling from the west carrying precious furs and voyageurs ("pork eaters") coming from the east bearing valuable trade goods and supplies. This allowed for an exchange of important materials-all within a single season.

Every year, an annual meeting known as The Great Rendezvous was held at Fort William. Every summer in July, Fort William became the centre of frenzied activity as hundreds of Natives, voyageurs, clerks, partners and agents arrived. These Rendezvous meetings required much work but there was also time for fun, with numerous campfires and many stories told.

Today, the Great Rendezvous is re-enacted each year in July, when hundreds of period re-enactors from across Canada and the United States gather at Fort William Historical Park to re-live the lively fur trade spirit much like their predecessors of centuries past. If you ever decide to attend one of these reenactments, remember your kinfolk Charles, Jean Baptiste, Mautherin (Marin) and Joseph Guidry dit Labine who worked as Voyageurs for the Northwest Company.

Note: Much of the information I obtained in this article I took from my book "La Verdure de Mirligueche" which lists a number of references, including "Five Fur Traders of the Northwest", by Theodore C. Blegen and edited by Charles M. Gates, (Minnesota Historical Society, St. Paul, 1965), and "The Voyageur" by Grace Lee Nute, (Minnesota Historical Society, St. Paul, 1955).

NEW RESEARCH REVEALS GUÉDRY'S EXILED TO NORTH CAROLINA
By Marty Guidry

Recently two genealogists independently discovered that several Guédry's were deported to North Carolina in early 1756. Mr. Paul LeBlanc, a Les Guédry d'Asteur member from Louisiana, through diligent research postulated in mid-2008 that some of the 50 Acadians disembarked at North Carolina in early 1756 were from the Guédry family.[1] In August 2008 Ms. Helen Morin Maxson of North Carolina after several years of research reached the same conclusion.[2] But who were these Guédry's and how did they arrive in North Carolina?

The Snow to North Carolina That Never Made It

Famous in Acadian annals, the snow Pembroke departed Goat Island near Port-Royal on 8 December 1755 under the helm of Captain Milton destined for North Carolina with 232 Acadians crowded aboard.[3] The Pembroke, however, never left the Bay of Fundy as the Acadians mutinied, took control of the Pembroke and made landfall at the entrance to the St. John River. There the Acadians disembarked on 8 February 1756 and with the help of Charles Deschamps de Boishébert, commandant of the French Fort Mènagoéche nearby, escaped to the interior of New Brunswick – some successfully trudging to Québec, but many dying during the cold winter months.

And the Sloop That Did

On 30 December 1755 Captain Samuel Barron sailed the sloop Providence from Halifax with approximately 50 Acadians aboard bound for North Carolina. These Acadians had been imprisoned briefly at George's Island in the harbor of Halifax. Although to date researchers have not located a manifest list for the Providence, other records strongly suggest the identities of most Acadians on the Providence.

Noted Acadian historian Placide Gaudet believed these deportees were Acadian deputies imprisoned on George's Island by the British in July 1755.[4] In fact, earlier the British had allowed these deputies to return to their families in other areas of Acadia and they eventually were deported with their families.[5]

After long hours of combing the archives in Nova Scotia and North Carolina during the past decade, researchers have been able to determine that most of the Acadians deported to North Carolina on the Providence were t related to Augustin Guédry and Jeanne Hébert. Augustin Guédry was the son of Claude Guédry and Marguerite Petitpas and his wife Jeanne Hébert very likely was the daughter of Jean Hébert and Jeanne Doiron. They had seven children: the twins Marie-Josephe and Hélène Guédry (born 1723), Jeanne Guédry (born 1725), Jean-Baptiste Guédry (born ca. 1728), Ursule Guédy (born 1731), Joseph Guédry (born 1735) and Pierre Guédry (born 1741).[6]

The Augustin Guédry & Jeanne Hébert Family

Information on the early lives of Augustin Guédry, Jeanne Hébert and their children is quite sketchy. Augustin Guédry first appears in the historical record as the 8-year old son of Claude Guédry and Marguerite Petitpas in the 1698 Census of Port-Royal, Acadia.[7,8,9] At this time his father Claude had ten cattle, two sheep, eight pigs, eight arpents of land and one gun. Claude Guédry had no fruit trees or domestic servants. It is not known with certainty where Augustin Guédry was born. We do know that his parents were living at Merligueche

NEW RESEARCH REVEALS GUÉDRY'S EXILED TO NORTH CAROLINA

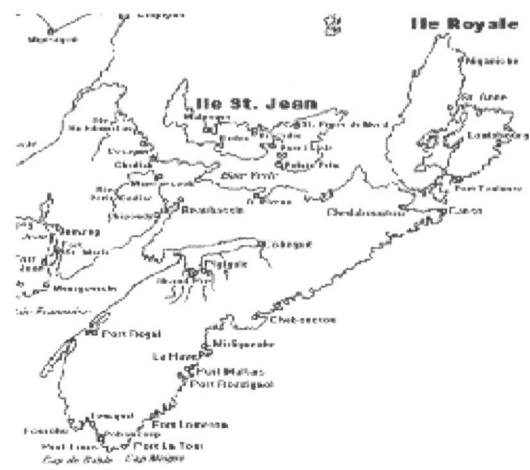

Early map of Nova Scotia showing the town of Merligueche

Photo of Lunenburg, Nova Scotia (formerly known as Merligueche)

(near present-day Lunenburg) in 1686[10,11,12,13]; however, it appears that by 1695 the family had moved to the Port-Royal area for Claude Guédry signed his name on 16 August 1695 to an Oath of Allegiance to the King of England administered by Commander Fleetwood Emes of the frigate Sorlings while he was at Port-Royal.[14,15,16,17]

By 1701 Claude Guédry and Marguerite Petitpas and their family had returned to Merligueche as their youngest son Paul Guédry was conditionally baptized there in January 1701 by Joseph Guyon (Dyon), husband of Paul's step-sister Marie Dugas.[18,19,20] On 14 January 1703 Baptiste Guédry conditionally baptized his younger sister Françoise Guédry at Merligueche on the day of her birth.[21,22] Later Father Félix Pain from St-Jean-Baptiste de Port-Royal Catholic Church visited Merligueche during a missionary journey to the East Coast and baptized both Paul Guédry and Françoise Guédry on 8 September 1705 with full church ceremonies. He entered the two baptisms in the register of St-Jean-Baptiste de Port-Royal Catholic Church on 27 October 1705 after returning from his missionary journey.[18,19,20,21,22,23]

In 1708 Augustin Guédry, now a young man of 16 years, was living in the Merligueche area with his parents and eight of his siblings. His brother Jean-Baptiste Guédry and wife Madeleine Mius were living nearby.[24,25]

War broke out between the Indians of the East Coast of Acadia and the English of New England in the summer of 1722. Caused by the ambushing and capture of Joseph d'Abbadie de Saint-Castin, highest chief of the Indians, by the English and by the plundering of the village of Nanrantsouak by the Bostonians in which they burnt the church, rectory and 33 wigwams, this war was the fourth between the Indians and the English since 1675. Officially begun by Governor Shute on 25 July 1722 with a declaration, this war was known variously as The Three Years War, Rale's War, Lovewell's War and Governor Dummer's Indian War. Nova Scotia Govenor Richard Philipps, who was at Canseau during the height of the fishing season, received news of the war from Governor Shute of Massachusetts. Immediately he organized a defense of the harbor there since the Indians had already seized 16 or 17 boats and fled to the harbors of the East Coast. Additionally, he sent several of his officers to the East Coast where they blamed both the Indians and the Acadians living among the Indians.[26]

NEW RESEARCH REVEALS GUÉDRY'S EXILED TO NORTH CAROLINA

At Merliguèche these officers captured Claude Guédry and Marguerite Petitpas and four of their sons with their families and brought all to New Hampshire. The sons were Claude Guédry, Phillipe Guédry, Augustin Guédry and Paul Guédry. It is uncertain who Phillipe Guédry was as no other record to date mentions a son of Claude Guédry and Marguerite Petitpas by this name. Perhaps it was another son of the family mistakenly called Phillipe. Shortly after they arrived in New Hampshire, Jacob Parker sent them to Boston; however, Bostonians did not want to admit them to their town because of a law forbidding foreigners from settling in the town. On 16 October 1722 the Acadians received an order from the councilors of Boston requiring them to go elsewhere. The officer charged with maintenance of the peace in Boston apparently never executed this order since he considered the Acadians prisoners, not immigrants to Boston.

On 9 January 1723 Jeanne Hébert, wife of Augustin Guédry, gave birth to twin daughters Hélène and Marie-Josephe in Boston. On the day of their birth their grandfather Claude Guédry conditionally baptized his new twin granddaughters.[26,27,28,29] A short time after these births the Acadians must have been released and returned to their homes for on 26 September 1723 Hélène Guédry and Marie-Josephe Guédry were baptized with full church ceremonies and their baptisms were recorded in the baptismal register of St-Charles-aux-Mines Catholic Church in Grand-Pré, Acadia.[27,28]

In September 1726 Jean-Baptiste Guédry and his son Jean-Baptiste Guédry fils along with three Mi'kmaq Indians were captured in the bay at Merliguèche, brought to Boston and charged with piracy. After quick trials all five were found guilty and hung on 13 November 1726. Shortly after Jean-Baptiste and his son had captured the boat, the captain of the boat asked Jean-Baptiste's mother, Marguerite Petitpas, and his brother Augustin Guédry to intercede and convince Jean-Baptiste to disembark from the boat. They attempted to convince Jean-Baptiste to leave the boat, but he would not.[30,31,32,33,34,35,36]

SITE OF THE GREAT ELM
Located on Boston Common, where many hangings took place in Boston in the 1700's.

Old State House, Boston, MA, where the trial of Jean-Baptiste Guédry and his son took place.

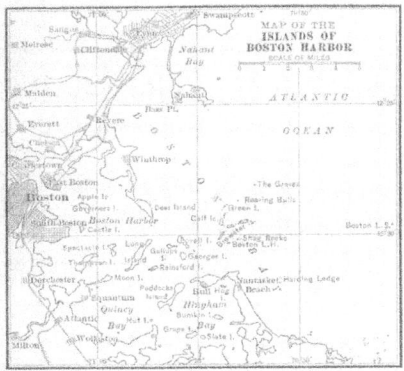

Map of Boston Harbour. Bird Island, which barely exsists now, is believed to be the burial site for Jean-Baptiste

After 1726 no record of Augustin Guédry or his family can be found for almost 26 years. Eventually, because of the heightened tension and increasing threats from the British, almost all Acadians at Merliguèche including Augustin Guédry and his family left their homes at Merliguèche and resettled in Île Royale (today Cape Breton).

Cont'd. on page 16

BON APPETIT - Recipes from The Guédry-Labine Family Cookbook

TACO BEEF SOUP by
Carolyn Guidry Hilderbran

1/2 lb. ground beef
1/2 cup chopped onion
1-1/2 cups water
1-16 oz. can cut stewed tomatoes (I've noticed that can sizes have become small so adjust accordingly)
1-15 1/2 oz. can pinto beans (I prefer Trappey's with jalapenos) if not available, substitute kidney beans
1-8 oz. can tomato sauce
2 Tbsp. Taco seasoning mix (1/2 envelope)

Toppings:
Corn chips
Shredded cheddar cheese
1 small avocado, peeled and chopped
Sour cream

In a large saucepan (a Dutch oven works great) cook meat and onion in about 2 tbs. of olive oil until brown. Drain off excess fat, add water, tomato sauce, un-drained tomatoes, beans and taco seasoning mix. Simmer covered for about 15 minutes.

Serve in bowls and use chips, shredded cheese, avocado and sour cream for guests to top their soup as they like.

FRANNIE'S BEER BREAD by
Charlene Guidry Lacombe-Jennings, LA

3 cups self-rising flour
3/4 cup sugar
1-1/3 bottle or can of your favorite beer
1 stick butter or margarine

Mix flour, sugar and beer, like a cake batter. Melt margarine, coat the pan and keep the excess to pour over the bread after baking. Pour batter in pan and bake at 350 degrees F for 35 minutes. Pour the excess margarine over the baked bread and put back in the oven for 10 minutes.

This was given to me by Frannie Deshotel. Her grandmother, Mrs. Richard from Evangeline, LA, made this for their snacks with coffee. - Charlene

NEW RESEARCH REVEALS GUÉDRY'S EXILED TO NORTH CAROLINA

Arsenault believed they stayed a few years near Cobequid (today Truro) before going to Île Royale.[37] There is evidence, however, that they may have gone directly from Merliguèche to Île Royale in 1749 or 1750. The Acadian settlement at Merliguèche persisted until at least June 1749 when Cornwallis anchored the Sphinx in the harbor at Merliguèche on his way to Chebucto (today Halifax). Here he stated:

> We came to anchor in Merliguiche Bay where I was told there was a French settlement. I sent ashore to see the Houses and manner of living of the Inhabitants – there are but a few Families with tolerable wooden Houses covered with Bark, a good many Cattle and clear ground more than serves themselves – they seem to be very peaceable, say they always looked upon themselves as English Subjects, have their Grants from Colonel Mascarene the Governor of Annapolis, and showed an unfeigned joy to hear of the new Settlement. They assure us the Indians are quite peaceable and not at all to be feared – there are none hereabouts.
>
> I have, &tc.,
> ED. CORNWALLIS[38,39]

Later in the summer of 1749 Cornwallis returned to Merliguèche for some "garden stuff".[39] Earlier on 12 September 1745 the governor and intendant from Québec, Messieurs Beauharnois and Hocquard, visited Merliguèche and commented in their report:

> At Merligueche, a small harbour five leagues east of LaHeve, are only eight settlers, among the rest Paul Guidry, alias Grivois, jovial or jolly, a good coast pilot.[39,40,41]

The above reference to "eight settlers" probably meant eight adult males and thus several families. In 1746 Abbé Le Loutre wrote a "Description de L'Acadie" in which he said:

> From Chegekkouk he went to Misliguesch et Haivre which is 25 leagues further; here there are a dozen French families and 3 to 400 Indians who assembled here.[39,42]

Finally in 1748 a "Description de L'Acadie" indicates that there were 20 families at Mirliguèche:

> The 2nd is Mioligueche at three leagues from la Haïve, the missionary has started constructing a church, it has twenty French families and 300 to 400 Indians assembled there since the month of June.[39,43]

By 1753 only one French family remained at Merliguèche – that of "Old Labrador".[44]

Return of Acadians to Merliguèche from Louisbourg in August 1754

On arriving in Halifax in August 1754 to avoid starvation on Île Royale, a group of nine Acadian men with their families stated that they had been enticed to leave Acadia after the founding of Halifax in 1749.[44] These people primarily were children of Augustin Guédry and Jeanne Hébert and their families. Several members of the Guédry family of Merliguèche were known for their excellent coasting pilot skills and thus could easily have made the short voyage to Île Royale about 1750.[39]

NEW RESEARCH REVEALS GUÉDRY'S EXILED TO NORTH CAROLINA

In 1752 M. le Comte de Raymond directed a survey of the French possessions Île Royale and Île Saint-Jean (present-day Prince Edward Island) to census the growing population and to establish boundaries of present and future concessions on the islands.[45,46] Sieur Joseph de la Roque, King's Surveyor, commenced the survey on 5 February 1752 to the southeast of Louisbourg. About the 2nd of April 1752 Sieur de la Roque reached the Baie des Espagnols (today North Sydney, Cape Breton). Here among the resettled Acadians were several children of Augustin Guédry and Jeanne Hébert with their families including Marie-Josephe (called Joseph), Hélène (called Eleine), Ursule (called Eustache) and Pierre.[45,47(a)] In his typical detailed style of recording each family he encountered, Sieur de la Roque wrote:

> Paul Boutin, ploughman, native of la Cadie, aged 25 years. Married to Eustache Guedry, native of la Cadie, aged 21 years.
>
> They have Pierre Guedry their brother, aged 11 years.
> They have two sheep and one hen.
> The land on which they are was given to them verbally by Messieurs Desherbiers and Prevost. They have made a clearing in which to sow a peck of oats and a bushel of peas.
>
> Charles Boutin, ploughman, native of la Cadie, aged 29 years. Married to Joseph Guedry, native of la Cadie, aged 28 years.
> They have three children, two sons and a daughter.
> Jean Charles, aged 5 years;
> Olive, aged 3 years;
> Marie Françoise, aged 3 months;
> Eleine Guédry, her sister, native of l'Acadie, aged 29 years.

Living nearby were the families of their uncle Paul Guédry married to Anne Mius and their aunt Françoise Guédry married to Jean LeJeune as well as their cousins Judith Guédry (daughter of Paul Guédry) with her husband Jean Cousin and their children, Marie Guédry (daughter of Jean-Baptiste Guédry) with her husband Germain LeJeune and their children and Joseph Guédry with his wife Josette Benoît and their children. Although we don't know the year in which Marie-Josephe, Hélène, Ursule and Pierre Guédry migrated to Île Royale, it was probably in mid to late 1750 as this was when most of the Acadians of Baie des Espagnols arrived.[45,48] Paul Boutin and Ursule Guédry received their marriage certificate at Louisbourg on 9 November 1750.[49]

Leaving the Baie des Espagnols on the 5th of April 1752, Sieur de la Roque continued around the eastern coast of Île Royale surveying the shores of the Baie de l'Indienne, the Baie de Mordienne and the Baie de Miré at which he arrived the 9th of April 1752. Here he found Jeanne Guédry, the daughter of Augustin Guédry and Jeanne Hébert, with her husband Julien Bourneuf, their four daughters, Julien's sister Renée Guillaume Bourneuf and Jeanne's brother Joseph Guédry.[45,50] Sieur de la Roque thus recorded:

> Julien Bourneuf, ploughman, native of Médrillac, bishopric of St. Malo, aged 36 years. Married to Jeanne Guedry, native of la Cadie, ages 27 years.
> They have four daughters: --
> Anne, aged 12 years;
> Jeanne, aged 9 years;

Continued on page 19

IN THE NEWS-HISTORICAL NEWS TIDBITS

Hadacol Helps Thousands of All Age Groups

Countless thousands have proved that HADACOL is beneficial to folks of all ages. That is the reason so many purchase the large economy size bottle so all the family can benefit from nature's Vitamins and Minerals in HADACOL.

For instance, Miss Ethel Guidry, 822 Montgomery St., Port Neches, Texas, only 17 years old, was "feeling nervous, had little appetite, her face was pale and drawn and she suffered from gas on the stomach."

Her system lacked the B vitamins and Minerals which HADACOL contains and this may cause digestive disturbances such as heart burns, indigestion, and often times Miss Guidry says she could not eat the kind and type of food she wanted without feeling terrible afterwards.

Miss Guidry, who recently graduated from high school, is already working in a bank. She said that after taking several bottles of HADACOL she is now "feeling wonderful," and has "lots of pep and energy."

Most folks take HADACOL because it has worked such wonders for relatives or friends. Miss Guidry took HADACOL because her mother had taken 12 bottles with excellent results.

Above: Ethel Guidry featured in an ad for Hadacol. Lafayette Advertiser

Below: Lafayette Advertiser, August 30. Isaure & Hilda Guidry

SISTERS ARE INJURED WHEN TRAIN HITS BUGGY

Lafayette, La., August 30.—Miss Isaure Guidry was probably fatally injured and her sister, Hilda, was dangerously hurt here tonight when a buggy in which they were riding was struck at a grade crossing by a Southern Pacific passenger train. The two young women are members of a widely known Louisiana family, and are granddaughters of former Governor and United States Senator Alex Mouton.

Below: Lafayette Advertiser, Lafayette, LA September 19, 1891

SCOTT SCRAPINGS.

Scott, La., Aug. 24th, 1891. Don't forget the champion base ball game between the Breaux Bridge team and the Montez Club, purse $50 to $150, Saturday, 29th inst., at Scott. That night there will be a grand ball. Mr. Guidry has completed the gailery to his Hall, and has had it painted. This will afford more dancing room and give the stags and steers a chance to witness the fun without obtruding their forms upon the dancing floor.

♦ ♦ ♦

A DELIGHTFUL EVENT OF the week was the surprise planned by Miss Bernice Overton on last Thursday in honor of the fourteenth birthday of Miss Mary May Guidry at the home of Mr. and Mrs. P. R. Guidry, 2348 Sixth street.

Little Miss Guidry was taken for an automobile ride, and upon her return home was surprised to find so many of her friends calling. The honoree received many lovely gifts.

Dancing and games were enjoyed throughout the evening. Several piano selections were given by Miss Overton.

Assisting Mrs. Guidry in entertaining the young folks were Misses Helen Potts and Eva Guidry.

Those participating in the enjoyable affair were Misses Bernice Overton, Helen Potts, Rena Melanson, Inez Higgs, Aileen Peckham, Aline Hudson, Mozelle Bryant, Margaret McDonald, Lois Ader, Bernice Trahan, Margaret McGrory and Charle Mac Abington; Messrs. Carl Carbitt, Thurston Goodwin, Fred Steussey, Byrd Brannon, Eugene Peveto, Weldon Davis, and Max Clarifield; Mr. and Mrs. P. R. Guidry and Misses Helen Porter and Eva Guidry.

♦ ♦ ♦

Above: Port Arthur News, Port Arthur, Texas, May, 27, 1923

LET ME TAKE YOUR ORDER FOR WOOD AND COAL.

I have opened a WOOD and COAL YARD at DeBlanc's old stand, and have a full supply of good Dry ASH WOOD on hand.

WILL HANDLE ONLY PITTSBURG COAL.

Also,

All kinds of FEEDSTUFFS.

Telephone 66 and you will get prompt service.

AYMAR GUIDRY.

NEW RESEARCH REVEALS GUÉDRY'S EXILED TO NORTH CAROLINA

>   Julienne, aged 7 years;
>   Sophie, aged 5 years;
>   Joseph Guedry, his brother-in-law, native of la Cadie, aged 17 years. Renée Guillaume, his sister, native of the parish of Argence, aged 20 years.
>   He owns in livestock: one pig and three fowls. He is in the colony three years, and has been given rations for that time.
>   The land on which he is settled is situated to the east of the dwelling place of Monsieur de la Borde, treasurer to the colony; it was given to him verbally by Messieurs Desherbiers and Prévost. He has made a good clearing in which he sowed two pecks of oats.

Note that the four daughters listed above are those of Julien Bourneuf and his first wife Anne Marie Hyaune, who died 10 February 1750. He and Jeanne Guédry wed about 14 January 1751 on which date their marriage certificate was recorded at Louisbourg.[51] Shortly after Sieur de la Roque censused Julien Bourneuf and Jeanne Guédry their first child François Bourneuf was born. He was baptized at Louisbourg on 26 July 1752.[52] Two years later they had a daughter Françoise Bourneuf, who was baptized on 30 June 1754 at Louisbourg.[53]

In the summer of 1753 Paul Boutin, his wife (i.e., Ursule Guédry), one boy (i.e., Pierre Guédry) and two girls were living at Baie des Espagnols on Bras du Sud. They had one sow and one arpent of cleared land. Residing next to Paul Boutin was Charles Boutin with his wife (i.e., Marie-Josephe Guédry), two boys and one girl. Apparently during the previous year Hélène Guédry, sister of Marie-Josephe Guédry, had left the home of Charles Boutin. They had one beef, one cow, two calves and one sow. Next to Charles Boutin lived François Lucas with his wife. This couple had one pig and one sow. The wife of François Lucas almost certainly was Hélène Guédry as we will see shortly. On the north side of the Rivière de Miré was Julien Bourneuf with his wife (i.e., Jeanne Guédry), one boy and four girls. They had one domestic servant and one cow.[54]

In August of 1754 twenty-five persons arrived at Halifax from Louisbourg, Île Royale stating that earlier they had been enticed to leave Acadia with the founding of Halifax in 1749, but now were returning to escape starvation on Île Royale. They professed that they would take the Oath of Allegiance. Of the 25 persons nine were adult males. They stated to William Cotterell, Secretary, at Halifax that they were "nearly related to old Labradore" - who was most likely Paul Guédry, youngest son of Claude Guédry and Marguerite Petitpas.

City and Harbour of Louisbourg   Map of 'Halifax', Nova Scotia, 1750

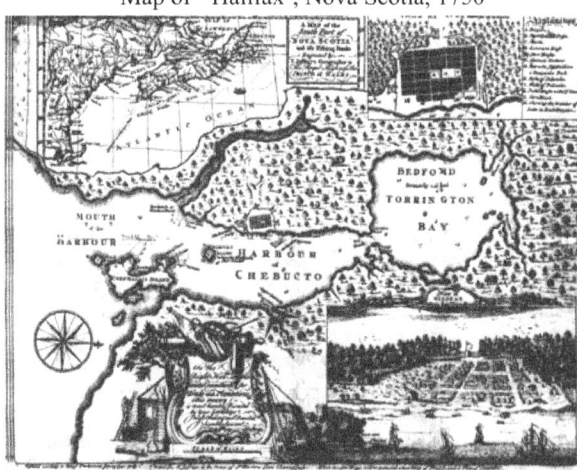

NEW RESEARCH REVEALS GUÉDRY'S EXILED TO NORTH CAROLINA

The nine men named were Paul Boutin, Charles Boutin, Julien Bourneuf, Sebastian Bourneuf, Joseph Gedri, Pierre Gedri, Pierre Erio, François Lucas and Claude Erot.[55,56,57,58] The land that they had cleared at Baie des Espagnols on Île Royale was rocky and had very poor soil, never able to produce enough to support their families. They had lived off the rations supplied by the French at Louisbourg. These ceased in 1754 and the Acadians realized that they could not support themselves so they had asked permission to leave.[59] Governor Lawrence determined to send these Acadians to the newly-established Lunenburg just below their former home of Merliguèche. Through his Provincial Secretary William Cotterell he instructed the Commander at Lunenburg Lt. Colonel Patrick Sutherland to victual the new arrivals and to give them tools and land.[55,56,58,60,61] They settled just above Lunenburg on their former lands at Merliguèche.

SECRETARY'S OFFICE, 24 August 1754.

DR. SIR,--
* * * * The Bearers hereof being in all twenty-five persons are just arrived here from Louisbourg, from whence they made their Escape to avoid starving. Some of them were formerly Inhabitants of this Country, and are nearly related to old Labrador; they have all taken the oaths; the Colonel desires you would treat them kindly, ordered them to be Vituelled, to have tools given them, and Land laid out for them where you shall see most convenient.

I am, Dr. Sir,
Yours, &c.,
WM. COTTERELL

To Col. Sutherland,
commanding at Lunenburg[56,58,61]

Above: Heading-Victual List - 1755

Left: Sample of family names on the Victual List showing family group #1420. Name 1424 reads Pierre Boutein (Pierre Guédry), brother of Ursule Guédry.

1425: Joseph Guedry (Joseph Guédry), son of Augustin Guédry and Jeanne Hebert

BOOK NOOK

Discovering New Brunswick
By Marianne and H.A. Eiselt

New Brunswick offers a unique partnership of French and English traditions. In this book, travel writers Marianne and H.A. Eiselt celebrate the natural landscape, the fine architectural heritage of cities, towns and villages and the festivals and events that bring the communities together each year.

This full color souvenir book covers all four corners of the province-its geography, its people and its history.

Highlights include: Hopewell Rocks, Saint John Market, St Andrews-by-the-Sea, St. Stephen's Chocolate Festival, Miramichi Irish Festival, Acadian Village, Sussex Balloon festival.

Full color photographs accompany the descriptive text which follows the main tourist routes as shown on the provincial maps.

New Brunswick Book of Everything

Everything you wanted to know about New Brunswick and were going to ask anyway. From the folks who brought you the best-selling *Nova Scotia Book of Everything* comes the **New Brunswick Book of Everything**. From the number of kilometers of coastline, to the stories behind those weird place names (hello Skeedaddle Ridge) to profiles of Stompin' Tom and Frank McKenna, no book is more comprehensive than the **New Brunswick Book of Everything**. No book is more fun. Well-known New Brunswickers weigh in on a whole range of subjects. Arthur Doyle's five most memorable New Brunswick political scandals; meteorologist Claude Cote tells us his five biggest New Brunswick weather stories and David Ganong tells us his five favorite memories of growing up in New Brunswick.

Stories of the First People, the worst weather, New Brunswick slang, the most infamous crimes. it is all here! Whether you are a life long resident or visiting for the first time, you will discover no more comprehensive book about your favorite province. If you love New Brunswick, you'll love the **New Brunswick Book of Everything!**

NEW RESEARCH REVEALS GUÉDRY'S EXILED TO NORTH CAROLINA

Between 16 June 1755 and 29 June 1755 one thousand five hundred and forty-eight persons were victualled at Lunenburg.[62,63] Almost all of the persons victualled were Germans recently settled at Lunenburg; however, a few were Acadians newly-arrived from Île Royale and Île Saint-Jean who had settled at Merliguèche just above Lunenburg. Below in the order that they appear on the 1755 Victual List for Lunenburg are the Acadians from Île Royale who arrived at Halifax in August 1754. The number to the right of each name is the number assigned that person on the 1755 Victual List for Lunenburg. Note that the Acadians that arrived in August 1754 appear as one contiguous group (Nos. 1402-1425) on the 1755 Victual List for Lunenburg. Family groups are separated by a blank for convenience. In parentheses beside each name are the usual spelling of the name and key relationships.

1402 – Francois Loucas (Francois Lucas)

1403 – Helena Loucas (Hélène Guédry, his wife)
    [daughter of Augustin Guédry & Jeanne Hébert]
1404 – Maria Loucas (Marie Lucas, their daughter)

1405 – Charles Boutein (Charles Boutin)
1406 – Maria Boutein (Marie-Josephe Guédry, his wife)
    [daughter of Augustin Guédry & Jeanne Hébert]
1407 – Jean Charles Boutein (Jean Charles Boutin, their son)
1408 – Pierre Oliver Boutein (Pierre Olivier Boutin, their son)
1409 – Maria Fran^s Boutein (Marie Françoise Boutin, their daughter)
1410 – Magd Perpeta Boutein (Magdeleine Perpetue Boutin, their daughter)

1411 – Julien Bourneuve (Julien Bourneuf)
1412 – Jeane Bourneuve (Jeanne Guédry, his wife)
    [daughter of Augustin Guédry & Jeanne Hébert]
1413 – Francois Bourneuve (François Bourneuf)
1414 – Jean Bourneuve (Jeanne Bourneuf, daughter of Julien Bourneuf & first wife)
1415 – Sophia Bourneuve (Sophie Bourneuf, daughter of Julien Bourneuf & first wife)
1416 – Francois Bourneuve (François Bourneuf, their son)
1417 – Sabastien Bourneuve (Sébastien Bourneuf, brother of Julien Bourneuf)
1418 – Leon Deran Bourneuve (Léon Deran Bourneuf)

1419 – Paul Boutein (Paul Boutin)
1420 – Ursula Boutein (Ursule Guédry, his wife)
    [daughter of Augustin Guédry & Jeanne Hébert]
1421 – Cathrina Boutein (Marguerite Catherine Boutin, their daughter)
1422 – Joseph Boutein (Joseph Boutin, their son)
1423 – Joseph Boutein (Joseph Boutin)
1424 – Pierre Boutein (Pierre Guédry, brother of Ursule Guédry)
    [son of Augustin Guédry & Jeanne Hébert]

NEW RESEARCH REVEALS GUÉDRY'S EXILED TO NORTH CAROLINA

1425 – Joseph Guedry (Joseph Guédry)
   [son of Augustin Guédry & Jeanne Hébert]

Of the nine adult males identified as coming with their families from Louisbourg to Halifax,[55,56,57,58] seven appear above. Neither Pierre Erio nor Claude Erot appear on the 1755 Victual List for Lunenburg. Furthermore, six of the seven known children of Augustin Guédry and Jeanne Hébert appear on the 1755 Victual List for Lunenburg. Only their son Jean-Baptiste Guédry does not appear. Where he and his family were residing in early 1750's is not known.

Pierre Erio and Claude Erot probably were Pierre Terriau and Claude Terriau. On 7 April 1752 Sieur de la Roque arrived at Baie de Mordienne, a small community not far from Baie des Espagnols. The first two families he surveyed were those of Claude Teriau and of Pierre Teriau.[45,47(f)] Claude Teriau was 56 years of age living with his wife Marie Guérin and their nine children - three sons and six daughters ranging in age from 6 years to 25 years. Pierre Teriau was 58 years of age living with his wife Margueritte Guérin and their nine children – four sons and five daughters ranging in age from 4 years to 24 years. These two men were much older than the other Acadians leaving the Louisbourg area for Merliguèche. It is doubtful that they came to Merliguèche with their families. The above letter[56,58,61] states that only 25 persons arrived from Louisbourg in August 1754. The families of the other seven men that are listed on the 1755 Victual List for Lunenburg number 24 persons.[62,63] Including Claude Teriau and Pierre Teriau by themselves in the number of Acadians arriving at Halifax closely matches the 25 Acadians mentioned in the letter.[56,58,61] Also, at their advanced age and that of their families it is likely that Pierre Terriau and Claude Terriau may have come to Merliguèche to determine if the "accommodations" were suitable for their families who planned to come later. Since they did not appear on the 1755 Victual List for Lunenburg, they probably returned to their families at Baie de Mordienne between August 1754 and June 1755.

Although to date we have not uncovered any definitive records proving that François Lucas married Hélène Guédry, daughter of Augustin Guédry and Jeanne Hébert, it certainly appeared likely from the 1755 Victual List of Lunenburg and other corroborative evidence that the Helena (Loucas) mentioned is in fact Hélène Guédry, the daughter of Augustin Guédry and Jeanne Hébert. In April 1752 Hélène Guédry was unmarried and living with Charles Boutin and Marie-Josephe Guédry, her brother-in-law and sister, at Baie des Espagnols, Île Royale.[45,47] By summer 1753 it appears that she was no longer living in the Charles Boutin home; however, living next to Charles Boutin was François Lucas and his wife. They had no children indicating they probably were newly married. In the 1755 Victual List for Lunenburg the wife of François Loucas was Helena and they have a daughter Maria Loucas – an infant born since the census in 1753.[54] Although circumstantial, this evidence certainly indicates that the wife of François Lucas was Hélène Guédry, daughter of Augustin Guédry and Jeanne Hébert.

Twenty-five Acadians traveled from Louisbourg to Halifax in August 1754 and then to Lunenburg.[56,58,61] Twenty-four Acadians from this contingent appear on the 1755 Victual List for Lunenburg as a contiguous group. Neither Pierre Terriau (Pierre Erio) nor Claude Terriau (Claude Erot) appears on the 1755 Victual List for Lunenburg. It is very likely that one or two Acadian children were born between the arrival of the Louisbourg Acadians in August 1754 and the enumerations in the June 1755 Victual List for Lunenburg. Possible births include Marie Lucas, infant daughter of François Lucas and Hélène Guédry, and Marie Perpetua Boutin, daughter of Charles Boutin and Marie-Josephe Guédry.

NEW RESEARCH REVEALS GUÉDRY'S EXILED TO NORTH CAROLINA

None of these Acadians appear on the 1756 Victual List for Lunenburg[64,65,66] which suggests that they were no longer in Lunenburg by February 1756.

A Second Group of Acadians Arrive at Merliguèche in October 1754

A second group of six Acadian families (28 persons) arrived at Halifax from Île Royale in early October 1754 under the leadership of Charles King. Four persons in this group returned to their former homes at Pisiquit and the remainder went to Lunenburg, settling just above the little community at Merliguèche. Like the August 1754 group, these people also had previous connections with Merliguèche.[67,68] They too had gone to Île Royale because of the threats of Father Le Loutre, but now wanted to return to their former lands due to the very poor soil on Île Royale and the starvation suffered by their families.

At a council holden at the Governors House in Halifax on Wednesday the 9th day of Oct., 1754

PRESENT

Chas. Lawrence, Esq., President.
Jno. Collier,
Willm. Cotterell, | Councs.
Robt. Monckton,
Jno. Rous,

The President acquainted the Council that six French Families, consisting of Twenty-eight Persons, who had deserted their Lands in this Province were arrived at Halifax, and desired to be permitted to return to their said Lands. The Heads of the said Families being called in and asked the Reason of their quitting their Lands, They declared that upon the first Settling of the English at Halifax, they were so terrified by the Threats that Mr. Le Leutre had used and his declaring the great distresses they would be reduced to if they remained under the Dominion of the English, That they, on that account, had retired and were set down on the Island of Cape Breton, where they had remained ever since; but that the Land there being so very bad they were utterly incapable of subsisting their Families, and had applied to the Governor of Louisbourg for leave to return to their former Habitations, to which he had consented. They further declared that if the Council would permit them to enjoy their former Lands, that they were willing to take the Oath of Allegiance to His Majesty, and that their future Behaviour should be unexceptionable.

The Council being of Opinion that the return of these People might have a good Effect, not only on the German Settlers, many of whom had formerly deserted to the French, but also on the other French Inhabitants, by voluntarily taking the Oath of Allegiance to His Majesty, unqualified by any reservation. And it appearing that they were in very great distress being intirely destitute of all necessaries, It was Resolved that they should be permitted to return to their former Possessions, and that Twenty-four of them being the most necessitous, should be allowed Provisions during the Winter, and that the other four should have a Week's Provisions given them to Subsist them till they returned to their former Habitations at Pisiquid where they would be assisted by their Friends and Relations.

NEW RESEARCH REVEALS GUÉDRY'S EXILED TO NORTH CAROLINA

The said Inhabitants then very chearfully took the Oath of Allegiance to his Majesty, appointed to be taken by the french Inhabitants.

JNO. DUPORT, Secy.   CHAS: LAWRENCE[67,68]

At the Baie des Espagnols in early April 1752 Sieur de la Roque censused Joseph Guédry, nephew of Augustin Guédry and Jeanne Hébert, with his wife Marie-Joseph Benoît and their three children;[45,47(b)] Honoré Trahan with his wife Marie Corperon and their three children;[45,47(c)] Jean Baptiste LeJeune and Margueritte Trahan and their three children;[45,47(d)] Jean Benoît with his wife Anne Trahan[45,47(e)] and Charles Roy with his wife Marguerite LeJeune.[45,47(d)]

> Joseph Guedry, ploughman, native of la Cadie, aged 38 years. Married to Josette Benoist, native of la Cadie, aged 24 years. They are in the country two years and have had food from the King for the said time.
> They have three children, one son and two daughters.
> Servant, aged 10 days.
> Perrine, aged 13 years.
> Jeanne, aged 3 years.
> Their live stock consists of one pig.
> The dwelling or the land in which they are settled, has been given to them verbally by Messieurs Desherbiers and Prevost. They have made a clearing of about twelve arpents from which they have gathered a large quantity of very fine turnips, cabbage and beans.
>
> . . . .
>
> Honoré Trahan, ploughman, native of la Cadie, aged 26 years. Married to Marie Corperon, native of the same place, aged 33 years.
> They have been in the colony three years, and have been given rations for that time.
> They have one son and two daughters:
> Pierre, aged 2 years.
> Marie, aged 5 years.
> Marguerite, aged 3 weeks.
> In live stock they own two oxen, two cows, two calves, two pigs and one hen.
> The land in which they are settled was given to them verbally by Messieurs Desherbiers and Prévost. They have made a clearing of four arpents.
>
> . . . .
>
> Jean Bte. Le Jeune, ploughman, native of la Cadie, aged 24 years. Married to Margueritte Trahan, native of same place, aged 24 years.
> They have three children, two sons and a daughter:
> Jean, aged 3 years.

NEW RESEARCH REVEALS GUÉDRY'S EXILED TO NORTH CAROLINA

Blaise, aged 2 years.
Margueritte, aged 2 months.
Two pigs are all their live stock.
They are in the colony two years and a half, and have been granted rations for 33 months.
The land they occupy has been given them by Messieurs Desherbiers and Prévost. They have made a clearing on it half an arpent square.

. . . .

Jean Benoist, ploughman, native of la Cadie, aged 25 years. Married to Anne Trahan, native of the place, aged 21 years.
They have been two years in the colony and have been given rations for the said time.
The land they occupy was given to them verbally by Messieurs Desherbiers and Prévost. They have made a clearing on it of an arpent square and has two arpents of fallow land.

. . . .

Charles Roy, ploughman, native of Port-Royal, aged 34 years. Married to Margueritte Le Jenne, native of the same place, aged 30 years.
They have been in the colony for one year, and have been given rations for the said time.
The land that they occupy was given to them by Messieurs Desherbiers and Prévost. They have made a clearing where they can sow half a peck in oats and peas.

Like the Acadians that arrived at Halifax in August 1754, the Acadians that arrived in October 1754 also appear as one contiguous group (Nos. 1448-1471) on the 1755 Victual List for Lunenburg.[62,63] Family groups below are separated by a blank for convenience. In parentheses beside each name are the usual spelling of the name and key relationships.

1448 – Charles King (Charles Roy) [1st cousin of Marguerite Trahan]
1449 – Margretta King (Marguerite LeJeune, his wife)
1450 – Peter King (Pierre Roy, their son)
1451 – Olive King (Olive Roy, their son)

1452 – Joseph Laberdore (Joseph Guédry, son of Jean-Baptiste Guédry & Madeleine
          Mius dit dAzy and the nephew of Augustin Guédry & Jeanne Hébert)
1453 – Joseph Laberdore (Marie-Josephe 'Josette' Benoît, his wife)
1454 – Bering Laberdore (Perrine Guédry, their daughter)
1455 – Jeane Laberdore (Jeanne Guédry, their daughter)
1456 – Servant Laberdore (Servant Guédry, their son)

1457 – Nore Trahan (Honoré Trahan)
          [1st cousin of Anne Trahan below]
1458 – Maria Trahan (Marie Corperon, his wife)
1459 – Maria Trahan (Marie Trahan, their daughter)
1460 – Pierre Trahan (Pierre Trahan, their son)
1461 – Pellage Trahan (Marguerite Trahan, their daughter)

NEW RESEARCH REVEALS GUÉDRY'S EXILED TO NORTH CAROLINA

1462 – Jean Lejeune Lejeune (Jean Baptiste LeJeune)
1463 – Margretha Lejeune (Marguerite Trahan, his wife) [1st cousin of Charles Roy]
1464 – Jeane Lejeune (Jean LeJeune, their son)
1465 – Margretha Lejeune (Marguerite LeJeune, their daughter)
1466 – Blaise Lejeune (Blaise LeJeune, their son)
1467 – Marie Lejeune (Marie LeJeune, their daughter)

1468 – Jean Bonneau (Jean Benoît)
1469 – Anna Bonneau (Anne Trahan, his wife)
    [1st cousin of Honoré Trahan above]
1470 – Anna Bonneau (Anne Casimere Benoît, their daughter)
1471 – Roze Bonneau (Rose Benoît, their daughter)

Like the Acadians that arrived in August 1754, the Acadians that arrived in October 1754 also came from the area near Baie des Espagnols, Île Royale.

None of these Acadians that arrived in October 1754 appear on the 1756 Victual List for Lunenburg[64,65,66] which suggests that they were no longer in Lunenburg by February 1756.

Acadians from Île Saint-Jean Join Their Cousins at Merliguèche

At least one other Acadian family appeared on the 1755 Victual List for Lunenburg. In early May 1752 Sieur de la Roque recorded at Anse au Comte Saint-Pierre, Île Saint-Jean (today Keppoch, Prince Edward Island):

> Joseph Deschamps dit Cloche, ploughman, native of l'Acadie, aged 42 years, he has been in the country three years. Married to Judict Duaron, native of l'Acadie, aged 32 years.
> They have five sons and three daughters: --
> Philippe Deschamps, aged 16 years;
> Louis, aged 14 years;
> Augustin, aged 12 years;
> Jean Baptiste, aged 6 years;
> François, aged 14 years;
> Eufrozinne, aged 18 years;
> La Blanche, aged 8 months
> Elisabeth, aged 18 months.
> Their live stock consists of: eight pigs and twenty fowls.
> The land on which they are settled is situated as in the preceding case, it was given to them verbally by Monsieur de Bonnaventure. On it they have made a clearing for the sowing of three bushels of wheat.[45,75(a)]

Joseph Deschamps, whose full name was Nicolas Joseph Deschamps, was at Lunenburg at least by June 1753 when the first German settlers arrived. Father Clarence d'Entremont (see below) discusses Governor Lawrence mentioning Vieux Labrador and Deschamps nicknamed Cloverwater. Although Father d'Entremont appears uncertain as to the identity of these two men, they almost certainly were Paul Guédry, youngest son of Claude Guédry and Marguerite Petitpas, and Nicolas Joseph Deschamps dit Cloche, husband of Judith Douaron (Doiron),[78] who was the daughter of Philippe Doiron and Marie-Josephe Guédry.[79]

NEW RESEARCH REVEALS GUÉDRY'S EXILED TO NORTH CAROLINA

Marie-Josephe Guédry was the daughter of Claude Guédry and Marguerite Petitpas[80,81] and thus was the sister of Paul Guédry. Joseph Deschamps, therefore, was the nephew through marriage of Paul Guédry. Of course, as with Paul Guédry, Marie-Josephe Guédry is referred to as an "Indian" because of her close association with Mi'kmaq living near the Guédry and Petitpas families at Merliguèche from the late 1600's to the mid-1700's. Father Clarence-Joseph d'Entremont wrote:

> Charles Lawrence, while he was overseer for establishing some Foreign Protestants at Lunenburg, they arriving here, the 8th of June 1753, with some new colonists, found there the Vieux Labrador (Old Labrador), who was an Indian or at least a half-breed, as he said in his journal. He found likewise his nephew, he called Deschamps, nicknamed Cloverwater, whose services were very useful to Lawrence. It is not a question of the family of Vieux Labrador.
>
> As for Deschamps, Captain Charles Morris said the 15th of May 1754 that he was a neutral French, in the employ of the English (a). In reality, however, his father was Acadian and his mother an Indian. Winthrop Bell, in his Index, identifies him with Joseph (or René) Deschamps (b). The census of Île Saint-Jean of 1752 places at Anse au Comte Saint-Pierre "Joseph Deschamps dit Cloche, resident farmer, native of Acadia, age of 42 years ... married to Judit Duaron, native of Acadia, age of 32 years", having with them five boys and three daughters, Philippe, the oldest of the family being then 16 years. The following year, the 12th of February, when he married at Port-Lajoie with Madeleine Trahan, daughter of Jean-Baptiste and of Catherine Joseph Boudrot, he said that his father was "Nicolas Joseph Deschamps of Saint Martin de Ray, (sic, for Île de Ré), diocese of La Rochelle". Consequently the Deschamps of the journal of Lawrence cannot be this Joseph, of whom the father was not Acadian and the mother was not an Indian. Notice that this family of Joseph Deschamps was sent in exile to Pennsylvania where one of his daughters, Blanche, wed the 14th of February 1763 René LeCore (c).
>
> There were in Acadia two other persons of the name of Deschamps, namely Isaac, later judge in Nova Scotia, perhaps descendant of the Huguenot Isaac Deschamps of Boston and afterwards of Narragansett and Marie Broussard; and Charles Deschamps de Boishébert, military officer, from Québec, whom we find in Acadia from 1747. But both are born in 1722 and could not be the father of our Deschamps (d).
>
> We find at Massachusetts with a number of the exiles Jean Deschamps, born about 1798 (sic 1698), his wife Jeanne, called here Joan, born about 1703 and their daughter Anne or Nannette, called Nanny, born about 1739, married to Joseph La Noue. They have been put first at Malden, the 28th of November 1755, but were transferred to Stoneham the 17th of March following. Both parents were sick and crippled and unable to work. It is rather strange to find in 1760 some bills of Joseph La Noue for having taken care of these persons. Jean Deschamps and his wife, at the same time as Nannette and her two children, were transferred to Boston the 28th of August 1760. Notice that in 1763 Joseph La Noue and Anne Deschamps had two sons and a daughter (a). We do mention that family in exile at Stoneham in the 40th chapter in connection with one the children of François Mius who was sent here the 3rd of September 1760. This Jean Deschamps, whom we met here for the first time, but of whom we no longer hear after 1760, could be the Deschamps of the journal of Lawrence, who disappeared from the public records of Acadia after 1754 or 1755.

NEW RESEARCH REVEALS GUÉDRY'S EXILED TO NORTH CAROLINA

Be that as it may of the identity of our Deschamps, he must have wanted to settle at Merliguesh, became Lunenburg, having requested a share of land with gardens, in order to send to Pisiquid for his wife and his children; they having passed through Halifax. His Indian mother must be sister to Vieux Labrador since Deschamps called him his uncle. Is it possible that this one whom we consider as the eldest of the children of Pierre Guidry would have been likewise half-bred, therefore, he called himself Labrador, the name that his real father had born? Moreover, would not Vieux Labrador himself have been half-bred instead of pure-blooded Indian?[76]

On the 1755 Victual List for Lunenburg was the family of Nicolas-Joseph Deschamps:[62,63]

1312 – Joseph Deschamps (Nicolas-Joseph Deschamps)
1313 – Judith Deschamps (Judith Doiron, his wife)
1314 – Louis Deschamps (Louis Deschamps, their son)
1315 – Gustave Deschamps (Augustin Deschamps, their son)
1316 – Leblanch Deschamps (La Blanche Deschamps their daughter)
1317 – Jean Deschamps (Jean Baptiste Deschamps, their son)
1318 – Francois Deschamps (François Deschamps, their son)
1319 – Isabella Deschamps (Elisabeth Deschamps, their daughter)
1320 – Maria Deschamps (Marie Deschamps, their daughter)

The Deschamps did not appear on the 1756 Victual List for Lunenburg[64,65,66] which suggests that they were no longer in Lunenburg by February 1756.

At least a few of the Acadians victualled at Lunenburg in June 1755 left the area voluntarily. Julien Bourneuf, Jeanne Guédry and their family returned to the Louisbourg area between late June 1755 and September 1755. Likewise, Sébastien Bourneuf returned to the Louisbourg area with his brother and sister-in-law. On 28 September 1755 Françoise Bourneuf, just 15 months old and the daughter of Julien Bourneuf and Jeanne Guédry, was buried in the cemetery at Louisbourg.[69] At this time Jeanne Guédry was expecting another child within a few days. Shortly after the death of her daughter Françoise, Jeanne Guédry gave birth to another daughter Marie. Unfortunately, complications in the birth developed and both Marie Bourneuf and Jeanne Guédry died shortly after Marie's birth. *(see page 39 for copy of Jeanne Guédry's death record)* Marie Bourneuf was baptized on 12 October 1755 at Louisbourg[70] – just three days before her mother was buried in the nearby cemetery.[71] The next day young Marie was buried near her mother.[72] With the fall of Louisbourg in 1758 the British exiled Julien Bourneuf, his four young children François, Julienne, Sophie and Jeanne, his daughter Anne and her husband Guillaume Mervin and Julien's brother Sébastien Bourneuf to France on the ship Le Duc Guillaume. They disembarked from the Le Duc Guillaume at St. Malo, France on 1 November 1758. Sébastien Bourneuf died shortly afterwards on 15 May 1759.[73,74] Apparently Pierre Terriau (Pierre Erio) and Claude Terriau (Claude Erot) left Merliguèche before June 1755 as they did not appear on the 1755 Victual List for Lunenburg.

In addition to the Acadians discussed above, Stephen White at the Centre d'Etudes Acadiennes in Moncton, New Brunswick suspects that the family of Paul Hébert was at Halifax in late December 1755 and was deported from there.[79]

NEW RESEARCH REVEALS GUÉDRY'S EXILED TO NORTH CAROLINA

Censused by Sieur de la Roque in early May 1752 at Rivière du Moulin-à-scie on Île Saint-Jean not far from the home of Joseph Deschamps were:

Paul Hébert, imbecile, ploughman, native of l'Acadie, aged 35 years, he has been three years in the country. Married to Marie Michel, native of l'Acadie, aged 32 years.
They have two sons and two daughters:
François Hébert, aged 10 years;
Louis, aged 8 years;
Théotiste, aged 17 years;
Margueritte, aged 6 months.
The land of which they are settled is situated on the Anse aux Pirgoues, it was given to them verbally by Monsieur de Bonnaventure. On it they have made a clearing for the sowing of six bushels of wheat.[45,75(b)]

Paul Hébert and his family were not on the 1755 Victual List for Lunenburg,[62,63] but did appear in June 1763 on the census taken of Acadians in Pennsylvania.[102,103,104] They apparently were not deported directly to Pennsylvania in late 1755 as they were not on the "List of Acadian Families in Pennsylvania at the Beginning of 1757"[105] indicating that they arrived in Pennsylvania after this time. Although we have no documentation of their being in Merliguèche in late 1755, they may have come to Merliguèche with or shortly after Joseph Deschamps and his family since they lived near the Deschamps family on Île Saint-Jean. Furthermore, the parents of Paul Hébert were Jean Hébert and Jeanne Doiron. Paul Hébert, therefore, was the brother of Jeanne Hébert, wife of Augustin Guédry, and thus the uncle of Hélène, Marie-Josephe, Ursule, Jeanne, Joseph and Pierre Guédry, who were at Merliguèche in 1754 and 1755.

Acadians at Merliguèche Imprisoned on George's Island

What happened to the fifty or so Acadians remaining in Merliguèche after June 1755? They seem to disappear from the record for several years. A clue may lie tucked in a small article on page 2 of the 23 October 1755 edition of the Pennsylvania Gazette newspaper.

Halifax, in *Nova-Scotia*, Sept. 27
On Monday last arrived here the Jolly Bacchus (a Tender belonging to the Fleet) from Lunenburg, with the Inhabitants of a small French Settlement a little above that Place; they brought with them all except two, who we hear are fled to the Indians for Succour and Assistance.[82]

After agreeing in August and October 1754 to aid the Acadians from Louisbourg, the British apparently changed course and determined to exile these Acadians. They brought the fifty or so Acadians living at Merliguèche to Halifax in the tender Jolly Bacchus and imprisoned them on George's Island in the Halifax harbor. Originally called Île à la Raguette or Snowshoe Island until 1749, George's Island became a British prison island where many Acadians were held in the mid-1700's.

NEW RESEARCH REVEALS GUÉDRY'S EXILED TO NORTH CAROLINA

October 23, 1755.

The PENNSYLVANIA  GAZETTE.

Containing the Freshest Advices, Foreign and Domestick.

NUMB. 1400.

HALIFAX, in Nova-Scotia, Sept. 27.

On Monday last arrived here the Jolly Bacchus (a Tender belonging to the Fleet) from Lunenberg, with the Inhabitants of a small French Settlement a little above that Place; they brought with them all except two, who we hear are fled to the Indians for Succour and Assistance.

Wednesday last arrived here the Hon. Rear Admiral Holbourne, in his Majesty's Ship Edinburgh, also his Majesty's Ships Centurion, Austria, and Norwich, from their Cruize off the Harbour of Louisbourg: On their Passage they met with three French Men of War, who had made their Escape from Louisbourg, to whom they gave Chace for some Time, but theirs being clean Ships, and ours considerably foul, they soon lost Sight of them. Yesterday arrived his Majesty's Ship the Dunkirk, who had been upon the Cruize with Admiral Holbourne.

There are now in this Harbour Thirty-nine Ships and other Topsail Vessels, viz.

Twelve English Ships of War of 74 and 64 Guns.

Three of 20 Guns, and two Snows.

Two French Ships of War of 74 Guns, viz. the Alcide and Lys.

Fourteen French Merchant Ships and Snows---lately sent in by our Fleets, now cruizing off Louisbourg, and the Mouth of St. Lawrence River. (And three more are hourly expected.)

Six English Merchant Snows and Brigantines, besides a great Number of Sloops and Schooners.

Acadians Deported to North Carolina

Earlier on 3 October 1755 Samuel Brown, Master of the Transport Sloop <u>Providence</u> received sailing orders from Colonel Charles Lawrence.

HALIFAX, 3 Oct. 1755.

SIR, --

You are to receive on Board your Sloop from George's Island a number of French Inhabitants a list whereof you will receive from the Commanding Officer there and you are to proceed therewith to the province of North Carolina and upon your arrival you are to deliver the Letter you have herewith as addressed and use your utmost diligence to get the people put on shore and will obtain a certificate of their being so landed.

NEW RESEARCH REVEALS GUÉDRY'S EXILED TO NORTH CAROLINA

You will take care to see the allowance of provisions properly served during the voyage agreeable to the following proportion viz 1 lb. Beef 2 lb. of Bread and five pounds of Flour each person per week, and you are to be accountable for what shall remain of the provisions after the people are landed and for what arms you have received from His Majesty's Stores for your defence.

C. LAWRENCE

To Samuel Barron,
Master of the Sloop Providence[83,84,85]

In early 1756 Charles Apthorp and Thomas Hancock of the Boston mercantile company Apthorp & Hancock, which supplied most of the ships used to deport the Acadians, submitted an account to Governor Charles Lawrence.

The Government of Nova Scotia, to John Campbell, Dr.

1755
Nov. 15th to the freight of fifty French people brought from Halifax
to N. Carolina, in the Sloop Providence, Samuel Barron Mr.,
per Certif. at 12s. 6d.   £31 5 0
North Carolina, Jany. 13th, 1756   JNO. CAMPBELL.[85,86,87]

The British loaded approximately fifty Acadians imprisoned on George's Island onto the Providence in late December 1755 and on 30 December 1755 she sailed under Captain Samuel Barron bound for North Carolina. Although the exact date of arrival at North Carolina is not known, it must have been in early January 1756 as the account for services of the Sloop Providence was filed on 13 January 1756.[85,86,88,89]

George's Island, Halifax Harbour, Nova Scotia   *Acadian Memorial Halifax, N.S.*

To date no manifest or list of the Acadians deported from Halifax to North Carolina has been located. Although we know that most, if not all, the Acadians deported to North Carolina on the Providence were those captured at Merliguèche, who were they? The fifty Acadians noted as arriving in North Carolina may not be an exact account of those loaded on the Providence in Halifax. A few may have died on the voyage to North Carolina, an infant or two may have been born on the trip and, of course, the number fifty may be an approximation of the actual number of Acadians landed on the Albemarle shore.

NEW RESEARCH REVEALS GUÉDRY'S EXILED TO NORTH CAROLINA

Based on records from North Carolina, Pennsylvania and Maryland as well as those from Acadia, a reconstructed list of Acadians by family group likely deported from Halifax on the <u>Providence</u> in December 1755 is:

* Nicolas-Joseph Deschamps, Judith Douaron (his wife), Augustin Deschamps, Louis Deschamps, LaBlanche Deschamps, Jean Baptiste Deschamps, François Deschamps, Elisabeth Deschamps, Marie Deschamps, Eufrozinne Deschamps (10)
* François Lucas, Hélène Guédry, Marie Lucas (3)
* Paul Boutin, Ursule Guédry, Catherine Boutin, Joseph Boutin (4)
* Pierre Guédry (1)
* Joseph Guédry (1)
* Charles Boutin, Marie-Josephe Guédry, Jean Charles Boutin, Pierre Olivier Boutin, Marie Françoise Boutin, Magdeleine Perpetue Boutin (6)
* Joseph Guédry, Marie-Josephe Benoît, Perrine Guédry, Jeanne Guédry, Servant Guédry (5)
* Honoré Trahan, Marie Corperon, Marie Trahan, Pierre Trahan, Marguerite Trahan (5)
* Jean Baptiste LeJeune, Marguerite Trahan, Jean LeJeune, Marguerite LeJeune, Blaise LeJeune, Marie LeJeune (6)
* Jean Benoît, Anne Trahan, Anne Casimere Benoît, Rose Benoît (4)
* Paul Hébert, Marie Michel, François Hébert, Louis Hébert, Théotiste Hébert, Marguerite Hébert (6)

What was the fate of the several other Acadians that returned to Merliguèche, but are not on the above list? We know that Julien Bourneuf with his wife Jeanne Guédry and their four children along with Julien's brother Sébastien Bourneuf returned to Île Royale between late June 1755 and September 1755. The fate of Léon Duran Sébastien is unknown. Further, what happened to Charles Roy, his wife Marguerite LeJeune and their two children is not known. No further information could be found in the records after they appeared on the 1755 Victual List for Lunenburg.

Several of the Acadians at Merliguèche in 1754 and 1755 died between 1755 and 1763. The death of Jeanne Guédry in October 1755 at Louisbourg was discussed above. Charles Boutin and his wife Marie-Josephe Guédry both died sometime between 1755 and 1763. The June 1763 census of Acadians in Pennsylvania indicates that Paul Boutin and Ursule Guédry had six children living with them. In fact, at this time Paul Boutin and Ursule Guédry only had three children: Marguerite Boutin, Joseph Boutin and Suzanne Catherine Boutin. The other three children were those of Charles Boutin and Marie-Josephe Guédry, both deceased. Those children were: Jean-Charles Boutin, Pierre-Olivier Boutin and Marie-Françoise Boutin. Additionally, it appears that at least two of the children of Joseph Guédry and Marie-Josephe Benoît died between 1755 and 1763. In 1755 they had two daughters and a son: Perrine Guédry (age 16 years), Jeanne Guédry (age 6 years) and Servant Guédry (age 3 years). When the family was censused in July 1763 at Port Tobacco, Maryland, they had three children Genevieve Guédry, Gabriel Guédry and Joseph Guédry. It would appear that Jeanne Guédry and Servant Guédry and possibly Perrine Guédry died between 1755 and 1763. Jean Benoît, husband of Anne Trahan, died before July 1763 for on the 1763 petition of the Acadians at Port Tobacco, Maryland, Anne Trahan had remarried to Louis Latier and her children were called orphans. Likewise, both Jean LeJeune and his wife Marguerite Trahan had died prior to July 1763 as their son Blaise LeJeune was an orphan living with the family of Honoré Braux at Port Tobacco when the 1763 petition of the Acadians at Port Tobacco was written.

NEW RESEARCH REVEALS GUÉDRY'S EXILED TO NORTH CAROLINA

Where on the North Carolina shore did Captain Barron unload the Acadians? Although not known with certainty at this time, these Acadians likely first touched North Carolina soil on the shores of Albemarle Sound and possibly in today's Chowan County.[87] Chowan County lies on the northwestern edge of Albermarle Sound. Chowan County, originally formed in 1670 as Shaftsbury Precinct of old Albermarle County, was named after the Chowan Indians living there. After several changes during the next century, the boundaries of Chowan County became stable after 1778. Edenton, the seat of Chowan County since 1720, was incorporated in 1715 as the town of Queen Anne's Creek. In 1722 it became Edenton honoring Governor Charles Eden. From its earliest days Edenton was a thriving town and seaport lying on Albermale Sound at the confluence of the Chowan and Roanoke Rivers. In 1728 it became the colonial capital of North Carolina and was the cultural and economic hub of the state. During this period its docks constantly buzzed with activity as hundreds of ships docked there annually. Certainly known to Captain Barron, Edenton may have been the location where in early January 1756 the <u>Providence</u> docked and Barron unloaded his weary cargo of Acadians.

Chowan County, N. C.

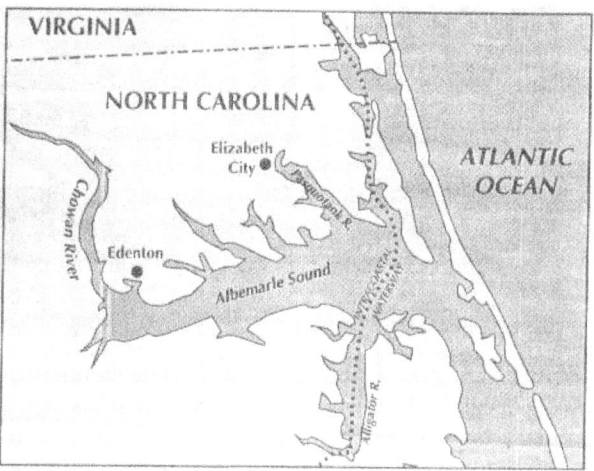

Edenton, N.C. and the Albemarle Sound

Few records of Acadians in North Carolina survive. On Thursday, 24 November 1757 the "Minutes of the Lower House of the North Carolina General Assembly" recorded:

> Mr. Vail moved that a Sufficient Sum be allowed and paid to the Neutral French in and about Chowan County towards their subsistence.

> Resolved, That the sum of Twenty five pounds proclamation Money be laid out in provisions and other necessaries by the Treasurer of the Northern District and delivered the said Neutrals and that the said sum be allowed him in account with the Public.[87,90,91,92,93]

Augustin Deschamps Remains in North Carolina

By late 1757 a substantial number of the Merliguèche Acadians had settled along Albermarle Sound in and around Chowan County. No other records of these Acadians has surfaced except those involving a lone

NEW RESEARCH REVEALS GUÉDRY'S EXILED TO NORTH CAROLINA

Acadian Augustin Deschamps, son of Nicolas-Joseph Deschamps and Judith Douaron (Doiron). Shortly after being deported to North Carolina, Augustin met Elizabeth White, daughter of Luke White (of Chowan County, North Carolina) and Sarah Copeland. Augustin and Elizabeth wed shortly before 8 October 1758 as on that date Luke White gave "my beloved daughter Elizabeth Dishon or formerly called Elizabeth White" 50 acres of wood land in Chowan County.[94,95]

Built in 1758, The Cupola House is located on the north shore of Edenton Bay and was present at the time the Acadians were at Chowan County, N.C. (right-Cupola House in 1918,, below-view of back of house)

The 17 November 1770 will of Luke White mentioned Augustin Deshon by his full name. In this will he left to his daughter Elizabeth Deshon one-half of his land and property. He left the other half of his land and plantation to his wife Sarah Copeland. In his will he stated "I give and bequeath to my Daughter Elizabeth Deshon one half of all my Land and Plantation to her Heirs forever, I likewise give her my said daughter my Negro man Christo and all my Boats and Canoes." The executors of this will were Augustin Deshon and John Copeland.[95,96,97]

In a letter dated 1887 from Tampa, FL, Dr. Louis Deshong, grandson of Augustin Deschamps and Elizabeth White, stated "Father's mother, Elizabeth White, was a dark skinned, coarse woman of no culture, and her offspring took of the same quality – not one of them was taught to write. They were honest, industrious, and hard working men." He then describes Augustin Deschamps, his grandfather, as "a well-made man about five feet ten inches, fair-skinned, blue-eyed, with black hair. He was a good disposition, inoffensive person. If he had any predominating trait it was that of planting and caring for trees – he had a large peach orchard." Of his father and uncles, sons of Augustin Deschamps and Elizabeth White, Dr. Deshong stated that all of them were farmers and "They had no use of tools or inventive genius; not one of them was taught to read or write. They were honest, industrious and hard working men. The only child that was ever anything of note was Henderson, a son of Augustine Deshon Jr." Ironically, "the only child that was ever anything", Henderson Deshon, moved to Giles County, Tennessee after 1820 and was killed by lightning. Dr. Louis Deshong stated that he lived near his grandparents and parents for twenty years and knew them well.[98]

NEW RESEARCH REVEALS GUÉDRY'S EXILED TO NORTH CAROLINA

According to Chowan County records and United States Censuses for 1790 through 1820, Augustin Deschamps and Elizabeth White had at least nine sons and three daughters. For several years Augustin Deschamps operated a ferry in Chowan County for which he was paid 1256 pounds and 1516 pounds at different times by the Colonial Government. Augustin Deschamps and his family lived in Chowan County until 1793 when they all moved to Orange County, North Carolina. In Orange County Augustin Deschamps had a farm with a large peach orchard and on this farm he lived from 1793 until his death in 1820. In describing Augustin Deschamps' last days, Dr. Louis Deshong said "My grandfather Dishong remained in Chowan County, North Carolina until the close of the War of 1776 when he and all of his family removed to Orange County some 200 miles west where he lived and died of a pollypud of the nose; he was 80 years of age, and had been a member of the Baptist Church for many years". The American Revolution ended with the Treaty of Paris in 1783 thus it appears that Dr. Deshong may have been confused by ten years on the date that Augustin Deschamps moved to Orange County. Records in Chowan County after 1793 are devoid of any mention of Augustin Deschamps or his family.[97] Today descendants of Augustin Deschamps and Elizabeth White live in North Carolina as well as many other states including Mississippi, Oklahoma, Texas and Florida.[95,97,98]

Acadians Leave North Carolina for Pennsylvania or Maryland

With the lone exception of Augustin Deschamps the Merligueche Acadians deported to North Carolina did not remain long there. Many stayed at least until late 1757 as seen above and may have remained as long as 1760.[99] It appears reasonable that the Acadians left North Carolina in late 1760 after the surrender of Montréal on 8 September 1760 ending the French and Indian War and ensuring British control of all lands from Georgia to the Hudson Bay.[79] Exactly when and how they left North Carolina is not known at this time.

St. Joseph's Catholic Church- Courtyard entrance

Interior-St. Joseph's Catholic Church, Philadelphia, PA

St. Joseph's Catholic Church- Philidelphia, PA

St. Joseph's Catholic Church, Philadelphia, PA, built in 1733, located at 321 Willings Avenue (south of Walnut St., between 3rd & 4th Streets)

The Marriage Register of St. Joseph's Catholic Church (Philadelphia, Pennsylvania) for the year 1761 records the marriage of one of the Acadians deported to North Carolina - Simon Guétry.[100] The Simon Guétry mentioned is Joseph Guédry, son of Augustin Guédry and Jeanne Hébert.

NEW RESEARCH REVEALS GUÉDRY'S EXILED TO NORTH CAROLINA

Also, this register for the year 1763 contains the marriage of René Le Core and Blanche Dechamps, daughter of Joseph Dechamps and Judith Douaron (Doiron).[100]

> Guétry-Melançon: January 22d, Simon Yetry (Guétry) to Magdalen Melançon
>
> Le Core-Dechamps: February 14th, René Le Core to Blanche, daughter of Joseph Dechamps; witnesses Halin d'Aigre and Joseph Ribaud; the nuptial blessing was given afterwards at Mass.

The Baptismal Register of St. Joseph's Catholic Church (Philadelphia, Pennsylvania) for the year 1762 records the baptism of Susan Catharine Butin.[101] She was Susan Catherine Boutin, daughter of Paul Boutin and Ursule Guédry. The sponsor (i.e., godfather) of Susan Catherine Boutin, called "Peter Dietry" in the Register, was Pierre Guédry, the brother of Ursule Guédry and uncle of Susan Catherine Boutin.

> Butin, Susan Catharine, of Paul and Ursula Butin, born December 17, 1761, baptized June 24, sponsors Peter Dietry and Christina Geiger, *ibid.*

At least some of the Acadians deported to North Carolina left for Pennsylvania by late 1760 as indicated by the marriage of Joseph Guédry to Magdalen Melançon on 22 January 1761 in Philadelphia, Pennsylvania. Why they left North Carolina and how they traveled to Pennsylvania is not known at this time.

In 1763 we find many of the Merilguèche Acadians in Pennsylvania and Maryland. On 10 February 1763 the Treaty of Paris ended the Seven Years War (French and Indian War) and a new phase in Acadian – British relations began. The French government petitioned England to send the Acadians imprisoned there to France. Once on French soil, these Acadians sent copies of the petition to their relatives in British North America. By mid-1763 the Acadians in each English colony sent a petition to the French government requesting repatriation to France or a French colony. Each petition included a list of the Acadians in the particular colony. In the petitions from Pennsylvania and the Maryland communities of Snowhill and Port Tobacco we find many of the Acadians captured in Merliguèche in September 1755 and deported to North Carolina from Halifax in December 1755.

On 20 June 1763 in Pennsylvania[102,103,104] were:
* Paul Boutin, Ursulle Boutin, his wife with six children
* Joseph Guedry, Magdelaine his wife with three children
* Pierre Guedry single
* Allen Daigle and Frosine Deschamps and three children
* René Le Corps and LaBlanche Deschamps his wife
* Paul Ebert, Marie Ebert his wife with five children

None of the above Acadians appeared on the "List of Acadian Families in Pennsylvania at the Beginning of 1757"[105] indicating that they arrived in Pennsylvania after early 1757.

In Snowhill, Maryland on 7 July 1763[106,107,108,109] were:
* Francois Lucas, Anne Lucas his wife, Rose Lucas, Marie Lucas, Margueritte Lucas
* Louis Déchamp, Marie Déchamp his wife, Marie Déchamp [NOTE: Louis Déchamp was the son of Augustin Deschamps and Elizabeth White.]

NEW RESEARCH REVEALS GUÉDRY'S EXILED TO NORTH CAROLINA

At Port Tobacco, Maryland on 7 July 1763[110,111,112,113] were:
* Joseph Gaidris, Marie Benoist Gaidris his wife, Gabriel Gaidris, Joseph Gaidris, Genevieve Gaidris
* Honoré Trahan, Marie Trahan his wife, Marie Trahan, Pierre Trahan, orphan Joseph LeJeunne, orphan Antoine LeJeune
* Honoré Braux, Magdelaine Braux his wife, Magdelaine Braux, Marie Breaux, Margueritte Braux; Blaise LeJeune orphan. [NOTE: Apparently both Jean LeJeune and his wife Marguerite Trahan died before July 1763 as their son Blaise LeJeune is listed as an orphan.]
* Louis Latier, Anne Latier his wife, Antoine Latier, Anne Benoist orphan, Rose Benoist orphan, Margueritte Benoist orphan. [NOTE: Anne Trahan Latier, wife of Louis Latier, was the first cousin of Honoré Trahan and the widow of Jean Benoît. Anne, Rose and Margueritte Benoist were not truly orphans, but the children of her first marriage to the deceased Jean Benoît.]

Within these three petitions from Acadians at Snowhill and Port Tobacco, Maryland and at Pennsylvania are found at least one member of each family from the reconstructed list of Acadians deported to North Carolina from Halifax on 30 December 1755. Several of these Acadians continued their search for a new Acadian homeland and migrated to Louisiana in 1767, 1768 and 1769 including the families of Paul Boutin (Ursule Guédry) [with two of the children of the late Charles Boutin and Marie-Josephe Guédry], Pierre Guédry, Honoré Trahan (Marie Corperon), Blaise LeJeune, Joseph Guédry (son of Joseph Guédry & Magdeleine Melançon), Joseph Guédry (Marie-Josephe Benoît) and Louis Latier (Anne Trahan). A few families stayed in Maryland after 1763 including the families of Louis Déchamp and François Lucas (Hélène Guédry).

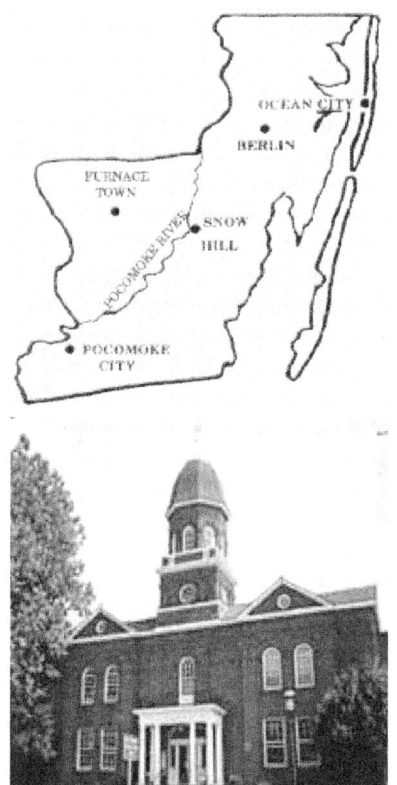

Left: Map showing Snow Hill, Maryland, settled in 1642.

Lower left: Snow Hill Courthouse, built in 1742. In 1834 the courthouse burned to the ground and was rebuilt, receiving many renovations over the years, then was lost to fire once again. The current structure was built in 1894.

Top right: Historical marker in front of St. Ignatius Catholic Church located in Port Tobacco, Maryland.

Bottom left: St. Ignatius Catholic Church and cemetery, Port Tobacco, MD

GENERATIONS   Volume 7 Issue 1 Page 39

NEW RESEARCH REVEALS GUÉDRY'S EXILED TO NORTH CAROLINA

A long journey indeed was suffered by these Merliguèche Acadians exiled to North Carolina in 1756. Fearing the harsh policies of the British and threatened by their priest Father Le Loutre, they left the Acadian mainland in 1749-1750 to resettle on Île Royale or Île Saint-Jean. Facing near starvation from drought and poor soils they returned to Merliguèche in 1754 where they were captured by the British in late 1755, imprisoned on George's Island at Halifax and then deported to North Carolina on 30 December 1755. Leaving North Carolina about 1760, they went either to Pennsylvania or Maryland where they remained until the late 1760's. Still seeking a new Acadian homeland, many journeyed to Louisiana in 1767-1769; however, even within Louisiana they had to relocate several times within the next fifteen years. The tenacity and courage of these Acadian people to preserve their culture and religion is almost unparalleled in human history.

References at end of this issue.

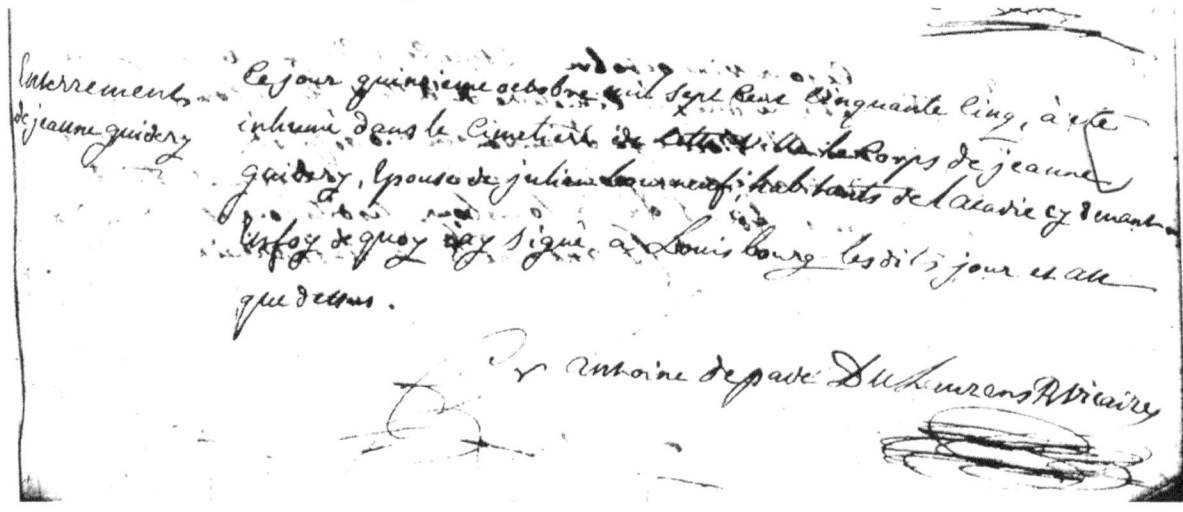

RECORDS

FORTRESS OF LOUISBOURG
ILE ROYALE, ACADIA

DEATH RECORD OF JEANNE GUEDRY

(DAUGHTER OF AUGUSTIN GUEDRY AND JEANNE HEBERT
& WIFE OF JULIEN BOURNEUF)

15 OCTOBER 1755

AT
NATIONAL ARCHIVES OF CANADA
OTTAWA, CANADA

DEPOT DES PAPIERS PUBLICS DES COLONIES;
ETAT CIVIL ET RECENSEMENTS
SERIE G1, VOLUME 409, REGISTRY 1, FOLIO 74
MICROFILM F-593

Left: Citation information for the death record of Jeanne Guédry

Below: Copy of actual death record of Jeanne Guédry.

JUDGE GREG G. GUIDRY [1961 -]
ASSOCIATE JUSTICE – LOUISIANA SUPREME COURT

Judge Greg G. Guidry

Born in the New Orleans, LA area in 1961, the Honorable Greg Gerard Guidry currently sits as one of the six Associate Justices of the Louisiana Supreme Court where he represents the 1st District. Justice Guidry lives in Westwego, LA with his wife Cathy and their three children Gavin Matthias, Gaye M. and Lorraine M. Guidry.

After graduating magna cum laude in 1982 with a B.A. degree from Louisiana State University in Baton Rouge, LA, Greg Guidry attended the Louisiana State University Law Center where he received his Juris Doctorate in 1985. After receiving his Juris Doctorate, he was inducted into the prestigious Order of the Coif and selected for the Louisiana Law Review on the basis of grades. An honorary scholastic society promoting excellence in legal education, the Order of the Coif only accepts the top 10% of the graduates from a member law school. He also has received a Judicial Studies Master's Degree from the National Judicial College.

While at the Louisiana State University Law Center, Greg Guidry was awarded a Rotary Foundation Scholarship for International Understanding. Through this scholarship he studied classical civilization and Roman law at the University of Witwatersrand in Johannesburg, Republic of South Africa. After returning from South Africa, Justice Guidry began his legal career in the New Orleans office of Liskow & Lewis in the commercial litigation section. From 1990-2000 he served as an Assistant United States Attorney within the United States Attorney's Office for Eastern District of Louisiana.

As an Assistant United States Attorney, he prosecuted scores of federal public corruption and commercial fraud cases. During his decade of service with the United States Attorney's Office he served variously as a division supervisor, ethics officer, trial advocacy instructor and grand jury coordinator. The United States Attorney General, the Director of the FBI and the Chief Postal Inspector formally commended Greg Guidry for his work with the United States Attorney's Office.

In 2000 Greg Guidry successfully won election to the Division E seat in the 24th Judicial District Court, Louisiana for the Parish of Jefferson. After serving six years as a judge on the 24th Judicial District Court, Judge Guidry sought and won a seat in 2006 on the Louisiana Fifth Circuit Court of Appeals. In November, 2008 Judge Guidry won a hard-fought election over challenger Jimmy Kuhn to represent the 1st District on the Louisiana Supreme Court. He began service on the Court in January, 2009.

Justice Guidry is an advisory board member for the New Orleans Chapter of the Federalist Society, is President of the Judge John C. Boutall American Inn of Court and is a member of the Louisiana Bar Foundation. In the past he has served as President of the Louisiana Fifth Circuit Judges Association. Judge Guidry is a frequent lecturer for the Louisiana Judicial College, the Louisiana State Bar Association and the New Orleans Chapter of the Federal Bar Association.

2009 GUÉDRY-LABINE & PETITPAS REUNION INFORMATION

Congres Mondial Acadien (CMA) for 2009 will be held on the Acadian Peninsula in New Brunswick from 7 August - 23 August 2009. CMA activities will be centered around Caraquet, New Brunswick. You can click on this website to keep up with the events planned for the 2009 CMA.

http://www.cma2009.ca/

We are having our Guédry-Labine & Petitpas Reunion on Sunday, 16 August 2009 in the Conference Center of Danny's Inn in Bereford, New Brunswick. Beresford is just five miles north of Bathurst, New Brunswick and Danny's Inn is on Highway 134 just south of Beresford. Bathurst has a rich Acadian history that we'll explore in the coming months.

We will begin about 8:30 am and have activities until 5:00 pm. Our agenda, activities and displays will include formal sessions with music, presentations, etc. as well as time to mingle and get to know your cousins. The tentative agenda is:

8:30 am - Opening ceremony and French Mass with French Rosary at
        Sainte-Famille (Holy Family) Catholic Church in Bathurst
9:30 am - Registration at Danny's Inn Conference Center & Display Browsing
10:00 am - Cajun Music with a Louisiana flavor
10:45 am - Meeting Cousins, Display Browsing and Sales Table
11:00 am - Presentation: Cajun and Acadian Music & Culture
11:45 am - Meeting Cousins, Display Browsing and Sales Table
12:00 noon - Buffet Lunch
1:00 pm - Presentation: Petitpas Family - New Results through DNA Research
1:45 pm - Meeting Cousins, Display Browsing and Sales Table
2:00 pm - Acadian Musical Entertainment: New Brunswick Style
2:45 pm - Meeting Cousins, Display Browsing and Sales Table
3:00 pm - Presentation: History of the Acadian Peninsula and the Acadians
3:45 pm - Meeting Cousins, Display Browsing and Sales Table
4:00 pm - TBD
5:00 pm - Closing Ceremony

There will be a superb buffet lunch. It'll be a Hot & Cold Dinner Buffet that includes roast beef smothered in peppercorn gravy, sweet & sour meat balls, lasagna, chicken wings, potato casserole, coleslaw, tossed green salad, carrot salad, rolls, carrot cake, cherry cheesecake, fresh fruit salad, coffee and tea.

Registration information was sent out in August to those on our distribution list. A copy of the registration form will be attached to the next few issues of this newsletter. It is not too early to secure lodging.

The website below contains a number of motels, hotels and bed & breakfasts in the Bathurst area.

http://www.bathurst.ca

NEW BRUNSWICK ACCOMMODATIONS - CMA 2009

The Guédry-Labine family reunion is scheduled to take place August 16, 2009, in the town of Bathurst, not far from Caraquet, New Brunswick, CA. Here are a few more links for accommodations in those areas. We'll add more details about our reunion in the next few months.

BATHURST - http://www.bathurst.ca/english/home/

Authentique Bed & Breakfast Enjoy our 4 star B&B in a heritage home of the 20's with 'Arts & Craft's influences, conveniently located in the heart of Bathurst. You are welcome to relax in a cozy atmosphere with personalized service. Spacious rooms with very comfortable beds, cable TV, DVD, MP3, wireless internet, work desk and telephone. Each room has a private bathroom. Breakfast 'A la Carte' will be served in our elegant dining room.

Comfort Inn Bathurst Conveniently located on St. Peter Avenue. Close to shopping and offices. 35 person meeting room available.

John's Motel Our rooms have a full bath and shower, color television with cable, and most importantly comfortable beds! We also boast a swimming pool and an area for picnics. We also have in-room coffee.

Sea'scape Cottage This is our fully equipped beach house located on the beautiful Bay of Chaleur in Bathurst, New Brunswick. Select the virtual tour button to have a closer look.

The official New Brunswick Tourism Website is at the link below. You can learn about interesting locations, sites and activities at this website. By clicking on the word "Guides" in the left column of the page, you can order a free 2008 Experience New Brunswick Vacation Planner" which is excellent.

http://www.tourismnewbrunswick.ca

The 2009 CMA website has an excellent page on accommodations within the Acadian Peninsula. Visit it by clicking on this link:

http://www.cma2009.ca

CARAQUET - http://www.ville.caraquet.nb.ca/

Hotel Paulin "The Pearl of Baie des Chaleurs", Caraquet.

Motel Colibri 12 rooms smoking and non-smoking. 2 double beds. Continental breakfast.

Super 8 Motel 50 guest rooms including 18 junior suites.

ON THE WEB

Les Guédry d'Asteur

http://freepages.genealogy.rootsweb.ancestry.com/~guedrylabinefamily/

The Guédry-Labine Family Genealogical Database

Developed by the Les Guédry d'Asteur, Inc. Genealogy Committee

http://freepages.genealogy.rootsweb.ancestry.com/~guidryrm/Guedry-Labine/

The Louisiana State Archives

This is the official website for the Louisiana State Archives. It provides a very nice overview of the archival holdings and services. Although there are no images of original documents at this time, there is a very nice index to Confederate Pension Applications with numerous Guidry records. Click on Research Library under Sections of Organization, then Confederate Pension Applications to the left of the top photograph, then Search the Database.

http://www.sos.louisiana.gov/archives/archives/archives-index.htm

DUES REMINDER

Attached at the back of this issue is a membership application for renewing your membership in Les Guédry d'Asteur. Our dues are very reasonable at $6.00 for individuals and $10 for a family.

By joining and paying your dues, you provide us with the financial resources to participate in many projects, one being the CMA 2009 reunion in Bathurst, New Brunswick.

Please take a moment, complete the Membership Application, enclose a check and send it to the address on the application. It will help all of us do so much for the family.

REFERENCES - GUÉDRY'S EXILED TO NORTH CAROLINA

REFERENCES

1. Conversation between Mr. Paul LeBlanc and Martin Guidry on 28 June 2008 in Lafayette, LA.

2. Maxson, Helen Morin, "The Acadians of North Carolina", Le Réveil Acadien (Acadian Cultural Society; Fitchburg, MA), Volume. XXIV No. 3 (August 2008), pp. 66-75.

3. Faragher, John Mack; A Great and Noble Scheme – The Tragic Story of the Explusion of the French Acadians from Their American Homeland (W. W. Norton & Company; New York, NY; 2005), pp. 372-373.

4. Richard, Edouard; Acadie – Roeconstitution d'Un Chapitre Perdu de l'Histoire d'Amerique (The Marlier Publishing Co.; Boston, MA; 1921), p. 448 (Appendice VI – "Genealogie des Familles Acadiennes avec Documents" par Placide Gaudet).

5. Letter, Stephen A. White (Genealogist, Centre d'études acadiennes, Université de Moncton, Moncton, New Brunswick, Canada) to Mrs. Helen Morin Maxson (Charlotte, North Carolina), 9 February 2006.

6. Arsenault, Bona, Histoire et Généalogie des Acadiens (Les Editions Leméac Inc., Québec, Canada, 1978) pp. 1491, 2499.

7. Census of Acadia in 1698 ("Recensement des habitants du Port-Royal leurs familles terre en valeur Bestiaux Arbres fruitiers et fusils Pour l'année 1698"), [Archives Nationales de France – Le Centre des Archives d'Outre-Mer (29 Chemin du Moulin Detesta, Aix-en-Provence, France 13090), Col, G1 466, nos. 18-20, 29]. Microfilm at Centre d'Etudes Acadiennes (Université de Moncton, Moncton, New Brunswick, Canada E1A 3E9), Microfilm No. CEA F1801. Transcribed copy at the National Archives of Canada (395 Wellington Street, Ottawa, Ontario, Canada K1A 0N3), Archives des Colonies, Series G1, MG1, Vol. 466, Nos. 18-20 (Microfilm No. C-2572).

8. White, Stephen A., Dictionnaire Généalogique des Familles Acadiennes – Première Partie 1636 á 1714 en Deux Volumes (Centre d'Etudes Acadiennes (Université de Moncton, Moncton, New Brunswick, Canada E1A 3E9), pp. 771-773.

9. Arsenault, Bona, L'Acadie des Ancêtres (Le Conseil de la Vie Française en Amérique; Québec, Canada; 1955), p. 95.

10. Census of Acadia in 1686 ("Recensement fait par Monsieur De Meules … de tous le Peuples de Beaubassin, Rivière St. Jean, Port-Royal, Isle Percée et autres Costes de L'Acadie, … commencement de lannée 1686"). Acadia (Port-Royal, Cap-Sable, Port-La Hève, Mirliguèche, Baie des Mines, Rivière St-Jean, Passamaquoddy,

Mégais, Pentagouet, Beaubassin, Miramichi, Chédabouctou, Nipisiguit, Île-Percée). [Archives Nationales de France – Le Centre des Archives d'Outre-Mer (29 Chemin du Moulin Detesta, Aix-en-Provence, France 13090), Col, G1 466, no. 10]. Microfilm at Centre d'Etudes Acadiennes (Université de Moncton, Moncton, New Brunswick, Canada E1A 3E9), Microfilm No. CEA F1801. Transcribed copy at the National Archives of Canada (395 Wellington Street, Ottawa, Ontario, Canada K1A 0N3), MG1, Series G1, Vol. 466, Nos. 10 (Microfilm No. C-2572).

11. White, Stephen A., Ibid., p. 771.

12. Hébert, Rev. Donald J., Acadians in Exile (Hebert Publications; Cecilia, LA; 1980), pp. 475, 508.

13. LeBlanc, Dudley J., The Acadian Miracle (Evangeline Publishing Company; Lafayette, LA; 1966), p. 381.

14. Oath of Allegiance in 1695 ("Liste des Acadiens qui ont prêtre le serment d'allégeance au roi d'Angleterre, 1695"), Acadia (Port-Royal), 16 August 1695 [Massachusetts Archives (Secretary of the Commonwealth, 220 Morrissey Boulevard, Boston, MA 02125.), Vol. 2 (Colonial Chapter 8 (Nova Scotia and Canada from 1643 to 1719), Folio 540. Transcribed copy at the National Archives of Canada (395 Wellington Street, Ottawa, Ontario, Canada K1A 0N3), Volume II, Folio 540 (Microfilm No. F-579). Fascimile of the document on page facing page 317 of "Mémoires de la Societé Généalogique Canadienne-Françoise", volume 6 pp. 316-317 (1955).

15. Mémoires de la Societé Généalogique Canadienne-Françoise, (Société Généalogique Canadienne-Française, 3440 Rue Davidson, Montréal, Québec, Canada H1W 2Z5), Volume 6 pp. 316-317 (1955).

16. Labine, Mark; La Verdure de Mirligueche. The Story of the Guidry dit Labine Family in North America (Mark Labine; St. Paul, MN; 2002), pp. 32-33.

17. White, Stephen A., Ibid., p. 773, Supplement p. 158.

18. St-Jean-Baptiste de Port-Royal Catholic Church, Public Archives of Nova Scotia (6016 University Avenue, Halifax, Nova Scotia B3H 1W4), [Baptism of Paul Guédry, 8 September 1705]; Microfilm at Centre d'Etudes Acadiennes (Université de Moncton, Moncton, New Brunswick, Canada E1A 3E9), Microfilm No. CEA F1018.

19. Rieder, Milton P. and Rieder, Norma Gaudet, Acadian Church Records (Milton P. Rieder, Jr. and Norma Gaudet Rieder; Metairie, LA; 1977), Volume III (Port-Royal, 1702-1721) p. 17.

20. White, Stephen A., Ibid., p. 790, Supplement p. 160.

21. St-Jean-Baptiste de Port-Royal Catholic Church (Port-Royal, Acadia), Public Archives of Nova Scotia (6016 University Avenue, Halifax, Nova Scotia B3H 1W4), [Baptism of Françoise Guédry, 8 September 1705]; Microfilm at Centre d'Etudes Acadiennes (Université de Moncton, Moncton, New Brunswick, Canada E1A 3E9), Microfilm No. CEA F1018.

22. Rieder, Milton P. and Rieder, Norma Gaudet, <u>Acadian Church Records</u> (Milton P. Rieder, Jr. and Norma Gaudet Rieder; Metairie, LA; 1977), Volume III (Port-Royal, 1702-1721) p. 18.

23. d'Entremont, Father Clarence-Joseph; <u>Histoire du Cap-Sable de l'An Mil au Traité de Paris, 1763</u> (Hebert Publications; Eunice, LA; 1981), pp. 1927-1929, 1932, 1939-1940, 1942-1943.

24. Census of Acadia in 1708 ("Recensement genal fait au mois de Novembre mile Sept cent huit de tous les Sauvages de l'Acadie qui resident dans la Coste de l'Est, Et de ceux de Pentagouet et de Canibeky: ... des francois Establis a La delle Coste de l'Es"), Acadia (Port-Razoir, Cap-Sable, La Hève, Rivière St-Jean), November 1708 [Newberry Lbirary (E. E. Ayer Collection) (60 W. Walton Street, Chicago, IL 60610-7324), Ms. 751. Transcribed copy at the National Archives of Canada (395 Wellington Street, Ottawa, Ontario, Canada K1A 0N3), MG18, F18. Unpublished transcribed copy at Centre d'Etudes Acadiennes (Université de Moncton, Moncton, New Brunswick, Canada E1A 3E9).

25. White, Stephen A., <u>Ibid.</u>, pp. 771-772.

26. d'Entremont, Father Clarence-Joseph, <u>Ibid.</u>, pp. 1595-1597, 1615-1616, 1622-1623, 1625.

27. St. Charles-aux-Mines Catholic Church (Grand-Pré, Acadia), Archives of the Catholic Diocese of Baton Rouge (1800 South Acadian Thruway, P. O. Box 2028, Baton Rouge, LA 70821), Volume 2 (1707-1748) #42 of baptismal records.

28. Pollard, Nora Lee; <u>Diocese of Baton Rouge Catholic Church Records</u> (Catholic Diocese of Baton Rouge – Department of Archives, Baton Rouge, LA, 1978, 1999), Volume 1 p. 59 and v. 1A (Revised) p. 88.

29. White, Stephen A., <u>Ibid.</u>, p. 773, Supplement p. 158.

30. d'Entremont, Father Clarence-Joseph, <u>Ibid.</u>, pp. 1042, 1601-1604, 1617-1618, 1623, 1625.

31. Supreme Judicial Court, County of Suffolk (Clerk's Office, Boston, MA 02108), "Criminal Case – Piracy of Jean-Baptiste Guédry & son Jean-Baptiste Guédry fils", v. 211 document 26283 nos. 4 & 5; v. 216 document 28868.

32. "The Trial of Five Persons for Piracy, Felony and Robbery: Who Were Found Guilty and Condemned, at a Court of Admiralty for the Trial of Piracies, Felonies and Robberies Committed on the High Seas, Held at the Courthouse in Boston, with His Majesty's Province of Massachusetts-Bay in New-England, on Tuesday the Fourth Day of October, Anno Domini, 1726", Printed by T. Fleet, for S. Gerrish, at the lower end of Cornhill, 1726. (Early American Imprint Series. First Series: No. 2818; Evans 2818). Transcript of trial of Jean-Baptiste Guédry pere and Jean-Baptiste Guédry fils on pages 2-19. Transcript of trial of Philippe Mius, Jacques Mius and John Missel on pages 19-34. (See page 8 for Augustin Guédry reference.)

33. Coleman, Benjamin, Collections of the Massachusetts Historical Society (Massachusetts Historical Society; Boston, MA), v. 6 (1799) pp. 108-112.

34. Le Reveil Acadien (Acadian Cultural Society, P. O. Box 2304, Fitchburg, MA 01420), v. 8 pp. 15-16.

35. La Société Historique Acadienne – Les Cahiers (La Société Historique Acadienne, Case Postale 632, Moncton, New Brunswick, Canada E1C 8M7), v. 16 p. 31.

36. White, Stephen A., Ibid., p. 774, Supplement p. 158.

37. Arsenault, Bona, Ibid., pp. 588, 1491.

38. Akins, Thomas B.; Selections from the Public Documents of the Province of Nova Scotia (Charles Annand, Publisher; Halifax, Nova Scotia; 1869) pp. 559-561. [Reprint Edition: Acadia and Nova Scotia – Documents Relating to the Acadian French and the First British Colonization of the Province, 1714 – 1758 (Polyanthos; Cottonport, LA; Reprint Edition, 1972), pp. 559-561.

39. Bell, Winthrop P.; The "Foreign Protestants" and the Settlement of Nova Scotia - The History of a Piece of Arrested British Colonial Policy in the Eighteenth Century (Centre for Canadian Studies, Mount Allison University; Sackville, New Brunswick, Canada; 2nd edition, 1992), pp. 403-404.
[1st edition, 1961 by University of Toronto Press; Toronto, Ontario, Canada]

40. Murdoch, Beamish; A History of Nova-Scotia or Acadie (James Barnes, Printer and Publisher; Halifax, Nova Scotia, Canada; 1866), p. 81.

41. "Letter of Messrs. Beauharnois & Hocquart to the Count de Maurepas, 12 September 1745, Québec, Canada". Transcribed copy at the National Archives of Canada (395 Wellington Street, Ottawa, Ontario, Canada K1A 0N3), MG1, Series C^{11}A, Vol. 83. (Microfilm No. F-83).

42. Rameau, M. E.; Collection de Documents Inédits sur le Canada et l'Amérique Publiés par Le Canada-Français (L.-J. Demers & Frère; Québec, Québec, Canada; 1888-1890), Volume 4, Tome Premier, p. 43.

43. Rameau, M. E., Ibid., volume 4 pp. 44, 47.

44. Bell, Winthrop P., Ibid., pp. 404, 483.

45. Census of Île Royale and Île Saint-Jean in 1752 ("Voyage d'inspection du Sieur de La Roque. Recensement 1752") [Archives Nationales de France – Le Centre des Archives d'Outre-Mer (29 Chemin du Moulin Detesta, Aix-en-Provence, France 13090), Col, G1 466, no. 81]. Microfilm at Centre d'Etudes Acadiennes (Université de Moncton, Moncton, New Brunswick, Canada E1A 3E9), Microfilm No. CEA F1802.

46. Gaudet, Placide; Report Concerning Canadian Archives for the Year 1905 in Three Volumes (S. E. Dawson, Printer; Ottawa, Canada; 1906), Volume II, Appendix A, Part I - "Tour of Inspection Made by the Sieur de la Roque. Census 1752"; pp. 3-165.

47. (a) Gaudet, Placide, Ibid., p. 47. (b) Gaudet, Placide, Ibid., pp. 46-47.
(c) Gaudet, Placide, Ibid., p. 49. (d) Gaudet, Placide, Ibid., p. 50.
(e) Gaudet, Placide, Ibid., pp. 49-50. (f) Gaudet, Placide, Ibid., pp. 55-56.

48. Gaudet, Placide, Ibid., pp. 45-48.

49. National Archives of Canada (Ottawa, Canada); Depot des Papiers Publics des Colonies; Etat Civil et Recensements; Serie G1, Volume 408, Registry 1, Folio 127v (Microfilm F-593). (Marriage Certificate of Paul Boutin and Ursule Guédry, 9 November 1750).

50. Gaudet, Placide, Ibid., p. 61.

51. National Archives of Canada (Ottawa, Canada); Depot des Papiers Publics des Colonies; Etat Civil et Recensements; Serie G1, Volume 408, Registry 1, Folio 130v (Microfilm F-593). (Marriage Certficate of Julien Bourneuf and Jeanne Guedry, 14 January 1751).

52. National Archives of Canada (Ottawa, Canada); Depot des Papiers Publics des Colonies; Etat Civil et Recensements; Serie G1, Volume 408, Registry 2, Folio 11v (Microfilm F-593). (Baptismal Certficate of Francois Bourneuf, son of Julien Bourneuf and Jeanne Guedry, 26 July 1752).

53. National Archives of Canada (Ottawa, Canada); Depot des Papiers Publics des Colonies; Etat Civil et Recensements; Serie G1, Volume 409, Registry 1, Folio 20v (Microfilm F-593). (Baptismal Certficate of Francoise Bourneuf, daughter of Julien Bourneuf and Jeanne Guedry, 30 June 1754).

54. Census of Île Royale in 1753. ("Recensement Général des habitans des Ports et havres de l'Isle Royale, de la quantité de Bestiaux, Batiments, Chaloupes et Chafaux pour la pêche, des terrains defrichés, auquel est joins un memoire des observations qui ont étés prises de la situation desdits Ports et havres, de la qualité des Terres, prairies et bois qui les avoisinent; fait en Juillet et Aout 1753.") [Transcribed copy at the National Archives of Canada (395 Wellington Street, Ottawa, Ontario, Canada K1A 0N3), Archives des Colonies, Series G1, MG1, Vol. 466, Part 3a].

55. d'Entremont, Rev. Clarence-Joseph, Ibid., p. 1854.

56. Roth, D. Luther, Acadie and the Acadians, (Press of L. C. Childs & Son; Utica, NY; 1891). pp. 204-205.

57. Bell, Winthrop P., Ibid., pp. 404-405, 483-484.

58. Akins, Thomas B., Ibid., pp. 214-215.

59. Bell, Winthrop P., Ibid., p. 484.

60. Bell, Winthrop P., Ibid., p. 483.

61. Public Archives of Nova Scotia; Letterbook; Letter of Mr. William Cotterell to Lt. Colonel Patrick Sutherland; 24 August 1754.

62. "A List of Foreign & Other Settlers Victualled at Lunenburg Between 16 & 29 June 1755 both Days Included"; [Harvard University – The Houghton Library, Hyde Collection (Cambridge, MA), fMS Can 76]; Microfilm Copy at the Nova Scotia Archives and Records Management (6016 University Avenue; Halifax, Nova Scotia, Canada B3H 1W4), MG1, Volume 113.

63. "1755 Victual List for Lunenburg"; http://freepages.genealogy.rootsweb.co/~ked1/1755vict.html

64. "A list of Foreign and other Settlers Victualled at Lunenburg and Halifax Between the 23 Feb. 1756 and the 16th May"; National Archives of Canada (395 Wellington Street, Ottawa, Ontario, Canada K1A 0N3), MG18, F19, N.S. 1749-1756.

65. Kaulback, Ruth E.; Historic Saga of Lehève (LaHave) (Ruth E. Kaulback; Petite Riviere, Nova Scotia, Canada; 1970), pp. 94-102 ("A list of Foreign and other Settlers Victualled at Lunenburg and Halifax Between the 23 Feb. 1756 and the 16th May").

66. "1756 Lunenburg Vitualling List"; http://www.seawhy.com/vict56.html

67. Bell, Winthrop P., Ibid., pp. 483-484.

68. Akins, Thomas B., Ibid., p. 228.

69. National Archives of Canada (Ottawa, Canada); Depot des Papiers Publics des Colonies; Etat Civil et Recensements; Serie G1, Volume 409, Registry 1, Folio 72v (Microfilm F-593). (Burial Certficate of Françoise Bourneuf, daughter of Julien Bourneuf and Jeanne Guédry, 28 September 1755).

70. National Archives of Canada (Ottawa, Canada); Depot des Papiers Publics des Colonies; Etat Civil et Recensements; Serie G1, Volume 409, Registry 1, Folio 73v (Microfilm F-593). (Baptismal Certficate of Marie Bourneuf, daughter of Julien Bourneuf and Jeanne Guédry, 12 October 1755).

71. National Archives of Canada (Ottawa, Canada); Depot des Papiers Publics des Colonies; Etat Civil et Recensements; Serie G1, Volume 409, Registry 1, Folio 74 (Microfilm F-593). (Burial Certficate of Jeanne Guédry, wife of Julien Bourneuf, 15 October 1755).

72. National Archives of Canada (Ottawa, Canada); Depot des Papiers Publics des Colonies; Etat Civil et Recensements; Serie G1, Volume 409, Registry 1, Folio 74v (Microfilm F-593). (Burial Certficate of Marie Bourneuf, daughter of Julien Bourneuf and Jeanne Guédry, 16 October 1755).

73. Rieder, Milton P. Jr. and Rieder, Norma Gaudet; The Acadians in France – Volume III Archives of the Port of Saint Servan (Milton P. Rieder, Jr.; Metairie, LA; 1973), pp. 6-7, 14, 16.

74. Robichaux, Albert J. Jr.; The Acadian Exiles in Saint-Malo, 1758-1785 (Hebert Publications; Eunice, LA; 1981), pp. 160-161, 620.

75. (a) Gaudet, Placide, Ibid., p. 108. (b) Gaudet, Placide, Ibid., p. 106.

76. d'Entremont, Father Clarence-Joseph, Ibid., pp. 1852-1854.

77. Bell, Winthrop P., Ibid., pp. 405, 443.

78. Arsenault, Bona, Ibid., p. 2085.

79. Letter (E-Mail), Stephen A. White (Centre d'Études Acadiennes, Université de Moncton, Moncton, New Brunswick, Canada) to Mrs. Helen Morin Maxson (Charlotte, North Carolina), 19 October 2007.

80. White, Stephen A., Ibid., p. 513.

81. Arsenault, Bona, Ibid., p. 1375.

82. Pennsylvania Gazette newspaper (Philadephia, PA; 23 October 1755, #1400), p. 2.

83. (a) Akins, Thomas B.; Ibid., p. 280. (b) Jehn, Janet; Acadian Exiles in the Colonies (Janet Jehn; Covington, KY; 1977), p. 219.

84. Jehn, Janet, Ibid., p. 219.

85. Public Archives of Nova Scotia; Order Book - Colonel Charles Lawrence; Order of C. Lawrence to Master Samuel Barron, Master of the Sloop Providence; 3 October 1755.

86. Maxson, Helen Morin; Ibid., p. 66.

87. Akins, Thomas B.; Ibid., p. 289.

88. Gipson, Lawrence Henry; The Great War for the Empire – The Years of Defeat, 1754-1757 [The British Empire Before the American Revolution – Volume VI] (Alfred A. Knopf; New York, NY; 1946), p. 299.

89. Landry, Don; "Ships of the Acadian Expulsion – A Compilation of Information on the Eighteenth Century Transport Vessels, Used by the British to Transport the Acadians ("Neutral French") during the Acadian Expulsion of 1755"; http://www.landrystuff.com/ExpulsionShips.html

90. Lafreniere, Albert N.; "Acadian Deportation Ships", Connecticut Maple Leaf (French-Canadian Genealogical Society of Connecticut, Inc.; Tolland, CT) Volume 6 No. 1 (Summer 1993), pp. 26 and Volume 6 No. 2 (Winter 1993), pp. 148-149.

91. Maxson, Helen Morin; Ibid., p. 71.

92. Saunders, William L.; The Colonial Records of North Carolina (P. M. Hale, Printer to the State; Raleigh, NC; 1886-1890), Volume V, p. 894.

93. Saunders, William L., Clark, Walter and Weeks, Stephen B.; The Colonial and State Records of North Carolina (State of North Carolina; Raleigh, NC, 1886-1907), Volume V, p. 894.

94. Saunders, William L., Clark, Walter and Weeks, Stephen B.; The Colonial and State Records of North Carolina ("Documenting the American South" [DocSouth]; Online Digital Collection; 2008-2009), Volume V, p. 894; http://docsouth.unc.edu/csr/index.html/volumes

95. Land Record of Luke White dated 8 October 1758, Chowan County, North Carolina; "Record of Deeds Book Q, 1773-1777, Chowan County". Located in the Chowan County Courthouse in Edeton, NC, it was registered on 26 February 1774.

96. Maxson, Helen Morin, Ibid.; pp. 72, 74.

97. Will of Luke White dated 17 November 1770, Chowan County, North Carolina; "Chowan Co. Wills, 1694-1938, Warner-White, Will Book A, Page 185". The will was executed at Edenton, Chowan County, NC and is located in the North Carolina State Archives in Raleigh, NC.

98. Johnson, Jeffrey Earl (Jay); "Deschamps Family History" (Website within FamilyTreeMaker Online of Genealogy.com; Updated September 6, 2000). http://familytreemaker.genealogy.com/users/j/o/h/Jeffrey-E-Johnson/index.html

99. Letter, Stephen A. White (Centre d'Études Acadiennes, Université de Moncton, Moncton, New Brunswick, Canada) to Mrs. Helen Morin Maxson (Charlotte, North Carolina), 9 February 2006.

100. Furey, Francis T.; "Father Farmer's Marriage Register, 1758-1786, Preserved at St. Joseph's Church, Philad'a.", Records of the American Catholic Historical Society of Philadelphia, Vol. 1 – 1884-1886 (American Catholic Historical Society of Philadelphia; Philadelphia, PA; 1887), pp. 279, 282.

101. Middleton, Rev. Dr.; "List of Baptisms Registered at St. Joseph's Church, Philadelphia. (First Series.) From August 29, 1758, to December 31, 1775.", Records of the American Catholic Historical Society of Philadelphia, Vol. 1I – 1886-1888 (American Catholic Historical Society of Philadelphia; Philadelphia, PA; 1889), p. 266.

102. Rieder, Milton P. Jr. and Rieder, Norma Gaudet; The Acadian Exiles in the American Colonies, 1755-1768 (Milton P. Rieder, Jr. and Norma Gaudet Rieder; Metairie, LA; 1977), pp. 2-3, 5.

103. Jehn, Janet; Acadian Exiles in the Colonies (Janet Jehn; Covington, KY; 1977), pp. 213-214, 216-218.

104. National Archives of Canada (Ottawa, Canada); "Liste Des noms et nombres de Tous Les accadiens qui sont dans la pinsilvenia, 20 juin 1763", MG 5, Volume 450, Folios 416-417.

105. Vincens, Simone; Les Indomptés (Hébert Publications; Rayne, LA; 1990), pp. 213-217.

106. Rieder, Milton P. Jr. and Rieder, Norma Gaudet; Ibid., p. 30.

107. Jehn, Janet; Ibid., pp. 132, 151.

108. National Archives of Canada (Ottawa, Canada); "Etat des gens neutrals Acadiens qui sont a Lewisville A Snow hill, En Maryland, 7 Juillet 1763", MG 5, Volume 450, Folio 441.

109. Wood, Gregory A.; <u>A Guide to the Acadians in Maryland in the Eighteenth and Nineteenth Centuries</u> (Gateway Press, Inc.; Baltimore, MD; 1995), pp. 112-113, 165.

110. Rieder, Milton P. Jr. and Rieder, Norma Gaudet; <u>Ibid.</u>, pp. 33-34.

111. Jehn, Janet; <u>Ibid.</u>, pp. 133, 137, 152-153.

112. National Archives of Canada (Ottawa, Canada); "Etat des gens neutrals Acadiens qui sont a portabaco, En Maryland, 7 Juillet 1763", MG 5, Volume 450, Folio 442.

113. Wood, Gregory A.; <u>Ibid.</u>, pp. 98-99, 122, 154, 186.

Les Guédry d'Asteur

To share your ideas for the newsletter, contact:

Marty Guidry
6139 North Shore Drive
Baton Rouge, LA 70817
225-755-1915
guidryrm@cox.net

'GENERATIONS' newsletter is now in its seventh year. We hope to provide our readers with an interesting, informative and entertaining newsletter. Your input is always welcome and we look forward to another year of sharing family history and news with you.

The Guédry-Labine Family Newsletter 'GENERATIONS' serves as a focal point for family members to share and learn about us.

Allie Guidry
txguidry2000@yahoo.com

Marty Guidry
guidryrm@cox.net

Les Guédry d'Asteur Officers and Committees

OFFICERS:
President - Martin Guidry (LA)
Vice-President - Elaine Clement (LA)
Secretary - Billy Harrell Guidry (LA)
Treasurer - Daniel "Chuck" Guidry (LA)

COMMITTEES:
Website - Becky Boggess (IA) - Chairperson
　　　Annie Grignon-Labine (QU) - Translator
　　　Elaine Clement (LA) - Translator
　　　Martin Guidry (LA)

Genealogy - Daryl LaBine (FL/ON) - Chairperson
　　　Bernard Geddry (AZ)
　　　Mark Labine (MN)
　　　Daniel "Chuck" Guidry (LA)
　　　Martin Guidry (LA)

Finance - Cheryl Guidry Tyiska (MD) - Chairperson
　　　Paul Labine (IL)
　　　Marshall Woolner (OR)
　　　Gloria Parrent (TX)
　　　Chuck Guidry (LA)

Membership - Charlene Guidry Lacombe (LA) - Chairperson
　　　Gayle Guidry (LA) - Special Projects
　　　Warren Guidry (TX)

Sales - Cindy Guidry Herdt (WA) - Chairperson
　　　Wayne Simoneaux (LA)
　　　Billy Harrell Guidry (LA)

Publicity - Elaine Clement (LA) - Chairperson
　　　Margaret Jeddry (MA)
　　　Warren Guidry (TX)

Newsletter - Allie Guidry Hardee (VA)
　　　Rachel Hardee (VA)
　　　Lindsey Hardee (OH)
　　　Martin Guidry (LA)

CAFA Board Member - Jeanette Guidry Leger (LA)

SPRING 2009

Volume 7, Issue 2

Les Guédry d'Asteur

GENERATIONS

IN THIS ISSUE

AN INTERESTING GENEALOGICAL PUZZLE by Marty Guidry — 2

DUAL ROLES-Ray Labine: Chemist, Pilot — 6

BON APPETIT: Recipes from the Guédry/Labine Family Cookbook — 10

HOTEL LABINE- Fort Coulonge, Quebec, CA — 11

BOOK NOOK — 13

THINGS TO SEE & DO: New Brunswick Tourism — 25

As our Guédry-Labine and Petitpas Reunion approaches, another edition of "Generations" providing the latest details about the reunion and the Congres Mondial Acadien rolls off the presses. This issue of "Generations" has several interesting articles about our family. Despite the idyllic image of the typical Acadian life incorrectly portrayed in Longfellow's "Evangeline", our Acadian ancestors led extremely complex lives – experiencing much travel, deep tragedies, great joys, an intense work ethic, strong moral values, a great sense of humor, a wiseness often unrecognized and a profound religious conviction that gave them the strength to persevere through the toughest of times. They had their inner squabbles, their 'falling from the proverbial wagon' morally and other problems, but they stayed together as a family, guarded their treasured culture and religion and persevered – handing us a unique heritage and a wonderful life in today's world.

Occasionally in researching our ancestral heritage, we hit the proverbial 'brick wall' – not being able to find the parents of an ancestor. For many years this happened to descendants of Jean-Baptiste Guédry and Anne Magdeleine Dupuis; however, recently research by Daniel 'Chuck' Guidry and Audrey Westerman broke through the wall using extant land records and identified the parents of Jean-Baptiste Guédry. "An Interesting Genealogical Puzzle: Using Land Records to Determine Parentage" recounts the lives of Jean-Baptiste Guédry and Anne Magdeleine Dupuis and how land records and other civil records can provide genealogical gems.

In "Dual Roles" we learn how Ray Labine fell in love with flying during World War II and was able to continue that love affair for the rest of his life while leading a normal working life in Sudbury, Ontario.

"Bon Appetit" provides recipes for a very tasty Chicken Fricot and delicious Smothered Okra. Perfect for these early summer days.

Did you know that some Acadians were pirates? Have you visited the remains of Fort Beausejour on the border of Nova Scotia and New Brunswick and wondered what really happened there? The "Book Nook" features two books that answer these questions. Two other books in the "Book Nook" discuss the history of our Acadian ancestors in Acadia and after their exile.

For many years the Labine Hotel was a landmark in Fort Coulonge, Québec. Its story is an interesting one that begs to be told. Its proprietress Wilda Laporte Labine, a unique woman, was an excellent businesswoman that knew how to handle both the rough lumbermen and the family vacationers. In "Labine Hotel – Fort Coulonge, Québec, Canada" the Labine Hotel tells its interesting story from construction through its final days.

AN INTERESTING GENEALOGICAL PUZZLE: USING LAND RECORDS TO DETERMINE PARENTAGE - JEAN-BAPTISTE GUÉDRY, HUSBAND OF ANNE MAGDELEINE DUPUIS *by Marty Guidry*

For many years genealogists in Louisiana diligently traced ancestry to Jean-Baptiste Guédry and Anne Magdeleine Dupuis; however, they had difficulty bridging the gap between Jean-Baptiste Guédry and Claude Guédry, the first known Guédry in Acadia. In 1994, Daniel C. "Chuck" Guidry and Audrey Westerman published a paper in Terrebonne Life Lines in which they used extant land records to identify the parents of Jean Guedry as Jean-Baptiste Guédry and Anne Magdeleine Dupuis.[1] Through their excellent research the parents of Jean-Baptiste Guédry are identified.

The earliest known record of Jean-Baptiste Guédry, husband of Anne Magdeleine Dupuis, is the 7 July 1763 list of Acadians at Port Tobacco, MD desiring to return to France.[2,3] *(see pages 15 & 16)* Here one finds:

> *Etat des gens neutrals acadiens qui sont a portabaco. En Maryland 7 juillet 1763*
>
> ...
>
> *jean Gaidris, anne Gaidris son epouse, firmin Gaidris, magdelaine Gaidris, jean Gaidris, Monique Gaidris 6*

> [Translation: *List of the Neutral Acadians who are at Portabaco. In Maryland 7 July 1763*]

On 4 February 1768 Anne Dupuis, widow Guédry (age 35), and her five children Fermin (age 16), Magdalena (age 14), Monica (age 6), Isabel (age 3) and Jean-Baptiste (age 2) disembarked from the ship Jane in New Orleans, LA.[4,5] *(see pages 17 & 18)* They had departed the North Potomac River (Port Tobacco, MD) along with 144 other Acadians on 17 December 1767. The Jane was a plantation-built, seventy-five ton vessel commanded by Captain Richard Ryder with a crew of seven. Captain Ryder received his permit to sail to New Orleans at Patuxent, MD on 2 March 1767.[6,7] *(see page 19 for 'Permit to Sail')*

Arriving on the Jane with Anne Dupuis and her children were Pierre Guédry (called Pedro Lledri on the manifest and Pedro Lledre on the list of settlers), his wife Margarita, one child Maria and an orphan Olivier Baven (Boutin). Also sailing on the Jane were Joseph Guédry (called Joseph Landri on the manifest and the list of settlers), his wife Magdalena, three children Joseph, Simon and Magdalena and an orphan Margarita Baven (Boutin).[4,5] Pierre Guédry and Joseph Guédry were brothers and the sons of Augustin Guédry and Jeanne Hébert

Between March 1765 and February 1768 Jean-Baptiste Guédry died – probably near Port Tobacco, MD. Little of his early life is known although from the ages of his wife and children he likely was born in Acadia about 1731 and married Anne Magdeleine Dupuis in Acadia about 1750.

Shortly after arriving in New Orleans, Anne Magdeleine Dupuis and her children along with Pierre Guédry and his family and Joseph Guédry with his family were forced by Spanish officials to settle far up the Mississippi River at Fort San Luis de Natchez (near present-day Vidalia, LA). This swampy, insect-infested area was too far from New Orleans by river for profitable commerce and a great distance from other Acadian communities. A large number of the Acadians at Fort San Luis de Natchez died within the first eighteen months of settlement including Pierre Guédry's wife and two young children and probably Joseph Guédry's wife and three children. In December 1769 the Spanish relented and let the Acadians move downriver – close to other Acadian communities.[4,5,8] *(see page 20 for 'Distribution of Land')*

AN INTERESTING GENEALOGICAL PUZZLE

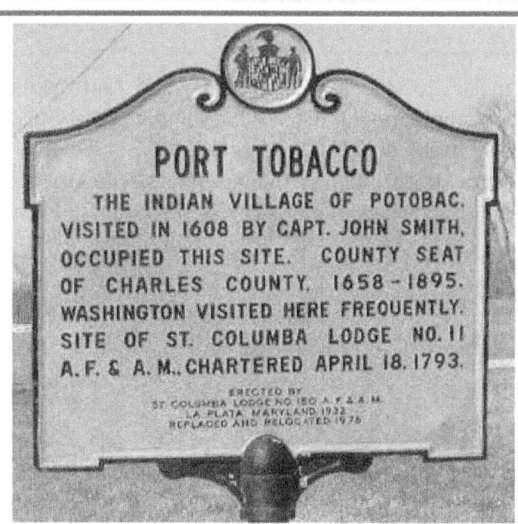

Anne Magdeleine Dupuis and her children along with Pierre Guédry and his new wife Claire Babin and Joseph Guédry immediately left Fort San Luis de Natchez and resettled in Ascension Parish, LA. On 1 August 1770 they were living near each other on the left bank (east side) of the Mississippi River in Ascension Parish near the Isle aux Marais. With Anne Magdeleine Dupuis (widow Guédry, age 40) were her children Firmin (age 18), Magdeleine (age 16), Jean (age 8) and Monique (age 6). Isabel Guédry apparently died at Fort San Luis de Natchez. Pierre Guédry (age 26) was with his second wife Claire Babin (age 26) and their new son Pierre (age 5 months). Also censused near the households of Anne Magdeleine Dupuis and of Pierre Guédry was Joseph Guédry (age 30) living alone – apparently having lost his entire family at Fort San Luis de Natchez.[9,10,11]

In Ascension Parish on 24 May 1773 Joseph Guédry, son of Augustin Guédry and Anne (Jeanne) Hébert of L'Assomption Parish in Pisiguit, Acadia, married Anne Monique Dupuis, daughter of Jean Dupuis and Anne Braud. Witnesses to their marriage were Joseph Buten (Boutin) and Joseph Dupuis.[12,13] This was the second marriage for Joseph Guédry. At St. Joseph's Catholic Church in Philadelphia, PA on 22 January 1761 he married Magdelen Melancon.[14,15,16]

Joseph Guédry and Magdalen Melançon had three children: Joseph (b. ca.. 1755), Simon (b. ca. 1763) and Magdalena (b. ca.. 1765).[4,5] Magdalen Melançon and her three children apparently died at Fort San Luis de Natchez during their brief residence there in 1768-1769.[9,10]

Anne Magdeleine Dupuis and her family remained in Ascension Parish as did Joseph Guédry. On 23 April 1777 Anne Dupuis (widow Guédry, age 44) was living with her sons Firmin Guédry (age 27) and Jean Guédry (age 17) and her daughter Marie (Monique) Guédry (age 15) on the east side of Mississippi River near the Isle aux Marais. Firmin Guédry was listed as the head of the household. Joseph Guédry (age 45) and his wife Marie (Anne Monique) Dupuis (age 33) were living next to Anne Dupuis and her family.[17,18] By 1777 Pierre Guédry had moved his growing family to the Opelousas region.[19,20]

In December 1782 Joseph Guédry died. Shortly after is death on 10 December 1782 his widow Anne Monique Dupuis requested an inventory of the estate.

Acadian Settlement at San Luis de Natchez, circa 1768

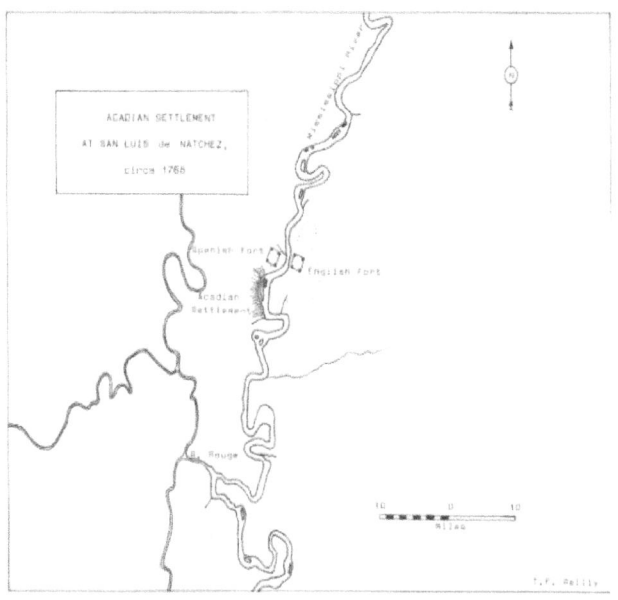

AN INTERESTING GENEALOGICAL PUZZLE

He lived in the community L'Anse de L'Isle aux Marais and present at the inventory were: Jean Guédry, nephew of the deceased, Pierre Dupuis, Pierre Landry, Pierre Brasseux, Joseph Braud, relatives, friends and neighbors of the deceased. The appraisers were Joseph Landry and Simon Richard. The property of Joseph Guédry adjoined that of Firmin Guédry, son of Ann Magdeleine Dupuis, the widow of Jean-Baptiste Guédry.[21,22]

As stated in his marriage certificate to Anne Monique Dupuis, Joseph Guédry was the son of Augustin Guédry and Anne Hébert.[12,13] One of the persons present at the inventory of Joseph Guédry's estate was Jean Guédry, *nephew of the deceased. (see page 21 for the first page of Joseph Guédry's inventory)*

Based on census and sacramental records, in 1782 in Louisiana there were only two known Jean Guédry's: Jean-Baptiste Guédry, the son of the late Jean-Baptiste Guédry and Anne Magdeleine Dupuis, who was born about 1761 and Jean-Baptiste Guédry, son of Pierre Guédry and Claire Babin, who was born 9 July 1776. It is improbable that a six-year old child would be mentioned as attending an estate inventory; therefore, the son of Pierre Guédry and Claire Babin is not the Jean Guédry mentioned in the above estate inventory. The Jean Guédry mentioned must be the son of the late Jean-Baptiste Guédry and Anne Magdeleine Dupuis.

Jean Guédry could only be the nephew of Joseph Guédry if his father and Joseph Guédry were brothers or if his mother Anne Magdeleine Dupuis and Joseph Guidry's wife Anne Monique Dupuis were sisters. As stated in her marriage certificate, Ann Monique Dupuis, widow of Joseph Guédry, was the daughter of Jean Dupuis and Anne Braud.[12,13]

Although we do not know with certainty the parents of Anne Magdeleine Dupuis, the available records do provide some clues. From Louisiana census records Anne Magdeleine Dupuis was born ca. 1730-1733. Her eldest child Firmin Guédry was born about 1750-1752; therefore, she married Jean-Baptiste Guédry about 1750. Furthermore, in 1763 she and her husband Jean-Baptiste Guédry were at Port Tobacco, MD with their children.

A review of Dupuis men who had daughters named Anne and/or Magdeleine born in the 1720 - 1740 timeframe yielded several potential sets of parents for Anne Magdeleine Dupuis.[23] They are:

1) Charles Dupuis and Madeleine Trahan – daughter Madeline was born in 1739; however, this family was exiled to Southampton, England and Madeleine Dupuis married Eustache Daigle there in 1759.

2) Antoine Dupuis and Marie-Joseph Dugas – daughter Madeleine was born in 1722; she married Joseph Hébert about 1740. Another daughter Anne-Marie was born in 1731; however, she married Michel Boudrot about 1751.

3) Germain Dupuis and Marie Granger – daughter Anne was born in 1738; however, she married Dominique Thibodeau. Another daughter Marie Madeleine was born in 1741; however, she wed Amand Breau about 1763.

AN INTERESTING GENEALOGICAL PUZZLE

4) Joseph Dupuis and Elizabeth LeBlanc – daughter Marie Magdeleine was born on 20 May 1737.[24,25] Nothing futher could be found of her life, but she does not have the name Anne.

5) Charles Dupuis and Elizabeth LeBlanc – daughter Anne was born on 7 May 1733.[26,27] This family was exiled to Maryland. Charles Dupuis and Elizabeth LeBlanc with two sons Jean-Baptiste and Joseph were at Annapolis, MD in 1763.[28,29,30]

Although to date no definitive record confirming the parents of Anne Magdeleine Dupuis has been located, it appears very probable that they were Charles Dupuis and Elizabeth LeBlanc. More importantly for this study, almost certainly they were not Jean Dupuis and Anne Braud, the parents of Anne Monique Dupuis, as they had only two daughters: Marie (born ca. 1739) and Monique (born ca. 1744).[31] The relationship of Joseph Guédry and Jean Guédry, therefore, was because Jean Guédry's father was the brother of Joseph Guédry.

Since the parents of Joseph Guédry were Augustin Guédry and Jeanne Hébert, **the parents of Jean-Baptiste Guédry, father of Jean Guédry and husband of Anne Magdeleine Dupuis, also were Augustin Guédry and Jeanne Hébert.**

Besides the evidence discussed above, collateral evidence supporting this conclusion stems from Anne Magdeleine Dupuis' close association with Joseph Guédry and Pierre Guédry, both sons of Augustin Guédry and Jeanne Hébert . They were, in fact, her brothers-in-law and certainly provided much needed support to her. From Port Tobacco, MD Anne Magdeleine Dupuis sailed to New Orleans, LA on the Jane with Pierre Guédry and Joseph Guédry, sons of Augustin Guédry and Jeanne Hébert. She settled near both of them at Fort San Luis de Natchez in 1768 and at L'Anse de L'Isle aux Marais in Ascension Parish, LA in 1770. In 1777 and 1782 she still was living near Joseph Guédry at L'Anse de L'Isle aux Marais. Furthermore, Charles Dupuis and Elizabeth LeBlanc were exiled to Maryland and were at Annapolis, MD in 1763 – not far from Anne Magdeleine Dupuis and Jean Baptiste Guédry at Port Tobacco, MD.

- References on page 22

DUAL ROLES-RAY LABINE, HIS JOB & HIS LIFELONG LOVE

In World War II Ray Labine served in the Royal Canadian Air Force, but was attached to the British Royal Air Force piloting Spitfires engaged in fighter and photo reconnaissance. With a deep love of flying engrained in him, after WWII Ray became a part-time flying instructor near Sudbury, Ontario while working full-time as a laboratory chemist at the International Nickel Company (INCO) Copper Cliff facility in Sudbury.

The article below from INCO's newsletter "The Triangle" of August 1975 describes Ray Labine's interesting dual roles as flight instructor and process chemist. Thanks to André Labine of British Columbia for finding this fascinating story and providing it to "Generations".

Dual Roles

As a summer wind chases wisps of cloud across the sky over Whitewater Lake, near Sudbury, a novice pilot casts a nervous side-long look at his instructor. The wind is pushing their pontooned aircraft off course.

"Apply a little aileron . . . Come on, use that arm . . . Keep that wing down . . . That's it . . ." The voice beside the student pilot coaches patiently as the plane banks, and then side-slips into a proper cross-wind landing approach.

For the novice at the controls, the "book learning" of cross-wind landings isn't helping much now. There's an odd feeling in the pit of his stomach . . . wing down, so close to the water . . . it feels unnatural. At the last minute, the plane levels out.

"That's got her!" The spray and resistance of water, a slight sinking sensation, and the aircraft lands gracefully on the sunlit lake. Our student awkwardly taxies to the dock, and the first man out is Ray Labine, flying instructor. Ray casually jockeys the plane to the fuel pump. His now pensive student clambers onto the dock, absently wipes his forehead on his shirt-sleeve, and heads for the small frame building that houses Sudbury Aviation. The clatter of a screen door, and Pearl McMahon, factotum, and wife of owner, John McMahon, looks up, and bestows a motherly smile. "Coffee's on downstairs", she says. Feeling more inclination for a stiff belt to get the wobble out of his knees, our man settles for a cup of coffee and looks around for anyone who will listen to a lengthy discussion of cross-wind landings.

Meanwhile, instructor Ray Labine is aloft again, patiently and methodically guiding another would-be pilot through the intricacies of float-plane flying. He prides himself on producing sound and safe pilots, reminding his students of the inherent danger of becoming "know-it-alls". "When you think you know it all, you should get out of flying", he claims. Among his successful students, he counts his brother, Maurice Labine, a senior

Dual roles

Preparing for a lesson aloft, student pilot, Ivan Leblanc, left, a garage mechanic at Copper Cliff South mine, and flying instructor, Ray Labine, a chemist in the process technology laboratory at Copper Cliff, plot their proposed course before heading for the "wide blue yonder".

captain with Air Canada, and his son Jim, captain of an Otter and flying the high Arctic.

Contrary to what one might expect, Ray and a good many of his students are not full-time flying "mavericks", but everyday gentlemen holding regular jobs. As a matter of fact, Ray is a full-time chemist at Inco's process technology laboratory in Copper Cliff, and a good sprinkling of his students are Inco miners, drillers, mechanics and engineers. So when the attention is not on the "ore below", eyes are turned to the "sky above".

Speaking of "sky above", that blue in Ray's eyes is not for naught. He's been a pilot a long, long time, and although he's not one for talking about himself, a few cold beers, a mention of Spitfires and Messerschmidts may ignite the necessary spark.

If you're lucky, he'll tell you some of it ... About the days he flew the Spitfires, tested the Fokke Wulfs and the chase of the German battleship, the Graf Spee.

Ray earned his wings at Uplands Airport in Ottawa. The year? 1941. He trained student pilots on Harvards and Tiger Moths. Soon after, he was commissioned, and attached to the R.A.F. in England, engaged in fighter and photo

At the Sudbury Aviation base on Whitewater Lake at Azilda, Ivan Leblanc and Ray Labine conduct a pre-flight check of the aircraft they'll be using. Air intakes, propeller, control surfaces and floats are all subjected to very close scrutiny before take-off.

reconnaissance. He flew every kind of Spitfire, the "Spit" fives, nines and elevens. He tells of plotting the daily bomb-lines through the use of remote-control aerial photography. He reminisces over the unending conflicts between ground personnel and air crews, particularly in the assessment of aerial mapping and photographs... problems arose from failure to grasp each other's difficulties. The ground crew demanded exact continuity of altitude and location in order to do accurate mapping and pin-point bomb targets. "When we say photograph at 502 feet, we don't mean at 500", was a normal kind of ground crew statement. The air crews were lacking accurate weather information, hard-pressed by enemy attacks and were flying through cloud, wind and storm over unfamiliar terrain.

As a test pilot of Spitfires, Messerschmidts and Fokke Wulfs for the assessment of the R.A.F. Ray attracted the attention of the de Haviland people. This English aircraft company of world renown wanted our man to continue with them as test pilot. Unfortunately, as with a good many of his fellow pilots who had come through the war in one piece, the stresses of losing friends and terrifyingly close calls had taken their toll in nerves. High blood pressure and

Ground school, and some of Inco's budding pilots. From left: Instructor Ray Labine, Ivan Leblanc, South mine; Tom Beaudry, Stobie mine; Kevin Thorpe, smelter; Charles De Rusha, Stobie mine; Josef Stanzinger, Creighton mine and Don Fournier, smelter.

states of acute stress disqualified many superlative war pilots from continuing in civil aviation.

Ray recovered from high blood pressure in due course, but changed his line of work in the interim. He started with Inco in 1946 and has stayed. He's successfully combined his flying enthusiasm with his job at Inco. However, he has a sneaky kind of pet thought... to have his own little Lear jet and fly off into the sunset... A Lear yet? Oh it's only worth about a million and a quarter!

Flight lieutenant, Ray Labine, overseas in Wales in 1943. The aircraft is a mark eleven Spitfire, a high-altitude photo reconnaissance plane. Ray was on loan to the R.A.F. at the time the picture was taken, and was flying photo forays over Berlin at an altitude of 40,000 feet.

IN THE NEWS-HISTORICAL NEWS TIDBITS

BACK HOME AFTER DETENTION—The four-man crew of the Shrimper Texas Clipper is greeted in Port Arthur after return there from a 22-day detention in Obregon, Mexico, by Mexican authorities. Left to right: Newell F. Allen; Aubrey Guidry; Joe Faveta; Capt. Albert N. Tabbot in command of the boat; Frank Taylor, owner of the boat, and Dusty Rhodes of Port Arthur. (AP Photo).

The Abilene, Texas, Reporter-News
February 5, 1947

Lafayette Advertiser, Scott, LA-1896

Mr. Jules Guidry,
Scott, La.

Dear Sir:

Your grandson, Eli, returns to his home to-day, after having completed the full Diploma Business Course, for which he has received the Diploma of the Kentucky University; under seal.

We hope he may return in September and complete the Short-hand and Type-writing Courses, which his scholarship, entitles him to do. He has been a courteous and polite young man to both teachers and students alike. Wishing him a safe journey home and with my best regards to yourself, I am, most respectfully,
W. R. Smith.

BABY FALLS THREE STORIES, UNINJURED

By United News.

SAN FRANCISCO, Nov. 16.—William Guidry, aged 11 months, is still able to do his daily "cooing" despite his tumble from a window of his parents' third floor apartment. Physicians who examined the child say he is none the worse for his long fall. "Not a scratch," was the official diagnosis.

San Antonio Express-San Antonio, TX, Nov. 17, 1924

New Castle News, New Castle Pennsylvania, December 16, 1913

Right: HUSBAND IS ABSOLUTE BOSS

Article reads: SPRINGFIELD, Mass. Dec. 16 -Judge Charles L. Long, who two years ago made the celebrated decision that "man, who pays the bills, is boss of the household and lord and master of the exchequer" yesterday ruled that a husband may eject his wife's relatives from the house.

Hormidas G. Labine, the defendant in a separate support suit, declared that it was a case of "too much brother-in-law".

Judge Long said that a husband has the right to remove from his home any of his wife's relatives and if he cannot do so alone, the police, if called upon must help him. In the end, however Labine was ordered by the court to contribute to the support of his wife and children.

HUSBAND IS ABSOLUTE BOSS

SPRINGFIELD, Mass., Dec. 16.—Judge Charles L. Long, who two years ago made the celebrated decision that "man, who pays the bills, is boss of the household and lord and master of the exchequer" yesterday ruled that a husband may eject his wife's relatives from the house.

Hormidas G. Labine, the defendant in a separate support suit, declared that it was a case of "too much brother-in-law."

Judge Long said that a husband has the right to remove from his home any of his wife's relatives and if he cannot do so alone, the police, if called upon must help him. In the end, however Labine was ordered by the court to contribute to the support of his wife and children.

BON APPETIT-Recipes from the Guédry-Labine Cookbook

CHICKEN FRICOT
by Margaret Jeddry-Nahant, MA & Meteghan, Nova Scotia

1 4-5 lb. chicken (2-3 kg.)
1/2 lb. salt pork (250 g)
2 large onions, chopped
2 tbsp. flour (30 ml.)
6 large potatoes, peeled & diced
2 medium carrots, peeled & diced
3 qts. Boiling water (3 l.)
1 tbsp. salt (15 ml.)
1 tsp. pepper (5 ml.)
1 tbsp. summer savory (15 ml.)

METHOD:

Cut the chicken into serving *pieces*. Score the salt pork into small squares and melt in a heated skillet. Fry chicken in salt pork fat until golden brown, turning pieces frequently. Remove chicken from skillet and sauté onion for 1 minute. Add the flour and sauté for an additional 1-2 minutes.

Place chicken and onion in large pot. Add water, potatoes, carrots, salt, pepper and summer savory. Bring to a boil. Reduce heat to simmer and cook for 1 hour or until chicken is tender. Taste and adjust seasonings. Serves 8.

SMOTHERED OKRA
By Alice Matte Guidry-Lake Charles, LA

2 lbs. fresh okra (sliced 1/4 inch thick or less)
1 tomato, peeled and chopped
1 lg. yellow onion, peeled and chopped
1/2 cup vegetable oil
Salt, black pepper and red pepper to taste

Cook okra on medium heat stirring often so as not to let it burn. It should take about 45 minutes to cook to the point that it is no longer 'ropey'. Add onions and tomato after 30 minutes and cook for the final 15 minutes. A few teaspoons of bacon drippings can be used with the oil for additional flavor. Season with salt, black pepper and red pepper.

You can adjust this recipe accordingly to cook an entire bushel in an 18-quart roasting oven. It is much easier and you shouldn't have to stir as often if the roasting pan has a non-stick coating. You should cook it covered in the roasting pan, stirring every 15 minutes.

Labine Hotel-Fort Coulonge, Québec, Canada by Marty Guidry

With the lumber industry of Pontiac County booming at the dawn of the twentieth century, Mr. George Jewell built a grand hotel in Fort Coulonge during 1901. Begun in the late 1690's as a trading post on the Ottawa River near the mouth of Rivière Coulonge, Fort Coulonge in the late 1890's was bustling with activity as lumbermen hired in Ottawa arrived by train, spent the night in town and then set out in the morning for the nearby lumber camps.

Fort Coulonge needed lodging for these men and George Jewell recognized the need. Constructed in 1901, the three-story Jewell House operated under the capable hands of Mr. Jewell until 1922 when Raoul Labine purchased it. The name changed to the Labine Hotel and Raoul's wife, Wilda Laporte Labine, operated the hotel for the next fifty-four years. Ironically, Mrs. Labine was born the same year that the Labine Hotel was constructed – 1901.

During the 1920's the Labine Hotel operated a horse-drawn bus to transport guests to and from the train station. At about eight each evening the train with whistle blowing would arrive at Fort Coulonge. Approximately twenty guests and their luggage would clamber aboard the waiting horse-drawn bus for the mile trip to the Labine Hotel. Each passenger paid twenty-five cents for the ride.

To house the horses needed for the bus, the Labine Hotel had its own stable - large enough to accommodate thirty horses.

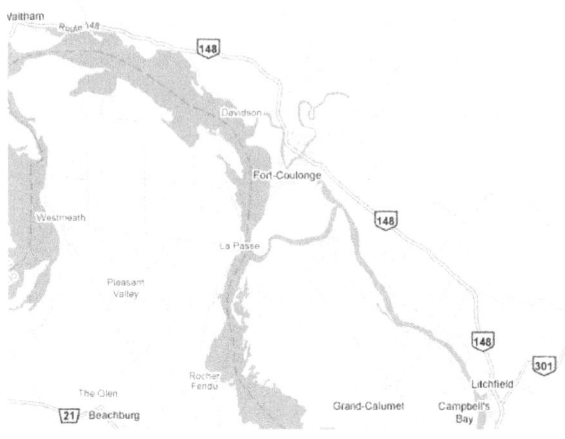

Labine Hotel-Fort Coulonge, Quebec, CA

If you brought your own horse to the hotel, the Labine's would stable it for you and add the costs of hay and oats to your bill.

Mrs. Labine's father, Paul Fabien Laporte, had thirty to forty horses that he used to take the lumbermen and their supplies to the lumber camps. Toward the end of March, the men broke camp and returned south. Of course, that meant another overnight stay at the Labine Hotel in Fort Coulonge. Since the wage during this time was a dollar per day, a lumberman would make one hundred to one hundred fifty dollars during the winter season. That first night outside the lumber camp, a night spent at the Labine Hotel, often was quite exciting. Fights among the men occurred, the best man won and it was all forgotten right there.

The men provided their own music – the juice harp, the mouth organ, spoons on a pan, a comb and paper and similar simple instruments kept the men's toes tapping and voices singing. Often local singers, fiddlers and step-dancers entertained the men for free.

Mrs. Labine operated the hotel with seven to ten employees including a cook, a kitchen girl, a dining room waitress, two chamber maids, a laundress and a man to stoke the fires. In the early years the hotel was without electricity so a young girl cleaned and filled the sixty to seventy oil lamps at the hotel. Later Mrs. Labine purchased a gas generator that eliminated this day-long job.

Labine Hotel-Fort Coulonge, Québec, Canada

The nearby river provided water for drinking, cooking and washing. The staff and guests daily used two drums of water brought from the river. One drum was for drinking and cooking and the other for washing.

The Labine Hotel had twenty-five rooms with a total of forty beds. When pressed, the hotel could accommodate up to one hundred beds. An agreement between the hotel and the lumber companies limited the men in transit to a maximum of fifty at any one time; however, occasionally as many as one hundred men arrived on the train. Straw mattresses were scattered about and everyone slept a little closer that night.

Hotel guests enjoyed excellent meals including boiled pork or sausage, potatoes, beans, superb soup and bread freshly-baked in the hotel ovens. Charlie Kenny's bakery down the street occasionally supplemented the supply of bread. At breakfast eggs were a special treat for the men who had not had any for the entire winter. There was no limit and some men ate as many six to eight eggs at a meal. Homemade, mouth-watering desserts as cakes and pies made with apples, prunes, raisins and dried peaches quickly disappeared from the table. Each morning at 4:30 a.m. the kitchen staff began preparing their desserts in the specially-made large baking tins.

Other guests besides lumbermen stayed at the Labine Hotel throughout the year. The Labine Hotel had an excellent reputation among its guests. From August until spring nearly all rooms were occupied each night. In the summer several guests would rent their room for several months at the rate of twenty dollars a month.

Mrs. Labine reserved one room at the hotel as a sample showroom for traveling salesmen. They would rent the room for a week and local townspeople would come to examine the merchandise on display and place their orders. Mr. Dowey Gamble of the J. M. Garland Company and Mr. Cleavens of the Jules Patry Co. often reserved the showroom.

A shrewd hotel manager, Mrs. Wilda Labine's motto was "I see nothing, I know nothing, I say nothing." She knew the value of minding one's own business and of confidentiality. She once remarked "In a hotel we know everyone's problems. People come here to have a good time and to forget. We had to try and make peace. That was number one!" She often attributed her success as a hotel manager to her faithful practice "Give a good measure, and give quality." Her clients appreciated her generosity and hospitality – returning to the Labine Hotel season after season. A few even visited every year for Mrs. Labine's entire fifty-four year tenure.[1]

In 1976 the Labine's sold the Labine Hotel to Mr. Leveillé. Shortly afterwards, on 1 September 1979 it burned down. Today the Bank of Nova Scotia occupies the site of the old Labine Hotel.[2]

Sadly, on 23 October 2005 Mrs. Wilda Laporte Labine died at Sacred Heart Manor in Fort Coulonge at the age of 104 years.[3] Her husband Raoul Labine had died earlier. The grand old Labine Hotel is no more, but the memories shared by several generations of guests are vivid and long-lasting.

1. LaBine, Daryl; The Guédry, Guidry, Geddry, Jeddry, Guildry dit LaBine, LaBine & LaBean Family – Descendants of Claude Guédry & Marguerite Petitpas (Daryl LaBine; St. Catharine's, Ontario, Canada; 1999), pp. 449-450. (Information in above article largely taken from this source.)

2. http://ww3.sympatico.ca/larry.kenney/oldcoulonge.html

3. Obituary of Wilda Laporte Labine; Ottawa Citizen (26 October 2005) (Ottawa, Ontario, Canada).

Labine Hotel - After the fire

BOOK NOOK

AN UNSETTLED CONQUEST-The British Campaign Against The Peoples of Acadia
By Geoffrey Plank

The story of the removal of the Acadians, some of whose descendants are the Cajuns of Louisiana, and the subsequent oppression of the Mi'kmaq has never been completely told. In this first comprehensive history of the events leading up to the ultimate break-up of Nova Scotian society, Geoffrey Plank skillfully unravels the complex relationships of all of the groups involved, establishing the strong bonds between the Mi'kmaq and Acadians as well as the frustration of the British administrators that led to the Acadian removal, culminating in one of the most infamous events in North American history.

The Siege of Fort Beauséjour 1755
By Chris M. Hand

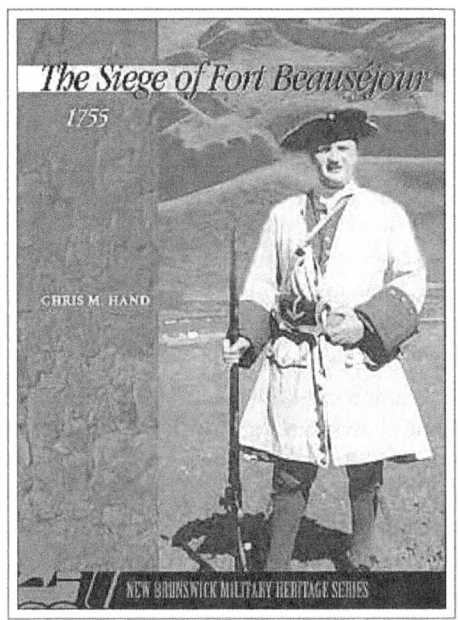

The British capture of Fort Beauséjour was the final act in a long struggle between Britain and France for control of Acadia. In The Siege of Fort Beauséjour, 1755, Chris M. Hand outlines the events leading up to the siege and gives a running account of the seige itself. In June, 1755, a combined force of New England volunteers and British regulars captured it after a brief siege. When Beauséjour fell, so too did Acadia, and the great expulsions followed soon after. Major Chris M. Hand, Royal Canadian Regiment, is currently serving overseas, seconded to the British Army, Warminster, England. The Siege of Fort Beauséjour, 1755 is based on his MA thesis in history at the University of New Brunswick. The Siege of Fort Beauséjour, 1755 is Volume 3 in the New Brunswick Military Heritage Series. Published in cooperation with the Military and Strategic Studies Program at the University of New Brunswick and the Canadian War Museum, this series is part of the New Brunswick Military Heritage Project.

BOOK NOOK

Les Flibustiers de l'Acadie - Coureurs des mers
By Armand G. Rocichaud

Armand G. Robichaud est un géographe-urbaniste de Shédiac, au Nouveau-Brunswick. Il est co-auteur du livre *Les bâtiments anciens de la mer Rouge* (Michel Henry, Éditeur, 1988) et auteur du livre *Des histoires de Robichaud* (Éditions de la Francophonie, 2002).

Dans cet essai, Armand G. Robichaud nous présente *Les Flibustiers de l'Acadie*, un sujet sur lequel peu d'historiens se sont penché. Il explique la différence entre un corsaire, un flibustier et un pirate et trace un portrait de plusieurs de ceux-ci qui ont participé à la course sur mer en Acadie. Il explique les liens de parentés entre plusieurs flibustiers acadiens et explique dans quels contextes ils ont agit. Ce sont les corsaires acadiens qui sont les derniers à avoir combattu pour la France en Amérique. Il est également question d'incidents du XIXe siècle, impliquant les corsaires et les pirates de la Nouvelle-Écosse et du Nouveau-Brunswick. Le livre traite aussi brièvement des trésors cachés des pirates, des trésors des Acadiens du Grand Dérangement et de quelques naufrages.

This book (in French) mentions the 1726 trial of Jean-Baptiste Guédry on pages 105-109.

HISTORY OF THE CAJUNS-From Ancient France to Nova Scotia to Louisiana to Colonial Texas *By Alex Loya*

During the French and Indian War one of the saddest episodes was the expulsion of the French population of what used to be the French Colony of Acadia in present day Nova Scotia. This human tragedy came to be known as the Great Acadian Exile. It was at this time that the people known as the French Acadians were scattered through the 13 British Colonies and to the Spanish Colony of Louisiana, where they became known as Cajuns, and where they gave Louisiana her character. In this thoroughly well researched book, drawing from primary and other sources, Alex Loya examines the incontrovertible evidence that a number of those first Cajuns moved on to Texas where they became a significant segment of the colonial population of Texas and that they participated in every aspect of American history starting with the American Revolution, when the tragedy of the French Acadians turned into victory.

Census of Acadians at Port Tobacco, MD desiring to go to France, 7 July 1763

263

442 État des gens neutrals acadiens qui sont a portabaco. En Maryland
7 juillet 1763

+ Charle Braux, claire Braux son epouse, marie Braux, margueritte braux, elizabeth Braux, anne Braux, magdelaine Braux, pierre braux, anne La jeunne orpheline .... 9.

+ charle commost veuf, anne commost, charle Commost, firmin commost .... 4.

+ joseph Babin, rosalite Babin son epouse, joseph babin 3

+ honoré trahan, marie trahan son epouse, marie trahan, pierre trahan, gens orphelin joseph le jeunne orphelin antoine le jeune 6

+ joseph gaidris, marie benoist gaidris son epouse, gabriel gaidris, joseph gaidris, genevieve gaidris, ... 5.

+ Louis Latier, anne Latier son epouse, antoine Latier; anne Benoist, orpheline, rose benoist orpheline, margueritte benoist orpheline 6

+ antoine Braux, margueritte Braux son epouse, joseph braux, charle Braux perpetue Braux, Scholastique Braux ... 6

Census of Acadians at Port Tobacco, MD desiring to go to France. 7 July 1763, Pg. 2

204

+ jean Broussard, anne Broussard son epouse, firmin broussard, magdelaine broussard jean broussard 5

+ antoine Babin, catherine babin son epouse, françois babin, firmin Babin, charle Babin, claire babin, rose Babin, anne Babin, marie Babin 9

+ jean Gaidris, anne Gaidris son epouse, firmin Gaidris, magdelaine Gaidris, jean Gaidris, monique Gaidris 6

+ jean Braux, marie Braux son epouse, michel Braux, margueritte Braux, remis Boudraux orphelin 5

+ jean Braux, osite Braux son epouse, pelagie Braux 3

+ anne Dupuis Veuve, marie Dupuis, margueritte Dupuis, monique dupuis, pierre dupuis 5

+ joseph Braux, marie josette braux son epouse, joseph marie Braux, margueritte Braux, marie Rose landri 5

442

+ pierre richard veuf, anne marie Richard 2

+ jean Dupuis, anne Dupuis son epouse, firmin Dupuis, marie dupuis 4

Arrival in New Orleans, 1768

[Lista de las familias Acadiana q.^e han venido a esta Provincia a establecerse de la Luisiana, y se hallan a lo pasado en la Avitacion del Rey oy dia de la fha. 2 de Feb.^ro de 1768]

Años / Meses

	Joseph Landri	32	Elena	02
	Magdalena	35	Agustin Nacido recién	
Hijos	Joseph	13	Mariana Nacida recién	
	Simon	05		
	Magdalena	03		
huerf.^a	Margarita Bauer	15	Agustin Landri	25
			Hermanos Alexandro	18
			Pedro	16
	Bacilio Landri	42	Magdalena	27
	Ursi	36	Genoveva	23
hija	Maria	12	Cecilia	21
	Mariana	02	Magdalena	14
	Joseph Bauer	38	Viuda: Rosa Landri	30
	Rosa	37	Hijos: Margarita	05
hijos	Simon murió el 15 del Corr.^te	06	Magdalena	03
	Maria Rosa	02	Maria	1
herm.^o	Joseph Bauer	14		
			Juan Baup.^ta de Pui	38
			Ana	32
viuda	Margarita Bauer	38	Hijos: Fermin	16
Hijos	Joseph	17	Maria	13
	Estevan	08	Cecilia	04
	Pedro	08		
	Margarita	13		
			Viudo Ana Bró	60
	Maximen Landri	31	Hijos Pedro de Pui	18
	Maria	28	Maria	22
h.^o	Marcelo	02	Monica	24
	Maria	06		
huerf.^a	Margarita Bró	20	Viuda: Ana de Pui	35
			Hijos: Fermin Lleni	16
	Margarita Landri	33	Juan Baup.^ter	02
	Pedro Bró	13	Magdalena	14
	Ana	14	Monica	06
			Isabel	05

Arrival in New Orleans, 1768, Page 2

	Pedro Ledai	26	Viuda: Margarita	26
	Margarita	27	Hijos: Pedro Chiacere	26
Hijos:	Maria	03	Joseph	18
Huerfan:	Olivie Baven	18	Ana	22
			Maria	20
	Miguel Ribet	28		Juan Carlos Bró	36
	Simil	25		Maria	32
Herm:	Blas	21	Hijos:	Miguel	13
	Mariana	28		Simon	02
	Margarita	18		Margarita	10
				Ludwin	06
Viuda:	Cathalina Baven	47	Herm:	Eronin Venua	18
Hijos:	Timan Baven	21		Remi Budró	13
	Carlos	18			
	Clara	24		Joseph Bró	34
	Luisan	22		Maria Josepha	30
	Rosa	14	Hijos:	Joseph	08
	Isabel	04		Margarita	06
				Clara	03
				Carlos recien nasido	—
	Fran.co Baven	26	Viuda:	Clara Bró	66
	Margarita	30		Pedro	17
Hijos:	Carlos	04	Hijos:	Isabel	25
	Pablo	6		Ana	23
Herm:	Maurien Binuan	12		Magdalena	21
	Ana	07			
				Olivie Baven	22
Viuda:	Margarita Bró	63		Maria	22
Hijos:	Maria Josepha	22	Hijos:	Maria Josepha	05
	Maria Rosa	20		Mariana	04
			Huerf:	Genobeva	21
	Juan Bró	32		Antonio Bró	32
	Maria	27		Margarita	32
Hijos:	Juan Baupta	6	Hijos:	Joseph	14
	Maria	03		Carlos	11

Permit to Sail to New Orleans for the "Jane" - 2 March 1767

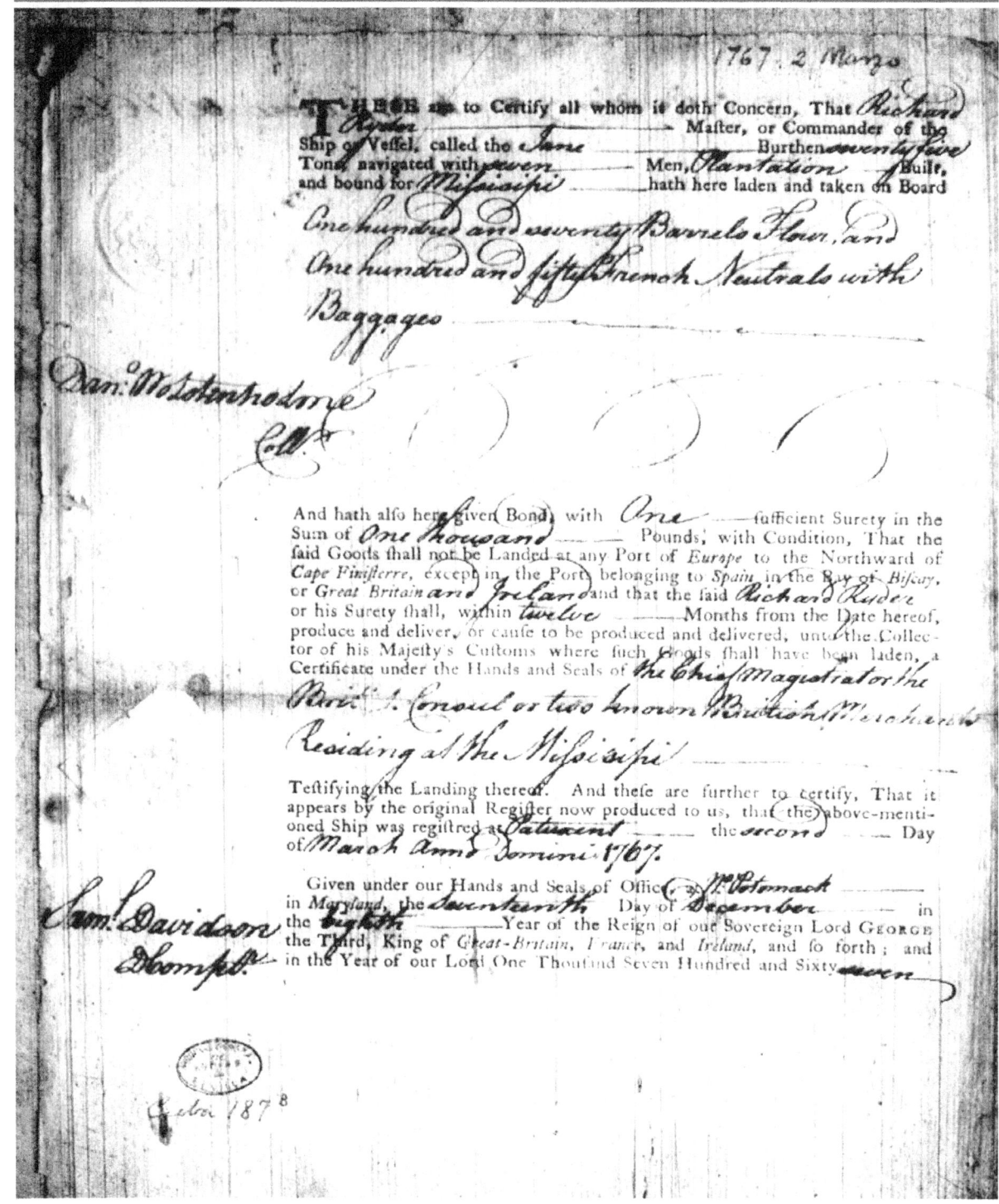

Distribution of Land to the Acadians Settling at Fort San Luis de Natchez, Feb. 1768

Distribución de Tierras p.̃ las Familias Acadianas q.̃ sean derinado à la Poblacion de S.̃ Luis en Nãrches

Arpanas

- Joseph Landri su muger tres hijos y una huerf.ª ...... 6 arp.ᵗᵃˢ
- Basilio Landri su muger y dos hijos .... 5.
- Joseph Baben su muger dos hijos y un huerf.ª ...... 5.
- Margarita Baben viuda con quatro hijos .... 4.
- Maturen Landri su muger dos hijos y una huerf.ª ... 5.
- Margarita Landri viuda con sinco hijos .... 6.
- Agustin Landri con seis Hermanos .... 6.
- Rosa Landri Viuda con tres hijos .... 4.
- Juan Bap.ᵗᵃ de Pui su muger y tres hijos .... 5.
- Ana Brò viuda con tres hijos .... 4.
→ Ana de Pui viuda con sinco hijos .... 6.
→ Pedro Andre su muger una hija y un huerf.ª .... 5.
- Miguel Ritec su muger y tres hermanos .... 6.
- Cathalina Baben viuda con seis hijos .... 6.
- Juan C.º Baben su muger dos hijos y dos herm.ˢ ..... 6.
- Margarita Brò viuda con dos hijos .... 5.
- Juan Brò su muger y dos hijos .... 5.
- Margarita viuda con quatro hijos .... 5.
- Juan Carlos Brò su muger quatro hijos y dos huerf.ª
- Joseph Brò su muger y quatro hijos

Inventory of Joseph Guédry's Estate

REFERENCES

1. Guidry, Daniel C. "Chuck" and Westerman, Audrey; "Guédry – Guidry – Gaidry", Terrebonne Life Lines (Terrebonne Genealogical Society; Houma, LA), Volume 13, No. 4 (Winter 1994), pp. 62-63.

2. Archives Nationales France, Archives du Ministère des Affaires étrangères, Correspondance politique, Angleterre (Paris, France), volume 450, folio 442. "Etat des gens neutrals acadiens qui sont a portabaco. En Maryland 7 juillet 1763" [Transcription: National Archives of Canada (Ottawa, Canada), MG 5, Volume 450, Folio 442.]

3. Rieder, Milton P. Jr. and Rieder, Norma Gaudet; The Acadian Exiles in the American Colonies, 1755-1768 (Milton P. Rieder, Jr. and Norma Gaudet Rieder; Metairie, LA; 1977), p. 33.

4. Archivo General de Indias "Audiencia de Santa Domingo (A.D.S.)" (Seville, Spain), Legajo 2585, Folios 577-604. "Acadians Families Who Came to Louisiana and Were Going to Settle at San Luis de Natchez in the Year 1768" and "Acadians Who Were Granted Land at San Luis de Natchez, 1768" [Microfilm available at the Center for Louisiana Studies; University of Louisiana at Lafayette; Lafayette, LA].

5. Voorhies, Jacqueline K.; Some Late Eighteenth-Century Louisianians – Census Records of the Colony, 1758-1796 (The USL History Series, University of Southwestern Louisiana; Lafayette, LA, 1973), pp. 435-436, 438.

6. Archivo General de Indias "Papeles Procedentes de Cuba (P.P.C.)" (Seville, Spain), Legajo 187-A-1 (2 Marzo 1767). "Passport for the Jane, 2 March 1767" [Microfilm available at the Center for Louisiana Studies; University of Louisiana at Lafayette; Lafayette, LA].

7. Voorhies, Jacqueline K.; Ibid., p. 200.

8. Brasseaux, Carl A.; The Founding of New Acadia – The Beginnings of Acadian Life in Louisiana, 1765-1803 (Louisiana State University Press; Baton Rouge, LA; 1987), pp. 78-89.

9. Archivo General de Indias "Papeles Procedentes de Cuba (P.P.C.)" (Seville, Spain), Legajo 188-A-1, Folios 454-466. "Etat, du habitants acadiens de la paroisse de L'assession a Commence Sur La Rive Droite du fleuve, chez jean jeansonne, autre fois chez La Veuve Lachance et finis a La pointe D'Enhaute Lisle aux marais. Année 1770" [Microfilm available at the Center for Louisiana Studies; University of Louisiana at Lafayette; Lafayette, LA].

10. Voorhies, Jacqueline K.; Ibid., p. 277.

11. Robichaux, Jr., Albert J.; <u>Colonial Settlers Along Bayou Lafourche – Louisiana Census Records, 1770-1798</u> (Albert J. Robichaux, jr.; Harvey, LA; 1974), p. 7.

12. Ascension Catholic Church; Donaldsonville, Ascension Parish, LA; Volume 1 page 124 of the Marriage Register (24 May 1773).

13. Pollard, Nora Lee Clouatre; <u>Diocese of Baton Rouge Catholic Church Records</u> (Diocese of Baton Rouge; Baton Rouge, LA; 1978-2008), v. 2 pp. 272, 340.

14. St. Joseph's Catholic Church; Philadelphia, Philadelphia County, PA; Marriages for the Year 1761 (Simon Yetry and Magdalen Melançon).

15. Furey, Francis T.; "Father Farmer's Marriage Register, 1758-1786. Preserved at St. Joseph's Church, Philad'a.", <u>Records of the American Catholic Historical Society of Philadelphia</u> (American Catholic Historical Society of Philadelphia; Philadelphia, PA; 1889), v. II (1886-1888) p. 279.

16. O'Keefe, Barbara Brady; "Father Farmer's Marriage Registers, 1758-1786. St. Joseph's Church, Philadelphia, Pennsylvania", Acadian-home.org website (Viewed 26 Jan 2006), p. 23 of 93.

    http://www.acadian-home.org/acadian-marriages-Philadelphia.html

17. Archivo General de Indias "Papeles Procedentes de Cuba (P.P.C.)" (Seville, Spain), Legajo 190. "General Census of the Inhabitants of the District of the Parish of Ascension of Lafourche des Chetimachas, which begins on the right bank of the river beginning below at Basil Prejean and ending above at the tip of the Isle aux Marais; and on the left bank, at Sieur Maruice Canoee formerly of the village of the Houmas and ending above at Francois Babin opposite the tip of the above mentioned isle, comprising five leagues, 1777" [Microfilm available at the Center for Louisiana Studies; University of Louisiana at Lafayette; Lafayette, LA].

18. Robichaux, Jr., Albert J.; <u>Ibid.</u>, p. 18.

19. Archivo General de Indias "Papeles Procedentes de Cuba (P.P.C.)" (Seville, Spain), Legajo 2358. "Opelousas General Census, May 4, 1777" [Microfilm available at the Center for Louisiana Studies; University of Louisiana at Lafayette; Lafayette, LA].

20. Voorhies, Jacqueline K.; <u>Ibid.</u>, p. 312.

21. Ascension Parish Courthouse; Donaldsonville, Ascension Parish, LA; Original Acts v. 15 "Invent & Sales", Judice N-1 "B" pp. 523-529.

22. Behrman, Eileen Larré; <u>Ascension Parish, Louisiana Civil Records 1770-1804</u> (Eileen L. Behrman; Conroe, TX; 1986), pp. 26-27.

23. Arsenault, Bona; Histoire et Généalogie des Acadiens (Les Éditions Leméac Inc.; Ottawa, Canada; 1978), pp. 1112, 1129, 1145, 1162-1165, 1187.

24. St. Charles-aux-Mines Catholic Church, Grand-Pré, Acadie (Currently maintained at the Diocese of Baton Rouge; Department of the Archives; Baton Rouge, LA); St. Gabriel Catholic Church Register, v. 2 p. 162.

25. Pollard, Nora Lee Clouatre; Ibid., v. 1 p. 46; v. 1a (Revised) p. 70

26. St. Charles-aux-Mines Catholic Church, Grand-Pré, Acadie (Currently maintained at the Diocese of Baton Rouge; Department of the Archives; Baton Rouge, LA); St. Gabriel Catholic Church Register, v. 2 p. 125.

27. Pollard, Nora Lee Clouatre; Ibid., v. 1 p. 44; v. 1a (Revised) p. 67.

28. Archives Nationales France, Archives du Ministère des Affaires étrangères, Correspondance politique, Angleterre (Paris, France), volume 450, folio 443. "Recencement des habitants Neutre de L'accadie détenus à Annapolis En Maryland. 7 juillet 1763" [Transcription: National Archives of Canada (Ottawa, Canada), MG 5, Volume 450, Folio 443.]

29. Jehn, Janet; Acadian Exiles in the Colonies (Janet Jehn; Covington, KY; 1977), p. 138.

30. Rieder, Milton P. Jr. and Rieder, Norma Gaudet; Ibid.; p. 27.

31. Voorhies, Jacqueline K.; Ibid., p. 435.

TOURIST ATTRACTIONS-NEW BRUNSWICK

VILLAGE HISTORIQUE ACADIEN-CARAQUET, N.B.

In this "living visual workshop" visitors can see how Acadians lived between 1780 and 1890. Museum staff, dressed in the original costumes of the period, perform old crafts such as spinning wool, weaving cloth and making clothes, forging iron, making furniture and wagons, printing books and posters, making soap, drying fish, and preserving vegetables and meats.

http://www.villagehistoriqueacadien.com/

FESTIVAL ACADIEN de CARAQUET-August 1-15, 2009

Year after year, thousands of people converge on Caraquet to celebrate the vitality of the Acadian culture. The Acadian Festival is not only a cultural event of Acadia, but one of the most important attractions of the Atlantic. Its mission is to promote Acadian culture in all its shapes and forms, including music, theatre and the visual arts. Join the crowds to celebrate and encourage the approximately 200 artists in Acadia.

http://www.festivalacadien.ca/

VILLAGE de MEMRAMCOOK-Memramcook, NB

From the heights of Lourdes, formerly Village-du-bois, one can see the 15 smaller villages established in this serene valley. The Memramcook ecomuseum provides visitors with an overview of the numerous monuments and historical sites, of the people who made our past great, the customs, traditions and of the historical facts of Memramcook.

Once in the valley, you should not miss: The monument Lefebvre, the Parc LeBlanc Golf Course, the old Gayton covered bridge, Lourdes Church, Indians' Chapel in Beaumont, Belliveau Orchard & Acadian dishes at Leblanc Restaurant or the Au Vieux College Restaurant.

www.village.memramcook.com

2009 GUÉDRY-LABINE & PETITPAS REUNION INFORMATION

Congres Mondial Acadien (CMA) for 2009 will be held on the Acadian Peninsula in New Brunswick from 7 August - 23 August 2009. CMA activities will be centered around Caraquet, New Brunswick. You can click on this website to keep up with the events planned for the 2009 CMA.

http://www.cma2009.ca/

We are having our Guédry-Labine & Petitpas Reunion on Sunday, 16 August 2009 in the Conference Center of Danny's Inn in Bereford, New Brunswick. Beresford is just five miles north of Bathurst, New Brunswick and Danny's Inn is on Highway 134 just south of Beresford. Bathurst has a rich Acadian history that we'll explore in the coming months.

We will begin about 8:30 am and have activities until 5:00 pm. Our agenda, activities and displays will include formal sessions with music, presentations, etc. as well as time to mingle and get to know your cousins. The tentative agenda is:

- 8:30 am - Opening Service (Mass) at Holy Family (Sainte Famille) Catholic Church
  [Opening Procession honoring our ancestors, French Rosary, Mass, Closing Procession]
  (430 St. Peter Avenue; Bathurst, NB)
* 9:45 am - Reunion Registration at Danny's Inn Conference Center
* 10:00 am - Larry Miller and his Cajun Band (two-step & waltz demonstrations)
* 10:45 am - Break (View displays, meet cousins, sales table, etc.)
* 11:00 am - Presentation - Cultures of Louisiana Cajuns and Maritime Acadians
  (including a Cajun Mardi Gras Run)
* 11:45 am - Break (View displays, meet cousins, sales table, etc.)
* 12:00 pm - Dinner Buffet
* 1:00 pm - New Brunswick Acadian Musical Entertainment
* 1:45 pm - Break (View displays, meet cousins, sales table, etc.)
* 2:00 pm - Petitpas Genealogy - Recent Discovery Using DNA Techniques
* 2:45 pm - Break (View displays, meet cousins, sales table, etc.)
* 3:00 pm - Presentation - History of the Acadians of the Baie-des-Chaleurs Region
- * 3:45 pm - Break (View displays, meet cousins, sales table, etc.)
* 4:00 pm - Presentation - Louisiana Cajun French and Acadian French of Canada
- * 4:45 pm - Closing Ceremony

There will be a superb buffet lunch. It'll be a Hot & Cold Dinner Buffet that includes roast beef smothered in peppercorn gravy, sweet & sour meat balls, lasagna, chicken wings, potato casserole, coleslaw, tossed green salad, carrot salad, rolls, carrot cake, cherry cheesecake, fresh fruit salad, coffee and tea.

Registration information was sent out in August to those on our distribution list. A copy of the registration form will be attached to the next few issues of this newsletter. Now is a good time to secure lodging.

The website below contains a number of motels, hotels and bed & breakfasts in the Bathurst area.

http://www.bathurst.ca

NEW BRUNSWICK ACCOMMODATIONS - CMA 2009

The Guédry-Labine family reunion is scheduled to take place August 16, 2009, in the town of Bathurst, not far from Caraquet, New Brunswick, CA. Here are a few more links for accommodations in those areas. We'll add more details about our reunion in the next few months.

BATHURST - http://www.bathurst.ca/english/home/

Authentique Bed & Breakfast Enjoy our 4 star B&B in a heritage home of the 20's with 'Arts & Craft's influences, conveniently located in the heart of Bathurst. You are welcome to relax in a cozy atmosphere with personalized service. Spacious rooms with very comfortable beds, cable TV, DVD, MP3, wireless internet, work desk and telephone. Each room has a private bathroom. Breakfast 'A la Carte' will be served in our elegant dining room.

Comfort Inn Bathurst Conveniently located on St. Peter Avenue. Close to shopping and offices. 35 person meeting room available.

John's Motel Our rooms have a full bath and shower, color television with cable, and most importantly comfortable beds! We also boast a swimming pool and an area for picnics. We also have in-room coffee.

Sea'scape Cottage This is our fully equipped beach house located on the beautiful Bay of Chaleur in Bathurst, New Brunswick. Select the virtual tour button to have a closer look.

The official New Brunswick Tourism Website is at the link below. You can learn about interesting locations, sites and activities at this website. By clicking on the word "Guides" in the left column of the page, you can order a free 2008 Experience New Brunswick Vacation Planner" which is excellent.

http://www.tourismnewbrunswick.ca

The 2009 CMA website has an excellent page on accommodations within the Acadian Peninsula. Visit it by clicking on this link:

http://www.cma2009.ca

CARAQUET - http://www.ville.caraquet.nb.ca/

Hotel Paulin "The Pearl of Baie des Chaleurs", Caraquet.

Motel Colibri 12 rooms smoking and non-smoking. 2 double bed. Free breakfast.

Super 8 Motel 50 guest rooms including 18 junior suites.

ON THE WEB

Les Guédry d'Asteur

http://freepages.genealogy.rootsweb.ancestry.com/~guedrylabinefamily/

The Guédry-Labine Family Genealogical Database

Developed by the Les Guédry d'Asteur, Inc. Genealogy Committee

http://freepages.genealogy.rootsweb.ancestry.com/~guidryrm/Guedry-Labine/

The Louisiana State Archives

This is the official website for the Louisiana State Archives. It provides a very nice overview of the archival holdings and services. Although there are no images of original documents at this time, there is a very nice index to Confederate Pension Applications with numerous Guidry records. Click on Research Library under Sections of Organization, then Confederate Pension Applications to the left of the top photograph, then Search the Database.

http://www.sos.louisiana.gov/archives/archives/archives-index.htm

Archives of Canada

http://www.archivescanada.ca/english/index.html

DUES REMINDER

Attached at the back of this issue is a membership application for renewing your membership in Les Guédry d'Asteur. Our dues are very reasonable at $6.00 for individuals and $10 for a family.

By joining and paying your dues, you provide us with the financial resources to participate in many projects, one being the CMA 2009 reunion in Bathurst, New Brunswick.

Please take a moment, complete the Membership Application, enclose a check and send it to the address on the application. It will help all of us do so much for the family. And, if you would like to join at one of the Benefactor Levels, it would let us do even more.

Les Guédry d'Asteur

To share your ideas for the newsletter, contact:

Marty Guidry
6139 North Shore Drive
Baton Rouge, LA 70817
225-755-1915
guidryrm@cox.net

'GENERATIONS' newsletter is now in its seventh year. We hope to provide our readers with an interesting, informative and entertaining newsletter. Your input is always welcome and we look forward to another year of sharing family history and news with you.

The Guédry-Labine Family Newsletter 'GENERATIONS' serves as a focal point for family members to share and learn about us.

Allie Guidry
txguidry2000@yahoo.com

Marty Guidry
guidryrm@cox.net

Les Guédry d'Asteur Officers and Committees

OFFICERS:
President - Martin Guidry (LA)
Vice-President - Elaine Clement (LA)
Secretary - Billy Harrell Guidry (LA)
Treasurer - Daniel "Chuck" Guidry (LA)

COMMITTEES:
Website - Becky Boggess (IA) - Chairperson
    Annie Grignon-Labine (QU) - Translator
    Elaine Clement (LA) - Translator
    Martin Guidry (LA)

Genealogy - Daryl LaBine (FL/ON) - Chairperson
    Bernard Geddry (AZ)
    Mark Labine (MN)
    Daniel "Chuck" Guidry (LA)
    Martin Guidry (LA)

Finance - Cheryl Guidry Tyiska (MD) - Chairperson
    Paul Labine (IL)
    Marshall Woolner (OR)
    Gloria Parrent (TX)
    Chuck Guidry (LA)

Membership - Charlene Guidry Lacombe (LA) -
    Chairperson
    Gayle Guidry (LA) - Special Projects
    Warren Guidry (TX)

Sales - Cindy Guidry Herdt (WA) - Chairperson
    Wayne Simoneaux (LA)
    Billy Harrell Guidry (LA)

Publicity - Elaine Clement (LA) - Chairperson
    Margaret Jeddry (MA)
    Warren Guidry (TX)

Newsletter - Allie Guidry Hardee (VA) - Editor
    Rachel Hardee (VA)
    Lindsey Hardee (OH)
    Martin Guidry (LA)

CAFA Board Member - Jeanette Guidry Leger (LA)

SUMMER 2009

Volume 7, Issue 3

Les Guédry d'Asteur

GENERATIONS

IN THIS ISSUE

Michel Cantrell-   2
Commandant of
the First Acadian
Coast by Marty
Guidry

BON APPETIT: 11
Recipes from the
Guédry/Labine
Family Cookbook

BOOK NOOK   12

THINGS TO SEE   17
& DO: Bathurst &
New Brunswick
Travel /Tourism

CMA 2009 -   18
Guédry Family
Reunion Updates

With the Guédry-Labine & Petitpas Reunion only weeks away we are publishing an extra edition of "Generations" in 2009 to ensure everyone has the latest information on the Reunion. Although the article "Michel Cantrelle – Commandant of the First Acadian Coast" does not discuss directly the Guédry and Petitpas families, it does describe the governmental system under which the first Acadians, including members of the Guédry and Petitpas families, lived when they first reached the Louisiana shore. The French and later the Spanish had a rigorous system for settling and administering the Acadians in their villages.

As always, "Historical Tidbits" offers interesting insights into the lives of our Guédry ancestors using first-hand accounts from newspapers of the day. When you have a moment, grab "Generations" and read one of the news articles. You'll find it quite interesting.

Ready to cool down on a hot summer day? Why not try the Seafood Delight or a bowl of Homemade Creamy Banana & Pecan Ice Cream? Not sure know how to concoct these? Visit "Bon Appetit" and you'll be the hit at your house.

Bathurst, NB

After relaxing from a nice, cool treat, sit down and enjoy one of the interesting books from the "Book Nook".

Finally, study the information on our Reunion. The committees of Les Guédry d'Asteur have done an outstanding job organizing this year's Guédry-Labine & Petitpas Reunion. The agenda is varied and quite interesting with a very moving Mass to open the Reunion, Cajun and Acadian music, historical and genealogical talks, superb displays and a few surprises to keep everyone interested. And we'll enjoy a superb buffet lunch with perhaps a little "magic" thrown in. Haven't registered yet? It's not too late. You can simply show up at the door of Danny's Inn Conference Center and register there. Everyone with an interest in the Guédry, Labine and Petitpas families is invited to attend. So enjoy this extra edition of "Generations" and then rush to Bathurst, New Brunswick and visit with all of your cousins.

MICHEL CANTRELLE
COMMANDANT OF THE FIRST ACADIAN COAST
by R. Martin Guidry

The early life of the Cantrelle family in Louisiana is truly one of public service. Although they acquired vast tracts of land along the Mississippi River and enjoyed wealth, they devoted their lives to the people of Louisiana. The father of the family Jacques Cantrelle was influential in the affairs of New Orleans – being a warden of St. Louis Catholic Church and an employee of the Superior Council in New Orleans. Two of his sons-in-law Louis Judice and Nicolas Verret were commanders and commandants of the Acadians in today's St. James and Ascension Parishes. One son Michel Cantrelle was a commandant of the Acadian Coast and the Parish Judge of old Acadia Parish and of St. James Parish. Their story forms a significant part of the early history of this unique region of Louisiana.

Several members of the Guédry family who arrived in Louisiana between 1765 and 1785 settled in the St. James and Ascension Parish area. Among these was the very first Guédry to reach Louisiana soil – Joseph Guédry. After spending a brief period in the Attakapas region, Joseph Guédry relocated to Ascension Parish in September 1765.

ACADIANS ARRIVE IN LOUISIANA AND THE COMMANDERS

Beginning in 1764 as the first Acadians were arriving in Louisiana, the French authorities appointed commanders to assist the Acadians in settling their assigned lands. Additionally, these commanders, invested with limited civil and judicial authority, preserved the peace in their territory and with limited authority were judges. In 1769 the Spanish assumed full control of Louisiana and apportioned Louisiana into districts. The superior officer of each district was the commandant with significant military, civil and judicial powers. The commandants had a broader role in the district than did the earlier French commanders. The commandants not only preserved the peace, but also examined traveler's passports, aided new settlers in obtaining land grants, prevented smuggling, registered the sale of lands and slaves, served as a judge in minor cases, acted as a notary public and represented the Spanish governor in their districts. Additionally, the commandant awarded building contracts for public works and for furnishing provisions, issued land grants to settlers, employed many persons and could make 'cadets' of settlers' children. Cadets received a salary and could become officers in the army. In addition to his small salary, the commandant received fees that he collected and was given the title 'Don' and a commission as a lieutenant in the Spanish Army.

In early 1764 twenty Acadian exiles from New York arrived in Louisiana and in April of that year Governor d'Abbadie settled them on the right (west) bank of the Mississippi River near present-day Lagan, LA (St. James Parish). In February 1765 a second group of 193 Acadians from Halifax via St-Domingue reached New Orleans and in April 1765 they were sent to the Attakapas District (St. Martin Parish). In September 1765, to escape the raging malarial or yellow fever epidemic in the Attakapas District, 82 Acadians left their homes and resettled near Lagan, LA with the first group of Acadian immigrants. During May through November 1765 at least three other groups of approximately 300 Acadians from St-Domingue arrived at New Orleans and were settled on the west bank of the Mississippi River near present-day Welcome, LA (St. James Parish). Shortly thereafter, several of the Acadian families in this latter group moved downstream to a site near present-day Front Vacherie, LA (St. James Parish, LA).

MICHEL CANTRELLE-COMMANDANT OF THE FIRST ACADIAN COAST

Several groups of Acadians from Maryland arrived in New Orleans between 1766 and 1769. In September 1766 a chartered English ship delivered 224 Maryland Acadians to Louisiana. They soon were joined by an undetermined number of Acadians who arrived in December 1766. Governor Ulloa settled these groups along the Mississippi River in St. James and Ascension Parishes. Then in July 1767 another 211 Maryland Acadians arrived and in August 1767 were settled on the east side of the Mississippi River at Fort St. Gabriel located on the south side of Bayou Manchac near present-day St. Gabriel, LA (Iberville Parish). During February 1768 a group of 149 Maryland Acadians reached New Orleans. Governor Ulloa forced them to settle on the west side of the Mississippi River at San Luis de Natchez near present-day Vidalia, LA – a swampy, insect-infested land far from the other Acadian settlements and vulnerable to Indian raids. In December 1769 the Spanish permitted these Acadians to resettle downstream on the west side of the Mississippi River in present-day Ascension and northern Assumption Parishes just north of earlier Acadian settlements. In January 1769 the "La Bretana" (Brittania) left Port Tobacco, Maryland bound for New Orleans with 30 Acadians and approximately 70 Englishmen and Germans. As they neared the mouth of the Mississippi River, strong winds and fog caused them to miss the entrance and they landed near present-day Matagorda Bay, TX. After imprisonment by the Spanish as smugglers, they eventually reached Natchitoches, LA in October 1769 and in November 1769 settled on the east bank of the Mississippi River near present-day Galvez, LA (Iberville Parish).

No other groups of Acadians are known to have reached Louisiana until the seven Acadian expeditions of 1785 brought from France approximately 1500 new Acadian immigrants to Louisiana. The only other group of Acadians known to have arrived in Louisiana was an extended family of 19 Acadians who landed at New Orleans in December 1788 aboard the "Brigite" - having sailed from St. Pierre Island (St. Pierre and Miquelon). They settled in present-day Ascension Parish.[1,2]

In 1765 as the Acadians began arriving in Louisiana, Nicolas Verret and Louis Judice were appointed co-commanders of the territory along the Mississippi River above the German Coast. This territory became the Acadian Coast. Both Louis Judice and Nicolas Verret resided near present-day St. James, LA (St. James Parish) with Judice's home being a short distance upstream of Verret's home. Between them was the Spanish land grant of Jacques Cantrelle located in the section called Cabahanoce. Initially the Acadian Coast covered both banks of the Mississippi River from approximately five miles below present-day St. James, LA (near present Oak Alley Plantation) northward to the Ascension Parish line. As more Acadians settled in the area, the Spanish divided the territory into two parts with Verret being commander from his residence downriver to the southern edge of the territory and Judice being commander of the territory from the home of Jacques Cantrelle (present-day area of the St. James Catholic Church) upriver to the Ascension Parish line. Judice eventually extended the northern boundary of his territory into Ascension Parish. In January 1770 the jurisdictions changed with Verret as commandant of the Acadian Coast from Front Vacherie to the Ascension Parish line and Judice as commandant above the Ascension Parish line. When Verret died on 5 November 1775, the Spanish appointed Michel Cantrelle as commandant of Verret's territory.[3]

MICHEL CANTRELLE-COMMANDANT OF THE FIRST ACADIAN COAST

American Revolution plaque at the grave of Michel Cantrell, St. James Catholic Cemetery

JACQUES CANTRELLE – FIRST CANTRELLE IN LOUISIANA

Jacques Cantrelle, son of Claude Cantrelle and Marguerite Turpin and a native of St. Leger, Picardy, France,[4,5] was born about 1697. In 1720 he arrived in Louisiana on the braque *Le Profond* after a voyage of over three months. Initially, he was a worker on the Arkansas fort and by 1729 was in Natchez. On 28 November 1729 the Natchez Indians raided Fort Rosalie and killed over 200 inhabitants in less than two hours. Jacques Cantrelle had gone hunting for the day and escaped the massacre; however, his wife Marie Françoise Minquetz[4,5] was not so fortunate. She perished during the massacre[4,5]. There were no known children of this marriage. Many French left Natchez after the massacre including Jacques Cantrelle, who headed south, down the Mississippi River. He eventually settled at Cannes Brulées near present-day Kenner, LA.[6]

Shortly after settling in Louisiana, Jacques Cantrelle married Marie Marguerite Larmusiau, daughter of Jean Baptiste Larmusiau and Catherine Esternay and the widow of Pierre LeHoux, on 16 April 1730[4,5]. The couple lived at Gentilly ridge in eastern New Orleans along the shore of Lake Pontchartrain. Here Cantrelle became a warden of the St. Louis Church and was influential in New Orleans affairs[6]. He was employed by the Superior Council.

Granted a tract of land in 1762 with ten arpents frontage at Cabahanoce along the Mississippi River near present-day St. James, LA, Cantrelle opted to continue living in New Orleans. In the September 1763 Census of the Colony of Louisiana[7,8] Jacques Cantrelle was listed within Captain Guinault's district in New Orleans and had a wife, two sons less than fourteen years of age, three women slaves, two boy slaves, two girl slaves and a musket. From other records we know the family to be living with him at this time to be his wife Marie Marguerite Larmusiau[4,5] and their two sons Michel Cantrelle (baptized 24 March 1750)[9,10] and Jacques Cantrelle fils (born 1 April 1752)[11,12]. The couple also had three daughters who were married by 1763. Marie Marguerite Cantrelle married Nicolas Verret about 1748[13,14] and Marie Jeanne Cantrelle wed Louis Judice about 1751[13,15]. Nicolas Verret and Louis Judice were the two commanders of the Acadian Coast. A third daughter Marianne Cantrelle married first Pierre Songy about 1755[16,17] and then Jean Baptiste Poeyfarre on 23 May 1780[17,18]. All three daughters and their families resided along the Acadian Coast.

MICHEL CANTRELLE-COMMANDANT OF THE FIRST ACADIAN COAST

Other children of Jacques Cantrelle and Marie Marguerite Larmusiau were Jacques Cantrelle (baptized 25 October 1731)[20,21], Marie Josephe Cantrelle (born 11 January 1731)[20,22], Jean Baptiste Cantrelle (baptized 26 April 1744)[20,23], Jacque Cantrelle (baptized 27 March 1746)[20,24] and Marie Marguerite Cantrelle (baptized 11 September 1747)[25,26].

Not until approximately 1766 did Jacques Cantrelle move to his grant at Cabahanoce where he appeared on the census records of 1766[27,28], 1769[29,30] and 1777[31,32]. Extending from just below the present St. James Catholic Church downriver to almost the current St. James Co-Op Sugar Mill, Jacques Cantrelle's land grant was twenty-eight arpents. On 21 October 1777 Jacques Cantrelle was buried from St. James Catholic Church near Cabahanoce[30,33,34,35]. His wife Marie Marguerite Larmusiau lived to be 80 years old, dying in July 1785. Her funeral was held at the St. Louis Cathedral on 10 July 1785[36,37].

MICHEL CANTRELLE – SERVING THE FIRST ACADIAN COAST

Michel Cantrelle, the second to youngest child of Jacques Cantrelle and Marie Marguerite Larmusiau, certainly had a life filled with adventure as he lived in bustling New Orleans during his childhood and youth and then, as a young man, moved with his parents and brother Jacques Jr. to the largely unsettled region of Cabahanoce on the west bank of the Mississippi River above New Orleans. Here he experienced deep tragedy and setbacks as he rose to become commandant of the Acadians settled in that region.

On 24 March 1750 at St. Louis Cathedral in New Orleans Jacques Cantrelle and his wife Marie Marguerite Larmusiau watched silently as Father Dagobert baptized their infant son Michel Cantrelle. His godfather Michel Meilleur from whom he received his name was a master cobbler in New Orleans and his godmother Marie Jeanne

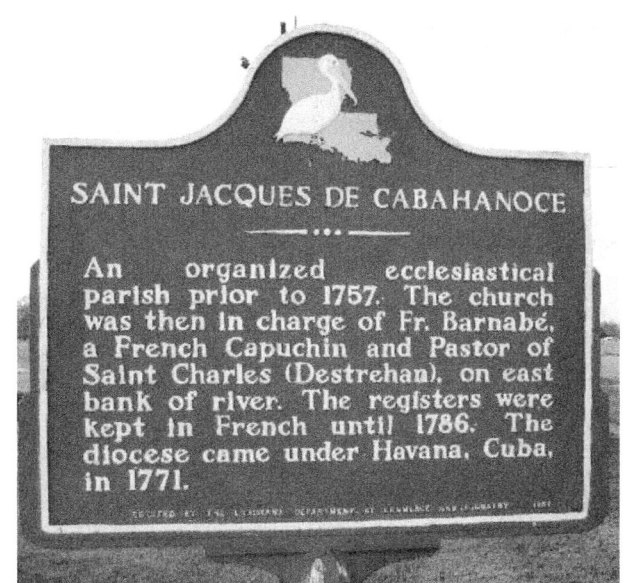

Cantrelle was his older sister who soon would marry Louis Judice.[9,10] After the ceremony he and his parents returned to their home on Gentilly ridge along the southeastern shore of Lake Pontchartrain.

In 1758 on the third of April Michel's sister and godmother Marie Jeanne Cantrelle and her husband Louis Judice had their fourth child, a son, and they named him Michel after his young uncle Michel Cantrelle. With 8-year old Michel Cantrelle as his godfather the infant boy Michel Judice was baptized on 5 April 1758 at St. Louis Cathedral. His aunt Marguerite LeHoux was his godmother[15,38]. Two years later at the age of ten Michel Cantrelle was the godfather of his niece Marie Verret baptized on 12 August 1760 at St. Louis Cathedral. She was the daughter of Nicolas Verret and Marie Marguerite Cantrelle, Michel's sister[39,40]. Interestingly, by the age of ten Michel Cantrelle was the godfather of a child of each of the first co-commanders of the Acadians.

In September 1763 Michel was living with his parents and younger brother Jacques at their home in New Orleans within Captain Guinault's military district[11,12]. By 1766 Acadians were beginning to arrive in Louisiana and were being settled by the Spanish along the

MICHEL CANTRELLE-COMMANDANT OF THE FIRST ACADIAN COAST

Mississippi River north of New Orleans. About 1765 Jacques Cantrelle, approaching his 69th birthday, established an indigo plantation on his 1762 land grant located near present-day St. James, LA in an area called Cabahanoce. His property on the west bank of the Mississippi River extended from just below the present St. James Catholic Church downriver to about the current St. James Co-Op Sugar Mill. His two sons-in-law Louis Judice and Nicolas Verret along with their wives (Jacques Cantrelle's daughters) and young families had already established homes in this area. Jacque's grant lay between their properties. Did he move here to be near his daughters and grandchildren? Initially his wife Marie Marguerite Larmusiau and their two sons Michel and Jacques Cantrelle did not accompany Jacques to Cabahanoce. Perhaps he traveled between New Orleans and Cabahanoce for a time to be with his family and to oversee the operations of his farm.

In 1766 Jacques Cantrelle was at Cabahanoce with his five slaves. He now had 28 arpents of land, 20 hogs and one gun. His wife and two sons were not with him[27, 28]. Between 1766 and 1769 Jacques Cantrelle brought his wife Marie Marguerite and his two sons Michel and Jacques to his Cabahanoce plantation. On the 14th of September 1769 Louis Judice censused the settlers at and near Cabahanoce. Jacques Cantrelle, his wife Marie Marguerite and his two sons Michel and Jacques are with him at Cabahanoce. By this time he had divided his property and livestock with his sons. He had retained eight arpents of land for himself and had given ten arpents each to his sons Michel, age 20, and Jacques, age 19. Michel Cantrelle had ten head of cattle, four pigs, six sheep and one gun[31,32].

As a young man and a son of a prominent plantation owner, Michel Cantrelle quickly gained status in the Cabahanoce area. In January 1770 at the age of 20 he was a lieutenant under his brother-in-law Captain Nicolas Verret in the Militia of the First Acadian Coast[41,42].

With death of his brother-in-law Nicolas Verret on 5 November 1775 Michel Cantrelle became the commandant of the Acadians in Verret's district extending from Front Vacherie to the Ascension Parish line.[41]. On 1 January 1777 Michel Cantrelle, 27 years of age and a Lieutenant Commandant, was still living on the Cabahanoce plantaion with his father, his mother, his brother Jacques and his widowed sister Marie Marguerite Cantrelle Verret and her seven children[31,32].

Even with his heavy responsibilities as Commandant of the First Acadian Coast and an unending workload managing the Cabahanoce indigo plantation, Michel Cantrelle still found time to court and fall in love. In 1777, shortly after the death of his father, Michel married Magdelaine Croiset of Pointe Coupee, the daughter of Francois Croiset and Marie Anne Trepagnier, in St. James Catholic Church at Cabahanoce. Witnesses at the wedding included Joseph Bourgois and Michel's brother Jacques Cantrelle[46,47]. Magdelaine Croiset was born on 10 February 1762 and baptized on 25 February 1762 at St. Francis Catholic Church in Pointe Coupee Parish, LA[44,45]. Unfortunately tragedy shortly stuck as Magdelaine died in September 1778 and was buried on 23 September 1778 in the cemetery near St. James Catholic Church[48,49]. It appears that she may have died in childbirth as a daughter of Michel Cantrelle and Magdelaine Croiset was baptized in St. James Catholic Church on 13 January 1779. Her mother Magdelaine Croiset is listed as deceased on the baptismal certificate[48,50]. Marie Magdelaine Cantrelle, the first and only child of Michel Cantrelle and Magdelaine Croiset, married Patrick Uriell, son of Jacques Uriell and Mary Mulvany of Ireland, at St. James Catholic Church on 29 September 1800[51,52].

Torn by the death of his young wife and with a new baby to raise, Michel Cantrelle met Madeleine Celeste Andry, daughter of Louis Antoine Andry and Marie Jeanne Lapierre, and again fell in love. Her father Louis Antoine Andry was adjutant major of the plaza of Louisiana and an infantry captain. Born on the thirteenth of April in 1760, Madeleine Celeste was ten years younger than Michel[53,54].

MICHEL CANTRELLE-COMMANDANT OF THE FIRST ACADIAN COAST

On 20 November 1779 Michel married Madeleine Celeste at St. Louis Cathedral in New Orleans. Witnesses at their wedding included Gilbert Antoine Maxent, the militia commandant, Joseph Ducros, city councilman of New Orleans, Jean Baptiste Poeyfarre, soon-to-be brother-in-law of Michel Cantrelle and Bernardo de Galvez, the governor of Louisiana[55,56]. The young couple and Michel's daughter Marie Magdelaine Cantrelle returned to the indigo plantation at Cabahanoce where they began their lives together. Soon Michel Cantrelle acquired the property of his deceased brother-in-law Nicolas Verret that was just downriver of his father's plantation. It included the present villages and plantations of Moonshine, Lagan, Pikes Peak, Home Place and Bessie K. to St. Joe, Felicity, Oak Alley and Baytree.

As Michel Cantrelle grew more prosperous and gained political stature in Louisiana, he and Madeleine Celeste watched their family grow. On 22 January 1781 they celebrated the baptism of their first child, Marie Josephe, at St. Louis Cathedral in New Orleans. She was born in late 1780 and had been conditionally baptized earlier at their Cabahanoce plantation – perhaps because she was ill at birth, but more likely because their home was a great distance from New Orleans and required a hazardous 60-mile trip by boat to reach the St. Louis Cathedral[57,58]. A second daughter Rose Carmelite was born 19 April 1782 and baptized at St. Louis Cathedral on 18 October 1784 after being conditionally baptized at the Cabahanoce plantation[59,60]. Madeleleine Celeste gave birth to Jean-Baptiste, their first son, on 19 June 1784. Initially, he was conditionally baptized at Cabahanoce and then brought to St. Louis Cathedral for the baptismal ceremonies on 13 October 1784[59,60]. Four years later on the third of January 1788 Michel and Madeleine Celeste had a son whom they named after his father. Little Michel Cantrelle was baptized at St. James Catholic Church in Cabahanoce on 23 March 1788[61,62].

On 4 February 1790 young Celeste Cantrelle was born to the couple. Conditionally baptized at St. James of Cabahanoce, she had the baptismal ceremonies supplied at St. Louis Cathedral on 8 February 1791[63,64]. On the 12th of May 1794 little Joseph Xavier Cantrelle entered the world and joined the now large family of Michel and Madeleine Celeste Cantrelle. After being conditionally baptized at Cabahanoce shortly after his birth, he received the baptismal ceremonies on 27 November 1794 at St. Louis Cathedral in New Orleans[63,65]. On 28 July 1798 Madeleine Celeste had her fourth son Louis Terence at Cabahanoce. He was baptized at St. James Catholic Church near the family plantation on 27 November 1798[48,66]. The last child born to Michel and Madeleine Celeste was a daughter Rose Aglae. She was born on 26 December 1805 and baptized at St. James Catholic Church on 4 January 1806[67,68]. Michel Cantrelle's importance in the government and politics of the day was reflected in the godparents of his children - especially their godfathers. These men often were military officers in the Spanish army or high-ranking government officials.

Michel Cantrelle began his government service as a young lieutenant in the Militia of the First Acadian Coast. In January 1770 he was serving under his brother-in-law Captain Nicolas Verret. With Nicolas Verret's death in November 1775 Michel Cantrelle was appointed commandant of Verret's district extending from Front Vacherie to the Ascension Parish line. He remained a commandant throughout the period of Spanish rule in Louisiana. When the Louisiana territory was transferred to the United States in 1803, his position as commandant was terminated; however, shortly thereafter in 1804 Governor Claiborne through his emissary Dr. Watkins reappointed Michel Cantrelle as Commandant of the Acadian Coast. In 1805 with the reorganization of parish government in Louisiana, the position of commandant was abolished. This did not end Michel Cantrelle's government service, however, as he was commissioned in 1805 as Parish Judge of the new parish of Acadia – the highest level parish official. When Acadia Parish was divided into St. James Parish and Ascension Parish in 1807,

MICHEL CANTRELLE-COMMANDANT OF THE FIRST ACADIAN COAST

Michel Cantrelle became the Parish Judge of St. James Parish – a position he held until 1812. He also was a member of the Louisiana legislative council of the first territorial government. As the residents of St. James Parish prospered during the American period, the growing Acadian population on the east bank of the Mississippi River needed a Catholic church of their own. In 1807 commissioners were selected and they began the construction of a church located on land at present-day Convent, LA. In honor of the long and dedicated service of Michel Cantrelle to St. James Parish, the commissioners named the new church St. Michel de Cantrelle[69,70]. In late October 1814 at 64 years of age Michel Cantrelle died. He was buried from St. James Catholic Church on 25 October 1814[71,72]. Thus ended one of the most important periods in the history of St. James Parish and the Acadian Coast.

See page 13 for References

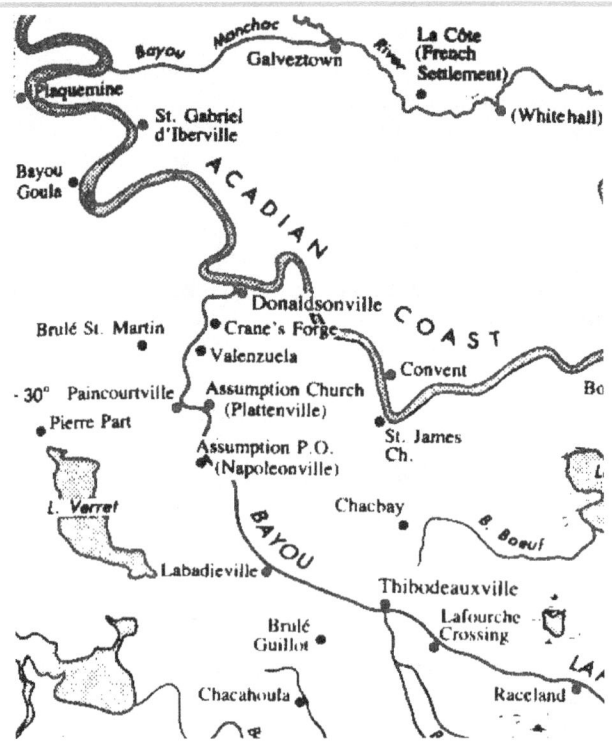

Vintage postcard: CARAQUET - Vue generale

IN THE NEWS-HISTORICAL NEWS TIDBITS

Joplin Globe, Joplin, MO, January 4, 1944

BIRDS MAKE A REFUGE FROM FARM SWAMPLAND

Jennings, La. — (AP) — A city of birds — population approximately 10,000—recently moved in on Frank Guidry, a planter.

He advised the state conservation commission that the birds have made a refuge out of a small swamp area. There are snowy egrets—once almost made extinct by commercial plume hunters—and glossy ibis.

Guidry said the birds maintain remarkable regularity of hours of work and sleep, scattering in the rice fields during the day to destroy insects and returning to their homes at the same time every night.

Port Arthur News, Port Arthur, Texas, March 12, 1928

Acadians To Have Music At Reunion

Plans for the reunion of descendants of Acadians deported by the British from Nova Scotia and who finally found refuge in Louisiana in 1765, to be held in Port Neches next Tuesday evening, are going forward, according to announcements made this morning, and a large crowd of Acadians are expected to gather in the Knights of Columbus hall in Port Neches.

The St. Mary's Catholic band of Port Arthur will play several selections as a part of the reunion program and speakers will be Vance Plauchette of Lake Charles, and Mayor J. W. Baker of Port Neches, with a dance to follow.

Pennsylvania Folklore
Mystery Shrouds Fate of Pennsylvania's 'Cajuns'

Wednesday, October 19, 1955

Harrisburg — Henry W. Shoemaker, Pennsylvania Folklore chief, says this year's two hundredth anniversary of the expelling of the Acadians or 'Cajuns' by the British Government of Nova Scotia was observed in Pennsylvania, although mystery shrouds the fate of the Pennsylvania Acadians.

It seemed that in 1755 there was fear that the sturdy Basque Colonists, mostly fishermen and small farmers located in Acadia, the name later was changed to Nova Scotia, might prove troublesome to the English power and hundreds of French, mostly of Basque origin were torn from their families and homes and loaded on ships and groups dumped in strong British Colonies along the Atlantic Coast from Cape Breton to Louisiana. Thousands were settled in Georgia, who pushed west to the French Colony of Louisiana and began active careers as fishermen and trappers.

"Looked upon as people apart by the ancient French Colonial families of Louisiana, they regarded the Basques almost as 'foreign interlopers' who spoke a language unknown to any French Dictionary." Shoemaker said.

"That great Frenchman of mysterious Colonial background, J. J. Audubon, came from Pennsylvania, near Pottstown, to Louisiana. He started as a painter of French Aristocratic women but became the idol of the Basque fishermen, and hunters who guided him in the wilderness Bayous, where he collected many of his rarest specimens which appear in his matchless volumes, 'The Birds of America.'

"As one old Cajun who was close to Audubon remarked, 'He was a great man, but unlike us was a French Colonial', meaning that the speaker was of Basque.

"The Basques are a handsome race, the men and women of fair complexion, blue or grey eyes with noble features, brown haired, slim, and erect, of medium height.

"What became of the Acadians in Pennsylvania remains a profound mystery. Perhaps most of the men resumed their hard journeys through British-held lands to Louisiana and the women intermarried with Germans, Huguenots, and Waldensians, losing their family names forever. There is a strong strain of Pennsylvania Dutch in Nova Scotia, shown by the names of old settlers, and by villages, townships, and natural features like streams and mountains. The Basques, like the Huguenots, intermarried probably with the German Pioneers from Pennsylvania.

"Likewise the Acadians found large groups of Pennsylvania Germans in Louisiana who befriended the weary Colonial refugees, helped them secure fishing and trapping materials and marked out their long, narrow farms and some of their daughters married Frenchmen forming a link between the early French aristocrats and the German Colonials from Pennsylvania.

"They made a tighter band among the population which was French to the last though there was much Pennsylvania Dutch blood among the refugees. Like in Pennsylvania, the composite race of Germans, Dutch, Huguenots, Waldensians, and Greeks made a people who have spread and prospered in all parts of America."

(Pennsylvania Folklore) Bedford Gazette, Bedford, PA, October 19, 1955

IN THE NEWS-HISTORICAL NEWS TIDBITS

Longfellow Memorial for Evangeline Park at Grand Pre

EVANGELINE AT GRAND PRE

LONGFELLOW WHO MADE EVANGELINE IMMORTAL

DISTINGUISHED GROUP AT GRAND PRE INCLUDING GOV COX OF MASSACHUSETTS

If the visitor to the beautiful Annapolis Valley of Nova Scotia is blessed with a true romantic spirit he may be able to conjure up the graceful, quiet figure of Evangeline, and, with Longfellow to help carry out the illusion, fancy he is back in the early days before the Acadians were driven sorrowfully from their little homes in 1755. The Annapolis-Cornwallis district, where the apple trees in their blossoming time make the valley a veritable paradise, is peculiarly romantic. The pathetic figure of Evangeline slips through the quaint streets of Grand Pre, and the plot of ground enclosing the large stone cross which marks the burial place of her forebears has been made into a memorial park and named after her. The gates are always open, and thousands of lovers of history and literature crowd there every year. A bronze statue of Evangeline, designed by an Acadian sculptor and fairly breathing the pathos of her story, now stands in the park. Nearby, admirers of Longfellow throughout Canada and the United States are planning to erect a memorial to the poet.

Not far from Grand Pre is Annapolis Royal, founded in 1604 and chiefly because of historic old Fort Anne, now a Canadian National Park. Few indeed are the actual descendants of the Acadians, but their ways and customs may be judged by the relics in the Acadian room in Fort Anne, furnished to represent exactly what their homes were in the past, and carefully looked after by L. M. Fortier, superintendent of the park.

Another pleasant spot for the visitor is Kentville, where the Cornwallis Inn attends to the material wants of its guests and abounds with suggestions for fishing, canoeing and hiking excursions. Still more entrancing, perhaps, is Digby, a town charmingly situated on the Annapolis Basin, where there is not only trout fishing but deep-sea fishing in the Bay of Fundy, and where visitors make The Pines a temporary home from which to take motor and boat trips to the beauty spots of Nova Scotia.

Indiana Gazette, 1925, Indiana, PA

BON APPETIT-Recipes from the Guédry-Labine Cookbook

SEAFOOD DELIGHT
from Julie Guidry-Abbeville, LA

4 1/2 cups water
1 1/2 lbs. medium sized fresh shrimp
1 (16 oz.) package linguine
1 (6 oz.) package frozen snow peas, thawed & drained
6 green onions, chopped
4 medium tomatoes, peeled, chopped & drained
1/2 cup olive oil
1/3 cup balsamic vinegar
1/4 cup fresh oregano, chopped coarsely
1/4 cup fresh basil, chopped coarsely
1 clove garlic, pressed
1/2 tsp. ground black pepper
Salt to taste
1/4 cup chopped fresh parsley

This chilled shrimp pasta, followed by a cold dish of homemade ice cream is perfect for a warm summer day. It doesn't get much better than this!

Peel and de-vein shrimp. Bring water to boil add shrimp and cook 3 to 5 minutes. Drain well, rinse with cold water. Chill. Set aside.

Cook linguine according to package directions, omitting salt, drain. Rinse with cold water and drain again. Combine shrimp and remaining ingredients, salt to taste. Toss gently. Cover and chill at least 2 hours.

HOMEMADE CREAMY BANANA & PECAN ICE CREAM
from Charlene Guidry Lacombe-Jennings, Louisiana

6 eggs, well beaten
2 cups sugar
1 can (16 oz.) evaporated milk
1 1/2 tbsp. all purpose flour
Dash of salt
3 tbsp. vanilla extract
4 ripe bananas, mashed
1 cup chopped pecans
Milk (to be added at the end)

Combine eggs, 1 1/2 cups sugar and milk. Beat one minute. Add 1/2 cup, flour, vanilla and salt. Beat until well blended. Fold in bananas and pecans.

Using an electric or hand turned crank-type home ice cream freezer, pour the mixture into the container. Add enough milk so that the container is 3/4 full. Follow the manufacturer's instructions to make the ice cream.

BOOK NOOK

French Fortresses in North America 1535-1763
Quebec, Montreal, Louisbourg and New Orleans
By Rene Chartrand

This title provides a detailed examination of the defenses of the three largest fortified cities in Canada - Quebec, Montreal and Louisbourg - and also covers New Orleans in America. Quebec City is the best known and most impressive of the sites covered, and was the strongest of the fortresses of New France: besieged twice by the British (1690 and 1759) and once by the French (1760), it was captured in 1759 by General James Wolfe. Montreal was also strongly fortified and its strategic location ensured its prominence in the fur trade early on. Fortress Louisbourg was built as a large fortified naval station between 1720 and 1743 and saw significant combat action.

Rene Chartrand was born in Montreal. A senior curator with Canada's National Historic Sites for nearly three decades, he is now a freelance writer and historical consultant. He has written numerous articles and books including some 20 Osprey titles and the first two volumes of 'Canadian Military Heritage'.

Sods, Soil, and Spades-The Acadians at Grand Pré and Their Dykeland Legacy
By J. Sherman Bleakney

French Acadians began settling in the Grand Pré area of Nova Scotia, a region plagued by salt-soaked tidal meadows, in the seventeenth century. By the middle of the eighteenth century, a complex system of sod barriers had enabled them to convert 3,000 acres of what had been tidal marshes into rich crop land. Four hundred years after the Acadian arrival in the Bay of Fundy region, the physical presence of their legacy is still intact.

Sherman Bleakney examines the unusual physical and biological features of this region of the Bay of Fundy, home to the only successful pioneer society in North America to farm below sea level. Using original photographs, diagrams, and graphs, Bleakney shows how and why the Acadians were successful. Sods, Soil, and Spades examines the unique and elegant engineering principles and practices used by the Acadians and looks at how their culture influenced their success in mastering this marshland region

References-Michel Cantrell

1. Oubre, Elton J.; Vacherie, St. James Parish, Louisiana – History and Genealogy (Oubre's Books, Thibodaux, LA, 2002), pp. 53-81.

2. Brasseaux, Carl A.; The Founding of New Acadia: The Beginnings of Acadian Life in Louisiana, 1765-1803 (Louisiana State University Press, Baton Rouge, LA, 1987), pp. 73-115.

3. Oubre, Op. cit., pp. 58-64.

4. Woods, Reverend Monsignor Earl C. and Nolan, Dr. Charles E.; Sacramental Records of the Roman Catholic Church of the Archdiocese of New Orleans (Archives of the Archdiocese of New Orleans, New Orleans, LA, 1987-2004), v. 1 pp. 39, 152, 163.

5. St. Louis Catholic Cathedral, New Orleans, LA, Marriage Register 1720-1730, pp. 81, 193.

6. Oubre, Op. cit., p. 64.

7. Voorhies, Jacqueline K.; Some Late Eighteenth-Century Louisianians – Census Records of the Colony, 1758-1796 (University of Southwestern Louisiana, Lafayette, LA, 1973), p. 15.

8. Archivo General de Indias, "Audiencia de Santa Domingo " (A.D.S.), (Seville, Spain), Legajo 2595.

9. Woods and Nolan, Op. Cit.; v. 1 p. 40.

10. St. Louis Catholic Cathedral, Op. Cit.; Baptismal Register 1744-1753, p. 180.

11. Woods and Nolan, Op. Cit.; v. 2 p. 40.

12. St. Louis Catholic Cathedral, Op. Cit.; Baptismal Register 1744-1753, p. 252.

13. Woods and Nolan, Op. Cit.; v. 1 p. 255.

14. St. Louis Catholic Cathedral, Op. Cit.; Baptismal Register 1744-1753, p. 165.

15. Woods and Nolan, Op. Cit.; v. 2 p. 156.

16. Woods and Nolan, Op. Cit.; v. 2 p. 257.

17. St. Louis Catholic Cathedral, Op. Cit.; Baptismal Register 1753-1759, p. 60.

18. Woods and Nolan, Op. Cit.; v. 3 p. 244.

19. St. Louis Catholic Cathedral, Op. Cit.; Marriage Register 1777-1784, p. 78.

20. Woods and Nolan, Op. Cit.; v. 1 p. 39.

21. St. Louis Catholic Cathedral, Op. Cit.; Baptismal Register 1731-1733, p. 13.

22. St. Louis Catholic Cathedral, Op. Cit.; Baptismal Register 1731-1733, p. 1.

23. St. Louis Catholic Cathedral, Op. Cit.; Baptismal Register 1744-1753, p. 9.

24. St. Louis Catholic Cathedral, Op. Cit.; Baptismal Register 1744-1753, p. 64.

25. Woods and Nolan, Op. Cit.; v. 1 pp. 39-40.

26. St. Louis Catholic Cathedral, Op. Cit.; Baptismal Register 1744-1753, p. 108.

27. Voorhies, Op. Cit.; p. 201.

28. Archivo General de Indias, "Papeles Procedentes de Cuba" (P.P.C.), (Seville, Spain), Legajo 187-A-1.

29. Voorhies, Op. Cit.; p. 441.

30. Archivo General de Indias, "Papeles Procedentes de Cuba" (P.P.C.), (Seville, Spain), Legajo 187-A-2.

31. Bourgeois, Lillian C.; Cabanocey – The History, Customs and Folklore of St. James Parish (Pelican Publishing Company, Gretna, LA, 1976), p. 183.

32. Archivo General de Indias, "Papeles Procedentes de Cuba" (P.P.C.), (Seville, Spain), Legajo 190.

33. Oubre, Op. cit., pp. 64-65.

34. Pollard, Nora Lee Clouatre; Diocese of Baton Rouge Catholic Church Records (Diocese of Baton Rouge, Baton Rouge, LA, 1978-2007), v. 2 p. 173.

35. St. James Catholic Church, St. James, LA, v. 1 p. 56a.

36. Woods and Nolan, Op. Cit.; v. 4 p. 48.

37. St. Louis Catholic Cathedral, Op. Cit.; Funeral Register 1784-1793, p. 4.

38. St. Louis Catholic Cathedral, Op. Cit.; Baptismal Register 1753-1759, p. 94.

39. Woods and Nolan, Op. Cit.; v. 2 p. 273.

40. St. Louis Catholic Cathedral, Op. Cit.; Baptismal Register 1759-1762, p. 37.

41. Bourgeois, Op. Cit.; p. 180.

42. Archivo General de Indias, "Papeles Procedentes de Cuba" (P.P.C.), (Seville, Spain), Legajo 161.

43. Oubre, Op. cit., pp. 64. Pollard, Op. Cit.; v. 2 pp. 173, 209.

44. St. James Catholic Church, St. James, LA, v. 1 p. 46.

45. Pollard, Op. Cit.; v. 1 p. 154, v. 1b p. 39.

46. St. Francis Catholic Church, Pointe Coupee Parish, LA, Book PCP-3 p. 108.

47. Pollard, Op. Cit.; v. 2 p. 173.

48. St. James Catholic Church, St. James, LA, v. 1 p. 63.

49. St. James Catholic Church, St. James, LA, v. 1 p. 59.

50. Pollard, Op. Cit.; v. 2 pp. 173, 711.

51. St. James Catholic Church, St. James, LA, v. 2 p. 51.

52. Woods and Nolan, Op. Cit.; v. 2 p. 5.

53. St. Louis Catholic Cathedral, Op. Cit.; Baptismal Register 1759-1762, p. 29.

54. Woods and Nolan, Op. Cit.; v. 3 pp. 6, 45.

55. St. Louis Catholic Cathedral, Op. Cit.; Marriage Register 1777-1784, p. 60.

56. Woods and Nolan, Op. Cit.; v. 3 p. 45.

57. St. Louis Catholic Cathedral, Op. Cit.; Baptismal Register 1777-1786, p. 116.

58. Woods and Nolan, Op. Cit.; v. 4 pp. 48-49.

59. St. Louis Catholic Cathedral, Op. Cit.; Baptismal Register 1777-1786, p. 341.

60. Pollard, Op. Cit.; v. 2 p. 174.

61. St. James Catholic Church, St. James, LA, v. 3 p. 14.

62. Woods and Nolan, Op. Cit.; v. 5 p. 61.

63. St. Louis Catholic Cathedral, Op. Cit.; Baptismal Register 1786-1796, p. 123.

64. St. Louis Catholic Cathedral, Op. Cit.; Baptismal Register 1786-1796, p. 337.

65. St. James Catholic Church, St. James, LA, v. 3 p. 175.

66. Pollard, Op. Cit.; v. 3 p. 193.

67. St. James Catholic Church, St. James, LA, v. 3 p. 296.

68. Oubre, Op. cit., pp. 63-64.

69. Bourgeois, Op. Cit.; pp. 41, 59, 88-92.

70. Pollard, Op. Cit.; v. 3 p. 192.

71. St. James Catholic Church, St. James, LA, v. 4 p. 39.

TOURIST ATTRACTIONS NEW BRUNSWICK

http://www.bathurstheritage.ca/index.asp

Watch for Bathurst's First Hand-I-Craft Fair at Gallery 360, **Bathurst Heritage Museum**, July & August, 2009. All handicrafts will be displayed: knitting; cross stitch; embroidery; needle point; felting and much, much more - even new crafts. Visit the website for upcoming events and hours of operation.

The Royal Canadian Legion War Museum in Bathurst displays military artifacts, such as weapons, medals, badges, pictures, and uniforms from the World War I, World War II, and the Korean war.

The Herman J. Good V.C. Branch No. 18 Royal Canadian Legion War Museum is located at:

575 St. Peter Avenue, Bathurst, New Brunswick.

1 (506) 546-3135

Golf Courses-Bathurst, New Brunswick

http://www.gowanbrae.ca/

Gowan Brae Golf Course
Younghall Drive
Bathurst, New Brunswick

(506) 548-9469

http://www.squiregreen.com/

Squire Green Golf Course
1290 Riverside Drive
Bathurst, New Brunswick

(506) 546-3309

CMA 2009-Guédry-Labine & Petitpas Reunion Information

We are having our Guédry-Labine & Petitpas Reunion on Sunday, 16 August 2009 in the Conference Center of Danny's Inn in Bereford, New Brunswick. Beresford is just five miles north of Bathurst, New Brunswick and Danny's Inn is on Highway 134 just south of Beresford.

We will begin about 8:30 am and have activities until 5:00 pm. Our agenda, activities and displays will include formal sessions with music, presentations, etc. as well as time to mingle and get to know your cousins. The agenda is:

* 8:30 am - Opening Mass at Holy Family (Sainte Famille) Catholic Church
    (430 St. Peter Avenue; Bathurst, NB)
    - French Rosary led by Pierrette Guidry of Colorado (8:15 am)
    - Opening Procession honoring our ancestors (8:30 am)
    - French Mass celebrated by Father Benoit Drapeau of Arizona
    - Closing Procession
* 9:45 am - Reunion Registration at Danny's Inn Conference Center
    [1223 Route 134 (Rue Principale) just north of Bathurst, NB]
* 10:00 am - Larry Miller and his Cajun Band
    (Including Cajun two-step & waltz demonstrations)
* 10:45 am - Break (View displays, meet cousins, sales table, etc.)
* 11:00 am - Presentation (Larry Miller of Louisiana) -
    Cultures of Louisiana Cajuns and Maritime Acadians
    including an actual Courir de Mardi Gras (Cajun Mardi Gras Run)
* 11:45 am - Break (View displays, meet cousins, sales table, etc.)
* 12:00 noon - Dinner Buffet
* 1:00 pm - Presentation (Sister Corinne LaPlant of New Brunswick) -
    History of the Acadians of the Baie-des-Chaleurs Region
* 1:45 pm - Break (View displays, meet cousins, sales table, etc.)
* 2:00 pm - Presentation (Eileen Avery [Petitpas] of California) -
    Petitpas Genealogy - Recent Discoveries Using DNA Techniques
* 2:45 pm - Break (View displays, meet cousins, sales table, etc.)
* 3:00 pm - New Brunswick Acadian Band
* 3:45 pm - Break (View displays, meet cousins, sales table, etc.)
* 4:00 pm - Presentation (Elaine Clement of Louisiana) -
    Louisiana Cajun French and Acadian French of Canada -
    How Similar Are They
* 4:30 pm - Break
* 4:45 pm - Closing Ceremony

There will be a superb buffet lunch. It'll be a Hot & Cold Dinner Buffet that includes roast beef smothered in peppercorn gravy, sweet & sour meat balls, lasagna, chicken wings, potato casserole, coleslaw, tossed green salad, carrot salad, rolls, carrot cake, cherry cheesecake, fresh fruit salad, coffee and tea. The cost is $25.00 CAN per person.

NEW BRUNSWICK ACCOMMODATIONS - CMA 2009

BATHURST - http://www.bathurst.ca/english/home/

Authentique Bed & Breakfast Enjoy our 4 star B&B in a heritage home of the 20's with 'Arts & Craft's influences, conveniently located in the heart of Bathurst. You are welcome to relax in a cozy atmosphere with personalized service. Spacious rooms with very comfortable beds, cable TV, DVD, MP3, wireless internet, work desk and telephone. Each room has a private bathroom. Breakfast 'A la Carte' will be served in our elegant dining room.

Comfort Inn Bathurst Conveniently located on St. Peter Avenue. Close to shopping and offices. 35 person meeting room available.

John's Motel Our rooms have a full bath and shower, color television with cable, and most importantly comfortable beds! We also boast a swimming pool and an area for picnics. We also have in-room coffee.

Sea'scape Cottage This is our fully equipped beach house located on the beautiful Bay of Chaleur in Bathurst, New Brunswick. Select the virtual tour button to have a closer look.

The official New Brunswick Tourism Website is at the link below. You can learn about interesting locations, sites and activities at this website. By clicking on the word "Guides" in the left column of the page, you can order a free 2008 Experience New Brunswick Vacation Planner" which is excellent.

http://www.tourismnewbrunswick.ca

The 2009 CMA website has an excellent page on accommodations within the Acadian Peninsula. Visit it by clicking on this link:

http://www.cma2009.ca

CARAQUET - http://www.ville.caraquet.nb.ca/

Hotel Paulin "The Pearl of Baie des Chaleurs", Caraquet.

Motel Colibri 12 rooms smoking and non-smoking. 2 double bed. Free breakfast.

Super 8 Motel 50 guest rooms including 18 junior suites.

ON THE WEB

Les Guédry d'Asteur

http://freepages.genealogy.rootsweb.ancestry.com/~guedrylabinefamily/

The Guédry-Labine Family Genealogical Database

Developed by the Les Guédry d'Asteur, Inc. Genealogy Committee

http://freepages.genealogy.rootsweb.ancestry.com/~guidryrm/Guedry-Labine/

The Louisiana State Archives

This is the official website for the Louisiana State Archives. It provides a very nice overview of the archival holdings and services. Although there are no images of original documents at this time, there is a very nice index to Confederate Pension Applications with numerous Guidry records. Click on Research Library under Sections of Organization, then Confederate Pension Applications to the left of the top photograph, then Search the Database.

http://www.sos.louisiana.gov/archives/archives/archives-index.htm

Archives of Canada

http://www.archivescanada.ca/english/index.html

DUES REMINDER

Attached at the back of this issue is a membership application for renewing your membership in Les Guédry d'Asteur. Our dues are very reasonable at $6.00 for individuals and $10 for a family.

By joining and paying your dues, you provide us with the financial resources to participate in many projects, one being the CMA 2009 reunion in Bathurst, New Brunswick.

Please take a moment, complete the Membership Application, enclose a check and send it to the address on the application. It will help all of us do so much for the family. And, if you would like to join at one of the Benefactor Levels, it would let us do even more.

Les Guédry d'Asteur

To share your ideas for the newsletter, contact:

Marty Guidry
6139 North Shore Drive
Baton Rouge, LA 70817
225-755-1915
guidryrm@cox.net

'GENERATIONS' newsletter is now in its seventh year. We hope to provide our readers with an interesting, informative and entertaining newsletter. Your input is always welcome and we look forward to another year of sharing family history and news with you.

The Guédry-Labine Family Newsletter 'GENERATIONS' serves as a focal point for family members to share and learn about us.

Allie Guidry
txguidry2000@yahoo.com

Marty Guidry
guidryrm@cox.net

Les Guédry d'Asteur Officers and Committees

OFFICERS:
President - Martin Guidry (LA)
Vice-President - Elaine Clement (LA)
Secretary - Billy Harrell Guidry (LA)
Treasurer - Daniel "Chuck" Guidry (LA)

COMMITTEES:
Website - Becky Boggess (IA) - Chairperson
    Annie Grignon-Labine (QU) - Translator
    Elaine Clement (LA) - Translator
    Martin Guidry (LA)

Genealogy - Daryl LaBine (FL/ON) - Chairperson
    Bernard Geddry (AZ)
    Mark Labine (MN)
    Daniel "Chuck" Guidry (LA)
    Martin Guidry (LA)

Finance - Cheryl Guidry Tyiska (MD) - Chairperson
    Paul Labine (IL)
    Marshall Woolner (OR)
    Gloria Parrent (TX)
    Chuck Guidry (LA)

Membership - Charlene Guidry Lacombe (LA) - Chairperson
    Gayle Guidry (LA) - Special Projects
    Warren Guidry (TX)

Sales - Cindy Guidry Herdt (WA) - Chairperson
    Wayne Simoneaux (LA)
    Billy Harrell Guidry (LA)

Publicity - Elaine Clement (LA) - Chairperson
    Margaret Jeddry (MA)
    Warren Guidry (TX)

Newsletter - Allie Guidry Hardee (VA) - Editor
    Martin Guidry (LA)

CAFA Board Member - Jeanette Guidry Leger (LA)

FALL 2009

Volume 7, Issue 4

Les Guédry d'Asteur

GENERATIONS

IN THIS ISSUE

Highlights of the Guédry-Labine & Petitpas Reunion by Marty Guidry — 1

Photo gallery from the Guédry-Labine and Petitpas Reunion in Bathurst, N. B. — 3

Historical Tidbits — 8

BON APPETIT: Recipes from the Guédry/Labine Family Cookbook — 10

BOOK NOOK — 11

Guédry Family Merchandise — 13

In this special 2009 Reunion issue of "Generations" we hope you can experience the fun and companionship that all had at our 2009 Guédry-Labine & Petitpas Reunion in Bathurst, New Brunswick on August 16th. With outstanding entertainment, informative talks, an exceptional buffet and wonderful friends, everyone had a memorable time. The 2014 Congrès Mondial Acadien will be in Madawaska, Maine. Congrès activities and reunions will be in southwestern Québec, northwestern New Brunswick and the Madawaska, ME area. We are already beginning plans for a Guédry-Labine & Petitpas Reunion there.

Last week Louisiane Acadie, the organization that developed Louisiana's bid for the 2014 Congrés Mondial Acadien, announced that there will be a major international Acadian festival in southern Louisiana in October 2011. The State of Louisiana has already committed funds for this event. Planning has begun and folks from throughout the United States, Canada and Europe will attend. Although the format is not known at this time, family reunions will be a major event of the festival and Les Guédry d'Asteur plans to have a Guédry-Labine & Petitpas Reunion at the Acadian festival. October is a wonderful time to visit Louisiana with cool temperatures and dry weather. This Acadian festival will not replace nor compete with the Congrés Mondial Acadien. It will be an additional opportunity for Acadians from throughout the world to gather, celebrate our heritage, renew acquaintances and meet our cousins. So mark your calendars for October 2011 with "Laissez les bon temps roulez en Louisiane".

HIGHLIGHTS OF THE GUEDRY-LABINE & PETITPAS REUNION
By Marty Guidry

Attended by 73 cousins, the 2009 Guédry-Labine & Petitpas Reunion provided exciting entertainment, great food and wonderful fellowship to all. Our Bathurst, New Brunswick hosts, Lorn Guidry and his son Jason, not only were instrumental in organizing the Reunion, but also welcomed us in grand style to New Brunswick.

As we all gathered at 8:30 am in Holy Family Catholic Church in Bathurst, Pierrette Guidry of Colorado led the French Rosary – a moving and unique experience. Father Benoit Drapeau, originally from Bathurst and now residing in Arizona, led the opening procession behind the banners of our forefathers – Claude Guédry/Marguerite Petitpas and each of their children. Father Drapeau celebrated a moving bilingual Mass to open the reunion. A. J. LeBlanc, Claudette Mancini and Albert Geddry read the scriptural verses and Pierrette Guidry sang a beautiful rendition of <u>Ave Maria</u> during communion. As the Guédry banners led the closing processional, everyone sang "Ave Maris Stella" – the Acadian National Anthem – to end the Mass. We all appreciate the outstanding efforts of Jeanette Guidry Leger in helping organize our beautiful opening Mass.

HIGHLIGHTS OF THE GUEDRY-LABINE & PETITPAS REUNION - by *Marty Guidry*

After Mass everyone drove the five miles to Danny's Inn in Beresford for remainder of the Reunion. On arriving, we were greeted by magician John Guidry, brother of Lorn. John roamed the room, baffling one person after another with his amazing feats of hand. I am still trying to discern how he poured water into his cupped hand, opened it to show it dry and then re-cupped it to return the water to the glass.

Shortly after we arrived at Danny's Inn, Lorn Guidry greeted each of the ladies with a special Bathurst seaglass pendant necklace that he crafted. Lorn and his wife Debbie have collected seaglass from the Bathurst beaches for several years and craft the beautiful pendants at their home. Thanks, Lorn, for this treasured gift to each of our ladies.

After Marty Guidry made brief introductory remarks welcoming everyone to Bathurst, Larry Miller and his Cajun Band from Iota, LA struck up a lively Cajun two-step. Feet were moving and hands clapping as we all enjoyed the music. Between songs, Larry discussed the origins of Cajun music, the similarities and differences of Louisiana Cajun and Acadian music of New Brunswick and the Louisiana Cajun culture. Later Larry and his lovely wife demonstrated the Cajun two-step and Cajun waltz. The surprise for many was when they invited several of us to dance with them. We soon had several couples on the dance floor. The excitement of the morning climaxed when the band struck up the traditional Cajun Mardi Gras song and six of our Guédry and Petitpas cousins came dancing into the room in traditional Courir de Mardi Gras costumes. With Larry Miller calling, they put on a lively Cajun Mardi Gras dance – teasing audience members, dancing with them and putting on a great show. Throughout the morning we had several breaks so we could meet each other, visit the various exhibits on our family and purchase souvenirs.

As the noon hour approached, we all gathered for a tasty buffet lunch that included roast beef in peppercorn gravy, sweet & sour meatballs, lasagna, chicken wings, potato casserole, coleslaw, tossed green salad, carrot salad, rolls and several desserts including cheesecake and carrot cake. Magician John was busy throughout lunch entertaining us all with his quick hands and devilish tricks. The decibel level throughout the room was high as folks discussed their families, their journeys to the reunion and their home areas. Between conversations, folks purchased special gifts of t-shirts, caps, pens, key chains, lapel pins and magnets – all personalized with our Les Guédry d'Asteur logo. Thanks to Rachel Hardee, Jeff Killingsworth and Allie Guidry for manning our sales table and registration booth.

As the afternoon began, Sister Corinne LaPlant of New Brunswick discussed the history of the Acadians of the Baie-des-Chaleurs region. Her discussion of Nicolas Denys and his brief venture in the Bathurst area and the origins and lives of the Acadians of Caraquet & Acadian Peninsula was quite interesting. Eileen Avery of California then presented the results of research into her Petitpas family. In a very interesting and informative talk, Eileen discussed recent discoveries that she has made through mtDNA tests. In the second half of her discussion, she presented a brief genealogy of the Petitpas family.

With the day winding down, the New Brunswick Acadian band, with Roger Lanteigne on accordion, played a lively set of Acadian and country music that had everyone toe-tapping, singing and clapping their hands. As the strains of the last tune reverberated in the room, folks made a last dash to the sales table and enjoyed the various family exhibits.

It was truly a memorable day for all of the Guedry, Labine and Petitpas cousins in New Brunswick. Many new friends were made and old friendships renewed.

On Monday, August 17th many of us ventured over to the town of Pokemouche for the Espace 2009 activities. Marty Guidry was one of the featured speakers, giving a short talk on the birds of Louisiana. Larry Miller again entertained the large crowds that gathered on the 18th for the Louisiana Day festivities which featured Cajun food & entertainment from Louisiana.

GENERATIONS   Volume 7, Issue 4   Page 3

Guédry-Labine & Petitpas Reunion-Holy Family Catholic Church, Bathurst, N.B.

Father Drapeau greeting family

Family members gathering at Holy Family Catholic Church for opening Mass

Family members gather for the opening Mass at Holy Family

L to R: Marty Guidry, Lorn Guidry, George Guidry

Family arriving for the opening Mass

Alter-Holy Family Catholic

Left: Elaine Clément greeting guests

Family Banners

French Mass celebrated by Father Benoit Drapeau of Arizona

Pierrette & Jerry Guidry

Displays Guédry-Labine & Petitpas Reunion, Danny's Inn-Bathurst, N.B.

Jeff Killingsworth setting up the registration desk

Guédry-Labine & Petitpas Reunion, Aug. 16, 2009-Danny's Inn, Bathurst, N.B.

Above: Marty Guidry

Below: Family members enjoying the music of Larry Miller. Elaine Clément joined in on the triangle

1 & 2-Marty Guidry presenting thank you gifts to Jason & Lorn Guidry

3-Marty presents appreciation gifts to A.J. LeBlanc, Claudette Mancini & Albert Geddry

Guédry-Labine & Petitpas Reunion, Aug. 16, 2009-Danny's Inn-Bathurst, N.B.

Standing: Lorn Guidry of Bathurst, N. B.

Top row: Family members enjoying the Mardi Gras run while Larry Miller's band performs (Larry & wife dancing in center picture).

Center-Top: John Guidry of Bathurst, N.B. entertains the group with magic tricks throughout the day. Center-below: Jeff Killingsworth from VA-working the sales table.

Lorn Guidry of Bathurst, N. B., made beautiful sea-glass necklaces to give to the ladies at the reunion.

Guédry-Labine & Petitpas Reunion, Aug. 16, 2009-Danny's Inn-Bathurst, N.B.

1-Martin "Marty" Guidry

2-Display for Sister Corinne LaPlant's presentation 'History of the Acadians of the Baie-des-Chaleurs Region'

4-Eileen Avery [Petitpas] of California presents 'Genealogy - Recent Discoveries Using DNA Techniques'

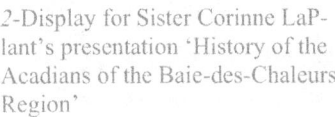

3-Sister Corinne LaPlant of New Brunswick

5,6 & 7-Local New Brunswick Acadian band with Roger Lanteigne on accordian entertains the group with music featuring Acadian & Louisiana styles.

8-Marie-Claude Geddry & Rachel Hardee

IN THE NEWS-HISTORICAL NEWS TIDBITS

Stars and Stripes Newspaper, Europe, Mediterranean, and North Africa Editions, 1942-1964
June 20, 1964

You'd Faint, Too

LAFAYETTE, La. (AP) — James Guidry, 23, fainted in the hospital corridor upon being told he was the father of triplets. Doctors had to be called to revive him.

Stars and Stripes Newspaper, Europe, Mediterranean, and North Africa Editions, 1942-1964
February 8, 1953

2 Airmen Rescue Yank Overcome In Smoky Room

LANDSBERG, Feb. 7 (Special) — A/1C Girard Guidry, of the 7030th Hq Sq, owes his life to two alert buddies, who forced their way into his smoke-filled room here to rescue him from almost certain asphyxiation.

Returning to their own room shortly after midnight recently, A/3C Leon Savard and A/2C Vincent LeMoine found the barracks corridor filling with smoke which smelled "like smoldering blankets."

The pair traced the odor to Guidry's room. Forcing the locked door, they found Guidry on his bed, unconscious from fumes generated by newspapers lying on a connected electric hot-plate.

Artificial respiration revived Guidry, who had been unconscious for about two hours. Questioning revealed he had fallen asleep after mistakenly connecting the hot-plate instead of a radio.

LeMoine and Savard were commended by Capt Paul Teegarden, CO of the 7030th.

MOTHERS' DAY AT MARBO-GUAM—Mothers at home were not forgotten by soldiers at Marbo, much thanks to Chaplain Pearce who made arrangements for flowers to be sent home from that area. Left to right, Sgt. John H. Neale, Larchmont, N.Y., Sgt. Richard Mansure, Prospect Park, Pa., Sgt. Robery G. Guidry, Cutt Off, La., PFC Leonard Whitgar, Red Bluff, California, and Chaplain Pearce.
(Signal Corps Photo)

Stars and Stripes Newspaper, Pacific Editions, 1945-1963, May 14, 1947

Just Like Home

The New Guinea version of the "old corner barber shop." Well, anyway, the chair is modern. The guy getting clipped is 2/Lt. Joseph Guidry, of Breaux Bridge, La., and all that's missing is the barber shop quartet. Even the shine boy's here.

Stars and Stripes Newspaper, Europe, Mediterranean, and North Africa Editions, 1942-1964, September 27, 1943

GENERATIONS Volume 7, Issue 4 Page 9

IN THE NEWS-HISTORICAL NEWS TIDBITS

Paul LaBine
Gary Laitinen
Margaret Lencione
Peter Lindsay
John Lindstrom

Above: Paul LaBine, U.S. Yearbooks-Hancock Central High, Hancock, Michigan 1958

Below: Gilbert Labine-Winnipeg Free Press-Manitoba, Canada, June 2, 1936

David Jeddry of Salmon River, Nova Scotia-WWII Draft Registration Card-1942

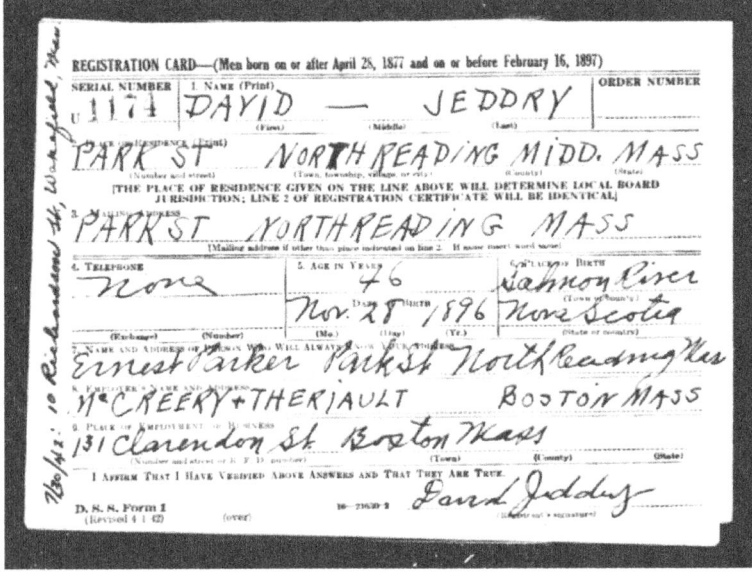

GILBERT LABINE, president of Gunnar Gold Mines, Ltd., who flew from Winnipeg, Monday, to the company's property in the central Manitoba area, to be present at the pouring of the first gold brick at the new mill. The brick will represent a clean-up from six weeks' operations.

John Guidry-1871 Census-Quebec West-St. Pierre Ward, Quebec, Canada

BON APPETIT-Recipes from the Guédry-Labine Cookbook

BABY LIMA BEANS AND TOMATO
Mary Guidry Dupont-Houma, LA

1 lb. fresh or frozen lima beans
1-14 1/2 ounce can stewed tomatoes or
4 fresh tomatoes peeled and diced
1 large onion diced
1 tbsp. olive oil

In medium size pot sauté onion in olive oil, on low fire, until soft, not brown. Add tomatoes and sauté for 10 minutes or so. Add lima beans and cook until beans are done; this may take up to 1 hour or longer.

Pickled pork or salt pork may be added, cut in small pieces and add to onions.

EGGPLANT FRITTERS
Jack Guidry, Lafayette, LA

"I used to live for "eggplant season" when my mom would fix a batch of these golden brown lip-smackers". - Jack Guidry

1 large eggplant
1 tsp. salt
3/4 cup sugar
1 egg, slightly beaten
2 tbsp. vanilla extract
1 tbsp. baking powder
2 cups flour (can vary)
Water to cook eggplant

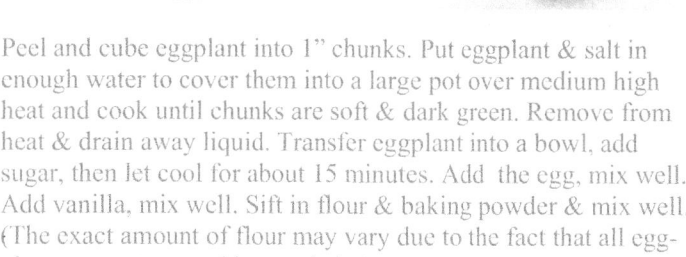

Peel and cube eggplant into 1" chunks. Put eggplant & salt in enough water to cover them into a large pot over medium high heat and cook until chunks are soft & dark green. Remove from heat & drain away liquid. Transfer eggplant into a bowl, add sugar, then let cool for about 15 minutes. Add the egg, mix well. Add vanilla, mix well. Sift in flour & baking powder & mix well. (The exact amount of flour may vary due to the fact that all eggplants are not created in equal size).

The difficult part of this recipe is getting the consistency of the batter correct. It shouldn't be so thin as to run off the spoon, nor so dry that it won't come off at all. Using your fingers to remove the batter from the spoon is ok.

Heat about 1" of oil in a deep frying pan to 350 degrees. Using a tablespoon, drop the batter, one spoonful at a time, into hot oil (they swell up). Fry each "glob" of batter until golden brown on both sides. You can flatten them a little with your spoon. Remove them when done and sprinkle a little sugar on them. These are best served hot!

BOOK NOOK

A Travel in Time to Grand Pré - *by Michele Doucette*

A Travel in Time to Grand Pré is an historically informative adventure, tying the history of the descendants of Yeshua to modern day Nova Scotia, Canada. Madeleine Sinclair feels disconnected with the era of her birth. Transported back to 1754, she comes to learn, live and experience firsthand the lives of the French Acadian people, meeting Michel (dit Sophie) LeBlanc.

Through the warm, loving and helpful guidance of fellow time traveler, Madame Pêche, she comes to understand the predetermined course of her Sinclair bloodline, beginning with Rollo the Viking, father of William Longsword, a line that is shown to be linked to the Merovingians, the Cathars and the Knights Templar (protectors of the Holy Grail).

Before long, the reader is led to the very apex of this time travel adventure. Madeleine has been decreed the one who is to introduce the words of Yeshua, spoken in Aramaic at the height of his ministry, to the modern world. Herein, Yeshua explains how individuals can find their way, their truth(s), so as to live their lives to the fullest.

http://germaindoucet.com/

Postcards from Acadia -*by Barbara LeBlanc*

Postcards from Acadie explores the cultural and symbolic resonance of Grand-Pré, Nova Scotia, Canada. Settled in the 1680s, Grand-Pré was one of the sites for the Acadian Deportation in 1755. From the settlement and deportation of the early Acadians, to the mass marketing of the Dominion Atlantic Railway and the federal reshaping as a National Historic Site, Grand-Pré has served "as a historical clue, a focal point, a catharsis, a catalyst and a motivator, both for Acadians and for others." Excavating the political and cultural symbols that have shaped Grand-Pré, Barbara LeBlanc explores the ways in which we negotiate personal and group identity.

In Acadian endeavors to direct and control a sense of identity in a changing world, Grand-Pré plays a significant role by serving as a place of heritage commemoration and celebration – of past, present and future.

GENERATIONS Volume 7, Issue 4 Page 12

Louisiane Day-Espace Neuf, August 17-18, 2009-Pokemouche, N.B.

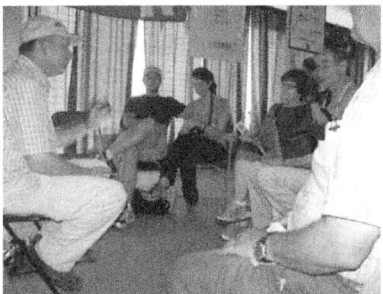

Left: Marty Guidry-Conference speaker on Aug. 17th on The Birds of Louisiana
Below: Waiting for the Courir de Mardi Gras

Below: Chef Roy Lyons joins Larry Miller on stage - Louisiane Day-Tuesday, Aug. 18th

The Louisiane booth-representing the culture, food and music of Louisiana

Left: Marty Guidry. Standing: Elaine Clément & Rachelle Dugas. Seated: Jeff Killingsworth & Rachel Hardee

Marty Guidry & Jeanette Leger-dancing a two-step as Larry Miller entertains the crowd (below)

Les Guédry d'Asteur Merchandise

We have a variety of items for sale on the *Guédry-Labine Family* website. A few of the items are souvenirs from our reunion in Bathurst and many are items that just have the *Les Guédry D'Asteur* name. These were a big hit at our gathering and there are lots of goodies left over for folks to enjoy.

Visit the 'Guédry Merchandise' page on our website to order:

http://freepages.genealogy.rootsweb.ancestry.com/~guedrylabinefamily

You can pay online through PayPal or download an order form and mail to:
Cindy Herdt, P.O. Box 6, Entiat, WA 98822.

Thanks again to Cindy Herdt for ordering all of our sales items and to Lindsey Hardee for designing our logo for the 2009 reunion.

Les Guédry d'Asteur Keychain-$6.00

Guédry-Labine Cookbook-$15.00

Les Guédry d'Asteur Reunion T-Shirts-several sizes available. $10.00-$14.00, depending on size. Also on our website you will find links to our Café Press page if you would like to order items bearing the family crest.

Les Guédry d'Asteur Reunion Magnet-$1.00

Les Guédry d'Asteur Pens - $3.00

Reunion Lapel Pin-2009-$3.00

Les Guédry d'Asteur Cap-$14.00

Les Guédry d'Asteur

What's in a name?

Guédry is the family to which you belong if your name is spelled Guédry, Guedry, Guidry, Gaidry, Guildry, Geddry, Jeddry, Labine, LaBine, LaBean or any of several dozen variations. The original name of our family is believed to have been Guédry. We are all descendants of Claude Guédry & Marguerite Petitpas.

Here are some common and uncommon variant spellings of the name.

Guédry	Guiddry	Geddrie	Jeddrie	Labeen
Guedry	Guiddery	Geddry	Jeddry	Labene
Guedrie	Guiedri	Gedree	Jederie	Labine
Guedris	Guiedry	Gedrie	Jedrey	LaBine
Guidry	Guildry	Gedry	Jedrie	LaBean
Gudiry	Guildrie	Gettry	Jedry	LaBeau
Guidery	Guitry	Gidrie		Labeau
Guidrey	Gaidry	Gidry	Lledre	
Guidrie	Gaidrie		Yedri	

Our **Petitpas** cousins likewise have several variations of their name including Petitpas, Pettipas, Petipas, Petitpa, Petit Pas and Pitts.

DUES REMINDER

Attached at the back of this issue is a membership application for renewing your membership in Les Guédry d'Asteur. Our dues are very reasonable at $6.00 for individuals and $10 for a family in 2009.

Please take a moment, complete the Membership Application, enclose a check and send it to the address on the application. It will help all of us do so much for the family. And, if you would like to join at one of the Benefactor Levels, it would allow us do even more.

HELP US SPREAD THE NEWS

Les Guédry d'Asteur maintains an email distribution list of our members so that we can keep you updated on upcoming events and family news. We also send this newsletter out to the members on that list. Help us continue to expand and reach new family & friends by encouraging other family members to forward their email addresses to Marty Guidry at guidryrm@cox.net

Les Guédry d'Asteur

To share your ideas for the newsletter, contact:

Marty Guidry
6139 North Shore Drive
Baton Rouge, LA 70817
225-755-1915
guidryrm@cox.net

'GENERATIONS' newsletter is now in its seventh year. We hope to provide our readers with an interesting, informative and entertaining newsletter. Your input is always welcome and we look forward to another year of sharing family history and news with you.

The Guédry-Labine Family Newsletter 'GENERATIONS' serves as a focal point for family members to share and learn about us.

Allie Guidry
txguidry2000@yahoo.com

Marty Guidry
guidryrm@cox.net

Les Guédry d'Asteur Officers and Committees

OFFICERS:
President - Martin Guidry (LA)
Vice-President - Elaine Clement (LA)
Secretary - Billy Harrell Guidry (LA)
Treasurer - Daniel "Chuck" Guidry (LA)

COMMITTEES:
Website - Becky Boggess (IA) - Chairperson
    Annie Grignon-Labine (QU) - Translator
    Elaine Clement (LA) - Translator
    Martin Guidry (LA)

Genealogy - Daryl LaBine (FL/ON) - Chairperson
    Bernard Geddry (AZ)
    Mark Labine (MN)
    Daniel "Chuck" Guidry (LA)
    Martin Guidry (LA)

Finance - Cheryl Guidry Tyiska (MD) - Chairperson
    Paul Labine (IL)
    Marshall Woolner (OR)
    Gloria Parrent (TX)
    Chuck Guidry (LA)

Membership - Charlene Guidry Lacombe (LA) -
    Chairperson
    Gayle Guidry (LA) - Special Projects
    Warren Guidry (TX)

Sales - Cindy Guidry Herdt (WA) - Chairperson
    Wayne Simoneaux (LA)
    Billy Harrell Guidry (LA)

Publicity - Elaine Clement (LA) - Chairperson
    Margaret Jeddry (MA)
    Warren Guidry (TX)

Newsletter - Allie Guidry Hardee (VA) - Editor
    Martin Guidry (LA)

CAFA Board Member - Jeanette Guidry Leger (LA)

WINTER 2010

Volume 8, Issue 1

Les Guédry d'Asteur

GENERATIONS

IN THIS ISSUE

BERNARD BUGARET 2
-An Acadian Pioneer
by Marty Guidry

SHERWIN JONAS 9
GUIDRY-by Sheri
Guidry Bergeron

BOBBY CHARLES 11
GUIDRY-Memorial

THEODULE GUIDRY 15
-Patent Application

BON APPETIT: Recipes from the Guédry/ 19
Labine Family Cookbook

DR. LEONARD 20
CHARLES LABINE
TURNS 90

RONALD GUIDRY - 21
Guidry Takes Gold by
Jeremy Theriot

BOOK NOOK 25

ALBERT GEDDRY 26
HONORED

THE DROUIN COL- 28
LECTION-A VALU-
ABLE RESEARCH-
SOURCE by Marty
Guidry

With the advent of a new year our Winter 2010 issue of "GENERATIONS" makes its appearance. This issue contains many interesting stories of our family that I believe you'll enjoy.

Many Acadian researchers try without success to locate the European origins of their ancestors. Our family is fortunate in that we have several records documenting the Basque origin of Bernard Bugaret, the father of Catherine Bugaret and grandfather of Marguerite Petitpas, wife of Claude Guédry. Three of those documents, discussed in this issue, present an interesting look into Bernard's life in France and Acadia.

We wish a very happy birthday to two of our family celebrating a true milestone of life – ninety years of age. Sherwin Guidry from Montegut, LA is not only a superb singer and public speaker, but also an avid writer on the preservation of our Acadian heritage. Dr. Leonard Charles Labine from Moscow, Idaho, is a dentist by profession and was a sports broadcaster by avocation in Moscow for almost forty years.

Did you know that a Guidry received a U. S. Patent for the hay baler that he invented? Theodule Guidry, a blacksmith and wheelwright of Church Point, LA, received this patent in 1908. Take a moment to learn a bit about his life and to peruse this interesting patent.

It is with sadness that we announce the passing of a Guédry family legend – Robert Charles Guidry (known in the music industry as Bobby Charles) from Abbeville, LA died in his hometown on 14 January 2010. Although a giant in his field as a songwriter, he was relatively unknown by the public.

Read his obituary and I am sure you'll recognize a few the songs he wrote such as "See You Later, Alligator" and "Walking to New Orleans".

Most of us recognize the name Ron Guidry as a Cy Young Award-winning pitcher with the New York Yankees, but I think you'll be equally impressed with our other Ronald Guidry who continues to win medals in golf, marksmanship, track and field and boxing. And he is doing so at the remarkable age of 72 years.

Retired Brigadier General Albert Geddry commanded the 12e Régiment blindé du Canada, an regiment of Acadians, during his distinguished military career. In April 2010 General Geddry will be honored by being named "Colonel of the Régiment" – an honor bestowed on him by the Queen of England.

Have you ever heard the term "Drouin Collection" in your genealogical research? Do you wonder what this collection is and what it contains? Now is your chance to discover the history of this collection and its remarkable value to Acadian researchers including the Guédry and Petitpas family. Marty Guidry reviews how the Drouin Collection developed and summarizes how this collection can aid your Guédry and Petitpas family research.

And don't forget the tasty recipes in "Bon Appetit", excellent reviews in the "Book Nook" and the interesting news articles of yesteryear in "Historical News Tidbits".

We hope you enjoy this issue of "Generations".

Marty Guidry

BERNARD BUGARET – AN ACADIAN PIONEER
by Marty Guidry

Today little evidence survives of the journeys our Acadian ancestors made when they left Europe to sail to Acadia. For Bernard Bugaret, however, an ancestor of the Guédry and Petitpas families, at least three records document his travels to Acadia from France.

About 1681 in Acadia Claude Guédry dit Grivois wed Marguerite Petitpas, widow of Martin Dugas and daughter of Claude Petitpas, Sieur de Lafleur and Catherine Bugaret. Between 1682 and 1703 Claude Guédry and Marguerite Petitpas had eleven children – nine sons and two daughters.[1,2] From these nine sons descend all the Guédry's (Guidry's, Jeddry's, Geddry's, Labine's, LaBean's and related families) in North America today.

Born in 1624, Claude Petitpas was well educated and served as syndicate (clerk of court) at Port-Royal, Acadia for many years.[2,3] About 1658 he married Catherine Burgaret, born in 1638 and the daughter of Bernard Bugaret. Between 1659 and 1682 Claude and Catherine had eight sons and five daughters.[2,3] All of the Petitpas and related families in North America descend from these eight sons. About 1690 Claude Petitpas died and his wife Catherine Bugaret married Charles La Tourasse also known as Charles Chevalier.[2,4]

Drawing of ship resembling the *Saint-Jehan*

Chevalier needed to obtain some information from Boston and in January 1693 he sent his wife Catherine Bugaret with a Mr. Boudrot to Boston to gather the needed information. The English authorities in New England had great confidence in and respect for Catherine Bugaret. Unfortunately, Catherine Bugaret died on the voyage to Boston.[4]

The first Bugaret to reach Acadia was Bernard Bugaret dit St-Martin du Gueret. On at least three occasions he sailed from France to Acadia. On 1 April 1636 he sailed from LaRochelle, France on the *Saint-Jehan* to Acadia.[5] One of nine ship's carpenters to sail, he appears on the *Saint-Jehan*'s manifest as:

> *Rôle des charpentiers qui sont allés faire navire et chaloupes en la Nouvelle-France,*
> . . .
> *Bernard Bugare, aussi charpentier basque*

Translation:
List of the carpenters who went to build ships and launches in New France
. . .
Bernard Bugare, also a Basque carpenter

Apparently, the carpenters including Bernard Bugaret completed their work in Acadia near the end of 1636 and sailed back to France in late 1636 or early 1637. On 15 September 1637 Bernard Bugaret signed a contract with Nicolas Denys in the presence of the notary Teuleron at LaRochelle, France. At this time Bugaret is listed as being a native of Villefranche in Gascony, France. In this document Bugaret contracts with Denys, a ship's captain, for passage for himself and ten men to sail to New France (Acadia). His return to Acadia at this time was to establish a fur hunting business for himself. This business venture can be discerned from a second contract Bugaret made less than four months later. On 14 January 1638 Bernard Bugaret, native of Villefranche-de-Queyran contracted with Barthélemi Redon dit la Borderye, native of Bordeaux and one of the ten men above.

BERNARD BUGARET – AN ACADIAN PIONEER

In the contract Bugaret agreed to transport Redon to La Hève, board him for one year, supply him with clothes, footwear, arms and munitions for the hunt and pay him 300 pounds in wages.[6] The year 1638 is significant because that also is the year in which Bernard's daughter Catherine Bugaret was born. Was she born in France after her father left for Acadia or was she born in Acadia while Bernard Bugaret was establishing his fur hunting enterprise? DNA testing of two direct descendants of Catherine Bugaret confirms that her parents were of European origin.[7] Where she was born is not known; however, no record of her mother going to Acadia has been found.

Bernard Bugaret did not remain in Acadia long for in 1648 he entered into another contract at La-Rochelle, France. On 24 March 1648, while living at du Mas in Agenois, he pledged to Emmanuel Le Borgne to sail again for New France. Bugaret was to go to La Hève in 1648 on a ship sent by Le Borgne to Governor d'Aulnay. At La Hève Burgaret would take charge of the ship at the stave-wood forest that he owned. Bugaret was to load the stave-wood on the ship and transport it back to Le Borgne in France. Two-thirds of the stave-wood would belong to Le Borgne and one-third would belong to Bugaret.

At the time of signing the document, Bugaret declared that he did not know how to sign his name.[8] (See below for a copy of this 1648 contract as well as a transcription and a translation of it.)

Although Bernard Bugaret apparently did not remain in Acadia for an extended time, his daughter Catherine married Claude Petitpas. At what time Catherine Bugaret arrived in Acadia is not known, but, once there, she remained for the rest of her life. Interestingly, several children of Claude Petitpas and Catherine Bugaret settled in the vicinity of Merliguèche (near today's Lunenburg) rather than in Port-Royal where their parents resided. Marguerite Petitpas and her husband Claude Guédry were one of the families that settled at Merliguèche. Near Merliguèche these families lived a rather primitive life among the local Mi'kmaq people – as woodsmen, farmers and coasting pilots. Why did they choose to live near Merliguèche? Was it because their grandfather Bernard Bugaret had a concession of land near Merliguèche that they could use? Had they heard tales from their mother about this area that enticed them to it? We may never know the answer, but their ties to Bernard Bugaret and his ventures at La Hève and Merliguèche certainly played a key role in their decisions.

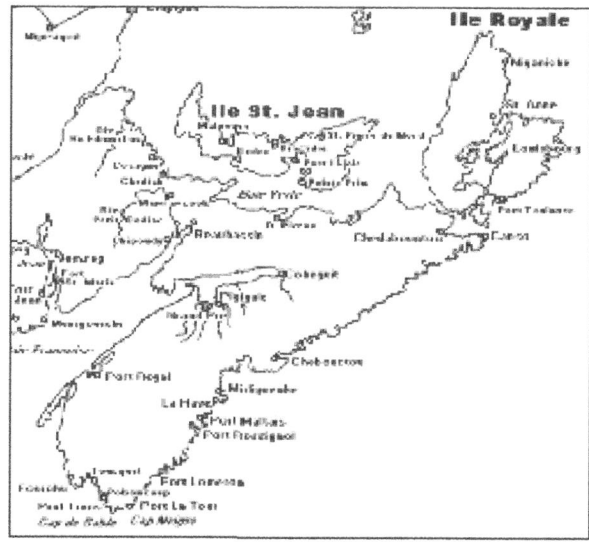

LIST OF CARPENTERS EMBARKING ON THE SAINT-JEHAN

Heading of the Roll of the Saint-Jehan

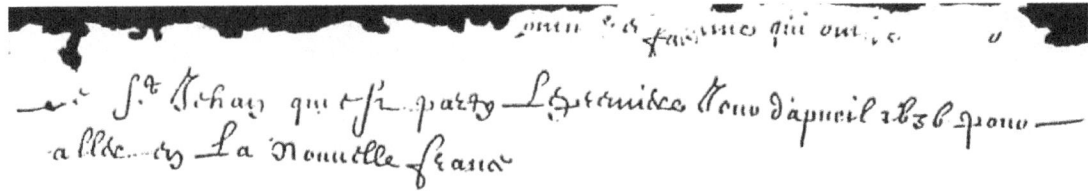

List of Carpenters on the Saint-Jehan
('Bernard Bugaret' appears on the 8th line from the bottom)

BERNARD BUGARET CONTRACT

Following on the next two pages are the transcription and translation of this contract.

Bernard Bugaret Contract-Transcription

Transcription:

Engagé
Bugaret
    a   134
Leborgne

Personnellement Establys bernard bugaret dict St-Martin
demeurant au lieu du Mas en Agenois d'une part, Et noble homme Emanuel
Le Borgne marchant demeurant en ceste ville d'autre part, Entre lesquelles parties ont
esté faictes les conventions suivantes, c'est assavoir que ledict S^r Le Borgne a consenti
par les présentes que ledict Bugaret s'embarque sure le navire que ledict
sieur Le Borgne doibt envoyer la présente année a Monsieur daulnay gouverneur
et lieutenant general pour le Roy de tout le païs et Coste de lacadie en la nouvelle
france, Et qu'il faict charger dans Icelluy navire au lieu de la heve
ou mervegue (?) au dict païs du bois merrain qu'il a dit luy apartenir
duquel bois merrain qui sera aporté dans ledict navire en apartiendra
les deux tiers audict sieur Le Borgne et l'autre tiers audict bugaret qui
sera partagé après l'arrivée dudict navire en l'une de ces raddes
sans que pour (le) tiers qui reviendra audict bugaret il soict obligé de payer
aulcun fret ny avarie par clause expresse ayant delaisse
audict sieur Le Borgne lesdicts deux tiers pour ledict fret et passage ce qui a esté
ainsi voulu et stipulé et accepté par lesdites partyes, et a ce faire et accomplir
par icelles sans venir au contraire a peyne de tous despens dommages
et interest ont obligé l'une a l'autre tous leurs biens Et ont renoncé
jugé et condempné etc. Faict a la rochelle en l'estude dudict notaire
apres midi le vingt quatriesme jour de mars mil six cent quarante
huit présents gilles Barré, Jean Bortuste clerqs demeurants en icelle, a ledict
Bugaret déclaré ne savoir signer de ce requis [dans tel navire
que bon luy semblera sauf et excepté]

(Extrait de la Série E, Notaires: Minutes TEULERON, notaire à La Rochelle (1646-
1648, f° 134 r°) [Archives Départementales de la Charente-Maritime].)

+

Bernard Bugaret Contract-Translation

Translation:

Pledged
Bugaret
   to   134
Leborgne

Personally Asserts bernard bugaret dit St-Martin
living at the place du Mas in Agenois of one part, And nobleman Emanuel
Le Borgne merchant living in this town of the other part, Between which parties have
been made the following conditions, that is to inform that the said sieur Le Borgne has
agreed by these presents that the said Bugaret embarks on the ship that the said
sieur LeBorgne is sending the present year to Monsieur d'aulnay governor
and lieutenant general for the King of all the country and Coast of Acadie in new
france And that he was put in charge of the said ship at the place of la hève
or mervegue at the said country of the stave-wood forest that he has said belongs to him
of which stave-wood forest which would be carried in the said ship by him will belong
two-thirds to the said sieur Le Borgne and the other third to the said bugaret which
will be divided after the arrival of the said ship at one of the harbors
unless the third that will accrue to the said bugaret he would be obliged to pay
no freight nor damage by the express clause being relinquished
by the said Le Borgne the said two thirds for the said freight and passage that has been
thus consented and stipulated and accepted by the said partners and has made that and accomplished by them without proceeding to the contrary has labored with all of the _____ damages
and interest have obliged the one to the other all their goods And have renounced,
judged and condemned etc. Made at la Rochelle in the office of the said notary
afternoon the twenty fourth day of march one thousand six hundred forty
eight by gilles Barré, Jean Bortuste clerks residing in the said place, has the aforesaid
Bugaret declared to not know how to sign of that required [in such ship
as he thought fit safe and excluded]

(Extrait de la Série E, Notaires: Minutes TEULERON, notaire à La Rochelle (1646-1648, f° 134 r°) [Archives Départementales de la Charente-Maritime].)

+

(NOTE: This translation is only approximate to give the general content of the contract. If anyone can provide a more accurate and complete translation, please send it to
guidryrm@cox.net)

References-Bernard Bugaret

1. Arsenault, Bona; Histoire et Généalogie des Acadiens (Éditions Leméac Inc., Ottawa, Canada, 1978), p. 588.

2. Arsenault, Bona; Ibid., p. 721.

3. "Familles establies a l'Acadie Port Royal - 1671", Archives Nationales Françaises (ANF), Le Centre des Archives d'Outre-Mer, (Aix-en-Provence, France), Col. G1, vol. 466, no. 8. (Census of Port-Royal – 1671). [Microfilm F1801 – Centre d'Études Acadiennes; Université de Moncton; Moncton, New Brunswick, Canada]. [Transcription: Report Concerning Canadian Archives for the Year 1905 (S. E. Dawson; Ottawa, Canada; 1906), Volume II, Appendix A, 3rd Part, pp. 1-6]

4. Webster, John Clarence: Acadia at the End of the 17th Century (The New Brunswick Museum; Saint John, New Brunswick, Canada 1934), p. 169.

5. "Rôle de tous les homes et femmes qui ont passé sur le Saint-Jehan, qui est parti le premier jour d'avril 1636 pour aller en la Nouvelle-France", Les Archives Départementales de la Charente-Maritime (35 rue François-de-Vaux-de-Foletier 17000 La Rochelle, France), Série B, prov 75, 5e dossier. [Transcription: A. Godbout, "Le role du Saint-Jehan et les origins acadiennes", Memoires de la Société Généalogique Canadienne Française (Montréal, Canada, 1944), Volume I, pp. 22-24]. [Fascimile: French Canadian and Acadian Genealogical Review (Québec, Canada, 1968), Volume I, pp. 61-65]

6. Memoires de la Société Généalogique Canadienne Française (Montréal, Canada, 1944), Volume I, pp. 29-30] [Translation: French Canadian and Acadian Genealogical Review (Québec, Canada, 1968), Volume I, p. 72]

7. Acadian & French Canadian Ancestral Home website by Lucie LeBlanc Consentino. "Mothers of Acadia – mtDNA Proven Origins" page at http://www.acadian-home.org/frames.html . Viewed 9 February 2010.

8. "Engagé Burgaret A Le Borgne – 4 March 1648", Les Archives Départementales de la Charente-Maritime (35 rue François-de-Vaux-de-Foletier 17000 La Rochelle, France), Extrait de la Série E, Notaires: Registre de Me Teuleron, notaire à La Rochelle (1646-1648, folio 134 r°) [Fascimile and Transcription: Massignon, Geneviève; Les Parlers Français d'Acadie – Enquête Linguistique, Volume II, pp. 963, 967-968]

SHERWIN JONAS GUIDRY by Sheri Guidry Bergeron

My father had his 90th birthday this January. He is an incredible, wholesome Cajun man who has a light-hearted personality and has used his 90 years loving, supporting and guiding our family. He was honored with a joyous birthday party and family reunion at Oak Alley on Sunday, January 3rd. He is dearly loved by everyone who knows him.

The youngest son of John Guidry and Ludovia Lirette, my father, Sherwin "Chabbie" Guidry, was born January 3, 1920, in Montegut, Louisiana, located south of Houma. After serving in WWII, he married on June 28, 1944, Lee Dora Peltier. They have two daughters, Sheri Guidry Bergeron and Kathy Guidry Henson. Sheri is married to Iven J. Bergeron, Jr. Iven and Sheri have two married sons, Troy and Todd, and seven grandchildren.

Chabbie, a leading citizen of Terrebonne Parish and throughout Acadiana, was acknowledged for contributing to the preservation of the history of our Acadian heritage with several awards. His wonderful insight into the past has been passed on through his artifact collection and narrative talks shared with youth groups throughout the state. He wrote articles for the Houma Courier and Bayou Catholic newspapers for many years covering Acadian and Terrebonne Parish history, folklore, and recaps of his studies and travels. He is known for articles such as: "History of the Acadians" and a compilation of his many articles that were published into books named, "Xplorin' Terrebonne" and "'Xplorin' Acadiana". These are available in various local libraries in Louisiana.

He has been gifted with a wonderful singing and speaking voice that has been shared in church and Master of Ceremonies events in various communities. He had an entertaining Dixieland band in which he played trumpet, and with his Bing Crosby style voice, sang popular dance tunes and top 40s songs and hits of WWII. He wrote several songs, one of which was adopted as the official Terrebonne Parish Song. His love for music and history were shared and appreciated throughout Acadiana. In his late 80s he was still entertaining other seniors living in nursing and assisted living homes in Baton Rouge.

Today in 2010, Chabbie and Lee are living in Baton Rouge, Louisiana. Chabbie is 90 years young and his health may have slowed him down, but he still sings and continues to entertain his family and friends.

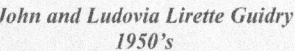

John and Ludovia Lirette Guidry 1950's

Kathy, Chabbie (90 years old), Lee, Sheri

SHERWIN JONAS GUIDRY *by Sheri Guidry Bergeron*

Sherwin Guidry's lineage:

Claude Guedry dit Grivois dit Laverdure (b. 1648, France; m. Marguerite Petitpas in Acadia)
|
Augustin Guedry (b. 1690 in Acadia, m. Jeanne Hebert)
|
Joseph Guedry (b. 1735 in Pisiquit, Acadia; m. Elizabeth Comeau in St. James, LA)
|
Jean-Baptiste Guidry (b. 1779 in St. James, LA; m. Marguerite Comeaux)
|
Edmond Guidry (b. 1813 in St. James, LA; m. Elmire Belanger, Elodie Foret)
|
Alidore Guidry (b. 1850 in Terrebonne, LA; m. Anazile Robichaux)
|
John Joseph Guidry (b. 1874 in Montegut, LA; m. Ludovia Lirette)
|
Sherwin Guidry (b. 1920 in Montegut, LA; m. 1944 Lee Dora Peltier)

Above: Alidore Guidry 1850-1935.

Top right: Alidore Guidry's 1870's home, South of Montegut.

Bottom right: John and Ludovia Lirette Guidry's Montegut home

Bobby Charles, Louisiana songwriter, dies at 71 (Story appeared on NOLA.com-January 14, 2010)

NEW ORLEANS MUSIC NEWS
The latest music updates from New Orleans and South Louisiana

Bobby Charles in 2007

By Keith Spera, The Times-Picayune
January 14, 2010, 1:39PM

Robert "Bobby" Charles Guidry, the reclusive south Louisiana songwriter of hits for Fats Domino, Frogman Henry and Bill Haley & the Comets, died early Thursday after collapsing at home in Abbeville, his manager said. He was 71.

Known professionally as Bobby Charles, he wrote "Walking to New Orleans," one of Domino's most beloved songs; "(I Don't Know Why I Love You) But I Do," an enduring classic by Henry; and "See You Later Alligator," a smash for Haley at the dawn of rock 'n' roll.

A reluctant performer, Mr. Charles largely disappeared after participating in the Band's 1976 farewell concert The Last Waltz. He preferred to **release the occasional album** while living quietly, an enigma whose songs were more famous than he was. Along the way he dealt with a litany of personal disasters ranging from fires to floods to cancer.
Mr. Charles agreed to stage a "comeback" at the 2007 New Orleans Jazz and Heritage Festival presented by Shell, only to **back out at the last minute,** citing health issues.

Mac "Dr. John" Rebennack, Marcia Ball, guitarist Sonny Landreth and other admirers performed his songs in his absence. "He was the champion south Louisiana songwriter," Landreth said. "Everybody had a favorite Bobby Charles song. He had the gift. "Mr. Charles grew up poor in Abbeville, the son of a gas company truck driver. At 14, he joined a band that entertained at high school dances. "Nobody in my family wanted me to get into the music business, but I always loved it," he said during a 2007 interview. "The first time I heard Hank Williams and Fats Domino, it just knocked me down. When I was a kid, I used to pray to be a songwriter like them. My prayers were answered, I guess."

Leaving a cafe one night, Mr. Charles bid farewell to friends with "see you later, alligator." As the cafe door closed behind him, a drunken stranger replied, "after while, crocodile." Not sure he heard correctly, he went back inside and asked the stranger to repeat it.

That couplet inspired him to write "See You Later Alligator." He sang it over the phone and landed a recording contract, sight unseen, from Chicago blues and R&B label Chess Records. The company's owners assumed he was black until he stepped off the plane in Chicago.

As a burgeoning teen idol, he hit the road with other Chess artists, the only white guy on the bus. Not all audiences appreciated such integration. The threats soured him on touring. So did the occasional bullet fired his way. "I never wanted to be a star," he said. "I've got enough problems, I promise you. If I could make it just writing, I'd be happy. Thank God I've been lucky enough to have a lot of people do my songs."

In the 1970s, Mr. Charles wrote a song called "The Jealous Kind." Joe Cocker recorded it in 1976, followed by Ray Charles, Delbert McClinton, Etta James and Johnny Adams. Kris Kristofferson and Gatemouth Brown covered Mr. Charles' "Tennessee Blues," as did newcomer Shannon McNally. Muddy Waters recorded "Why Are People Like That"; so did Houma guitarist Tab Benoit on his Grammy-nominated 2006 album "Brother to the Blues."

He could not play an instrument or read music. Songs popped into his head, fully formed. To capture them, he'd sing into the nearest answering machine; sometimes he'd call home from a convenience store pay phone. "I can hear all the chords up here," he said, pointing to his brain, "but I can't tell you what they are."

He counted Bob Dylan, Neil Young, Willie Nelson and James Taylor among his friends and fans. Mickey Raphael, the longtime harmonica player in Willie Nelson's band, appears on Mr. Charles' forthcoming CD. He once encountered Mr. Charles at Nelson's studio outside Austin, Texas. "He said he wanted to record some music, and he was bringing some musicians," Raphael recalled. He said, "This is my guitar player, Neil." And it was Neil Young. "He was so unpretentious and laid-back. On further investigation, you'd find out he wrote all these incredible songs."

In his younger years, Mr. Charles raised all kinds of hell. His rogue's resume included scrapes with the law, a busted marriage, and general excess. "To love and lose -- I know that pain," he said. "And cocaine killed so many of my friends."

For a time in the 1970s, he laid low in Woodstock, N.Y. But mostly Mr. Charles holed up in the bosom of south Louisiana, waiting for the next song to come along. Or the next calamity. For years, he lived on the Vermilion River outside Maurice, La. In the mid-'90s, his house burned down. He moved into a trailer on the grounds of Dockside Studios in Maurice, a favorite haunt. Despondent, he hit the road with one of his four sons and washed up at Holly Beach, a hamlet with 300 permanent residents on the Gulf of Mexico southwest of Lake Charles. "I'm a Pisces. I love water," he said. "There's nothing like a wave to wash away your problems and clean out your mind." In Holly Beach, Mr. Charles disappeared for a decade. But in the summer of 2005, Hurricane Rita found him. He escaped just ahead of the storm, then later returned to find his house had washed away.

The reclusive songwriter preferred to live quietly, out of the limelight. He moved to a two-bedroom trailer amid the grand oaks of an eight acre property outside Abbeville. He kept his address and phone number secret, and cast a wary eye toward strangers and acquaintances alike. "They all want to meet Bob Dylan or Willie Nelson. They say, 'Man, I got a song for Bob Dylan.' I think Bob Dylan writes most of his own. So does Willie. I don't even sing any of mine to them.

"Some people have to depend on somebody else to make a living. And that gets tiresome, man, carrying a load like that. It gets to the point where you're afraid to open your mouth in front of anybody."

Despite being swindled out of some publishing rights and songwriting credits along the way, his annual royalties afforded him a comfortable living. When, for instance, Frogman Henry's version of "But I Do" landed on the "Forrest Gump" soundtrack, Mr. Charles received a royalty check.

Mr. Charles was happiest in the studio. He often scheduled recording sessions to coincide with the full moon. "His approach was unorthodox," said Sonny Landreth, who often recorded with Mr. Charles at Dockside. "It wasn't like recording in Nashville, which is very organized, with musical charts."

Recent compositions occasionally contained ecological messages. The issue of clean water was especially important to him, Raphael said. "He'd call me up and say, 'I'm so mad about this, I had to write a song,'" Raphael said. "You'd listen to the song, and know he was mad as hell, but he always put a positive spin on it."

In 2003, Mr. Charles and Jim Bateman, his manager for the past three decades, gathered recordings spanning 20 years for the double-CD "Last Train to Memphis," released via Charles' own Rice 'n Gravy Records. Guest musicians included Neil Young, Fats Domino, Willie Nelson, Delbert McClinton and Maria Muldaur.

Mr. Charles' voice, graced with a slight, Randy Newman-esque drawl, remained strong in his later years, as did his gift for pairing lyrics and melody. He was due to release a new album, "Timeless," next month. Co-produced by Mr. Charles and Rebennack, it contains mostly new songs, and is dedicated to Domino. While recording, "he had lots of energy, and was very productive," Landreth said. Rebennack "had that affect on him."
Mr. Charles recently injured his back in a fall, but remained intensely focused on finishing "Timeless." "He kept saying, 'I've got to get this out. I want to hold it in my hands,'" Bateman said. "It's like he had a premonition."

Mr. Charles saw the final design for the album's artwork, but died weeks before its scheduled Feb. 23 release. Had he lived, he was unlikely to hit the road to promote his new CD. In recent years, he tended to keep to himself. Most days, he ate alone at an Abbeville seafood joint where the waitress mixed his preferred cocktail -- a Grey Goose martini on the rocks -- as he parked his car.

"I don't really have anybody," Mr. Charles said in 2007. "I just don't have a whole lot in common with the people I went to school with. I still love them as my friends, but I don't have anything to say to 'em. They wouldn't believe half the (stuff) that happened to me anyway. "But when I get around Mac Rebennack or Fats or somebody like that, then I'm in my world."

NOTE: Robert Charles Guidry was survived by his four sons Mark Emery Guidry, Barry Charles Guidry, Guy Paul Guidry and Robert Charles Guidry, Jr. as well as his brother Floyd Guidry of Export, PA and sister Emily Guidry Courtier of Abbeville, LA. He was preceded in death by his parents Emery Guidry and Edvina Richard Guidry and his sister Lula Mae Guidry Bernard. A Memorial Service was held at St. Mary Magdalen Catholic Church in Abbeville, LA on 27 January 2010 at 3:00 pm for his family and friends. Another Memorial Service will be held in New Orleans, LA at a date to be determined.

 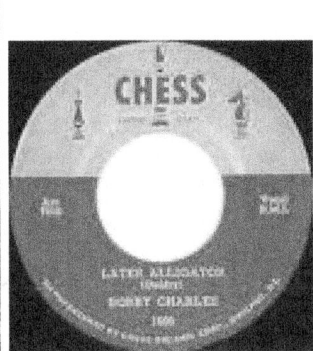 

In October, 2007, Bobby Charles was inducted into the Louisiana Music Hall of Fame.

THEODULE GUIDRY-PATENT APPLICATION

Theodule Guidry Patent Application filed February 21, 1908, Patented September 29, 1908

Excerpt: *NEWS FROM CHURCH POINT, LA-October 17, 1908*

Theodule Guidry, a son of Thelismare Guidry, of Church Point, has recently been granted a patent on a baler which people who has seen it pronounce to be the best of its kind they have ever seen. The baler is to be put on the market at once and Mr. Guidry is thinking of organizing a stock company for its manufacture.

The Guidry baler puts up two bales at once, one on each side of the feedbox. It is simple of construction and cheaply made.

T. Guidry has recently formed a partnership with Editor Ramsey, of the Church Point Democrat, under the name of Guidry and Ramsey, for the purpose of dealing in real estate business on an ambitious scale and with the purpose of booming Church Point property, which is said to be moving freely.

July 17, 1909 – The hay press factory being conducted by the Winkler brothers for the purpose of manufacturing the hay press recently invented by Theodule Guidry, is doing some fine work. They have so far made four presses all of which are sold, and have orders for seven more that will be delivered between now and fall.

Tuesday of this week one of their balers was experimented with while mounted on truck was rolled to some nearby field and two small creole horses attached, the baler did excellent work and turned out a good tight heavy bale. It is believed that this baler will put out from four to six hundred bales per day, and requires the use of only one horse and will not over work him. In every sense it is a desirable advantage over anything ever turned out in the baler line.

* *

Theodule Guidry (s/o Thelesmar Guidry & Herminia Daigle) was born October 13, 1883 in Church Point, Acadia Parish, Louisiana. He married Lulu Savoie on February 11, 1904 (d/o Francois Savoie & Eugenie David).

Theodule, was a blacksmith and wheelwright at the time he invented his hay baler. His brother, Pierre, owned a soda pop factory and his father, Thelesmar, owned several businesses in the town of Church Point, including shoemaker's shop which he expaned to include a saddler and barbering, and the three-story Guidry Hotel.

The three-story Guidry Hotel, built in anticipation of business to be brought in by Church Point's first railroad, the Opelousas, Gueydan and Northeastern. The hotel was one of the Thelesmar Guidry enterprises. (Freeland Archives photo, Acadia Parish Library)

The following 3-page document is the patent application filed with the U.S. Patent and Trademark Office Patents, 1790-1909

UNITED STATES PATENT OFFICE.

THEODULE GUIDRY, OF CHURCH POINT, LOUISIANA.

BALING-PRESS.

No. 899,666.   Specification of Letters Patent.   Patented Sept. 29, 1908.

Application filed February 21, 1908. Serial No. 417,101.

To all whom it may concern:

Be it known that I, THEODULE GUIDRY, citizen of the United States, residing at Church Point, in the parish of Acadia and State of Louisiana, have invented certain new and useful Improvements in Baling-Presses, of which the following is a specification.

The purpose of the present invention is to devise a press for forming hay, straw and other loose material into bales, the purpose being to provide a double acting press of novel structure so that each stroke of the plunger may be utilized for effective work.

For a full understanding of the invention and the merits thereof and also to acquire a knowledge of the details of construction and the means for effecting the result, reference is to be had to the following description and accompanying drawings.

While the invention may be adapted to different forms and conditions by changes in the structure and minor details without departing from the spirit or essential features thereof, still the preferred embodiment is shown in the accompanying drawings, in which:

Figure 1 is a perspective view of a double acting press embodying the invention. Fig. 2 is a vertical central longitudinal section of the baling chamber, the plunger operating mechanism and the mountings therefor being omitted. Fig. 3 is a transverse section on the line x—x of Fig. 1.

Corresponding and like parts are referred to in the following description and indicated in all the views of the drawings by the same reference characters.

The baling chamber 1 is double ended and is provided at a central point with a feed opening 2 through which the hay, straw or other material is supplied to the baling chamber to be compressed. Longitudinal sills 3 support the baling chamber and project beyond the ends thereof to receive the platforms 4 and 5. Frames 6 embrace the four sides of the baling chamber and stiffen and strengthen the same. A portion of the top of the baling chamber near each end is made movable, as indicated at 7, the outer end of said movable portion being pressed inward so as to reduce the opening at the end of the baling chamber through which the bale is discharged, thereby retarding the delivery of the bale with the result that the same is compressed simultaneously with its discharge. A bar 8 is secured to the upper side of each movable portion 7 near the extremity thereof and its ends are off-set and extend over the sides of the baling chamber and receive rods 9. A bar 10 is mounted upon the upper ends of the rods 9 and coil springs 11 are placed upon the rods 9 and confined between the parts 8 and 10. Set nuts 12 threaded upon the projecting ends of the rods 9 regulate the tension of the springs 11 and admit of varying the resistance of the movable portion 7 of the baling chamber to the outward pressure of the bale as the latter is discharged.

The plunger 13 mounted to reciprocate in the baling chamber, is arranged so as to move across the feed opening 2, thereby admitting of a quantity of material being supplied to the baling chamber upon either side of the plunger, whereby the latter performs compressive work at each stroke. To prevent binding of the plunger, anti-friction rollers 14 are located upon each side of the feed opening 2 and about in line with the inner side of the top of the baling chamber. The plunger is connected at its lower end with a slide 15 which is mounted in guides below the bottom of the baling chamber, said bottom having longitudinal slots 16 through which connections 17 pass and join the plunger to said slide. The connections 17 may be of any substantial structure to enable the plunger to withstand the strain to which subjected when in operation.

Follow blocks 18 separate the bales and when advanced in the baling chamber are prevented from rearward movement by means of catches 19, the latter being applied to opposite sides of the baling chamber and being spring actuated so as to yield and admit of the follow blocks passing by them, but which spring outward and engage with the follow blocks after the latter have cleared the catches in their forward movement.

A framework 20 is connected to one end of the longitudinal sills 3 and supports a vertically arranged crank shaft 21 to the upper end of which is fitted a sweep 22, a pitman 23 connecting the crank with a slide 15. As the crank shaft is rotated by means of the sweep 22, the slide 15 is reciprocated, thereby moving the plunger 13 backward and forward in the baling chamber and alternately pressing the material in the end baling compartments thereof. By having the slide 15 arranged below the bottom of the baling chamber and beneath the platforms 4 and 5, it does not interfere in the least with the bales or the operator when standing upon the platform.

It is proposed to arrange the baling chamber horizontally and for convenience of transportation it may be mounted upon a running gear, the latter being of any construction to admit of transporting the press from one place to another.

Having thus described the invention, what is claimed as new is:

In a press, the combination of a double ended baling chamber having a centrally disposed feed opening, platforms at opposite ends of the baling chamber and about in the plane of the bottom thereof, movable portions at the extremities of the bale compartments, transverse bars secured to the outer end portions of said movable portions and having their outer ends off-set, rods passed through the off-set ends of said bars, other bars mounted upon the upper ends of the rods, springs mounted upon the rods and confined between the outer ends of the said bars, set nuts fitted to the upper ends of the said rods, a plunger arranged within the baling chamber and adapted to reciprocate across the feed opening thereof, a slide arranged below the baling chamber and the said platforms and having connection with the lower end of the said plunger, and means for imparting a reciprocating movement to the said slide.

In testimony whereof I affix my signature in presence of two witnesses.

THEODULE GUIDRY. [L. S.]

Witnesses:
A. T. RICHARD,
HOMER BAROUSSE.

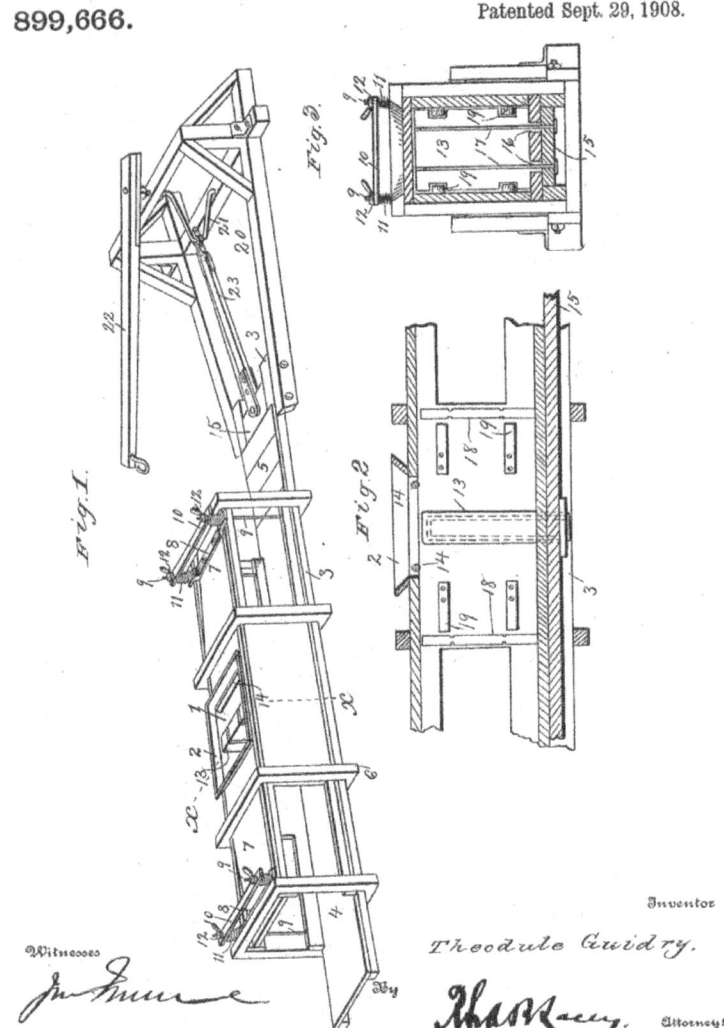

BON APPETIT

SAUSAGE JAMBALAYA
Charlene Lacombe - Jennings, LA

1 small onion, chopped
1 bell pepper, chopped
4 cloves garlic chopped
2 tablespoons margarine
1 pound smoked sausage sliced
1 can stewed tomatoes with green chilies (use Rotel tomatoes if available)
1 small can tomato paste
1/4 cup Worcestershire sauce
Seasonings to taste
Parsley
2-3 cups cooked rice

Saute onions, garlic and bell peppers in margarine. Add sausage, sauté well. Add tomatoes and tomato paste. Season to taste, add Worcestershire sauce. Add parsley. Let mixture cook for about 15-20 minutes, add water if needed. Add cooked rice to mixture.

Recipes from the Guédry-Labine Cookbook-A cookbook for and by descendants of Claude Guédry and Marguerite Petitpas, 2004

STUFFED BELL PEPPERS
Maudry Guidry Viator-Abbeville, LA

4 lg. bell peppers
1 cup cooked rice
1 lb. ground meat
1 tsp. salt
1 tsp. pepper
1 cup *Manwich* sauce
1 cup shredded cheese

Wash peppers & halve lengthwise and clean out seeds and membranes. Parboil for 5 minutes. Cook ground meat until it loses it's redness, then drain. Add rice, seasoning and half of the *Manwich* sauce and mix lightly. Spoon mixture into peppers. Arrange peppers in shallow baking dish and pour remaining *Manwich* sauce over them. Top with cheese and bake at 350 degrees for 20 minutes.

DR. LEONARD CHARLES LABINE TURNS 90

On 16 February 2010 Dr. Leonard Charles Labine will celebrate a milestone of his life - his 90th birthday. The son of Louis-Urgel Labine and Ila Lombarde, Leonard began life on 16 February 1920 in Nashua, New Hampshire.

Until he graduated from high school at age 18, Leonard lived with his mother and maternal grandparents in Nashua. He and his mother traveled to Moscow, Idaho in 1938 where Leonard attended the University of Idaho at Moscow to study pre-dentistry. After graduating from the University of Idaho, Leonard entered the University of Kentucky dental school in Louisville.

While attending college, he played both baseball and football. From the late 1950's until 1990 Leonard volunteered as the local sports broadcaster where he was known as the "Voice of the Moscow Bears". In 1994 Leonard was inducted into the Idaho Sports Hall of Fame.

While at the University of Idaho, Leonard enrolled in the U. S. Army R.O.T.C. program. He entered the University of Kentucky dental school in 1942 as an Army officer. The dental program at the University of Kentucky was cancelled while Leonard was there. He then served a short time overseas with the U. S. Navy Seabees before finishing dental school with the Army and serving an internship at the Presidio Hospital in San Francisco, California. On leaving the military in 1952, he returned to Idaho and opened a dental practice in Genesse before moving his practice to Moscow, Idaho in 1954 where he remained until his retirement.

Leonard married Camille Joyce Short in September 1943 in Moscow and they had three sons and a daughter. Their children are: Suzanne Lee Labine born in 1948, Lance Craig Labine in 1951, Leonard Charles Labine, Jr. in 1954 and Lon Labine in 1956. Today he has 11 grandchildren and 9 great-grandchildren.

Friends will visit Dr. Labine on his birthday at an open house where he will be surrounded by his children, grandchildren, nieces and nephews. It should be a memorable day for Dr. Labine as he celebrates this significant milestone of life.

Right/top: Leonard at his favorite hobby...sportscaster at age 70
Right/below: Chuck with dad at age 85
Below/left: Leonard in his college years
Below/center: Our family in 2000: Lon (youngest), Lance (2nd born), Leonard Labine (Dad), Suzanne (1st born), and Chuck (3rd born)

Guidry Gets Gold(s)

Words: Jeremy Theriot

Ronald Guidry

Golf, marksmanship, track and field, boxing... you name it, Ron Guidry has done it and still continues to do so. Considering the fact that he possesses medals in numerous competitive sports, one would (and should) think twice about hitting the greens or getting into a fistfight or shoot-out with Guidry.

A marksman since his army days in Germany from 1957-60, Guidry continued nurturing both his boxing and shooting skills while overseas.

"Back then, boxing was the sport," said Guidry. "Football just wasn't that popular yet."

Prior to being shipped off to Germany, Guidry earned the Louisiana State Golden Glove in 1955 – defeating a three-time champion. Although not favored to come out as the victor, Guidry knocked out his opponent in the first round.

"We used eight ounce gloves back then and no head gear," says Guidry.

Guidry later hung up his gloves in 1961 but not before winning the Louisiana State Golden Glove for that year.

"I didn't put on a glove or hit a bag for more than 40 years," says Guidry.

That was until in 2007, after perusing through an issue of GeezerJock (a magazine for athletes 40 years of age and older), Guidry discovered that a 68-year-old boxing champion had claimed the title two years in a row for the Ringside World Championship Tournament. It was this discovery that spurred on Guidry to once again lace up his gloves and re-enter the ring.

Just some of Guidry's awards

In his two months of training prior to the fight, Guidry lost 17 pounds – putting him in the 165lb. weight class.

"My cholesterol dropped by 50 points which prevented me from taking medication [to regulate his cholesterol]," says Guidry.

Similar to his fight in 1955, Guidry was once again the underdog. In addition to being the reigning champion and a couple of years his junior, Guidry's opponent also owned his own gym in Michigan where he could be found six days a week.

The fight took place in Kansas City and went down to the wire – lasting all three rounds. At the conclusion of the fight, the judges produced their decision that crowned Guidry the new champion.

At 72 years of age, Guidry still lives an exceptionally active lifestyle. A semi-retired electrical/instrument checker for R&D Engineering, Guidry is not satisfied with simply sitting still.

"I tried retirement for three months," says Guidry.

"I play golf in the morning," says Guidry. "What would I do for the rest of the day?"

After a three-month hiatus, Guidry returned to R&D but this time with a lighter workload that freed up his mornings.

In addition to his boxing accolades, Guidry has earned numer-

GUIDRY GETS GOLD (S) - *Jeremy Theriot*

Detail of Guidry's championship belt from 2007

ous titles with his golf game. Just some of his past accomplishments include amateur champion (70+ in 2007, 2008) for the Louisiana Golf Association (LGA), winner of the Senior Four Ball (in 2002 and 2004) as well as numerous Senior Olympic medals.

Currently, Guidry has more than 40 medals; proof of his numerous past victories.

"I used to compete more," says Guidry, "but now boxing takes up the majority of my time."

Recently, Guidry once again returned to Kansas City this past August to defend his title. Triumphantly, Guidry defeated the same opponent and maintain his champion title.

Guidry's recent 2009 fight can be viewed on www.youtube.com by searching under 'Ronald Guidry.'

> "All the time he's boxing, he's thinking. All the time he was thinking, I was hitting him."
> - Jack "Manassa Mauler" Dempsey
> 1895-1983
> World Heavyweight Titleholder 1919-1926

Volume 26; No. 10; October 2009
Published by
The East Baton Rouge Council on Aging

5790 Florida Blvd.
Baton Rouge, LA 70806
Phone: 225.923.8000
Website: www.ebrcoa.org

Published in the October, 2009 issue of 'the Platinum record' - The East Baton Rouge Council on Aging.

IN THE NEWS-HISTORICAL NEWS TIDBITS

Article from *History of La Salle County, Illinois* (Together with Sketches of it Cities, Villages and Towns, Educational, Religious, Civil, Military, and Political History, Portraits of Prominent Persons, and Biographies of Representative Citizens). Vol. I
Chicago: Inter-State Publishing Co.—1886

Rev. Felix Guedry, pastor of St. Patrick's Church, La Salle. was born April 5, 1833, in Louisiana, the third son of a family of eleven children of Gideon and Armelise (Landry) Guedry, natives of the same State. He received his primary education, first at a private school and later attended the district schools. At the age of twenty, in 1853, he went to Perry County, Mo., and attended St. Mary's Seminary until 1856 when he went to St. Vincent College, Cape Girardeau, Mo., where he pursued his ecclesiastical studies, and was professor of the college. He returned to St. Mary's Seminary in 1857, where he completed his theological studies and was raised to the priesthood in 1861. He was then professor in St. Vincent's College till 1863 when he became Treasurer of the same college, acting in this capacity until 1867, when he went to New Orleans and was assistant priest till 1868. He then went to Los Angeles, Cal., where he was Treasurer of St. Vincent's College, Los Angeles, Cal., until 1869 when he accepted the pastorship of St. Joseph's Church, Emmittsburg, Md., where he remained till 1872, after which he again returned to St. Vincent's College, Cape Girardeau, Mo., holding the position of professor until 1873, when he returned to Emmittsburg, Md., acting as Director of the Sisters of Charity until 1877. He was then engaged at New Orleans until 1878, and while there two of the four priests stationed there died of yellow fever. In December, 1878, Father Guedry returned to St. Mary's Seminary and acted as assistant pastor till 1880 when he was transferred to Chicago, and in June, 1880, he was appointed as assistant to Father Anthony, and after his death which occurred Feb. 18, 1881, he was appointed pastor of his present church.

St. Joseph's Catholic Church, Emmittsburg, MD

IN THE NEWS-HISTORICAL NEWS TIDBITS

Below: *The Lincoln Nebraska State Journal*
Lincoln, Nebraska - July 29, 1947

ARMY MILK IS TESTED several times before it is passed for consumption by GIs. S/Sgt. Abel Guidry, who inspects the bulk of milk brought in for army use, is shown testing a fresh batch from one of the large cans used before the milk is bottled.

(Official Photos By Lincoln Army Air Field).

Special Refrigerator Cars

The golden hued dairy product comes to the local creamery in specially designed refrigerator cars from as far as Chicago and is stored and inspected before it is released to the army.

One car of butter contains 30 or 40 750-pound churns of the butter and the veterinarians sample a pound from each of these churns. A taste test is run and is amazingly accurate in what it may reveal. For example, the acidity may be high. This is immediately detected by the trained sense of taste of the inspector. If the sample is found defective, a whole churning may be rejected.

S/Sgt. Abel Guidry, of the veterinary staff, an old hand at the inspection of eggs and dairy products, is partly responsible for the inspection and powdering of many of the eggs used right here at Lincoln. A certain portion of the powdered product is sent overseas.

Abbeville Meridional.

Official Journal of the Town of Abbeville and Vermilion Parish School Board

Abbeville, Louisiana, Saturday, June 14, 1919

The Soldiers Life.

July 1918 about 4:30 a. m. Over The Top (renewal of attack) our objective for the day, the Paris Soissons Road. Boches reinforced during night and withstand our first assault. Reform and make several attempt reaching slope (Bôches entrenched on hill across deep ravine through which we must debauch) but our lines too greatly deflected to hold ground. Retire several time, reform and await support. Support arrivals within 1-2 hour, make 3rd assult. This time we penetrate their lines and a hand to hand melange takes place—too hot for Fritz so they "break" and "beat it," we continue advance (or chase). That is my comrades do but I have to stay behind. Reason full of shrapnell. Had gone] about 100 meters after gaining of hill when a "77" whizes over and presents me with three "nice jogged" pieces of Shrapnel.

Have a tough time getting to 1st aid Station on account of very heavy shelling of back areas, but make it "somehow." Leg is fixed 1st aid man tells me that battalion chow wagons are only 3 kilometers back so its me for chow wagon. Pat Pullin (also wounded) comes along and we make kitchens O. K. Cookie gets busy and "toot sweet" begins to dish out, steak, fried spuds and fixing hot coffee. First meal in 3 days, oh Boy!

After getting a feed, an ambulance picked us up and conveyed us to Field Hospital 3. From there to Evacuation Hospital at Senlis I was taged a "latter" case and sent to The Hospital of The Legion of Honor (French) at Ecauin near Paris I was there about 20 days and then, being able to travel, was transferred to American Base Hospital 6 at Bordeaux, which ends my experiences in the 2nd Battle of The Marne I could tell you of many others in trenches, at Cantigny, in the St. Michiel offensive and in the Argonne Forest and will gladly do so if you wish it.

An enclosing G. O. 201 G. H. I It is the first and I believe only G. O. which the General issued mentioning singly but one division. We are all very proud of this order, in the 1st Division for if any one knows the worth of an outfit why to be sure General Pershing does and altho the newspapers have forgotten the Regulars I am sure he never will.

Well uncle as it is getting late and I am to turn out early tomorrow morning will close. With best wishes for health and success, I am as ever

Your nephew
Sgt. Martin Guidry
Co. F 28th Inf. American E. F.

Above: *Abbeville Meridional*-Abbeville, LA
June 14, 1919

HORIZONTAL

1. From what country were the settlers expelled in the poem "Evangeline?"

Crossword puzzle clue from *The Fitchburg Sentinel* (Sentinel, MA)-February 7, 1928

BOOK NOOK

The *Dictionary of Louisiana French (DLF)* provides the richest inventory of French vocabulary in Louisiana and reflects precisely the speech of the period from 1930 to the present. This dictionary describes the current usage of French-speaking peoples in the five broad regions of South Louisiana: the coastal marshes, the banks of the Mississippi River, the central area, the north, and the western prairie. Data were collected during interviews from at least five persons in each of twenty-four areas in these regions. In addition to the data collected from fieldwork, the dictionary contains material compiled from existing lexical inventories, from texts published after 1930, and from archival recordings.

The new authoritative resource, the *DLF* not only contains the largest number of words and expressions but also provides the most complete information available for each entry. Entries include the word in the conventional French spelling, the pronunciation (including attested variants), the part of speech classification, the English equivalent, and the word's use in common phrases. The *DLF* features a wealth of illustrative examples derived from fieldwork and textual sources and identification of the parish where the entry was collected or the source from which it was compiled. An English-to-Louisiana French index enables readers to find out how particular notions would be expressed in *la Louisiane*.

The Dictionary of Louisiana French (DLF)
As Spoken in Cajun, Creole, and American Indian Communities

LA VERDURE DE MIRLIGUECHE-
A STORY OF THE GUIDRY DIT LABINE FAMILY IN NORTH AMERICA
By Mark Labine

About the author:

Mark Labine is an Attorney who now works as a judicial officer for Hennepin County District Court. He enjoys history and genealogy and has written several family history books. He is married and has three children.

Mark's book can be purchased at:

Amazon.com

for $25.00

ALBERT GEDDRY HONORED

Brigadier-General Albert Geddry, Retired of the Canadian Army was appointed an Honorary Colonel of the 12th Armoured Regiment of Canada (le 12e Régiment blindé du Canada). He will assume this post on 4 June 2010 in Valcartier, Québec. Attached is the Letter of Appointment to General Geddry from the Minister of National Defence.

Honorary Colonels of regiments originated with the British and later was adopted by the Canadian armoured, artillery and infantry regiments. This appointment is both an honor for General Geddry and a working assignment. He is to promote the interests of the regiment whenever he can while respecting the chain of command.

He will preside over regimental functions as parades and cermonial occasions, be a grandfather figure to the troops and be a mentor to the commanding officer of the regiment. He may visit the regiment during training, be present at the repatriation of deceased regimental members from operations and ensure that regimental points of view are made known to those outside the chain of command.

The appointment is for three years and he serves at the Queen's pleasure. More importantly, this honor is bestowed by the Regimental Senate to those former officers of the regiment that are held in the highest esteem. General Geddry graduated from Université Ste-Anne (Church Point, Nova Scotia) in 1961 and joined the Canadian Army. He initially served in tanks with the Royal Canadian Dragoons (RCD). Later he served in the 12e Régiment blindé du Canada which he commanded during the 1976 Olympics and later in Cyprus. During the Olympics the Régiment provided security for the althletes and visitors. In 1983 he commanded the Canadian Forces Base Montréal. He became Commander of the Combat Training Center and Base in Gagetown, New Brunswick during 1986. General Geddry was appointed Director General of Public Relations at the National Defence Headquarters in 1988. After a distinguished military career serving the Canadian people, General Geddry retired from the Canadian Army after this last assignment.

Many of you know Albert from our Guédry-Labine Reunions. In 2004 he was instrumental in organizing our Meteghan reunion and served as the Master of Ceremonies. His wife Simone and daughters Marie-Claude and Nathalie helped with the preparations and setup and Nathalie entertained us with several songs. In our recent Reunion in Bathurst Albert attended with Simone, Marie-Claude and Nathalie and their husbands.

ALBERT GEDDRY HONORED

Minister of National Defence

Ministre de la Défense nationale

Le 09 OCT. 2009

Brigadier-général Albert L. Geddry, C.D. (Retraité)
Case postale 104
Meteghan River (Nouvelle-Écosse) B0W 2L0

Brigadier-général,

Je suis heureux de vous annoncer que, conformément à la recommandation du Chef d'état-major de la Défense, j'ai approuvé votre nomination en tant que colonel honoraire du 12ᵉ Régiment blindé du Canada.

La coutume de nommer des officiers régimentaires honoraires, au Canada, remonte à plus d'un siècle. Même si les fonctions et les rôles ont évolué au cours des années, les officiers honoraires continuent d'assurer la liaison entre les Forces canadiennes et la collectivité environnante. D'éminents Canadiens comme vous s'acquittent très bien de cette mission.

Je suis convaincu que, au cours des trois prochaines années, vous acquerrez une meilleure compréhension de la valeur de votre unité dans la région. En retour, votre nomination vous permettra de vivre des expériences uniques et satisfaisantes et profitera aux Forces canadiennes.

Je voudrais saisir l'occasion pour vous offrir mes plus sincères félicitations et vous remercier de l'intérêt que vous portez aux Forces canadiennes et à votre collectivité.

Veuillez agréer, Brigadier-général, l'expression de mes sentiments les meilleurs.

Peter G. MacKay

Ottawa, Canada K1A 0K2

THE DROUIN COLLECTION - A VALUABLE RESEARCH SOURCE

In uncovering their family history, genealogical researchers strive to use primary sources as birth and baptismal records, marriage records, death and funeral records, successions and other records created at the time of the actual life event. During the past decade with the recent dramatic improvements of computers in storage capacity, speed and software development and the rapid growth on the internet of both free and subscription genealogical websites as FamilySearch.com and Ancestry.com, increasing numbers of these records are becoming available to researchers on their home computers.

In 1899 a Canadian attorney Joseph Drouin founded *Les Généalogies Drouin enr.* In 1913 he renamed the business *L'Institut Généalogique Drouin* (The Drouin Genealogical Institute.) With a passion for genealogy Joseph Drouin researched Québec's vital records and sold family genealogies through the Institute. Between 1899 and 1937 he produced over 1500 genealogies of Québec families and compiled over 500,000 reference sheets for French-Canadian genealogical research.

With the death of Joseph Drouin in October 1937, his son Gabriel assumed leadership of The Drouin Genealogical Institute and continued his father's work. After completing his law degree, Gabriel Drouin opened a headquarters for the Institute in Montréal. Immediately Gabriel set a goal for the Institute to microfilm Québec's Vital Records – both civil and religious.

Québec had a unique document preservation procedure that greatly facilitated the work of the Institute. Until the late 1900's Québec church registers served as both the civil and vital records of the province. For all religious denominations a second copy of all church records was made and sent annually to the appropriate courthouse. During the 1940's researchers from the Institute filmed the entire set of records in the various courthouses. Limited filming of records continued into the mid-1960's.

Realizing the vast extent of his vision, Gabriel formed a team of contributors. After the records were microfilmed, these contributors accumulated genealogical data from the microfilms onto thousands of index cards. Today researchers can access these data in several formats including the Kardex, the series of 2366 microfilms, the *Dictionnaire nationale des canadiens-français* (also called the Red Drouin or the National Dictionary of French Canadians) and the *Feminine* (also called the Women Series or the Blue Drouin).

The Drouin microfilm collection contains approximately sixty-one million records on 2366 microfilm reels. To obtain these records, researchers microfilmed the vital records of more than three thousand parishes in Québec, Ontario, Acadia, Nova Scotia, New Brunswick, Maine, New York and Michigan. The records span the timeframe from 1621 to 1967 – almost 350 years of French Canadian history. Most of the microfilming was done in the 1940's; therefore, records beyond 1947 are scattered and few in number. Baptisms, marriages and burials from both Catholic and Protestant churches were researched and microfilmed as well as notarial records and other select documents of genealogical value. As with all original records of that time period, these records are handwritten and sometimes difficult to read.

Without any public funding Joseph and Gabriel Drouin invested their time, money and effort into creating an important genealogical resource for French Canadians. It is the largest and most valuable French-Canadian family history resource available – spanning almost 350 years and 37 million names. Understandably, the Drouin's never placed their vast collections in public librairies, archives or locations available without charge to researchers. They limited access to their collections to paying customers as this was the livelihood of the family.

With the death of Gabriel Drouin in 1980 the Drouin Genealogical Institute almost closed its doors. The heirs of Gabriel Drouin had to sell a part of their assets to Americans. Then genealogist Jean-Pierre Pepin became involved and created the Drouin Institute in a successful attempt to keep most of the Drouin collection in Québec.

Because of the genealogical significance of the Drouin Collection, Ancestry.ca negotiated with the Drouin Institute and secured the rights to host the Drouin Collection online. In 2007 it placed over 12 million of the original images online and in a partnership with the University of Montréal indexed the Collection making searching in French and English by name, date, place, church (institution) and religion an easy task. All of the Collection is now online through Ancestry.ca and the World Subscription of Ancestry.com.

On Ancestry the Drouin Collection is divided into six sub-collections. Additional information about the contents of each sub-collection can be found at the link below the sub-collection name. The sub-collection are:

- Québec Vital and Church Records (Drouin Collection), 1621-1967
  http://search.ancestry.com/search/db.aspx?dbid=1091

- Ontario French Catholic Church Records (Drouin Collection), 1747-1967
  http://search.ancestry.com/search/db.aspx?dbid=1109

- Acadia French Catholic Church Records (Drouin Collection), 1670-1946
  http://search.ancestry.com/search/db.aspx?dbid=1110

- Québec Notarial Records (Drouin Collection), 1647-1942
  http://search.ancestry.com/search/db.aspx?dbid=1112

- Early U.S. French Catholic Church Records (Drouin Collection), 1695-1954
  http://search.ancestry.com/search/db.aspx?dbid=1111

- Miscellaneous French Records (Drouin Collection), 1651-1941
  http://search.ancestry.com/search/db.aspx?dbid=1092

Although most of the records in the collection are specific to French-Canadians that initially settled the Québec and Montréal areas during the 1600's and early 1700's, there are a large number of records about Acadians. These records originate from three sources.

The "Acadia French Catholic Church Records (Drouin Collection), 1670-1946" sub-collection has birth, marriage and burial records of Acadians as well as confirmations, dispensations, censuses, statements of readmission to the church and various other records.

During the Acadian deportations from 1755-1763 approximately 2000 Acadians escaped deportation by fleeing to Québec. Many died during their travel to Québec; others died after reaching Québec. Their life in Québec was difficult initially; however, many of their descendants continued to live in the Québec region after the Treaty of Paris in 1763. Also, after 1763, when the Treaty of Paris allowed the Acadians along the Eastern seaboard of today's United States to resettle in other areas, groups of Acadians from Massachusetts, Pennyslvania, Connecticut and other colonies immigrated to Québec. Many of the Acadians reaching Québec have remained in the province while others ventured westward into Ontario.

Later in the 1820's an Acadian living in the St. Mary's Bay region of Nova Scotia immigrated to the Restigouche region of northern New Brunswick and southeastern Québec. The Gaspé region of Québec just across the New Brunswick border had a Catholic church parish – St-Joseph-de-Carleton Catholic Church - in the early 1800's. Baptisms, marriages and deaths of this family for the next 100 years were recorded in the registers of St. Joseph's and other Catholic churches of the Gaspé region of Québec. The records of this family are even more important when one considers that in 1893 a fire destroyed almost all the extant religious records for the entire St. Mary's Bay region in Nova Scotia. The only records remaining are a set of censuses taken by Father Jean-Mandé Sigogne of the St. Mary's Bay residents in 1818-1829 and in 1840-1844.

Is the Drouin Collection of value to Guédry, Labine and Petitpas researchers? Absolutely. One of the families that immigrated to Québec from Massachusetts in 1766 was Jean-Baptiste Augustin Guédry - often called Labrador and Jean Guidry in the Massachusetts records. Jean-Baptiste Augustin Guédry was the third child of Pierre Guédry dit Labine and Marguerite Brasseau and was the grandson of Claude Guédry and Marguerite Petitpas. During the early 1800's the Guédry name evolved into Guildry and in the latter part of the 1800's several descendants of Jean-Baptiste Augustin Guédry changed their name from Guildry to Labine. Today the Labine and Guildry families continue to reside in Québec and Ontario and are very numerous. Entries for this family are numerous in the Drouin Collection.

The Acadian that left the St. Mary's Bay region of Nova Scotia in the 1820's and resettled in the Restigouche region was Hilaire Guidry, son of Romain Guidry and Marie Comeau. The Drouin Collection contains a large number of birth, marriage and burial records for the family of Hilaire Guidry and Cécile Bourg. For today's Guidry, Geddry and Jeddry families of St. Mary's Bay these are the only religious records remaining of the family prior to 1893. Granted it is only one of many branches of Guidry's, Geddry's and Jeddry's from St. Mary's Bay, but it still remains a valuable resource for descendants of this couple.

Below are the number of records in each of the Drouin sub-collections for the Guédry, Labine and Petitpas families.

Drouin Sub-Collection	Labine	LaBean	Guildry	Guédry Guidry Gaidry Gidry	Geddry Jeddry Gedry Jedry	Petitpas Pettipas Petipas Petit Pas
Québec Vital & Church	1373	3	214	37	0	666
Ontario Church	454	0	2	0	0	9
Acadia Church	6	0	0	8	0	503
Québec Notarial	0	0	0	0	0	0
Early U.S. French Church	7	1	0	11	0	0
Misc. French	0	0	0	0	0	0

If you have ancestors from the Québec and Ontario provinces, consider using the Drouin Collection as part of your genealogical research. With over 37 million records online the Drouin Collection is the largest dababase of French Canadian genealogical records available to the public.

Below are three examples of records from the Drouin Collection - the 12 October 1832 baptismal record of Marie Justine Guildry dit Labine, the 20 November 1829 marriage record of Hilaire Guidry and Cecile Bourg and the 13 September 1640 burial record of Marguerite Petitpas. When viewing "Generations" online, increase the magnification level (percentage) at the top of the page to enlarge the original records for easier reading.

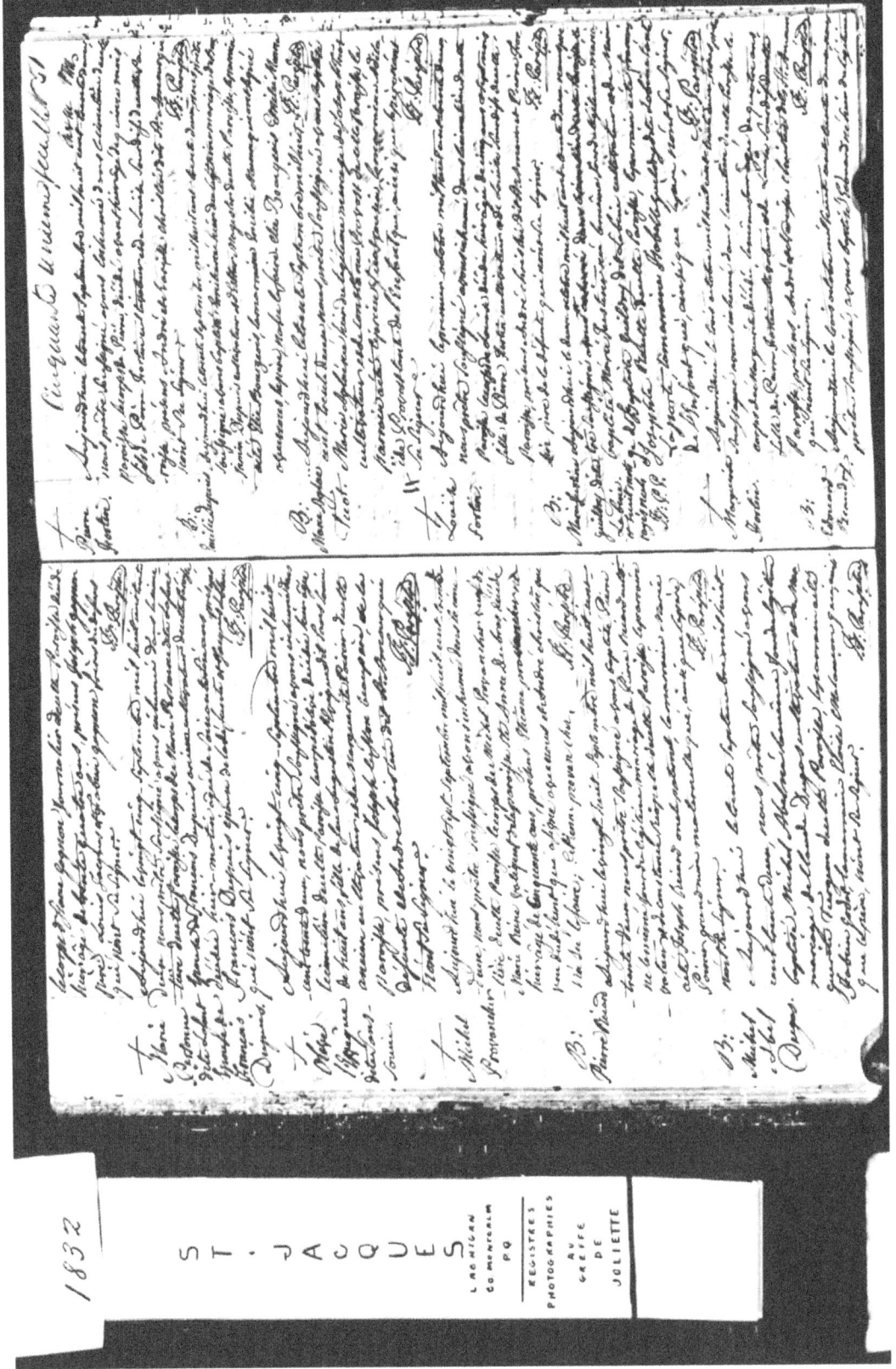

Baptismal record for Marie Justine Guildry dit Labine – right side of page, 5th entry from top

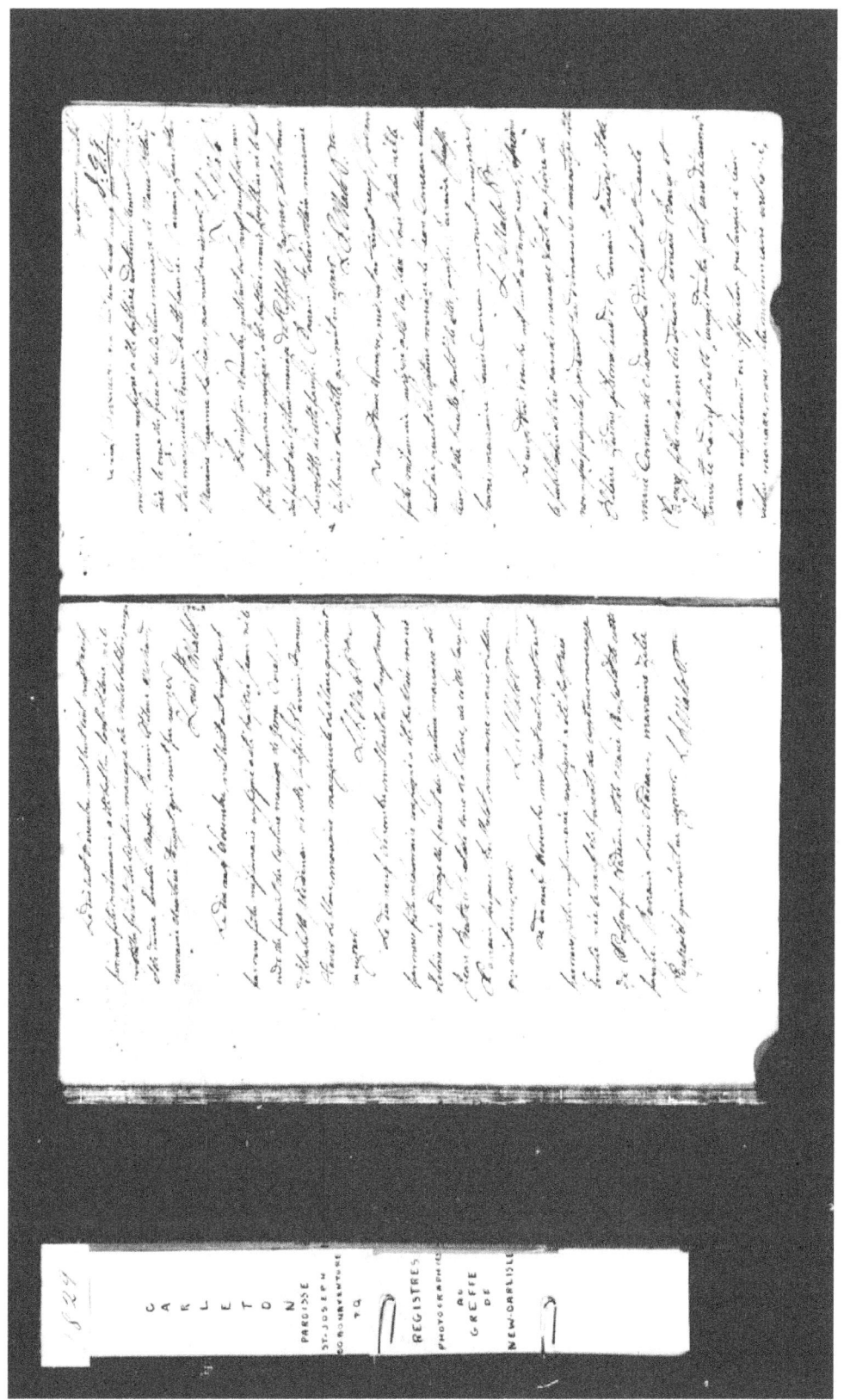

Marriage record of Hilaire Guildry & Cecile Bourg – last entry on right side of page

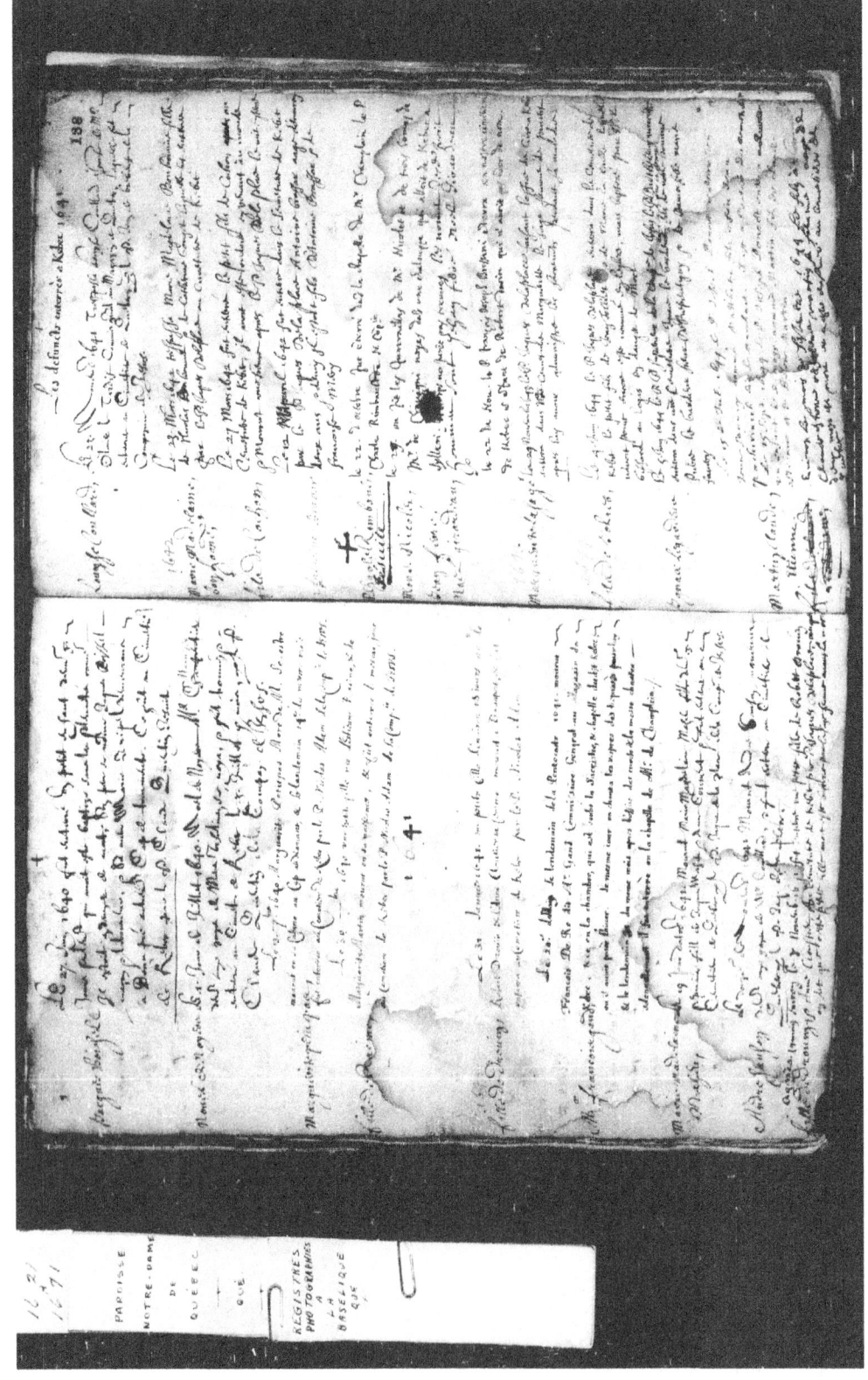

Burial record for Marguerite Petitpas – Third entry on left side of page

Les Guédry d'Asteur

What's in a name?

Guédry is the family to which you belong if your name is spelled Guédry, Guedry, Guidry, Gaidry, Guildry, Geddry, Jeddry, Labine, LaBine, LaBean or any of several dozen variations. The original name of our family is believed to have been Guédry. We are all descendants of Claude Guédry & Marguerite Petitpas.

Here are some common and uncommon variant spellings of the name.

Guédry	Guiddry	Geddrie	Jeddrie	Labeen
Guedry	Guiddery	Geddry	Jeddry	Labene
Guedrie	Guiedri	Gedree	Jederie	Labine
Guedris	Guiedry	Gedrie	Jedrey	LaBine
Guidry	Guildry	Gedry	Jedrie	LaBean
Gudiry	Guildrie	Gettry	Jedry	LaBeau
Guidery	Guitry	Gidrie		Labeau
Guidrey	Gaidry	Gidry	Lledre	
Guidrie	Gaidrie		Yedri	

Our **Petitpas** cousins likewise have several variations of their name including Petitpas, Pettipas, Petipas, Petitpa, Petit Pas and Pitts.

DUES REMINDER

Attached at the back of this issue is a membership application for renewing your membership in Les Guédry d'Asteur. Our dues are very reasonable at $6.00 for individuals and $10 for a family in 2009.

Please take a moment, complete the Membership Application, enclose a check and send it to the address on the application. It will help all of us do so much for the family. And, if you would like to join at one of the Benefactor Levels, it would allow us do even more.

Les Guédry d'Asteur is now on Facebook. Join us there and connect with other family members from all over the US and CAN. Feel free to post queries, photos, links, events or other items of interest to the family. Just search for 'Les Guédry d'Asteur' on Facebook to find our page.

Les Guédry d'Asteur

To share your ideas for the newsletter, contact:

Marty Guidry
6139 North Shore Drive
Baton Rouge, LA 70817
225-755-1915
guidryrm@cox.net

'GENERATIONS' newsletter is now in its eighth year. We hope to provide our readers with an interesting, informative and entertaining newsletter. Your input is always welcome and we look forward to another year of sharing family history and news with you.

The Guédry-Labine Family Newsletter 'GENERATIONS' serves as a focal point for family members to share and learn about us.

Allie Guidry
txguidry2000@yahoo.com

Marty Guidry
guidryrm@cox.net

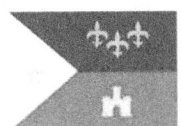

Les Guédry d'Asteur Officers and Committees

OFFICERS:
President - Martin Guidry (LA)
Vice-President - Elaine Clement (LA)
Secretary - Billy Harrell Guidry (LA)
Treasurer - Daniel "Chuck" Guidry (LA)

COMMITTEES:
Website - Becky Boggess (IA) - Chairperson
    Annie Grignon-Labine (QU) - Translator
    Elaine Clement (LA) - Translator
    Martin Guidry (LA)

Genealogy - Daryl LaBine (FL/ON) - Chairperson
    Bernard Geddry (AZ)
    Mark Labine (MN)
    Daniel "Chuck" Guidry (LA)
    Martin Guidry (LA)

Finance - Cheryl Guidry Tyiska (MD) - Chairperson
    Paul Labine (IL)
    Marshall Woolner (OR)
    Gloria Parrent (TX)
    Chuck Guidry (LA)

Membership - Charlene Guidry Lacombe (LA) - Chairperson
    Gayle Guidry (LA) - Special Projects
    Warren Guidry (TX)

Sales - Cindy Guidry Herdt (WA) - Chairperson
    Wayne Simoneaux (LA)
    Billy Harrell Guidry (LA)

Publicity - Elaine Clement (LA) - Chairperson
    Margaret Jeddry (MA)
    Warren Guidry (TX)

Newsletter - Allie Guidry Hardee (VA) - Editor
    Martin Guidry (LA)

CAFA Board Member - Jeanette Guidry Leger (LA)

SUMMER 2010

Volume 8, Issue 2

Les Guédry d'Asteur

GENERATIONS

IN THIS ISSUE

A LETTER FROM PRIVATE CYRILLE TRASIMON GUIDRY PÈRE DURING THE CIVIL WAR By Marty Guidry — 2

GENEALOGY- Ophelia Guidry Perry turns 102! — 8

GUIDRY'S HAVE LEADING ROLES IN DEEPWATER HORIZON OIL SPILL RESPONSE — 10

BOOK NOOK — 12

BON APPETIT: Recipes from the Guédry/Labine Family Cookbook — 13

ACADIAN MEMORIAL FESTIVAL, March 20, 2010-St. Martinville, LA and G.M.BRAUD Article- La Lettre — 14

MALVINA MENARD LABINE- Reeve of Rayside — 19

What a strange year 2010 has been thus far. Record colds this winter and record heat spells in the summer. And now a major oil spill in the Gulf of Mexico during prime hurricane season. For a few moments grab a nice beverage and enjoy the Summer 2010 issue of "Generations". It's another superb issue full of interesting stories about our Guédry-Labine and Petitpas families.

Interested in the War of Northern Aggression (sometimes called the Civil War in the U.S.) – then you'll enjoy the moving letter a father at the battlefront writes to his lonesome young son in "A Letter from Private Cyrille Trasimon Guidry during the Civil War". And speaking of youth, Ophelia Guidry Perry of Vermilion Parish, LA celebrated 102 years young this year. Her life story is quite interesting as she has seen so much occur in the last century.

The Deepwater Horizon oil spill in the Gulf of Mexico not only is harming fragile marshes where over 40% of the seafood in the U. S. spawns, but also is wreaking havoc on the culture and heritage of Acadians and other peoples living near and relying on the Gulf and marshes for their livelihood. Two persons leading the response effort in minimizing impact to the marshes and wildlife and to the response workers and residents are Roland Guidry, the Louisiana Oil Spill Coordinator, and Dr. Jimmy Guidry, the Louisiana State Health Officer.

During the 2010 Acadian Memorial Festival in St. Martinville, LA, the Guidry and Breaux families were honored as pioneer Louisiana Acadian families. The highlight of the Festival was the reenactment on Bayou Teche of the 1765 arrival of the Acadians to St. Martinville with the Guidry and Breaux families arriving by canoe and being greeted under the historic Evangeline Oak by a Spanish official. Enjoy the photographs of the events and the summaries of the Festival in English and French. Mr. Gérard-Marc Braud of Nantes, France attended the event and wrote a nice article in French of the Festival and of his scenic swamp cruise with Ron 'Black' Guidry on Bayou Black near Houma, LA.

In the political arena you'll be amazed at the fascinating story of Malvina Ménard Labine. Born into a poor family, she began working at thirteen. Married at nineteen, she had had twenty children when suddenly she became a widow at age 47. Struggling, but with a will of iron and a compassionate heart, she raised her family and then a second family of foster children while providing needed charity to many local families. Suddenly at age 65 she opted to run for reeve of her township and defeated the incumbent against great odds. Read how she did it in this interesting article.

Sit back, relax and get away from the doldrums of summer as you read the Summer 2010 issue of "Generations".

A LETTER FROM
PRIVATE CYRILLE TRASIMON GUIDRY PÈRE DURING THE CIVIL WAR *By Marty Guidry*

Born on 18 July 1828 in St. Martin Parish, LA, Cyrille Trasimon Guidry père married Azaliea Alzeninth Nunez on 23 May 1854 in Abbeville, Vermilion Parish, LA. He was the son Olivier Guidry fils and Isabelle Belzire Thibodeaux while Alzeninth was the daughter of Sebastien Nunez and Clementine Lapointe. Cyrille and Alzeninth raised a family of twelve children, eleven sons and one daughter, in Vermilion Parish, LA – Cyrille Trasimon fils (b. 1855), Olivier Hippolyte (b. 1857), Arthur (b. 1859), Numa Gilbert (b. 1861), Sebastien (b. 1864), the twins Adolphe and Rodolphe Anselme (b. 1868), Caliste (b. 1871), Socrates Odin (b. 1874), Luc (b. 1877), Xavier Nunez (b. 1880) and Modeste (b. 1881). To support his large family, Cyrille farmed near Abbeville. Cyrille Trasimon Guidry père died 5 December 1900 at his home near Abbeville, LA in Vermilion Parish. His wife Alzeninth Nunez Guidry died 3 May 1927 in Vermilion Parish, LA.

With the outbreak of the Civil War Cyrille Trasimon Guidry père enlisted in the Confederate Army in 1862 at Camp Pratt near New Iberia, LA in Iberia Parish. He was assigned the rank of private. The initial unit(s) in which he served are not known; however, by October 1864 he was a private in Company C of the 7th Louisiana Cavalry. He served in this unit until the surrender of the 7th Louisiana Cavalry at Chicot, LA in May, 1865. Captain William A. Whitaker commanded Company C while Colonel Louis Bush commanded the 7th Louisiana Cavalry Regiment until January 1865 when he was transferred. Colonel Louis A. Bringier replaced him and served until the surrender of the 7th Louisiana Cavalry.

The complete service record of Cyrille Trasimon Guidry père is not known; however, we do have sketchy information on his service. On 16 April 1915 his widow Alzeninth Nunez Guidry filed a Civil War Pension Application (Louisiana Civil War Pension Application No. 14260; Louisiana State Archives, Baton Rouge, Louisiana) and was granted a quarterly pension of $19.90 on 10 June 1915. On 6 September 1930 after the death of Alzeninth Guidry her family requested that the Board of Pension Commissioners return a letter written by Cyrille Trasimon Guidry during the Civil War and that was attached to the original application. The Board of Pension Commissioners responded on 30 September 1930 and stated that they were returning these four letters written by Cyrille Trasimon Guidry:

   dated Camp Pratt, LA, September 6, 1862
   dated Camp Bisland, January 9, 1863
   dated Camp Bisland, March 19, 1863
   dated Camp Bisland, April 1, 1863

A LETTER FROM PRIVATE CYRILLE TRASIMON GUIDRY PÈRE DURING THE CIVIL WAR

Camp Pratt was just north of New Iberia, LA near present-day Highway 82 in Iberia Parish, LA. Camp Pratt was a Confederate Enlistment Camp where young men enlisted and received their initial instructions on becoming a soldier. Camp Bisland was between Patterson, LA and Centerville, LA at the present-day Calumet Spillway along Bayou Teche in St. Mary Parish, LA. The Battle of Bisland was fought 12-13 April 1863. Almost certainly Cyrille Trasimon Guidry père fought in this engagement.

During late 1864 and early 1865 Companies A and C of the 7th Louisiana Cavalry made raids into the Bayou Lafourche region to acquire horses and supplies as well as to harass the enemy. By May 1865 the 7th Louisiana Cavalry had encamped near Alexandria, LA in Rapides Parish. They surrendered near here at Chicot, LA later that month.

The attached letter written by Cyrille Trasimon Guidry to his eldest son during the Civil War has survived over 140 years in our family. Written in Cajun French, no date or location is discernible. It appears that Alzeninth Guidry had written her husband Cyrille earlier that their eldest son Cyrille fils, who was about eight years old, was missing his father and needed a word of encouragement. In this brief letter the father tells his son that he is the "man of the house" now and that he needs to ensure the work is done and to care for the family. A transcription and translation of the letter follows.

The two photographs are of the father Cyrille Trasimon Guidry père and the son Cyrille Trasimon Guidry fils taking at different times in their lives. The original photographs in the author's possession are period tin-types. The graves of both father and son are located together in Old St. Mary Magdalen Catholic Cemetery behind the church in Abbeville, LA.

Cyrille Trasimon Guidry, fils

Cyrille Trasimon Guidry, père

A LETTER FROM PRIVATE CYRILLE TRASIMON GUIDRY PÈRE DURING THE CIVIL WAR

Transcription: **Cover**

Monsieur
Cyrille Trasimon Guidry
fils
Paroisse Vermillion
Abbeville
La

Letter

Mon cher fils ainé

Tu ma marquer sur la letter de ta mère que
me
vous ennuier beaucoup de moi ça   fait plaisir de
voir le naturel que mon grand fils a pour sont cher
papa et je m'ennuier beaucoup de toi aussi mon
cher fils. apprésent mon fils je demande de
fais travailler ces nègres là dans le lot et de
aller voir tout les jours. de m'envoyes les nouvelle
de ma récolte de m'envoyes comment et le
commencement de la récolte ci il y'a une jolie
aparance cette année et fair intention au
magasin de mais de ne pas le gaspiyer de fair
donner á mager de l'animeaux le vendre plain
pas plus qu'il ne faut rien de plus a te dire
pour le momes et tache de m'envoyer la réponce
de ma letter. Adieu adieu mon cher fils.
tu embrasses à ta manien pour moi et tes
petits frères aussi   ton cher papa   **C T Guidry**

Translation: **Cover**

Mr.
Cyrille Trasimon Guidry
fils
Vermillion Parish
Abbeville
La

Letter

My dear oldest son

You mentioned to me in your mother's letter that
me
you are very lonesome for me that pleases to
see the feelings that my big son has for his dear
father and I miss you very much also my
dear son. now my son I desire to
make those negroes work there in the field and to
go see everyday. to send me the news
of my crop to send me how and the
beginning of the harvest if it looks
good this year and take care of the
corncrib do not waste it to
feed it to the animals sell no
more than necessary nothing more to tell you
now and try to send me the answer
to my letter. Good-bye good-bye my dear son
kiss your mother for me and your
little brothers also your dear father   **C T Guidry**

A LETTER FROM PRIVATE CYRILLE TRASIMON GUIDRY PÈRE DURING THE CIVIL WAR

Cover page - Letter from Cyrille Trasimon Guidry père

A LETTER FROM PRIVATE CYRILLE TRASIMON GUIDRY PÈRE DURING THE CIVIL WAR

Letter from Cyrille Trasimon Guidry, père

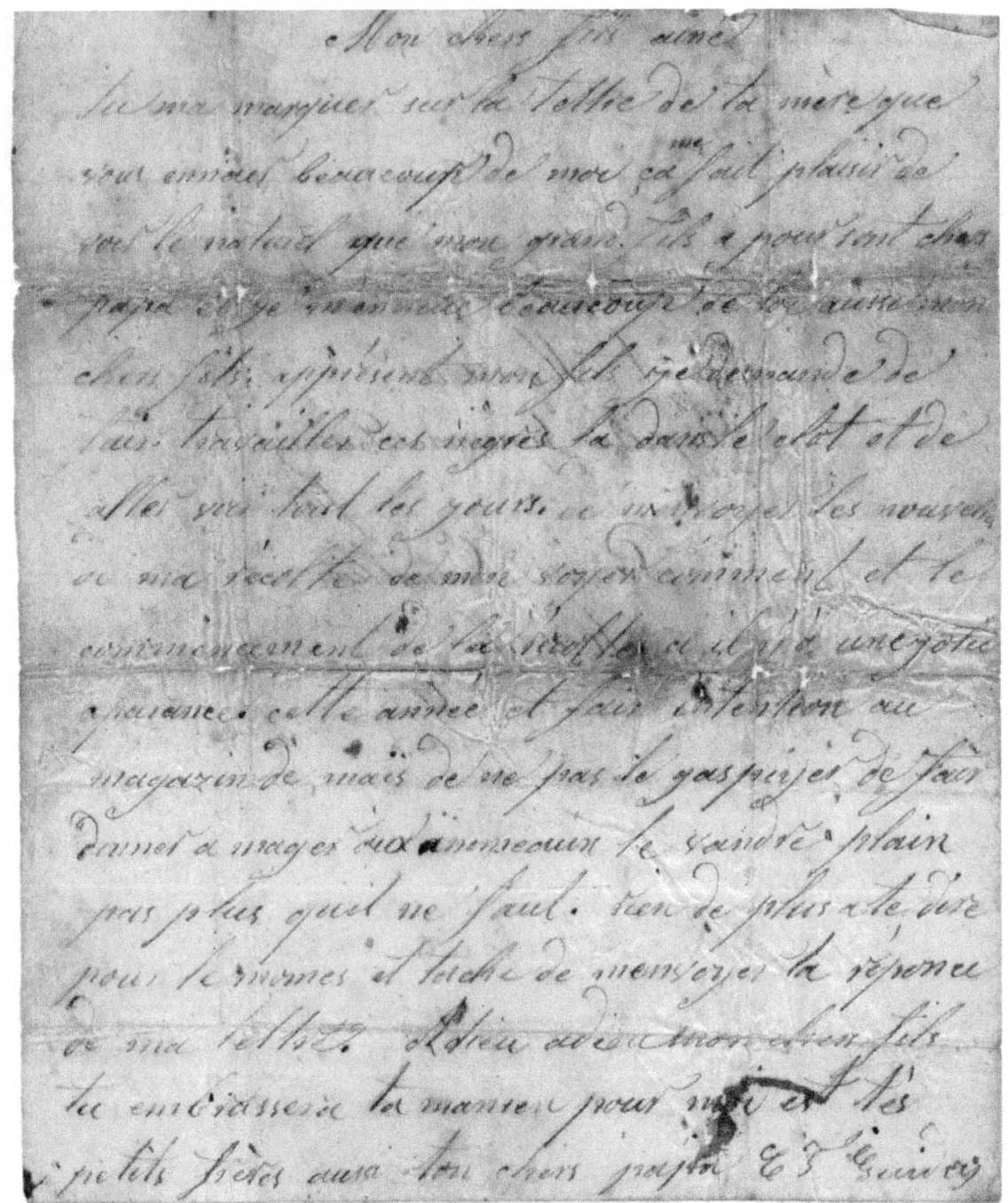

A LETTER FROM PRIVATE CYRILLE TRASIMON GUIDRY PÈRE DURING THE CIVIL WAR

Genealogy of Cyrille Trasimon Guidry fils

Cyrille Trasimon Guidry fils m. Uranie Mayard
|
Cyrille Trasimon Guidry père m. Azaliea Alzeninth Nunez
|
Olivier Guidry fils m. Elizabeth Belzire Thibodeaux
|
Olivier Guidry père m. Victoire Semere
|
Pierre Guédry m2. Claire Babin
|
Augustin Guédry m. Jeanne Hébert
|
Claude Guédry m. Marguerite Petitpas

Old St. Mary Magdalen Catholic Cemetery behind the church in Abbeville, LA

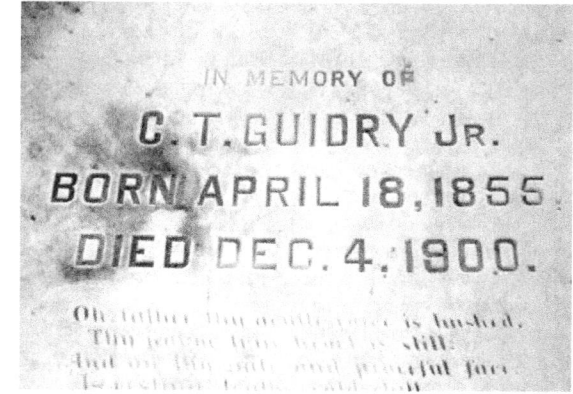

Ophelia Guidry Perry Celebrates Her 102nd Birthday!

The following article appeard in:
BONNES NOUVELLES, ABBEVILLE, LA, MAY 2010
By Cindy Luquette

Bonnes Nouvelles
Good news about people, places and things in Vermilion Parish

Over A Century of Living And Still Going Strong

By Cindy Luquette

Vermilion Parish mother, Ophelia Guidry Perry, was six years old when Americans celebrated the first nationally recognized Mother's Day on the second Sunday in May in the year 1914. The Cow Island native was born on April 30, 1908 and celebrated her 102 birthday on Friday, April 30, 2010.

Imagine living for over a century and imagine living during a time when people went from traveling by horse and buggy, to automobiles to airplanes and then jet planes, from telegraph, to telephone, to cell phones. Imagine going from listening to a radio, to watching television, from letters carried by pony express to email on the internet. Ophelia lived through all of these technological changes.

Her early years were spent in Cow Island. The details are sketchy but Ophelia and her brother, Walter, were adopted by Odilon and Laura Harrington Guidry when she was about four years old and her brother was two. Their birth mother died of yellow fever. Shortly after being adopted, around age five, Ophelia travelled to Abbeville to receive her education. She spent several years living in the convent with the Carmelite order of nuns and attended Mount Carmel school. She attended the school and lived with the nuns until she reached the sixth grade. (Tuition for attending the school in 1914 was $1.00 per month.) Upon reaching the sixth grade, she received word she was needed back in Cow Island to work in her parent's store. Her formal education ended and she left Abbeville to return home.

Ophelia wedded in 1932 at

Ophelia Guidry Perry turned 102 years on Friday, April 30, 2010.

Ophelia Guidry Perry Celebrates Her 102nd Birthday!

This is the house where she grew up in Cow Island. Photo at left is of Ophelia and her brother, Walter Guidry (dec).

age 24, Joseph E. Perry. The couple resided in Cow Island where Mr. Perry farmed property for Dr. P. J. Miller. The couple then had six children, four girls and two boys, which included a set of twins.

She was busy being a wife and mother until the flood of 1940 devastated Vermilion Parish and brought about a life changing experience for her and her family. An unnamed hurricane made landfall at Cameron, Louisiana on August 5, 1940. It was reported it brought with it a five foot tidal surge. The weather system stalled over south Louisiana for four days and dumped 21 inches of rain in a 24 hour period. The city of Abbeville reported receiving over 31 inches of rain. The unnamed weather system devastated Acadiana and Vermilion Parish. Crops, livestock as well as wildlife were all destroyed by the flood waters.

Life took and unexpected turn for Ophelia following the flood of 1940. Mr. Perry left her and the children shortly after the flood waters subsided. Many things are taken for granted or considered common place in today's modern world like automobiles, automatic washers/dryers and single parents, single mothers. However, in the 1940's, a single mother was not a common occurrence, but Ophelia took this unexpected turn in stride and did what she could to provide for herself and her six children. In 1942 she decided a move was in order so she and her children, ranging from ages two to 12, traveled the ten miles or so to the city of Abbeville.

Ophelia never owned an automobile in all of her 102 years of living. This idea is practically unheard of today, but she literally took it in stride and walked everywhere she went, be it work or church. "Mama worked several different jobs and we, her children, also worked little jobs. Some of the girls, myself included, had babysitting jobs to help with expenses," recalled her daughter, Hazel Roy. In 1957 Ophelia secured a job cooking for the doctors at the Palms Hospital. She retained that job until the hospital closed in 1962.

"We lived in various parts of the city, but wherever we lived, Mama walked with us to St. Mary Magdalene Catholic Church on Sundays. Mama prayed her rosary in French and still does each and every day," Hazel said.

She did not travel much and to modern-day standards she

Ophelia in her 40's

lived a sheltered or secluded life, but she did participate in the lives of her children attending PTA meetings and visiting their classrooms. (Imagine she participated in the lives of six children without the benefit of a vehicle.)

Ophelia's brother built two houses in 1949, the one in which she now resides and the other next door to it for their mother. She began caring for her mother in 1960 and cared for her until she passed away in 1968. Her brother moved into the house next door after his mother died. Ophelia was in her 80's at that time and she began cooking and caring for her brother just as she had done for her mother. "Mama cooked his meals and took her walker and would make her way across the yard to bring him his food. She did this until he passed away about seven years ago," recalled Hazel.

The question arises, "to what does she attribute her longevity?" She can answer that question with two simple words, "work and walk". Yes, she attributes living to age 102 to working and walking. There must be something to it as she has no health issues and is not on any medication. She has what some folks might call a vice. She enjoys eating two warm donuts with a glass of milk every morning. "Mama started doing that several years ago. She also loves shrimp gumbo and fried fish which she eats every Friday. If she had her way she would eat it everyday," Hazel said.

Ophelia and family celebrated her 100th birthday with a big party. For her 102nd birthday, she is keeping it simple, with no big celebration. There are four families with five generations including Ophelia, two daughters have great-grandchildren and one daughter has two great-grandchildren from the line of two of her children.

However, even with her two donuts a day, Ophelia is slight in stature and has flawless skin, free of wrinkles. She has a face that glows and clear blue eyes that have a hint of mischief. She puts her makeup on every morning and refreshes her lipstick throughout the day.

Ophelia Guidry Perry, many would consider this single mom of six to have lived a tough life, one void of riches and many would say few luxuries. However, spend just a few minutes with her and it will become crystal clear, she considers herself to be one of the richest people on earth, because of her treasure of six children, 28 grandchildren, 33 great grandchildren, 4 great great grandchildren, and the greatest treasure money cannot buy and time cannot steal - LOVE!!!!

Happy 102nd Birthday and Happy Mother's Day Ophelia! And all moms !

(Ophelia Guidry Perry, Cont'd.) / GUIDRY'S LEAD IN OIL SPILL RESPONSE

Adoptive Genealogy of Ophelia Guidry (Cow Island & Abbeville, Louisiana)

Ophelia Guidry m. Joseph E. Perry

(At birth Ophelia's mother was Rosa Backer; her father was not named.)

Ophelia adopted about age four by:

|
Odilon Guidry m. Marie Laura Harrington
|
Sebastien Guidry m. Nathilia Simon
|
Cyrille Trasimond Guidry père m. Azelima Alzineth Nunez
|
Olivier Guidry fils m. Isabelle Belzire Thibodeau
|
Olivier Guidry père m. Victoire Semere
|
Pierre Guédry m2. Claire Babin
|
Augustin Guédry m. Jeanne Hébert
|
Claude Guédry m. Marguerite Petitpas

GUIDRY'S HAVE LEADING ROLES IN DEEPWATER HORIZON OIL SPILL RESPONSE

On 20 April 2010 the Transocean oil rig Deepwater Horizon being operated by BP Oil exploded and caught fire in the Gulf of Mexico approximately 42 miles southeast of Venice, Louisiana. Of the 126 people on board the rig at the time of the explosion, seventeen were severely injured and eleven were killed. After a second explosion on 22 April the rig sank to the ocean floor resulting in a major oil leak into the Gulf of Mexico. Officials estimate that oil is flowing into the Gulf at a rate between 1.5 million and 2.5 million gallons per day.

Two Louisiana officials leading the response actions to the spill are Roland J. Guidry, Louisiana Oil Spill Coordinator, and Dr. Jimmy Guidry, Louisiana Medical Director and State Health Officer.

Roland Guidry directs the Louisiana Oil Spill Coordinator's Office – the mission of which is to provide innovative leadership and coordination in oil spill prevention, planning, response and natural resource damage assessment for the State of Louisiana. Roland is working directly with Coast Guard Admiral Thad Allen in overseeing and directing the response actions and natural resource assessments associated with the Deepwater Horizon oil spill.

Dr. Jimmy Guidry as the State Health Officer for Louisiana is responsible for investigating health issues that may impact the public and workers and developing strategies to combat diseases and other health issues in Louisiana. Dr. Guidry and his staff are investigating complaints of illnesses from oil cleanup workers, determining if public and worker health are being negatively impacted by the oil spill and its response activities and developing strategies to minimize any negative impacts.

GUIDRY'S LEAD IN OIL SPILL RESPONSE

Roland Guidry currently serves as Oil Spill Coordinator for the state of Louisiana. He has held this position since 1992. Prior to his appointment as Coordinator, he served as an elected member of the Greater Lafourche Port Commission for fifteen years, eight years as the Vice President. For over thirty years, he made his livelihood from Louisiana's abundant natural resources. First, he trapped and fished for a living. Then, as owner of a marine towing business, he worked in various types of oil related activities, ranging from drilling and exploration to transportation of crude oil and other hydrocarbons. As Oil Spill Coordinator, Mr. Guidry received a Public Service commendation from the United States Coast Guard for his participation in the Coast Guard negotiated rulemaking process and Certificate of Merit for his contributions during the Westchester Oil Spill in November 2000. Mr. Guidry has been designated by the Governor of Louisiana as the lead state trustee for assessing natural resources damages under the Oil Pollution Act of 1990. Additionally, Mr. Guidry serves as the primary state representative on the Region VI Regional Response Team for oil spill related matters, and has served on three different Area Committees designated under the Oil Pollution Act of 1990. He has attended a Training Workshop on Oiled Bird Rehabilitation, successfully completed Oil Spill Response Training with the United States Coast Guard Gulf Strike Team, and has completed a Hazardous Materials/Waste Training program certified by Louisiana State University. He has also completed an On-scene Coordinator Crisis Management Course by the United States Coast Guard Reserve Training Center in Yorktown, Virginia, an Inland Oil Spill Control Course at Texas A&M University, and the Qualified Individual Training Program OPA 90 from Massachusetts Maritime Academy at Buzzards Bay, MA. Mr. Guidry serves on several state wide committees including the BTNEP and Clean Gulf Conference Committee. Mr. Guidry has been a staunch advocate for preserving our coastal wetlands and is actively involved in the restoration and conservation of Louisiana's barrier islands as a comprehensive oil spill prevention measure. Roland Guidry, age 70, married to LouAnna Crosby for over 48 years. They have four children and eight grandchildren. They reside in Cut Off, LA and Roland works in Baton Rouge. Roland graduated from Larose Cut Off High School in 1954 and also served in the United States National Guard for eight years. He started researching the Guidry family history in the late sixties. Roland's hobbies are hunting, fishing, cooking, reading, carpentry and story telling.

Left: Roland Guidry, Oil Spill Coordinator for the State of Louisiana

Dr. Jimmy Guidry, State Health Officer of Louisiana

Jimmy Guidry, M.D., is currently the State Health Officer of Louisiana, and also serves as the Medical Director for the Department of Health & Hospitals (DHH). Prior to this, Dr. Guidry served as the Assistant Secretary for the Office of Public Health from October, 1996 through January, 2000, and as Medical Director of the Acadian Region from April 1990 through April, 1991. In addition, Dr. Guidry served as Director of Adolescent Services at LSU School of Medicine, Pediatric Department, Earl K. Long Hospital from January 1985 to March, 1990. He also worked in Pediatric Private Practice from July, 1981 through December, 1984.

Dr. Guidry presently chairs various task forces, including the DHH Obesity Task Force, the Child Death Review Panel, and the Governor's Task Force on Tuberculosis.

He has received numerous awards and honors. In 1997, Guidry was named the LPHA Award Recipient. He is well respected among his peers, and is sought-after for many speaking engagements. He also represents the state of Louisiana at many medical and environmental engagements across the country.

He received his Bachelors of Science from the University of Southwestern in 1974, earned his doctorate from the Louisiana State University School of Medicine in 1978, and completed his residency at Earl K. Long Hospital in 1981. He has been Board Certified since 1984 and is a Fellow of the American Academy of Pediatrics.

Dr. Guidry has a strong interest in the medical care of the citizens of Louisiana and works diligently towards the delivery of services in our state.

BOOK NOOK

When Clem Labine and his family abandoned Manhattan for an old brownstone in Brooklyn, Labine decided to launch a newsletter about the restoration and maintenance of antique houses. From these humble beginnings, *The Old-House Journal* grew until it had many thousands of subscribers in all fifty states.

Since its first publication in 1980, *The Old-House Journal Compendium* has been the go-to guide for anyone looking to buy, restore, or maintain an old house. This new edition combines the solid, detailed advice that made *The Old House Journal* newsletter famous, now in a modern, easy-to-use format. Fully redesigned with more than 800 black-and-white illustrations, this famous how-to reference provides sound and encouraging instructions for all at-home renovators.

Accessibly organized into chapters that correspond to the parts of a house, *The Old-House Journal Compendium* covers roofs, windows, wiring, plumbing, plastering, staircases, floors, painting, chimneys, fireplaces, stoves, moldings, woodwork, shutters, kitchens, bathrooms, as well as period design and decoration, and even landscaping--truly everything the new owner of an old home could need.

The Old-House Journal Compendium
Edited by Clem Labine & Carolyn Flaherty

American Roots
By Mark Labine

This book is about the ancestors of the children of Mark and Judy Labine. It is story of their American roots in North America and Europe.

Mark Labine is an attorney who now works as a judicial officer for Hennepin County District Court. He enjoys history and genealogy and has written several family history books.

Many of you may be familiar with Mark Labine's book, "La Verdure de Mirligueche: A Story of the Guidry dit Labine Family in North America", which was sold at our 2004 & 2009 reunions and has been featured here in GENERATIONS. That book is available for sale at Amazon.com.

BON APPETIT

Per Dana: This recipe is from a Cuban woman in Lafayette, Louisiana. The woman has since passed away. I sometimes add a ham bone when the seasonings are added. Can be served with sausage, cooked on the side, preferably fresh pork sausage. Use any sausage to suit your pallet. Also good served over rice.

CUBAN BLACK BEANS
from Dana Guidry-Lafayette, LA

1 lb. black beans
1 bell pepper, chopped
1 can whole black olives, pitted
2 onions, chopped
4 teaspoons olive oil

Salt, cayenne pepper, sugar, cumin, ground clove, ground oregano (all to taste-you be the judge as to what flatters your taste buds).

Soak beans overnight in full pot of water (a full 12 hour soak will soften those babies up a lot!). Next morning, drain the water & add new water (3 inches higher than beans). Boil for 20 minutes, drain & add the same amount of water you drained and add seasonings. Cook until the sauce gets really thick. Adjust seasonings before the end of the cooking session. Serves 6-8

FISH CAKES
From Simone Comeau Geddry, wife of General Al Geddry, Montreal, Canada

FISH CAKES

1 3/4 cup cooked, flaked fish, cod or haddock
2 cups seasoned mashed potatoes
1 tbsp. grated onion
2 tsp. lemon juice
1/2 tsp. summer savory, and/or pinch of ground ginger, and/or pinch of cayenne pepper
Salt & pepper to taste.

Mix together the fish, potatoes, onion, lemon juice and add seasonings to taste. Form into fish cakes about 3 inches in diameter and 1 1/2 inches thick. Sauté in butter until golden brown.

GUIDRY FAMILY HONORED AT 2010 ACADIAN MEMORIAL FESTIVAL *by Marty Guidry*

The 6th Annual Acadian Memorial Festival held in St. Martinville, LA on 20 March 2010 honored the Guidry and Breaux families during a reenactment of the 1765 arrival of the Acadians on Bayou Teche at St. Martinville. Martin Guidry and Elaine Clement represented the Guidry family during the reenactment. Karl Breaux and Gérard-Marc Braud (of Nantes, France) represented the Breaux family in the ceremonies. Arriving at the Evangeline Oak after paddling down Bayou Teche in canoes, members of the two families were greeted by a Spanish official welcoming them to the Attakapas country and offering them assistance in settling. After docking a short distance downstream, the two families were greeted by families honored in earlier years and escorted back to Evangeline Oak where Martin Guidry and Karl Breaux each presented a brief history of their families.

Throughout the day there were many activities for visitors to enjoy including listening to the Cajun Band "Moi -J'aime-Ça-Comme-Ça", tasting authentic Cajun delicacies as boudin, gratons, jambalaya and sweets, observing quilting demonstrations, riding in an authentic Cajun putt-putt boat and seeing the original Acadian silent film "Evangeline".

There were several presentations on Acadian topics including Martin Guidry discussing Pierre Guédry's difficult journey from Acadia to Louisiana and his life in Louisiana. Other talks presented during the day included renowned New Brunswick artist Georgette Bourgeois discussing her Acadian paintings, Gayle Breaux Smith tracing the journey of the Breaux family over 350 years and Debra Credeur discussing the Atchafalaya Natural Heritage Area. Storytelling for children, the Renaissance Cadienne Cajun Dance Troupe and Théâtre Acadien provided authentic, old-time entertainment for visitors of all ages.

Below are brief summaries in French by Gérard-Marc Braud of his experience at the 2010 Acadian Memorial Festival and a scenic swamp cruise that he enjoyed with Ron "Black" Guidry (Cajun Man's Swamp Cruise) on Bayou Black south of Houma, LA.

The Guidry and Breaux families in canoes arrive at the Evangeline Oak on Bayou Teche *Left:* Martin Guidry with banner and Elaine Clement in center listen to Spanish official welcoming them to the Attakapas country. *Right:* Gérard-Marc Braud with banner and Karl Breaux in center.

GENERATIONS Volume 8, Issue 2 Page 15

Article by G.M. Braud, appeared in
LA LETTRE, April, 2010 - Acadian Festival, St. Martinville, LA

N°73
Avril 2010

LA LETTRE

Bulletin de liaison

Association créée en 1984 pour entretenir les relations entre tous les membres du peuple Acadien et leurs amis :
- en FRANCE, au CANADA, en LOUISIANE, etc...

Siège Social : NANTES 06.10.78.79.62
Courriel (e-mail) : bretacadie@aol.com

Secrétariat Général : 6, avenue des Paludiers - 44380 - Pornichet - France 02.40.24.44.12
Courriel (e-mail) : isabelle.wyrat@free.fr

Article by G.M. Braud, appeared in
LA LETTRE, April, 2010 - Acadian Festival, St. Martinville, LA

Saint-Martinville – mars 2010

Dans la dernière « Lettre », nous avons évoqué le festival acadien de St Martinville qui, chaque année en mars, marque l'arrivée en Louisiane, des premiers acadiens fuyant les colonies anglaises de la côte est américaine, où ils avaient été retenus prisonniers pendant sept longues années.

Nous avons participé, le 20 mars dernier aux diverses manifestations qui ont marqué cette date mémorable pour la communauté acadienne de Louisiane.

Sous la férule de Ray Trahan, président des familles acadiennes, la fête s'est étalée tout au long de la journée avec, en point d'orgue, à l'heure de midi, la descente du bayou Teche, en pirogue, sur quelques centaines de mètres.

Deux familles étaient honorées en 2010, celle des Guédry (ou Guidry), et celle des Breau (avec toutes ses variantes)

L'arrivée des pirogues avait lieu au pied du fameux chêne dédié à l'héroïne Évangeline, en présence d'une représentation d'une vingtaine d'autres familles, tenant bannières.

Vêtus du costume acadien de l'époque (1765), nous eûmes l'honneur de porter la bannière des « Breau » et de faire cette « promenade » sur le bayou avec un vent assez fort qui menaçait notre frêle esquif, jusqu'au lieu de la cérémonie officielle où notre cousine Brenda Comeaux-Trahan, directrice générale du Mémorial acadien, animait l'ensemble des événements.

Ce fut une heure d'une grande intensité alors que Maryannick, pour sa part, sur la berge, en compagnie des autres membres des familles acadiennes, portant les bannières des différents patronymes acadiens et notamment des Trahan, nous souhaitait la bienvenue. Certes, bien que nombreuse, l'assistance n'était pas à la hauteur des espérances des organisateurs, mais l'ambiance était là, dans les rues proches de l'hôtel de ville, avec une présentation de vieilles voitures, des stands de nourriture et de boissons et... l'inévitable orchestre cadien qui distillait une musique à danser avec les classiques que tous les amoureux de la Louisiane connaissent bien.

Le Mémorial acadien était ouvert pour une visite et des commentaires assurés par Brenda qui n'a cessé de se dédoubler pendant toute cette journée de festivités.

Ce fut l'occasion de revoir de nombreux amis déjà rencontrés lors de nos précédents voyages, telle Jany Bulliard, l'une des fondatrices du Mémorial acadien, mais aussi de faire connaissance avec plusieurs autres familles pour parler de généalogie. Que du plaisir !... avant de rentrer sur Lafayette après un détour chez McGee's pour admirer l'immense plan d'eau du bassin de l'Atchafalaya.

De bien belles retrouvailles pour tous les acadiens présents.

Article by G.M. Braud, appeared in
LA LETTRE, April, 2010 - Swamp Tour, Houma, Louisiana

Bayou Black Sud de la Louisiane

Quand on cherche à rencontrer les alligators, dans le sud de la Louisiane, de nombreux « Swamptours » vous font leurs offres de services dans les revues touristiques et vous avez le choix.

Mais le parcours que je préfère pour aller à la rencontre de ces redoutables habitants des marais, se situe à proximité de Houma, sur le « bayou Black ». L'homme qui mène la barque s'appelle Guidry (tiens ! le même nom honoré à St Martinville). Nous nous connaissons depuis 1999 et le Congrès Mondial Acadien organisé cete année là dans cet État américain que les Acadiens du nord (ceux du Canada) appellent « l'Acadie tropicale ».

Ce 26 mars, en début d'après-midi, nous sommes un peu en retard à notre rendez-vous après avoir flâné à Thibodaux en compagnie de Rose Le Blanc et Irène Vicknair, nos deux sympathiques hôtesses.

À notre arrivée l'embarcadère est vide : Guidry est parti ! Mais, grâce au téléphone portable, son épouse l'ayant joint, il revient à notre rencontre. Ouf !

Alors commence une promenade au fil de l'eau, de bayou en bayou, un véritable labyrinthe que M. Guidry connaît par cœur. Hélas, son compagnon à quatre pattes, un chien, qui l'accompagnait les années passées, n'est plus de ce monde. Dommage ! car ses aboiements attiraient les « cocodrils » pour la plus grande joie des touristes prêts pour la photo-souvenir.

Et pendant près de deux heures, au milieu d'une nature sauvage, nous allons admirer une grande partie de la faune et de la flore de la Louisiane.

Les grandes aigrettes blanches, les ibis, et les petits rapaces s'envolent à notre approche, alors que le grand héron bleu, moins effarouché que ses congénères, pose pour la photo.

Le bateau à fond plat glisse sur l'eau, croise d'autres bateaux plus rapides, des pêcheurs sans doute, s'arrête de temps en temps pour un commentaire du capitaine, en français.

Des tortues qui se prélassent au soleil sur une branche d'arbre plongent dans l'eau saumâtre tandis que les premiers alligators font leur apparition. Des petits tout d'abord, puis d'autres de plus en plus imposants, que Guidry appelle... et nourrit parfois de morceaux de poulet.

Tout cela au milieu d'une nature luxuriante où les cyprès chauves et la mousse espagnole sont omniprésents, donnant au paysage traversé son caractère à la fois exotique et mystérieux.

Le capitaine nous prévient : pas question de mettre pied à terre... il n'y en a pas d'ailleurs ; les lentilles d'eau et les jacinthes donnent, en effet, l'illusion d'un sol agréable à piétiner, mais le danger guette l'imprudent !

Heureusement, aucun de nous n'a eu l'idée de s'aventurer hors du bateau.

Parfois un puits de pétrole (ou d'huile) vient gâcher cet environnement sauvage et harmonieux et nous rappelle que le monde des affaires n'est pas si loin de nous.

Notre capitaine termine cette balade par quelques chansons en s'accompagnant à la guitare et, bien sûr, nous avons droit à « Jolie blonde » et « la porte en arrière » entre autres.

Mais déjà nous voici de retour à l'embarcadère au milieu de nombreux bateaux de pêche. Une soirée festive nous attend avec nos amis acadiens et justement au repas il y aura de l'alligator pour les plus téméraires. Mais celui-là sera inoffensif !

G.M. Braud

Les Guédry d'Asteur photos from the Acadian Festival, March 20, 2010
St. Martinville, LA

Marty Guidry in 1760's period Acadian dress with Guédry banner

Marty Guidry & Georgette Bourgeois, Artist - New Brunswick

Above: A bateau with Evangeline sitting at bow and three Chitimacha Indians accompanying the Acadians on their journey down Bayou Teche approach the Evangeline Oak. *Below:* Visitors awaiting the arrival of Guidry and Breaux families

Above: Monsignor Courville blesses newly arrived Acadians in Guidry and Breaux families. Two grandmothers of Monsignor Courville are Guidry's. *Below:* Brenda Comeaux Trahan in gazebo discussing with visitors the reenactment ceremony

MALVINA MÉNARD LABINE (1893 – 1967) REEVE OF RAYSIDE TOWNSHIP

In late 1958 the lead story in northern Ontario was not the thousands of nickel miners out-of-work and in dire stress nor their upcoming Toronto meeting with Premier Leslie Font, but the upset victory of a 65-year-old grandmother with a grade school education as the reeve of Rayside Township, Sudbury District, Ontario. In Canadian provinces having rural municipalities the highest elected official of the municipality is a reeve – equivalent to a mayor in many other areas.

It seems that the only folks not surprised by Malvina Ménard Labine's upset win over the 41-year-old incumbent reeve were Malvina's neighbors and Malvina herself. So why would this elderly lady, untested in politics, run for reeve and, more importantly, how did she win?

Born into a poor family on 24 November 1893 in Azilda of Rayside Township, Malvina Ménard appreciated both hard work and sharing what she had with others. At thirteen she left home to work as a nursemaid. On the 12th of August 1912 she married Joseph Labine, a young blacksmith. They settled in a small shack on a farm just outside of Azilda.

Not afraid of hard work, Malvina farmed the property during the six months each year that Joseph left for the lumber camps. She hoed and sowed a one-acre garden, raised and milked the cows, picked fruit from the trees, fed the chickens and gathered the eggs and sold her farm products at market. During these years she also raised her family, which eventually reached twenty children. Every Saturday she hauled water up the hill, heated it in a wood stove and gave every child a bath. Sixteen of her children survived to adulthood - most raising families of their own. On 6 July 1940 Joseph Labine, a big jovial man of 228 pounds, went to market, ate a large lunch and dropped dead of a heart attack about 2:00 pm. Malvina had just given birth to their 20th child – a boy they called Bernard.

Malvina Labine, a widow at age 47 with nine children under sixteen years of age and nothing but debts to her name, reassessed her life. Born with a tough, never-give-up attitude, she sold five horses and her jalopy with bad brakes and bought a new tractor and truck. With the financial help of three sons working in the mines Malvina began life anew. Soon she replaced her shack of a home with a new home she built herself – a plain, strong home with room for all her family. She continued to work ever harder on the farm – pressing hay, threshing grain, picking potatoes and other crops, hoeing the garden, cooking meals and sewing and knitting clothes for the family. In addition, she worked odd jobs where she could find them – installing a heavy culvert on the roadway or serving as janitor at the new school. Her children helped where they could. With her children she was a loving, but strict mother – enforcing discipline and teaching them well.

Sooner than she expected, almost all her children had grown and left home. Now she had a big, empty home so she began to take in foster children. But she didn't just request a foster child, she asked for four foster children at once. After receiving two brothers and two sisters for foster care, Malvina then requested four additional foster children. Her new family continued to grow until she raised twelve foster children.

MALVINA MÉNARD LABINE (1893 – 1967) REEVE OF RAYSIDE TOWNSHIP

Born with a heart of gold and lots of compassion, Malvina was always there to help the less fortunate. A poor young boy never had the opportunity to fish; Malvina bought him a new rod and had her son take him fishing. A young girl's family could not afford a coat for her; Malvina helped the family buy a nice coat. More importantly, she kept up with each of 'her kids' to ensure they were doing well in school and often took them on outings. When a neighbor was sick, Malvina was there helping. When local miners went on strike and couldn't afford essentials for their family, Malvina quietly gave them cases of canned goods, children's clothes and baby food. She always kept ample supplies of meat, beans, corn, shortening, peanut butter, tomato juice and up to 400 loaves of day-old bread in the freezer.

When a neighbor lady saw hard times and needed help, Malvina quietly supplied her from her storehouse of goods – taking only a heartfelt "Thank You" for her good works.

Growing from a rural farming community to a suburb of Sudbury in the decade of the 1950's, Rayside Township with Azilda as its hub faced new challenges that were not being addressed to Malvina's and the townfolks' satisfaction. Tyne Castonguay, the incumbent reeve, seemed to care more for his patent medicine business than running the township. Malvina Labine had a reputation for getting things done so local folks asked her to run for reeve in the upcoming election. At first doubtful about running, she eventually consented. Once in the race, she ran hard and won the election. And, as is her style, her election party was at town hall where she passed out doughnuts, sandwiches and coffee to campaign workers of both sides.

So where did Malvina Labine garner all her support to defeat the incumbent reeve? Remember all those local children, women and families she helped over the years. They never forgot her and turned out in droves to vote for their dear friend. Of course, having sixteen children and numerous grandchildren didn't hurt either.

Malvina Ménard Labine served as reeve of Rayside Township from 1959-1961. In 1967 Malvina Labine died in Sudbury after living a hard, but fulfilling life. She is buried in Chelmsford – not far from where she lived most of her life.

Malvina Labine's political beginnings bore fruit when in 1988 her grandson Guy Labine, son of Robert Labine and Hortense Joliat, became one of the youngest members elected as Municipal Councillor of the Town of Rayside-Balfour that incorporated the former Rayside Township. Guy served two terms as Municipal Councillor from 1988 to 1993.

MALVINA MÉNARD LABINE (1893 – 1967) REEVE OF RAYSIDE TOWNSHIP

Genealogy of Guy Labine & of Joseph Labine, husband of Malvina Ménard

Guy Joel Labine m. Lyse Lavalée
|
Robert Bruno Labine m. Hortense Adrienne Joliat
|
Joseph Venance Aristide Labine m. Malvina Ménard
|
Aristide Guildry dit Labine m. Marie Louise Bélisle
|
Jérôme Guildry dit Labine m. Alice Beaudoin
|
Jean-Baptiste Guildry dit Labine Jr. m3. Marie Josette Vincent
|
Jean-Baptiste Augustin Guédry dit Labine m2. Marie-Marguerite Picot
|
Pierre Guédry dit Labine m. Marguerite Brasseau
|
Claude Guédry dit Grivois m. Marguerite Petitpas

Guy Labine

Top left: The first years of their family life, Joseph and Malvina Labine with Roméo, Lucienne, Germaine, and Yvonne. Top right: Malvina & son, Bernard.

Bottom left: Foster family Jacques with Bernard- second row on right. Bottom center & right: The Labine barn and out buildings in Azilda.

There is a large album of photos of this family on our Facebook page. Just follow this link to view:

http://www.facebook.com/photo.php?
pid=3745180&id=387769648496#!/album.php?
aid=164508&id=387769648496&page=5

IN THE NEWS-HISTORICAL NEWS TIDBITS

Rayne's giant "oua-oua-rons" can truly claim the title of the "jumpingest frogs in the world" as these big fellows go into orbit around the world as part of NASA's program for research for future space projects. Space-bound frogs attract the special attention of Rayne Mayor Bill Gossen, Frog Queen Sue Guidry, Congressman Edwin W. Edwards, David "Pete" Babineaux, and Ralph Stutes (Rayne councilman). These were some of the frogs selected by NASA for the OFO Program in the early 1970s. (Courtesy Fair Craig Hash.)

<u>Above</u>: *Frog Queen Sue Guidry, Rayne Louisiana;* <u>Below</u>: *Guidry Cleaners, Rayne, Louisiana*
Photos from <u>Images of America, Rayne</u>, Arcadia Publishing

Owner Danny Domingue is shown outside of Guidry's Cleaners with his delivery truck. (Courtesy Lucille Barrows.)

IN THE NEWS-HISTORICAL NEWS TIDBITS

Amarillo Daily News, Friday Morning, February 7, 1941

WAR 'GOT IN THEIR HAIR'—"Just for fun" these boys from Monroe, La., shaved their heads before war maneuvers at Camp Hulen, Tex. They belong to Battery G, 204th Coast Artillery, and wait'll the folks back home get a look at, left to right: Oliver Leonard, N. H. Knox, Robert Robinson, Claudius House, James Williamson, Herman Guidry, John Stewart, Shelly Brezeale.

Right: Mrs. Celeste Long, daughter of Mrs. A. Guedry-
The Constitution-Atlanta, GA, Wednesday, February 26, 1902

Dear Heloise:
When sewing, I have the hardest time threading the needle. So I found an easy way.
Spray a little hair spray on the end of the thread.
This will make the thread stiff and easy to push through the eye of the needle.

Sharon Guidry
Age 13

Hints from Heloise - Piqua Daily Call
July 22, 1972

ACADIAN CENTENARIAN DEAD.

MRS. CELESTE LONG, AGED 104, DIES IN NEW ORLEANS.

Her Family, the Broussards, One of the Most Famous in Louisiana.

New Orleans, La., February 21—(Special.)—Mrs. Celeste Long (nee Broussard), the oldest woman in New Orleans or Louisiana, died here yesterday aged 104 years and 11 months at the residence of her granddaughter, Mrs. William Dever, of 2710 Royal street.

Mrs. Long was born in St. Martinsville, La., March 23, 1797. Her birth is recorded in the parish church at St. Martinsville and is not disputed. Her family, the Broussards, is one of the most numerous and famous in southern Louisiana. Congressman Broussard, from the third Louisiana district, was a relative of hers, as was also Governor Alexander Morten, who was a cousin of her mother.

The family is of Acadian origin, and Mrs. Long's mother, Mrs. A. Guedry, was one of the refugees who came with Evangeline to Louisiana in 1769. She lived to a great age, and could tell all of the adventures of the refugees in their long trip from Nova Scotia to St. Martinsville.

Miss Broussard married Judge Alexander Hamilton, of Tennessee, in 1870. She had four children, all of whom are now dead. Many of them lived to be very old. Her second husband was John Long, of Washington. One child survives, Mrs. Numa Oliver, of Adeline, La. Long himself disappeared and was never afterwards heard of. Mrs. Long leaves five great grandchildren and five great great grandchildren, the latter residing in Cleveland, Ohio. Her husband was related to David Crockett and Bailey Peyton.

Mrs. Long was a typical Acadian, always hale and hearty, with snow white hair and fair complexion. She was never sick until Christmas, when she contracted a cold which ended her life.

She wore no glasses, even in her last days; spoke nothing but French, but read English, and was an enthusiastic reader of English newspapers and wrote correspondence well in English.

Les Guédry d'Asteur

What's in a name?

<u>Guédry</u> is the family to which you belong if your name is spelled Guédry, Guedry, Guidry, Gaidry, Guildry, Geddry, Jeddry, Labine, LaBine, LaBean or any of several dozen variations. The original name of our family is believed to have been Guédry. We are all descendants of Claude Guédry & Marguerite Petitpas.

Here are some common and uncommon variant spellings of the name.

Guédry	Guiddry	Geddrie	Jeddrie	Labeen
Guedry	Guiddery	Geddry	Jeddry	Labene
Guedrie	Guiedri	Gedree	Jederie	Labine
Guedris	Guiedry	Gedrie	Jedrey	LaBine
Guidry	Guildry	Gedry	Jedrie	LaBean
Gudiry	Guildrie	Gettry	Jedry	LaBeau
Guidery	Guitry	Gidrie		Labeau
Guidrey	Gaidry	Gidry	Lledre	
Guidrie	Gaidrie		Yedri	

Our **Petitpas** cousins likewise have several variations of their name including Petitpas, Pettipas, Petipas, Petitpa, Petit Pas and Pitts.

DUES REMINDER

Attached at the back of this issue is a membership application for renewing your membership in **Les Guédry d'Asteur**. Our dues are very reasonable at $6.00 for individuals and $10 for a family in 2010.

Please take a moment, complete the Membership Application, enclose a check and send it to the address on the application. It will help all of us do so much for the family. And, if you would like to join at one of the Benefactor Levels, it would allow us do even more.

Les Guédry d'Asteur is now on Facebook. Join us there and connect with other family members from all over the US and CAN. Feel free to post queries, photos, links, events or other items of interest to the family. Just search for 'Les Guédry d'Asteur' on Facebook to find our page.

Les Guédry d'Asteur

To share your ideas for the newsletter, contact:

Marty Guidry
6139 North Shore Drive
Baton Rouge, LA 70817
225-755-1915
guidryrm@cox.net

The Guédry-Labine Family Newsletter '*GENERATIONS*' serves as a focal point for family members to share and learn about us.

'*GENERATIONS*' newsletter is now in its eighth year. We hope to provide our readers with an interesting, informative and entertaining newsletter. Your input is always welcome and we look forward to another year of sharing family history and news with you.

Allie Guidry
txguidry2000@yahoo.com

Marty Guidry
guidryrm@cox.net

Les Guédry d'Asteur Officers and Committees

OFFICERS:
President - Martin Guidry (LA)
Vice-President - Elaine Clement (LA)
Secretary - Billy Harrell Guidry (LA)
Treasurer - Daniel "Chuck" Guidry (LA)

COMMITTEES:
Website - Becky Boggess (IA) - Chairperson
    Annie Grignon-Labine (QU) - Translator
    Elaine Clement (LA) - Translator
    Martin Guidry (LA)

Genealogy - Daryl LaBine (FL/ON) - Chairperson
    Bernard Geddry (AZ)
    Mark Labine (MN)
    Daniel "Chuck" Guidry (LA)
    Martin Guidry (LA)

Finance - Cheryl Guidry Tyiska (MD) - Chairperson
    Paul Labine (IL)
    Marshall Woolner (OR)
    Gloria Parrent (TX)
    Chuck Guidry (LA)

Membership - Charlene Guidry Lacombe (LA) - Chairperson
    Gayle Guidry (LA) - Special Projects
    Warren Guidry (TX)

Sales - Cindy Guidry Herdt (WA) - Chairperson
    Wayne Simoneaux (LA)
    Billy Harrell Guidry (LA)

Publicity - Elaine Clement (LA) - Chairperson
    Margaret Jeddry (MA)
    Warren Guidry (TX)

Newsletter - Allie Guidry Hardee (VA) - Editor
    Martin Guidry (LA)

CAFA Board Member - Jeanette Guidry Leger (LA)

FALL 2010

Volume 8, Issue 3

Les Guédry d'Asteur

GENERATIONS

IN THIS ISSUE

AND YOU SAID YOUR NAME IS WHAT? OR HOW GUÉDRY HAS EVOLVED INTO SO MANY VARIANTS *by Marty Guidry*	2
BOOK NOOK	6
THE LOUISIANA SLAVE DATABASE & THE LOUISIANA FREE DATABASE AND SLAVE NARRATIVES *By Marty Guidry*	7
BON APPETIT: *Recipes from the Guédry/Labine Family Cookbook*	25
HISTORICAL TIDBITS	26

As we end our eighth year publishing "Generations", we again have an excellent issue to read over the holidays. With the oil spill in the Gulf of Mexico finally abated, our thoughts are with our family members in southern Louisiana as they recover. We hope that their jobs and economy will return and they can overcome successfully this third major tragedy to impact them in less than six years.

The name of our family association is Les Guédry d'Asteur, but have you ever met anyone with the surname Guédry? I have not. So how did all of our names derive from the Guédry surname? For insight into how your name came about, you may want to read "And You Said Your Name Is What? Or How Guédry Has Evolved Into So Many Variants". It may not have all the answers, but it may provide some insights. If you have more information on your name, please let us know.

The Book Nook features two outstanding books about the Acadians of today. French, Cajun, Creole, Houma by Dr. Carl A. Brasseaux discusses how these several French cultures developed in the melting pot of southern Louisiana. Voyages: A Maine Franco-American Reader edited by Nelson Madore and Barry Rodrigue is a must read for those planning to attend the 2014 Congres Mondial in Madawaska, Maine. It is a series of literary articles on the Franco-American and Acadian experience in Maine.

And don't miss the delectable recipes in Bon Appetit. You are sure to want to try one during the holiday season.

"The Louisiana Slave Database & The Louisiana Free Database and Slave Narratives" provides an interesting insight into an under-researched area of our history and genealogy. Although the article centers on Louisiana and the Guédry family, it provides research tools that will let anyone research the African-American experience in the United States. The Slave and Free Databases provide a wealth of information on over 100,000 slaves and their masters in Louisiana. The Slave Narratives present first-hand autobiographical accounts of what it was to be a slave.

Thanks to Allie Guidry, our editor, for another superb issue of "Generations" just in time for the holidays.

Don't forget the Guédry-Labine & Petitpas Reunion on 8 October 2011 in Cutoff, LA. Registration information will be available soon.

And please remember to renew your membership in Les Guédry d'Asteur. Our dues are quite low and your financial help is how we fund our reunions, book donations, website, newsletter and other activities. Without you, Les Guédry d'Asteur would not exist.

Marty Guidry

AND YOU SAID YOUR NAME IS WHAT?
OR
HOW GUÉDRY HAS EVOLVED INTO SO MANY VARIANTS by Marty Guidry

Have you ever searched genealogical records and discovered that your family surname changes over time? Many a genealogist has acquired countless gray hairs trying to sort out variants of his surname and ensure that he researches all of these variants.

For most families the surname variants are rather straightforward. They often result from poor spelling and the less restrictive attitude of long ago – where if it sounded right, it was okay. Spelling really didn't matter. For example, the Acadian surname Breau often was written Brot, Brau, Brault, Bro and Breaux over the past 200 years. Most of these variants survive today in various localities.

The surname Guédry likewise has several "spelling" variants including Guedry, Guidry, Gaidry, Guildry and Gidry; however, there are several other variants as Jeddry, Jedry, Labine, LaBean and Lledri that have roots elsewhere. Often someone asks me, "If my name is Labine, how am I related to the Guédry family?" It is not a difficult answer if you know the history of our family.

Obviously, with modern means of transportation and relocations due to jobs, during the 20th century our family members have moved throughout the United States and Canada and even to other parts of the world. The analysis below will discuss where pockets of Guédry surname variants are found today and how variants in the surname may have developed. It would be impracticable to identify every location where a variant of the Guédry surname occurs today. Most folks of our family, however, can trace their variant of the Guédry surname to one of the locations below.

Let's explore how our distinctive Guédry surname has changed and how we are all related.

Guédry

A study of extant records of the 17th and 18th century strongly indicates that the original spelling of our surname was **Guédry**.

To the best of my knowledge the surname **Guédry** is no longer used in North America.

The name Guédry apparently has German origins being derived from one of several old German words: "wido" meaning forests or woods, "waido" meaning hunting place, park or forest or "wid" meaning wood in the sense of a weapon. Note that the old German "W" sounds similar to the French "Gui" as, for example, the German name Wilhelm is Guillaume in French.

Some researchers believe the Guédry name may have originated at Cuébris – a commune in the town of Puget-Théniers in the Alpes-Maritime Department, Provence-Alpes-Côte d'Azur Region of France. It is 18 miles northwest of Nice, France. Today there is a Hotel le Guitry in Nice, France.

Other researchers believe the Guédry family emigrated from the area of Alsace-Lorraine near the French-German border. Today in this region is Mount Gédry located in the village of Arpenans in the Haute-Saône Department, Franche-Comté Region in eastern France about fifty miles from the German border.

Interestingly, 43 miles northwest of Paris is the village of Guitry in the Eure Department, Haute-Normandie Region of France.

AND YOU SAID YOUR NAME IS WHAT?
OR
HOW GUÉDRY HAS EVOLVED INTO SO MANY VARIANTS *by Marty Guidry*

Guedry, Guidry, Gaidry

The spellings Guedry, Guidry and Gaidry today occur primarily in south Louisiana and southeast Texas.

The surname **Guedry**, closest in spelling to the original Guédry, is used today by folks in several pockets of Louisiana. These include St. Landry Parish near Opelousas, Terrebonne Parish near Houma and Ascension Parish near Prairieville and Gonzales. Additionally, many folks with the Guedry surname live in Hardin County, Texas near Batson. Just outside Batson is the historic, well-maintained Guedry Cemetery.

Apparently **Guedry** resulted from folks in the early 19th century dropping the accent acute from Guédry. Since many of the Acadians of that day could not write, non-French government clerks and priests may have been responsible for omitting the accent acute when Guédry's conducted business as land sales and censuses and recorded baptisms, marriages and burials.

The most common surname of our family in Louisiana and Texas is **Guidry**. In southern Louisiana the areas of the highest concentration of Guidry are Lafayette Parish, St. Martin Parish around Breaux Bridge and Cecilia, Acadia Parish near Rayne, Crowley and Church Point, throughout Terrebonne Parish and Lafourche Parish (with a large pocket along the Larose to Golden Meadow corridor), Ascension Parish near Donaldsonville and Calcasieu Parish near Lake Charles. In southeast Texas one finds pockets of Guidry's in Jefferson County near Beaumont and Port Arthur and in Orange County near Orange.

Although proof is lacking, it appears that the surname **Guidry** resulted from poor penmanship in the early 19th century when the accented 'e' of Guédry was closed and the accent acute was reduced to a dot to form an 'i'. The transition of Guédry to Guidry occurred slowly in the records during the first half of the 19th century in south Louisiana.

The surname **Gaidry** occurs in Louisiana in Terrebonne Parish near Houma and in Lafayette Parish near Lafayette. It appears to have originated in the Houma, LA area about 1872 and spread to the Lafayette, LA area in the 20th century.

Probably the surname **Gaidry** resulted from the 'u' of Guidry being closed due to poor penmanship. The first known record using the surname Gaidry was a 20 April 1872 Petition for Inventory after the death of Paul Gaidry on 27 February 1872. After 1872 we see the surname Gaidry appear regularly in a small number of church and civil records in Terrebonne Parish, LA.

Jeddry, Jedry, Jedrey, Geddry, Gedry

The surnames **Jeddry**, **Jedry**, **Jedrey**, **Geddry** and **Gedry** today occur principally in the St. Mary's Bay area of Nova Scotia and the New England states of Massachusetts and Connecticut. The Jeddry, Jedry and Jedrey surnames thrive in the Digby County, Nova Scotia communities of St. Alphonse and Salmon River while the Geddry and Gedry surnames dominate in the community of Meteghan less than five miles distant.

AND YOU SAID YOUR NAME IS WHAT?
OR
HOW GUÉDRY HAS EVOLVED INTO SO MANY VARIANTS *by Marty Guidry*

In the late 1800's and early 1900's many Acadians from Nova Scotia immigrated to New England to find work. Certainly they intended to earn money and return to their homes in Nova Scotia; however, many remained permanently in their new homes. Massachusetts and Connecticut attracted a large number of the Acadians including both Jeddry and Geddry families.

The **Jeddry, Jedry, Jedrey, Geddry** and **Gedry** families descend from Augustin Guédry and Marie Jeanson who founded a small community on St. Mary's Bay called Chéticamp. Later the name of this community was changed to St. Alphonse. Augustin Guédry's name was often spelled Augustin Gedree probably due to English clerks writing the name as they heard it spoken. As the children and grandchildren of Augustin began to register their lands and conduct other business with the English government, their names gradually evolved into Jeddry, Jedry, Jedrey, Geddry and Gedry – again because the English clerks wrote the names phonetically as they heard them spoken.

Labine, LaBine

Although **Labine** initially appears to be an entirely different surname than Guédry, the Labine and LaBine surnames are variants of Guédry. The Labine surname originated in the St. Alexis area near Montréal, Canada and is now found throughout the lower parts of the Québec and Ontario provinces. Family preference apparently determines whether the Labine or LaBine variant is used.

The **Labine (LaBine)** family descends from Pierre Guédry dit Labine, son of Claude Guédry and Marguerite Petitpas. Jean-Baptiste Augustin Guédry dit Labine, son of Pierre Guédry dit Labine and Marguerite Brasseau, was deported from Acadia to Boston, Massachusetts in November 1755 and remained with his growing family in the Boston area until 1766 when he was allowed to resettle near Montréal, Canada. In 1767 he established his family at St-Alexis near Montréal. In the late 1700's several of his children and grandchildren began calling themselves Labine and Guildry rather than Guédry with the Labine surname being derived from the 'dit' name of their ancestor Pierre Guédry dit Labine. The families prospered, grew and gradually resettled westward. Today the Labine (LaBine) surname is found throughout the southern regions of the Québec and Ontario provinces.

Guildry

Like the Labine surname, the **Guildry** surname originated in the St-Alexis area near Montréal, Canada. Today one finds Guildry's in areas near Montréal and Québec.

The **Guildry** family also descends from Pierre Guédry dit Labine, son of Claude Guédry and Marguerite Petitpas in the same manner as the Labine (LaBine) family. Jean-Baptiste Augustin Guédry dit Labine, son of Pierre Guédry dit Labine and Marguerite Brasseau, was deported from Acadia to Boston, Massachusetts in November 1755 and remained with his growing family in the Boston area until 1766 when he was allowed to resettle near Montréal, Canada. In 1767 he established his family at St-Alexis near Montréal. In the late 1700's several of his children and grandchildren began calling themselves Guildry and Labine rather than Guédry. The exact way that the Guildry surname derived from the Guédry surname is not known. The number of Guildry families is much smaller than that of Labine families and they are concentrated in the Montréal and Québec areas.

AND YOU SAID YOUR NAME IS WHAT?
OR
HOW GUÉDRY HAS EVOLVED INTO SO MANY VARIANTS by Marty Guidry

LaBean

The **LaBean** surname originated in Bay County, Michigan and today the majority of LaBean family members still reside in Bay County and the nearby counties of Arenac, Gladwin and Genesee.

One of only two children of Jean Baptiste Guildry dit Labine and Angélique Rivet to survive beyond 21 years of age, Jean Baptist Guildry dit Labine Jr. was born at St. Jacques de Montcalm, Québec on 31 July 1825. As a young man not yet 15 years of age, he left the Québec area and headed southwest toward Michigan. By 1840 he had settled in Monroe County in southeast Michigan. There on 7 November 1848 he married Edwidge Senever dit Lamarbre, who also had immigrated to Michigan from St. Jacques de Montcalm, Québec.

Over the next 27 years Jean Baptiste and Edwidge had 17 children in Monroe County – eleven of whom survived childhood. During this time Jean Baptiste Guildry dit Labine changed his name to Jean Baptiste Labine. In the early 1880's he moved his family north from Monroe County to Pinconning Township in Bay County, MI. About 1888 Jean Baptiste Labine died at Pinconning Township. The children prospered in Bay County and purchased property for their farms and homes. As they registered their lands and conducted other government business, they saw their surname change from Labine to **LaBean**. Apparently the English-speaking government clerks wrote the name as they heard it. The 'i' of Labine is pronounced as a long 'e' in French so 'bine' became 'bean' and Labine became LaBean. The new spelling stuck and today this branch of our Guédry family carries the surname LaBean.

"Extinct" Variants (Lledri, Lledre, Yedri)

There have been several other variants of the surname Guédry that have not survived to the present day – the most unusual being **Lledri (Lledre, Yedri)**.

In December 1767 Pierre Guédry and his young wife Marguerite Dupuis with their daughter Marie stepped aboard the "Jane" at Port Tobacco, MD for their journey to a new home in Louisiana. The Spanish scribe recorded a manifest of the Acadians disembarking at New Orleans in February 1768. As Pierre Guédry pronounced his name "Guédry" in his fluent French tongue, the Spanish scribe diligently wrote "Lledri" – the sounds he heard Pierre saying. This looks strange to an English speaker; however, the "Ll" in Spanish sounds similar to the English 'Y'. Thus the 'Gué' sounds pronounced in French sounds somewhat similar to the "Lle" in Spanish. The 'dry' sound in French sounds similar to 'dree' in English and 'dri' in Spanish.

The Lledri (Lledre, Yedri) appeared only on a few early documents recorded by Spanish clerks and priests and never was used by the Guédry family as their surname.

Other Variants

There are many other variants of the Guédry surname; however, each is similar in spelling to one of the surnames above. These include Guedrie, Guedris (**Guedry**); Guidiry, Guidery, Guidrey, Guidrie, Guiddry, Guiddery, Guiedry, Guiedri, Guitry, Gidry, Gidrie (**Guidry**); Guildrie (**Guildry**); Gaidrie, (**Gaidry**); Geddrie, Gettry (**Geddry**); Gedree, Gedrie (**Gedry**); Jeddrie, Jeddrey (**Jeddry**); Jederie, Jedrey, Jedrie (**Jedry**); Labeen, Labene (**Labine**) and LaBeau, Labeau (**LaBean**).

BOOK NOOK

In recent years, ethnographers have recognized south Louisiana as home to perhaps the most complex rural society in North America. More than a dozen French-speaking immigrant groups have been identified there, Cajuns and white Creoles being the most famous. In this guide to the amazing social, cultural and linguistic variation within Louisiana's French-speaking region, Carl A. Brasseaux presents an overview of the origins and evolution of all the Francophone communities.

Brasseaux examines the impact of French immigration on Louisiana over the past three centuries. He shows how this once-undesirable outpost of the French empire became colonized by individuals ranging from criminals to entrepreneurs who went on to form a multifaceted society—one that, unlike other American melting pots, rests upon a French cultural foundation. A prolific author and expert on the region, Brasseaux offers readers an entertaining history of how these diverse peoples created south Louisiana's famous vibrant culture, interacting with African Americans, Spaniards and Protestant Anglos and encountering influences from southern plantation life and the Caribbean. He explores in detail three still cohesive components in the Francophone melting pot, each one famous for having retained a distinct identity: the Creole communities, both black and white; the Cajun people and the state's largest concentration of French speakers—the Houma tribe.

Carl A. Brasseaux is of Acadian/Cajun ancestry and was raised in a bilingual home in the heart of Louisiana's French-speaking region. The author of more than thirty books, he is a professor of history and the director of the Center for Louisiana Studies at the University of Louisiana at Lafayette.

VOYAGES: A Maine Franco-American Reader

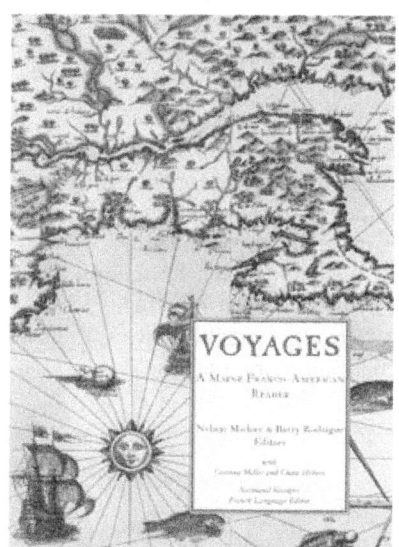

Voyages: A Maine Franco-American Reader, Edited by Nelson Madore and Barry Rodrigue, is an immense anthology of texts about the French and Canadian presence in Maine by U.S. scholars, with a few notable contributions from four Canadian academics. It was published in the Franco-American Collection series, linked to a research centre at the University of Southern Maine at Lewiston-Auburn, not far from the neighborhood that used to be called Little Canada because of the presence of French-Canadians in previous centuries.

Dozens of voices celebrate—in essays, stories, plays, poetry, songs and art—the Franco-American and Acadian experience in Maine. They explore subjects as diverse as Quebec-Maine frontier history, immigrant drama, work, genealogy, discrimination, women, community affairs, religion, archeology, politics, literature, language and humor. The voices, themselves, are equally diverse, including Norman Beaupré, Michael Michaud, Ross and Judy Paradis, Susann Pelletier, John Martin, Béatrice Craig, Michael Parent, Linda Pervier, Alaric Faulkner, Ray Levasseur, Yves Frenette, Paul Paré, Yvon Labbé, Rev. Clement Thibodeau, Bob Chenard, Denis Ledoux, Josée Vachon, Greg Chabot, Jean-Paul Poulain, Stewart Doty, Rhea Côté Robbins and many others. This is a rich resource and an engaging read, one that will resonate with many.

THE LOUISIANA SLAVE DATABASE & THE LOUISIANA FREE DATABASE AND SLAVE NARRATIVES
By Marty Guidry

With the unprecedented success of the ABC TV miniseries "Roots" in 1977 and the earlier-published book of the same title by Alex Haley, African-Americans and other began researching the genealogy and history of American slaves in earnest. Initially, as Haley discovered, records were difficult to locate and information within the records was tantalizing, yet incomplete. As time passed, researchers have found new sources and techniques for researching American slave genealogy and history. It is not unusual today for a person to trace their African-American genealogy to a tribe in Africa although few have the money, time and resources as Haley did to visit Africa on extended trips and seek their genealogy further back in time through the oral history of the tribe.

Louisiana Slave Datatase & Louisiana Free Database

Dr. Gwendolyn Midlo Hall[1,2], a Louisiana native and then-professor of history at Rutgers University in New Jersey, was doing research at the courthouse in Pointe Coupee Parish, Louisiana in 1984 when she discovered boxes of old notarial records containing a wealth of information on the slaves of that region. Captured by this intriguing information, Dr. Hall spent the next fifteen years gathering additional slave information from throughout Louisiana as well as from French, Spanish and Texan records.

Through her diligent, painstaking research, Dr. Hall amassed an unimaginable amount of information on over 100,000 slaves from Louisiana. The data included not only the slaves' names, but also their genders, ages, occupations, illnesses, family relationships, ethnicity, places of origin, owners, prices paid by owners and other tidbits of their history rarely known before.

In addition to compiling extensive information on 100,666 Louisiana slaves, Dr. Hall also recorded information on the manumissions of 4,071 slaves in their route to freedom. She divided her work covering the time period 1719-1820 into two databases: the "Louisiana Slave Database" and the "Louisiana Free Database".

In March, 2000 LSU Press published the two databases on a Compact Disk (CD) entitled "**Louisiana Slave Database and Louisiana Free Database 1719-1820**"[3]. The CD's soon sold out; however, the database was very cumbersome to use and difficult to search.

In 2001 ibiblio.org maintained by the University of North Carolina requested that Dr. Hall let them place the databases on their website. She agreed with the condition that they create a search engine for accessing the records easily. Unfortunately, ibiblio.org created a search engine only for the Slave Database and not the Free Database. They also made some changes to the databases; however, these are minor in nature. In November, 2001 ibiblio.org published the databases on their web portal under the name "**Afro-Louisiana History and Genealogy 1719-1820**"[4]. In addition, to the searchable database, the website also includes Dr. Hall's statistical calculations and three pre-set searches "African Names", "Revolts" and "Runaways". To access the "Afro-Louisiana History and Genealogy 1719-1820" database on ibiblio.org, click on this link:

http://www.ibiblio.org/laslave/   (Slave Database)

THE LOUISIANA SLAVE DATABASE
& THE LOUISIANA FREE DATABASE
AND SLAVE NARRATIVES
By Marty Guidry

Later Ancestry.com asked Dr. Hall for permission to incorporate the two databases into their search engine. Dr. Hall agreed provided Ancestry.com did not charge for their use. In 2003 Ancestry.com opened the two databases to the public free of charge under the titles "**Louisiana Slave Records, 1719-1820**"[5] and "**Louisiana Freed Slave Records, 1719-1820**"[6]. The two databases can be accessed on Ancestry.com at:

http://search.ancestry.com/search/db.aspx?dbid=7383   (Slave Database)

http://search.ancestry.com/search/db.aspx?dbid=7382   (Freed Database)

Before searching either the ibiblio.org or the Ancestry.com databases, one should read the brief explanation on how to conduct a search and tips for improving the search at:

http://www.ibiblio.org/laslave/explain.php   (How-To Search the Databases)

Dr. Hall's detailed description of the Louisiana Slave Database and the Louisiana Free Database[7] discusses the underlying format of these databases and provides statistical analyses of the information in the databases. Read her description at:

http://www.afrigeneas.com/library/louisiana/   (Description of Databases)

Although the Slave and Free databases provide a wealth of information on slaves in Louisiana during the 1700's and early to mid-1800's, these records do not include all slaves in Louisiana during this time period. Often additional information on slaves can be found in estates and conveyance records in Louisiana parish courthouses. Also, slaves during this period almost always were known by their given names as they did not have surnames. In searching the records, it is often more productive to search by the master's surname. Furthermore, searching spelling variations of the master's surname often provides more complete results.

A brief search on the Guédry surname and several of its variants produced these results:

Database	**Master's Surname - No. of Records**		
	Guedry	**Guidry**	**Geddry**
ibiblio.com (Slave)	13	119	1
Ancestry.com (Slave)	13	133	1
Ancestry.com (Freed)	0	1	0

No results were found for Guidery, Guidrey, Guedrey, Guedery, Gaidry, Guildry, Guildery, Guildrey, Gindry, Gindery, Gindrey, Gidry, Gudry, Gedry, Jeddry, Jedry, Labine, LaBean, Petitpas and Pettipas.

THE LOUISIANA SLAVE DATABASE
& THE LOUISIANA FREE DATABASE
AND SLAVE NARRATIVES
By Marty Guidry

Slave Narratives

During the 1930's the Works Progress Administration (WPA) established the Federal Writers' Project in which historians in the United States interviewed former slaves and compiled their narratives. The Slave Narrative Collection contains the autobiographical accounts of ex-slaves from 17 states. Compiled from over 2300 interviews during 1936-1938, these narratives are a unique glimpse into the life of a slave in the United States and are often difficult to read for the horrors suffered.

In 1941 the U. S. government microfilmed the narratives as the seventeen-volume Slave Narratives: A Folk History of Slavery in the United States from Interviews with Former Slaves[8]. Recently the Manuscript and the Prints and Photographs Divisions of the Library of Congress placed the original interviews and over 500 photographs of former slaves online on the website "**Born in Slavery: Slave Narratives from the Federal Writers' Project, 1936-1938**"[9] at the link:

http://memory.loc.gov/ammem/snhtml/snhome.html   (Born in Slavery)

Former slaves living in Louisiana were not interviewed as part of the Federal Writers' Project; however, 308 ex-slaves in Texas were. Many former slaves from Louisiana had moved to Texas after the Civil War. In 1974 Texas narratives of the Federal Writers' Project were published in four-volumes as The Slave Narratives of Texas[10]. Later in 1940-1941 ex-slaves in Louisiana were interviewed after the Federal Writers' Project had closed. Their narratives were published in 1990 in Mother Wit: The Ex-Slave Narratives of the Louisiana Writers' Project[11].

Recently Ancestry.com has compiled the slave narratives from the Federal Writers' Project as well as those from several others sources into a searchable database entitled "**Slave Narratives**"[12]. This extensive collection has over 3500 interviews with ex-slaves and spans the period from 1929-1939. "Slave Narratives" can be accessed on Ancestry.com at:

http://search.ancestry.com/search/db.aspx?dbid=4342   (Slave Narratives)

Examples of plantation slave quarters in Louisiana

THE LOUISIANA SLAVE DATABASE
& THE LOUISIANA FREE DATABASE
AND SLAVE NARRATIVES
By Marty Guidry

Although none of the former slaves interviewed had the surname Guidry (or a variant of it), several of the interviews mentioned a person named Guidry as the slave owner (master). These are:

Agatha Babino – Born a slave near Carencro, LA, Agatha Babino was living at Beaumont, TX when interviewed. She had lived near Carencro, LA most of her early life with a short stay in Opelousas, LA after marrying. About 25 years before the interview, she moved to Beaumont, TX.

Agatha was a slave of Ogis Guidry and his wife Laurentine and was the daughter of Dick and Clarice Richard from the Carolinas and slaves of Placide Guilbeau. She married Tessifor (Telesphore) Babino (Babineaux) and had twelve children. In her testimony Agatha gave a vivid description of her life as a slave during the Civil War era. According to Agatha, her master was very cruel - beating the slaves and providing only rudimentary living quarters and minimal food. Ogis Guidry had a large, one-story house with gallery and brick pillars. He owned many acres of land and had about 50 slaves.

Mentioned in the interview was a Dr. Guidry, a relative of Ogis Guidry, who told the slaves of their freedom after the Civil War. Also mentioned was Charlie Guidry, a judge, who married the slaves.

{From the information provided in the interview, we know that Ogis Guidry and his wife Laurentine were Augustin Guidry and Marie Leontine Guilbeaux, the sister of Placide Guilbeaux, who owned Agatha Babino's parents.

Augustin Guidry m. Marie Leontine Guilbeaux (sister of Placide Guilbeaux)
|
Augustin Guédry m. Adelaide Robichaud
|
Pierre Guédry m. Marie Claire Babin
|
Augustin Guédry m. Jeanne Hébert
|
Claude Guédry m. Marguerite Petitpas

The Dr. Guidry mentioned probably was Dr. Alexis Onesime Guidry, born in 1816 and the husband of first Celestine Laperle Dupre and then Palmyre Dupre. He was a physician and planter in St. Landry Parish, LA. He was the son of Charles Alexis Onesime Guidry and Julie Euphrasie Potier. Augustin Guidry, husband of Marie Leontine Guilbeaux, and Dr. Alexis Onesime Guidry were first cousins once removed.}

Lou Turner (also called Lou Eumann) – Born a slave at the Richard West plantation at Rosedale, TX near Beaumont, Lou Turner spent her entire life within three miles of the Beaumont, TX. She lived in Beaumont at the time of the interview.

THE LOUISIANA SLAVE DATABASE & THE LOUISIANA FREE DATABASE AND SLAVE NARRATIVES
By Marty Guidry

Lou Turner was owned by Richard West and his wife Mary Guidry. They had a plantation near Rosedale, TX where Lou was a slave. The West family had only a few slaves. Lou's parents were Sam Marble from Mississippi and his wife Maria. Lou discusses her life as a young girl living in the Big House with the master's wife treating her very kindly. She indicated that Mary Guidry was a 'doctor' and would go to other plantations to treat the folks there. The children of Richard West and Mary Guidry were grown, had moved away and had children of their own. Lou Turner would get to go with Mary Guidry to visit the grandchildren and would play with them. Richard West generally treated his slaves well especially before the Civil War.

After being freed, Lou Turner married George Turner in Beaumont when she was 19 years old. They had one daughter Sarah.

{Richard West, born at Mansura in Avoyelles Parish, LA on 31 July 1802 and the son of Thomas West and Susanne 'Nancy' Folk, was married three times: (1) Ann Foreman, daughter of Edward Foreman and Nancy Perry, on 27 March 1819 in Opelousas, LA; (2) Sara Lyons, daughter of Jean Michael Lyons and Mary Hayes, on 22 Jun 1824 in Lafayette, LA and (3) Mrs. Mary Guidry on 30 May 1854 in Jefferson County, TX. The wedding license of Richard West and Mary Guidry has "Mrs. Mary Guidry" indicating that Mary Guidry may have been married previously and Guidry was her former husband's surname.}

Lou Turner, also called Lou Eumann

Orelia Alexie Franks

THE LOUISIANA SLAVE DATABASE & THE LOUISIANA FREE DATABASE AND SLAVE NARRATIVES
By Marty Guidry

Louis Evans – Born near Grand Coteau, LA, Louis Evans was living at Beaumont, TX at the time of the interview.

Louis Evans was a slave of John Smith and his wife Carmellite who lived in a six-room, sawed-plank house on cypress pillars about three feet off the ground. Smith owned 140 acres of land on which he grew corn, cotton and potatoes and raised cattle and horses. John Smith owned about ten slaves – seven were Louis Evans, his brothers and sisters and his father Tom Evans and mother Rachel. From his early youth Louis was the personal servant of John Smith and was treated very well. His master treated all the slaves well. In the interview Louis discusses his life as a young slave and his observations of the Civil War around Grand Coteau, LA.

During the interview Louis Evans briefly discussed a slave Harry owned by Joe Guidry. Mr. Guidry let Harry work for money at times and Harry was able to buy his freedom and some land. He also mentioned that during the Civil War one of the Guidry boys deserted from the army. He was caught and punished. Young Guidry's father borrowed money from another man during the Civil War. After the War the lender seized all of Guidry's property except Harry's land because Guidry's son had deserted.

When he was 20 years old, Louis Evans married a quadroon lady Cora Gindry, who was the daughter of Old Dr. Gindry.

{In the interview Cora Guidry is called Cora Gindry. Here Gindry is a variant of the surname Guidry. A quadroon was a person of mixed race with ¼ African ancestry and ¾ Caucasian ancestry.

Louis Evans was the son of Tom Evans and Rachel. Cora Guidry probably was the daughter of Alexis Onesime Guidry, a physician and planter in St. Landry Parish, LA, and a mulatto woman (possibly Virginia Barker). The identity of the other Guidry's mentioned in the interview are not known.

Cora (Corinne) Guidry m. Louis Evans
|
Alexis Onesime Guidry with mulatto woman
(Wives: Celestine Laperle Dupre & Palmyre Dupre - sisters)
|
Charles Alexis Onesime Guidry m. Julie Euphrasie Potier
|
Louis David Guédry m. Marie Modeste Borda
|
Pierre Guédry m. Marie Claire Babin
|
Augustin Guédry m. Jeanne Hébert
|
Claude Guédry m. Marguerite Petitpas}

THE LOUISIANA SLAVE DATABASE & THE LOUISIANA FREE DATABASE AND SLAVE NARRATIVES
By Marty Guidry

Orelia Alexie Franks – Born a slave on the plantation of Valerian Martin near Opelousas, LA, Orelia Alexie Franks lived in Beaumont, TX for many years before her interview there.

She was the slave of Valerian Martin and his wife Malite Guidry. Her parents were Alexis Franks and Fanire Martin. Valerian Martin had a large plantation on which he raised sugar cane and cotton as wells as hogs and beef. He treated his slaves very well, checking on them every morning and ensuring they got treated properly if sick. He did not allow anyone to beat his slaves. The slaves had rudimenttary quarters, but ate well and enjoyed holidays together. Valerian Martin provided a cabin for his slaves to have prayer meetings. In the interview Orelia discusses several aspects of her life as a slave.

{Valerian Martin was André Valerien Martin, son of Jean André Martin and Gertrude Sonnier. Malite Guidry was Emelie Guidry, daughter of Louis David Guédry and Marie Modeste Bordat.

Emelie Guidry m1. Alexandre Dugas; m2. André Valerien Martin
|
Louis David Guédry m. Marie Modeste Bordat
|
Pierre Guédry m. Marie Claire Babin
|
Augustin Guédry m. Jeanne Hébert
|
Claude Guédry m. Marguerite Petitpas

[Note: Emelite Guidry and Augustin Guidry (husband of Marie Leontine Guilbeaux) were first cousins.]}

Amos Lincoln – Born a slave on the Elshay Guidry plantation in the lower delta country of Louisiana about 50 miles south of New Orleans, Amos Lincoln was living in Beaumont, TX during the interview. He had lived in Beaumont for 52 years.

While a slave, Amos Lincoln was owned by Elshay Guidry. During the interview Amos stated that Elshay Guidry was quite mean and whipped his many slaves. The slaves had very rudimentary cabins with dirt floors and very rustic furniture. They hunted, trapped and gathered most of their food. Amos married twice – first to Massage Florshann and then to Annie. After being set free, he sharecropped briefly in Louisiana and then moved to Texas where he again sharecropped.

Mary Scranton – Born near Lafayette, LA, Mary Scranton was living in Texas at the time of the interview.

Mary Scranton remembered that her first owner was called Valiere, but did not recall his last name. Her second owner was LaSan Guidry, who was very good to his slaves – always ensuring they could practice their religion and never mistreating them.

THE LOUISIANA SLAVE DATABASE & THE LOUISIANA FREE DATABASE AND SLAVE NARRATIVES
By Marty Guidry

Mary's parents were Joseph Johnson and his wife Clara Bell. When she was about twenty, she married George Scranton in Louisiana. They had five children together before George died in Port Arthur, TX.

{The LaSan Guidry mentioned in the interview was very probably Lessin Guidry, born 1829 in Lafayette Parish, LA and son of Alexandre Guidry and Marie Carmelite Broussard. He married Louisianaise Breaux, daughter of Valiere Breaux and Marcelite Fostin, in 1852 in Lafayette, LA. They had five children including Marie Eusiede Guidry, born in 1855. The first slave owner mentioned in the interview may have been Valiere Breaux, the father of Lessin Guidry's wife Louisianaise Breaux. He actually would have been the owner of Mary Scranton's parents, not Mary Scranton, as Valiere Breaux died before 1853 and Mary Scranton was born in 1859.

Lessin (Laisin, Lessaint, Lessaurt, Laison) Guidry m. Louisianaise Breaux
|
Alexandre Lessin Guidry m. Marie Carmelite Broussard
|
Joseph Guidry m. Scholastique Hébert
|
Pierre Guédry m. Marie Claire Babin
|
Augustin Guédry m. Jeanne Hébert
|
Claude Guédry m. Marguerite Petitpas }

Other Afro-Louisiana Resources

A new database on Ancestry.com is the "**New Orleans, Louisiana, Slave Manifests, 1807-1860**"[13]. Although the international slave trade was banned in 1807, within the United States slaves could still be marketed. The 1807 law banning the international slave trade also required that captains of vessels carrying slaves within the continental waters to prepare a manifest of their slave cargo. These are the surviving slave manifests prepared for ships entering and leaving the Port of New Orleans. Some inward and outward manifests have been lost over time. The records are not indexed at this time so each individual manifest must be searched. There are 29,875 individuals on the manifests.

http://search.ancestry.com/search/db.aspx?dbid=1562 (New Orleans Slave Manifests)

The "**Louisiana Digital Library**"[14] is a massive database containing over 144,000 photographs and documents on all aspects of Louisiana history and culture from the 1500's to the present day. Within the digitized collection are several hundred photographs and documents on slaves, the slave trade and slavery in Louisiana. Some are of a general nature, but many name the individuals and provide information on their lives. For best results use the "Search All Collections" feature on the homepage. See below for an example of one document from this collection on two slaves Henry and Don Louis belonging to Augustin Guedry. The original documents can be downloaded from the website at:

http://louisdl.louislibraries.org/ (Louisiana Digital Library)

THE LOUISIANA SLAVE DATABASE & THE LOUISIANA FREE DATABASE AND SLAVE NARRATIVES
By Marty Guidry

The "**Digitial Library on American Slavery**"[15] contains detailed information on over 150,000 slaves, free people of color and whites. The information was gleaned from over 17,000 legislative and county petitions as well as wills, inventories, bills of sale, court proceedings and other civil government documents filed between 1775 and 1867 in 15 southern states and the District of Columbia. There are six entries for Guidry (no other variants mentioned) in the database – Cilesie Savoy Guidry, Firmin Guidry, Louis Guidry, Onezime Louis Guidry, Onezime Guidry Esq. and Theodule Guidry. The "Digital Library on American Slavery" is at:

http://library.uncg.edu/slavery/about.aspx (Digital Library on American Slavery)

A team of international historians has compiled a superb website entitled "**The Trans-Atlantic Slave Trade Database**"[16] with information on almost 35,000 slave voyages from 1501 to 1866 destined for the United States and six other regions of the world. The names provided in this database are the African names of persons being transported as well as the names of the ship captains. Although not specific to Louisiana, this database provides a superb, detailed overview of slave trade from Africa to the United States and other regions of the world. It is available at:

http://www.slavevoyages.org/tast/index.faces (Trans-Atlantic Slave Trade Database)

Another excellent resource for Afro-American History and Genealogy is the AfriGeneas (African Ancestored Genealogy) website and particularly its **AfriGeneas Library**[57] at

http://www.afrigeneas.com/library/ (AfriGeneas Library)

There are many sources of information on slaves and slavery in Louisiana in texts and on the internet. The above are but a select group of the better ones readily available on the internet. With the expanded resources available today one can now trace his African ancestry well beyond the post-Civil War period. Additionally, there are professional genealogists specializing in Afro-Louisiana Genealogy with whom one can contract to get help.

See page 28 for References

Slave Quarters, Violet, Louisiana-1930's

Slave quarters at the former home of Colonel Daniel Edwards in Tangipahoa Parish Louisiana in 1955

SLAVE NARRATIVES-AGATHA BABINO

420280

EX-SLAVE STORIES
(Texas)

Page One

AGATHA BABINO, born a slave of Ogis Guidry, near Carenco, Louisiana, now lives in a cottage on the property of the Blessed Sacrament Church, in Beaumont, Texas. She says she is at least eighty-seven and probably much older.

"Old Marse was Ogis Guidry. Old Miss was Laurentine. Dey had four chillen, Placid, Alphonse and Mary and Alexandrine, and live in a big, one-story house with a gallery and brick pillars. Dey had a big place. I 'spect a mile 'cross it, and fifty slaves.

"My mama name was Clarice Richard. She come from South Carolina. Papa was Dick Richard. He come from North Carolina. He was slave of old Placid Guilbeau. He live near Old Marse. My brothers was Joe and Nicholas and Oui and Albert and Maurice, and sisters was Maud and Célestine and Pauline.

"Us slaves lived in shabby houses. Dey builded of logs and have dirt floor. We have a four foot bench. We pull it to a table and set on it. De bed a platform with planks and moss.

"We had Sunday off. Christmas was off, too. Dey give us chicken and flour den. But most holidays de white folks has company. Dat mean more work for us.

"Old Marse bad. He beat us till we bleed. He rub salt and pepper in. One time I sweep de yard. Young miss come home from college. She slap my face. She want to beat me. Mama say to beat her, so dey did. She took de beatin' for me.

"My aunt run off 'cause dey beat her so much. Dey brung her back and beat her some more.

-1-

SLAVE NARRATIVES-AGATHA BABINO

Ex-slave Stories
(Texas)

Page Two   38

"We have dance outdoors sometime. Somebody play fiddle and banjo. We dance de reel and quadrille and buck dance. De men dance dat. If we go to dance on 'nother plantation we have to have pass. De patterrollers come and make us show de slip. If dey ain't no slip, we git beat.

"I see plenty sojers. Dey fight at Pines and we hear ball go 'zing--zing.' Young marse have blue coat. He put it on and climb a tree to see. De sojers come and think he a Yankee. Dey take his gun. Dey turn him loose when dey find out he ain't no Yankee.

"When de real Yankees come dey take corn and gooses and hosses. Dey don't ask for nothin'. Dey take what dey wants.

"Some masters have chillen by slaves. Some sold dere own chillen. Some sot dem free.

"When freedom come we have to sign up to work for money for a year. We couldn't go work for nobody else. After de year some stays, but not long.

"De Ku Klux kill niggers. Dey come to take my uncle. He open de door. Dey don't take him but tell him to vote Democrat next day or dey will. Dey kilt some niggers what wouldn't vote Democrat.

"Dey kill my old uncle Davis. He won't vote Democrat. Dey shoot him. Den dey stand him up and let him fall down. Dey tie him by de feet. Dey drag him through de brash. Dey dare his wife to cry.

"When I thirty I marry Teasifor Babino. Pere Abadie marry us at Grand Coteau. We have dinner with wine. Den come big dance. We have twelve chillen. We works in de field in Opelousas. We come here twenty-five year ago. He die in 1917. Dey let's me live here. It nice to be near de church. I can go to prayers when I wants to.

SLAVE NARRATIVES-ORELIA ALEXIE FRANKS

420002

EX-SLAVE STORIES Page One   60
(Texas)

ORELIA ALEXIE FRANKS was born
on the plantation of Valerian
Martin, near Opelousas, Louisiana. She does not know her
age, but thinks she is near
ninety. Her voice has the musical accent of the French Negro.
She has lived in Beaumont, Texas,
many years.

"I's born on Mr. George Washington's birthday, the twenty-second of February but I don't know what year. My old massa was Valerian Martin and he come from foreign country. He come from Canada and he Canada French. He wife name Malite Guidry. Old massa a good Catholic and he taken all the li'l slave chillen to be christen. Oh, he's a Christian massa and I used to be a Catholic but now I's a Apostolic, but I's christen in St. Johns Catholic Church, what am close to Lafayette, where I's born.

"My pa name Alexis Franks and he was American and Creole. My ma name Fanire Martin and I's raise where everybody talk French. I talks American but I talks French goodest.

"Old massa he big cane and cotton farmer and have big plantation and raise everything. and us all well treat. Dey feed us right, too. Raise big hawg in de pen and raise lots of beef. All jes' for to feed he cullud folks.

"Us quarters out behind de big house and old massa come round through de quarters every mornin' and see how us niggers is. If us sick he call nuss. She old slavery woman. She come look at 'em. If dey bad sick dey send for de doctor. Us house all log house. Dey all dab with dirt 'tween de logs. Dey have dirt chimney make out of sticks and dab with mud. Dey

-1-

SLAVE NARRATIVES-ORELIA ALEXIE FRANKS

Ex-slave Stories   Page Two   G1
(Texas)

"Lots of time we eat coosh-coosh. Dat make out of meal and water. You bile de water and salt it, den put in de cornmeal and stir it and bile it. Den you puts milk or clabber or syrup on it and eat it.

"Old massa have de graveyard a purpose to bury de cullud folks in. Dey have cullud preacher. Dey have funeral in de graveyard. Dat nigger preacher he a Mef'dist.

"Old massa son-in-law, he overseer. He 'lew nobody to beat de slaves. Us li'l ones git spank when we bad. Dey put us 'cross de knee and spank us where dey allus spank chillen.

"Christmas time dey give big dinner. Dey give all de old men whiskey. Everybody have big time.

"Dey make lots of sugar. After dey finish cookin' de sugar dey draw off what left from de pots and give it to us chillen. Us have candy pullin'.

"Dey weave dey own cloth. Us have good clothes. Dey weave de cloth for make mattress and stuff 'em with moss. Massa sho' believe to serve he niggers good. I see old massa when he die. Us see old folks cry and us cry, too. Dey have de priest and burn de candles. Us sho' miss old massa.

"I see lots of sojers. Dey so many like hair on your head. Dey Yankees. Dey call 'em bluejackets. Dey a fight up near massa's house. Us climb in tree for to see. Us hear bullets go 'zoom' through de air 'round dat tree but us didn't know it was bullets. A man rid up on a hoss and tell massa to git us pickaninnies out dat tree or dey git kilt. De Yankees have dat battle and den sot us niggers free.

-2-

Ex-slave Stories
(Texas)

Page Three

"Old massa, he de kind man what let de niggers have dey prayer-meetin'. He give 'em a big cabin for dat. Shout? Yes, Lawd! Sing like dis:

> "'Mourner, fare you well,
> Gawd 'Mighty bless you,
> Till we meets again.'

"Us sings 'nother song:

> "'Sinner blind,
> Johnnie, can't you ride no more?
> Sinner blind,
> Your feets may be slippin'
> Your soul git lost.
> Johnnie, can't you ride no more?
> Yes, Lawd',
> Day by day you can't see,
> Johnnie, can't you ride no more?
> Yes, Lawd.'"

****

SLAVE NARRATIVES-LOU TURNER

420001

EX-SLAVE STORIES
(Texas)

Page One

118

LOU TURNER, 89, was born at Rosedale, near Beaumont, Texas, on the Richard West plantation. She has spent her entire life within three miles of Beaumont, and now lives in her own little home, with her daughter, Sarah.

"I hears you been 'round to see me befo', but you ain't never gwine find me to home. I sho' love to go 'round visitin'. You know dey say iffen you treats the cat too good, you ain't never know where the cat is.

"I's gwine on seventeen year old when freedom come. I's born right here near Beaumont, on the big road what they calls the Concord Road, in the place what they calls Rosedale. I's a growed-up young lady befo' I ever sees Beaumont. I's gwine on 89 year old now.

"Richard West, he's my massa and Mary Guidry she my missy. Dey used to call her the 'Cattle King.' Dey have a big plantation and jes' a few slaves. Dey raises my mammy since she eleven year old. Her name Maria and she marry Sam Marble. He come from Miss' ippi.

"I stay up at the big house and missy fix my plate when she fix hers. God bless her heart, she kind to me. I know now I's sassy to her but she didn't pay me no 'tention 'cause I's li'l. I slep' on a trundle bed by missy's side and I git so smart I allus smell my bed to see iffen dey puts nice, clean sheets on mine like dey did on hers. Sometime I play sick, but old missy a good doctor and she gimme beefoot oil and it so nasty I quit playing off. She French and she so good doctor they send for her to other folks houses.

-1-

Ex-slave Stories
(Texas)

Page Two

"Old missy was real rich. I's taken her money out of de wardrobe ane make tall playhouse out of gold and silver money. Iffen she have to buy somethin' she have to come and borrow it from me. Us allus has to figger how to take dat money out of de corners so de house won't fall down. I cried and cried iffen she tored it up.

"She'd take me with her when she go to see her grandchillen in de French settlement. Us come in buggy or hack and bring jelly and money and things. I thought I's gwine to Heaven, 'cause I gits to play with li'l chillen. Us play 'ring place', dat's draw a ring and hop 'round in it. Us jump rope and swing. Dey have a hair rope swing with a smooth board in it so it ain't scratch us behin'.

"Old missy so kind but what got 'way with me, I couldn't go to school. I beg and beg, but she kep' sayin', 'Some day, some day,' and I ain't never sit in a school in my life.

"Old massa didn't work 'em hard. He make 'em come in when the sun got bad, 'cause he feared dey git sunstroke. He mighty good in early days, but when he figger dey gwine loose he slaves he start bein' mean. He split 'em and sold 'em, tryin' to make he money out of 'em.

"De house what the white folks live in was make out of logs and moss and so was the quarters houses. Better'n New Orleans, dem quarters was. Us slaves have de garden patch. The white folks raises hogs and kilt 'em by the twenties. Dey smoke hams and shoulders and chittlin's and sich and hang 'em up in the smokehouse. Us allus have plenty to eat and us have good, strong clothes. Missy buy my dresses separate, though. She buy me pretty stripe cotton dress.

-2-

Ex-slave Stories　　　　　　　　　　　　　　　　　Page Three　　120
(Texas)

"Bout the only work I ever done was help watch the geese and turkeys and fill the quilts. I larn to card, too. Old missy never whip me much, she jes' like to scare me. She whip me with big, tall straw she git out the field or wet a towel and whip my legs. My old massa done a trick I never forgit while I's warm. I's big gal 'bout sixteen year old and us all 'lone on the place. He tells me to crawl under the corncrib and git the eggs. I knowed dey ain't nothin' dere but the nest egg, but I have to go. When I can't find nothin' he pull me out backwards by the feet and whip me. When old missy come home I ain't know no better'n to tell her and she say she ought to kill him, but she sho' fix him, anyway. He say she spile me and dat why he whip me.

"Old missy taken to preachin'. She was real good preacher. Dey have de big hall down the center of the house where they have services. A circuit rider come once a month and everybody stop workin' even if it wasn't Sunday.

"When war was on us there wasn't no sojers 'round where I was, but dat battle on Atchafalia shook all the dishes off the dresser and broke 'em up. Jes' broke up all the fine Sunday and company dishes.

"After de trouble my mammy have gettin' me 'way from there when freedom come, she gits me after all. Old missy have seven li'l nigger chillen what belong to her slaves, but dey mammies and daddys come git 'em. I didn't own my own mammy. I own my old missy and call her 'mama'. Us cry and cry when us have to go with us mammy. I 'members how old missy rock me in her arms and sing to me. She sing dat 'O, Susanna' and telt me a story:

-3-

SLAVE NARRATIVES-Slaves Executed

Daily Picayune (26-B)
9/30/1840
P.2-c.1

Negroes Executed. - Henry and Don Louis, two slaves belonging to Mr. Augustin Guedry, of the Parish of Lafayette, and connected in the late attempt at insurrection, have been apprehended, tried, found guilty and executed.

Source: Daily Picayune (New Orleans, LA)
30 September 1840
Page 2
(Louisiana Digital Library)

Slave cabin at Barbara Plantation, Louisiana.
Early 19th century construction.
Photograph from Library of Congress

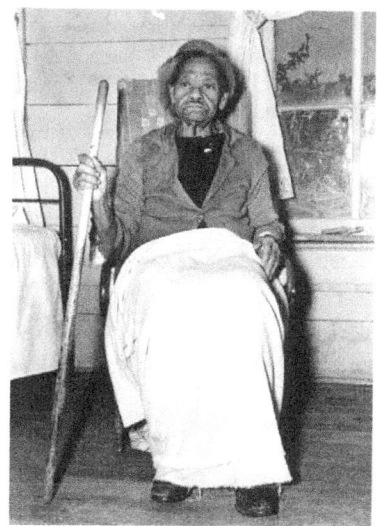

Mary Reynolds, former slave from Catahoula Parish, Louisiana.
(Photographer unknown, ca. 1938)

BON APPETIT

RAY'S CAJUN HOT BRISKET

This recipe comes from the Cajun Grill Master, Ray Guidry of Percy Guidry manufacturing in Lafayette, Louisiana. Their Cajun Grill is one of the hottest pieces of outdoor cooking equipment on the market. Additionally, Ray has written a great cookbook, The Cajun Grill Cookbook. http://www.cajungrill.com

1 beef brisket
1 C jalapeno peppers, chopped
2 large onions, chopped
Salt, cayenne pepper, and celery salt to taste
2 sweet green peppers, chopped
Vinegar or Zesty Italian salad dressing
5 large cloves of garlic, minced

Combine all seasonings in a large bowl. Trim excess fat off brisket. Lay the brisket flat on a table. Cut a slice in the meat on one of the long ends of the brisket to create a pocket. Put all of the seasonings in the pocket. Reserve the seasoning juices. Sew the pocket closed with a string. Create a rub of salt, cayenne pepper and celery salt. Spread this evenly on the outside of the brisket. Place the brisket on the Cajun grill with a full hot bed of coals with the coal tray at the highest position and with the cover of the Cajun Grill left open. Cook in this position for 30-40 minutes on each side or until the brisket becomes blackened. When this is done, take the brisket off and lay it in an aluminum baking pan. Pour the reserved seasoning liquid over the brisket and cover with aluminum foil. Place it back on the Cajun Grill with the coal tray in the lowest position, air controls completely closed, and cover closed for an additional 4 hours. Take the brisket off the grill at about the 3 1/2 hour mark and cut into thin strips with electric knife. Make sure to cut against the grain of the meat. Place the strips of brisket back into the pan which is full of juices and put it back on the Cajun grill for the additional 30 minutes.

BROCCOLI SALAD
From Ron & Joanne Pitts
Toronto, Ontario

1 large bunch broccoli
1 medium onion
8 slices cooked crisp bacon
1-1 1/2 cup mayonnaise
1/4 cup white sugar
2 tbsp. vinegar
3/4 cup salted sunflower seeds 1 cup raisins

Cut the broccoli in small pieces. Also cut up the onion and the cooked crisp bacon. Mix the mayonnaise, sugar and vinegar together and then toss all of the ingredients together.

Refrigerate an hour or so before serving.

Enjoy!

IN THE NEWS-HISTORICAL NEWS TIDBITS

The Kerrville Times, Kerrville, TX.
Friday, August 12, 1955

OCEAN FRESH
Shrimp and Oysters
and a variety of
FRESH FISH
Sea Food Dinners
Served Daily except Sunday
from 11 00 A. M. to 8 00 P. M.

Guidry's Sea Food
814 Main   Phone 1199

Remy Guidry, Owner - Jefferson Drug Store, 1966, Lafayette, LA

JEFFERSON DRUG STORE
REMY GUIDRY, Owner
610 Jefferson Blvd.   CE 4-1428

Galveston Daily News, 1925
Galveston, TX

MAN IS QUESTIONED IN FARMER'S DEATH

BODY IS FOUND BURIED ON FARM; HAD BEEN SHOT THROUGH HEAD.

By Associated Press.

Beaumont, Tex., Nov. 16.—A man is being held for questioning in connection with the death of Albert Guidry, well-to-do farmer, whose body was found this morning buried on a farm near here. Guidry had been shot through the head with a 12-gauge shotgun. He was last seen on Nov. 7.

The body was discovered by a searching party headed by Deputy Sheriff Artie Pollack. Marks of blood near the field and a freshly plowed path of ground twenty yards away attracted the searchers to the spot.

The man had purchased his farm, located at Voth, ten miles from Beaumont, from Guidry and a remainder of $2,100 was past due on the place, according to Guidry's family and the sheriff's department. On Nov. 7 the man called for Guidry to take him to the farm, where payment of the indebtedness was to have been made. The two left the home of Guidry's daughter together and the farmer was not seen since.

Les Guédry d'Asteur

What's in a name?

<u>Guédry</u> is the family to which you belong if your name is spelled Guédry, Guedry, Guidry, Gaidry, Guildry, Geddry, Jeddry, Labine, LaBine, LaBean or any of several dozen variations. The original name of our family is believed to have been Guédry. We are all descendants of Claude Guédry & Marguerite Petitpas.

Here are some common and uncommon variant spellings of the name.

Guédry	Guiddry	Geddrie	Jeddrie	Labeen
Guedry	Guiddery	Geddry	Jeddry	Labene
Guedrie	Guiedri	Gedree	Jederie	Labine
Guedris	Guiedry	Gedrie	Jedrey	LaBine
Guidry	Guildry	Gedry	Jedrie	LaBean
Gudiry	Guildrie	Gettry	Jedry	LaBeau
Guidery	Guitry	Gidrie		Labeau
Guidrey	Gaidry	Gidry	Lledre	
Guidrie	Gaidrie		Yedri	

Our **Petitpas** cousins likewise have several variations of their name including Petitpas, Pettipas, Petipas, Petitpa, Petit Pas and Pitts.

DUES REMINDER

Attached at the back of this issue is a membership application for renewing your membership in **Les Guédry d'Asteur**. Our dues are very reasonable at $6.00 for individuals and $10 for a family in 2010.

Please take a moment, complete the Membership Application, enclose a check and send it to the address on the application. It will help all of us do so much for the family. And, if you would like to join at one of the Benefactor Levels, it would allow us do even more.

Les Guédry d'Asteur is now on Facebook. Join us there and connect with other family members from all over the U.S. and CAN. Feel free to post queries, photos, links, events or other items of interest to the family. Just search for 'Les Guédry d'Asteur' on Facebook to find our page.

REFERENCES-SLAVE NARRATIVES

1. "Gwendolyn Midlo Hall", Wikipedia, the Free Encyclopedia; Internet at: http://en.wikipedia.org/wiki/Gwendolyn_Midlo_Hall

2. "Gwendolyn Midlo Hall"; ibiblio.org; Internet at: http://www.ibiblio.org/laslave/hall/vitajune2007.html

3. Hall, Gwendolyn Midlo; Databases for the Study of Afro-Louisiana History and Genealogy (Louisiana State University Press; Baton Rouge, LA; March, 2000). Compact Disk.

4. Hall, Gwendolyn, Midlo; Afro-Louisiana History and Genealogy, 1719-1820 (ibiblio.org; University of North Carolina; Chapel Hill, NC; November 2001). Searchable Internet Database: http://www.ibiblio.org/laslave/

5. Hall, Gwendolyn Midlo; Louisiana Slave Records, 1719-1820 (Ancestry.com; Ancestry.com Operations, Inc.; Provo, UT; 2003). Searchable Internet Database: http://search.ancestry.com/search/db.aspx?dbid=7383

6. Hall, Gwendolyn Midlo; Louisiana Freed Slave Records, 1719-1820 (Ancestry.com; Ancestry.com Operations, Inc.; Provo, UT; 2003). Searchable Internet Database: http://search.ancestry.com/search/db.aspx?dbid=7382

7. Hall, Gwendolyn Midlo; The Louisiana Slave Database and the Louisiana Free Database: 1719-1820 (Afrigeneas Library; Atlanta, GA). Internet Site: http://www.afrigeneas.com/library/louisiana/

8. Works Progress Administration; Slave Narratives: A Folk History of Slavery in the United States from Interviews with Former Slaves (Works Progress Administration; Washington, D.C.; 1941). Microfilm, 17 volumes.

9. National Digital Library Program (NDLP), Library of Congress: Born in Slavery: Slave Narratives from the Federal Writers' Project, 1936-1938; Searchable Internet Database: http://memory.loc.gov/ammem/snhtml/snack.html

10. Tyler, Ronnie C. & Murphy, Lawrence R., editors; The Slave Narratives of Texas (Encino Press; Austin, TX; 1974).

11. Clayton, Ronnie W.; Mother Wit: The Ex-Slave Narratives of the Louisiana Writers' Project (Peter Lang; New York, NY; 1990).

12. Works Progress Administration, et al.; "Slave Narratives" (Ancestry.com; Ancestry.com Operations, Inc.; Provo, UT; 2003). Searchable Internet Database: http://search.ancestry.com/search/db.aspx?dbid=4342

13. National Archives and Records Administration; New Orleans, Louisiana, Slave Manifests, 1807-1860 (Ancestry.com; Ancestry.com Operations, Inc.; Provo, UT; 2003). Searchable Internet Database: http://search.ancestry.com/search/db.aspx?dbid=1562

14. Louisiana Library Network; Louisiana Digital Library (State Library of Louisiana; Baton Rouge, LA; 1992). Searchable Internet Database: http://louisdl.louislibraries.org/

15. ERIT, University Libraries, UNCG; Digital Library on American Slavery (University of North Carolina; Greensboro, NC; 1993). Searchable Internet Site: http://library.uncg.edu/slavery/about.aspx

16. Eltis, David & Halbert, Martin; The Trans-Atlantic Slave Trade Database (Emory University; Atlanta, GA; 2008).

17. Nelson, Valencia King (webmaster); AfriGeneas (African Ancestored Genealogy) Library (Afrigeneas Library; Atlanta, GA). Searchable Internet Site: http://www.afrigeneas.com/library/

Les Guédry d'Asteur

To share your ideas for the newsletter, contact:

Marty Guidry
6139 North Shore Drive
Baton Rouge, LA 70817
225-755-1915
guidryrm@cox.net

The Guédry-Labine Family Newsletter '*GENERATIONS*' serves as a focal point for family members to share and learn about us.

"*GENERATIONS*' newsletter is now in its eighth year. We hope to provide our readers with an interesting, informative and entertaining newsletter. Your input is always welcome and we look forward to another year of sharing family history and news with you.

Allie Guidry
txguidry2000@yahoo.com

Marty Guidry
guidryrm@cox.net

   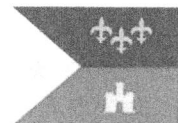  

Les Guédry d'Asteur Officers and Committees

OFFICERS:
President - Martin Guidry (LA)
Vice-President - Elaine Clement (LA)
Secretary - Billy Harrell Guidry (LA)
Treasurer - Daniel "Chuck" Guidry (LA)

COMMITTEES:
Website - Becky Boggess (IA) - Chairperson
    Annie Grignon-Labine (QU) - Translator
    Elaine Clement (LA) - Translator
    Martin Guidry (LA)

Genealogy - Daryl LaBine (FL/ON) - Chairperson
    Bernard Geddry (AZ)
    Mark Labine (MN)
    Daniel "Chuck" Guidry (LA)
    Martin Guidry (LA)

Finance - Cheryl Guidry Tyiska (MD) - Chairperson
    Paul Labine (IL)
    Marshall Woolner (OR)
    Gloria Parrent (TX)
    Chuck Guidry (LA)

Membership - Charlene Guidry Lacombe (LA) -
    Chairperson
    Gayle Guidry (LA) - Special Projects
    Warren Guidry (TX)

Sales - Cindy Guidry Herdt (WA) - Chairperson
    Wayne Simoneaux (LA)
    Billy Harrell Guidry (LA)

Publicity - Elaine Clement (LA) - Chairperson
    Margaret Jeddry (MA)
    Warren Guidry (TX)

Newsletter - Allie Guidry Hardee (VA) - Editor
    Martin Guidry (LA)

CAFA Board Member - Jeanette Guidry Leger (LA)

Made in the USA
Coppell, TX
04 September 2025

54282500R00195